My Body, My Health

The Concerned Woman's Book of Gynecology

My Body,
The Concerned

FELICIA HANCE STEWART, M.D.
Practicing in Gynecology
Associate Medical Director
Planned Parenthood Association of Sacramento
Clinical Instructor in Obstetrics and Gynecology
University of California, Davis
School of Medicine

GARY K. STEWART, M.D., M.P.H., F.A.C.O.G.
Practicing in Obstetrics and Gynecology
Medical Director
Planned Parenthood Association of Sacramento
Clinical Assistant Professor in
Obstetrics and Gynecology
University of California, Davis
School of Medicine

My Health
Woman's Book of Gynecology

FELICIA JANE GUEST
Health Educator, Medical Sciences Writer
Training Specialist for Patient Education and Counseling
Regional Training Center for Family Planning
Emory University School of Medicine
Department of Gynecology and Obstetrics
Atlanta, Georgia

ROBERT A. HATCHER, M.D., M.P.H., F.A.A.P.
Director of Family Planning Program
Emory University—Grady Memorial Hospital Family Planning Program
Associate Professor of Gynecology and Obstetrics
Emory University School of Medicine
Atlanta, Georgia

With Illustrations by **NELVA B. RICHARDSON**
Medical and Dental Illustrator,

BANTAM BOOKS
Toronto • New York • London • Sydney

MY BODY, MY HEALTH:
THE CONCERNED WOMAN'S BOOK OF GYNECOLOGY
A Bantam Book / published by arrangement with
John Wiley & Sons, Inc.

PRINTING HISTORY
John Wiley edition published April 1979
3 printings through December 1979
Bantam edition / March 1981

ISBN 0-553-01299-1

Published simultaneously in the United States and Canada

Bantam Books are published by Bantam Books, Inc. Its trademark, consisting of the words "Bantam Books" and the por-
trayal of a bantam, is Registered in U.S. Patent and Trademark
Office and in other countries. Marca Registrada. Bantam
Books, Inc., 666 Fifth Avenue, New York, New York 10103.

PRINTED IN THE UNITED STATES OF AMERICA

FG   0 9 8 7 6 5 4

This book is dedicated to
Fumiko Mallory, with gratitude

and to our mothers
Lena J. Hance
Janie C. Guest
Della Jensen Stewart
Meta Lieber Hatcher, 1899–1965

Foreword

"What do women want?" is a question ascribed to Freud which became a riddle in Victorian times. Answers are more obvious today. Among other things, women want basic tools for self direction and growth—among these tools are knowledge of themselves as soma and psyche, knowledge of their body's rhythms, knowledge of their inner space and how to protect it. As more is known about the reproductive sciences, the task of presenting such knowledge to the public grows more challenging. Women must be informed about their anatomy and functioning from an early age; they must learn how to prevent sexually transmitted diseases and unwanted pregnancy; they must be encouraged to become students of their own individual condition—surely an interesting quest, if occasionally an uncomfortable one.

In *My Body, My Health* the authors have taken on the task of such education and motivation—with wisdom, warmth, and clarity. Their book is exceedingly thorough, scientific, and understandable. The reader becomes a colleague in the quest for accurate information and its application to unique individuals. *My Body, My Health* will please the women's movement and consumer medicine advocates with its honesty and emphasis on self-care and informed choice. Yet it will reach an even larger audience, as it has humor and balance and is never doctrinaire. Counselors, sexologists, and perusers of birth control manuals will be delighted to find—at last—a thorough discussion of the sexual aspects of various contraceptive measures and an acknowledgment of the importance of sexuality in the birth control choice.

One need spend only a day in a woman's clinic or hospital emergency room to appreciate the difficulties that can visit the female reproductive system when women are not educated to be vigilant in self-protection. May this new book be widely read and wisely heeded!

Sadja Goldsmith Greenwood, M.D.
University of California
San Francisco Medical Center
San Francisco, California

Preface

Some of the most momentous decisions a woman makes have a direct and immediate impact on the health of her reproductive organs. As you decide whether to have a baby or to begin a sexual partnership, health probably is not your primary consideration; nor should it be. But health certainly is one factor that you will want to consider and plan for.

This book provides facts about your body and your health that you will need for making plans and decisions when your reproductive system demands your attention. You may be trying to become pregnant or trying to avoid pregnancy; you may have questions about an infection or about fibroid tumors; you may be considering whether to take estrogen hormones for menopause problems, or you may be worried about surgery that your clinician has recommended. Almost every woman faces one or more of these problems at some time during her life, and almost every woman has unanswered questions.

We have written about gynecology because our patients have asked so many good questions, and because it is hard for anyone outside the medical profession to obtain reliable information about even the most common gynecologic problems. The sad truth is that without our medical credentials we would not have been able to find and evaluate the dozens of books and articles we used in writing this book. We have tried to be scrupulously accurate and thorough in presenting the facts, as they are known today, including potential problems, risks, and complications.

The barriers that make medical information accessible only to members of the profession are intolerable if you believe as we do that each person has the right to know all the facts that are germane to personal health care decision making. As you decide about medical treatment or surgery, you have the right and the responsibility to learn about your problem, your treatment alternatives, and the possible complications. Your clinician has a legal obligation to provide the information you need, and your consent to treatment is your acknowledgment that you do understand. This book can help insure that your consent is truly informed.

No book can recommend or prescribe medical treatment specifically for you. You and your clinician are obviously in a better position to assess your needs. Also, your clinician may not agree with some of the recommendations in this book. Don't be concerned about such disagreement; it is the rule in medicine. Even the four authors of this book didn't always agree. One important reason for disagreement is that there are many gaps in knowledge in the field of gynecology, just as there are in almost all areas of medical science.

You may not be familiar with the term "clinician." We have used clinician throughout the book to mean physician, nurse practitioner, or physician assistant because we enthusiastically support the expanded roles of nurses and other specially trained members of the health care field. Their skills are especially well adapted to the field of gynecology.

Reference citations in the text are intended for those who want to find the medical articles we have used as sources for statistics. Most of these sources are available only in medical libraries. If you want to read more, but do not have an extensive medical background, the Suggested Reading list at the end of the book may be of help.

We expect to keep this book current by revising it regularly. Some of the issues in reproductive health need to be reevaluated almost weekly. Nothing would be more helpful to us and to future readers than your constructive comments for improving the next edition. We would like to hear from you. Please send your criticisms and suggestions to Felicia Stewart, Planned Parenthood Association of Sacramento, 1507 21st Street, Suite 100, Sacramento, California 95814.

Felicia Hance Stewart
Felicia Jane Guest
Gary K. Stewart
Robert A. Hatcher

Acknowledgments

Most of all, we are indebted to our patients. Their questions and their experiences are the backbone of this book.

Without Susan Worth this book would still be a 5-foot stack of handwritten yellow pages. No one else could type 90 error-free words per minute and at the same time absorb, evaluate, and gently identify our lapses in content and clarity. We were also very fortunate to have a hospitable home base at Planned Parenthood Association of Sacramento. Almost every member of the staff, and many patients as well, contributed their ideas, criticisms, comments, personal histories, and support to this book.

We are very fortunate to be able to include sections on puberty and teenage sexuality written by Geraldine Oliva, M.D. Her insight and unique professional background, as a Pediatrician and an expert in public health and family planning, bring clarity and depth to these thorny topics. We also appreciate the contribution of Mina B. Robbins, Ph.D., who provided a summary of common sexual problems which helped us with the chapter on that subject.

We are grateful for the help we received from friends, patients, and colleagues who reviewed and contributed to our manuscript. For their generous time, effort, and insight, we especially thank Rita R. Harris (Biomedical Photographer), Ward Cates, Ann Reed, Michael Castleman, Matelle Goldstein, Lorrie Morris, Robin Bernard, Marsha Ross, Jane Sugarman, Judy Wolen, Elinor Hackett, Martha Kayne, Karen Shaffer, Lena Hance, Carol Binns, Beverly Richardson, Florence Winship,

xii   MY BODY, MY HEALTH

Nancy Clark, Doug Cook, Mattie Baker, Sylvia Kelly, Mike Bennett, and Ed Brann.

And for special help in preparing the index, we want to thank Robin Bernard, Gene Bessent, Carol Binns, Paula E. Bunnell, Beverly Daves, Nancy E. Dimick, Mary Driscoll, Sarah Freeman, Sandra Beers Garese, Charlie Godwin, Jennie Godwin, Elizabeth Hervert-Gaines, Priscilla Munson Johnson, Kathy Kallvet-Webber, Dick King, Kathey Stubbs, and Therese Techman.

Contents

My Body, My Health

The Concerned Woman's Book of Gynecology

1 | How a Woman's Reproductive System Works

Components of a Woman's Reproductive System

UTERUS

The uterus is a rosy, glistening mass of muscle deep inside the lower middle abdomen (see Illustration 1). It is pear-shaped, domed at the top and narrowing to a neck at the bottom. It can be as small as a lime or as large as a good-sized pear. It feels firm and rubbery and becomes very tense and hard when it is touched or stimulated in any way.

Muscle layers about ½ inch thick cover a central cavity shaped like a flattened funnel. Colors deepen from pink to raspberry to vivid blood red between the outer muscle layers and the soft, velvety endometrium, the lining of the inner cavity. The endometrium is sloughed away and renewed during each menstrual cycle. Menstrual discharge is nothing more than shreds of endometrial tissue and blood from endometrial vessels.

The uterus has three openings. Near the domed top (the fundus), two fallopian tubes open into the central cavity, one on each side. At the narrow neck (the cervix), an inch-long canal opens into the vagina.

The uterus is supported by strong, supple ligaments and can be

1

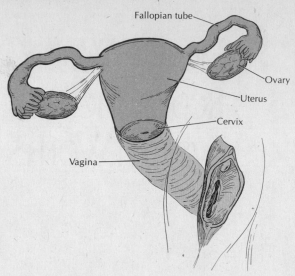

Illustration 1   Internal reproductive organs include the uterus, fallopian tubes, ovaries, cervix, and vagina.

moved easily in several directions. A rich network of uterine blood
vessels lies within folds of the supporting ligaments, and, especially
after pregnancy, blood vessels may crisscross the outer muscle layer of
the uterus.

The primary function of the uterus is to house and protect a fetus
for 40 or so weeks. In late pregnancy, the formerly pear-sized uterus
looks more like a medium-sized watermelon as muscle fibers stretch to
accommodate a growing fetus (or two). The uterus feels hard, and the
pregnant woman may notice waves of slow, tightening sensations long
before true labor contractions begin. No one knows what signals the
uterus to begin the powerful, rhythmic contractions of labor. The
uterus may be responding to hormonal messages or perhaps to something the fetus itself does.

Almost any pain message from the uterus, during menstruation or
during an IUD insertion, for example, will be felt as a cramp. Sometimes uterine cramping is perceived as back pain, or even leg pain,
because uterine nerves enter the spinal cord in the lower back very near
nerves from the upper thighs, and the brain may have trouble sorting
out the exact source of the pain message.

CERVIX

The cervix is the narrow neck of the uterus, and it connects the main body of the uterus with the vagina. You can feel its firm, smooth, rubbery surface (much like the tip of your nose) with a finger inside your vagina. When your vaginal walls are held apart with a speculum, your cervix is plainly visible; it looks like a small, pink glazed doughnut, an inch or so in diameter.

Right in the middle of your cervix is the opening (os) of the inch-long canal that connects the vagina with the uterine cavity. The os is a tiny round hole. Once you have delivered a baby, the os looks more like a ¼-inch-long horizontal slit. Sperm traverse this canal to reach the uterus, and menstrual discharge and babies leave the uterus through this same passageway.

Powerful muscle fibers in the cervix hold the fetus inside the uterus until labor begins, and then they stretch dramatically so that the cervical canal is fifty or more times its normal width at the time of delivery.

Glands line the cervical canal and produce a constant downward flow of mucus to protect the uterine cavity from bacterial invasion. Mucus characteristics are determined by cyclic hormone levels: thick and scanty mucus when estrogen levels are low; thin, slippery, abundant mucus at the time of ovulation when estrogen levels are high. Sperm have a better opportunity to penetrate the cervical canal when mucus is slippery and abundant; they are more likely to survive the journey up the fallopian tubes and have the opportunity to fertilize an egg.

If you perceive a pain message from your cervix, during an IUD insertion or during delivery, for example, it will feel like pressure, a bearing-down sensation sometimes accompanied by cramping. Even when a portion of your cervix is frozen during cryosurgery, pricked with a needle, or pinched with a clamp, what you perceive is pressure and cramping. The cervix has a short memory for pain; for example, your clinician may leave a clamp on your cervix for five minutes to hold it steady for IUD insertion, but your perception of pain will usually subside after a minute or so.

FALLOPIAN TUBES

A limp, delicate 5-inch-long fallopian tube droops from each side of the uterus. The soft, glistening pale pink tubes lie beneath folds of translucent membrane (peritoneum). Each tube is about an inch thick where it joins the uterus, narrow as a telephone cord in the middle, and flared at the open end. The trumpet-shaped ends (infundibula) are lined with white, ruffled *fimbria,* millions of tiny feathery fingers that are constantly in motion to draw an egg into a tube once it has left an ovary. The passageway that runs the length of the tube is no wider than a single strand of spaghetti.

Fertilization occurs when the egg has completed about one-third of the distance down the tube toward the uterus. The fertilized egg completes the journey in four to five more days, with cell multiplication and growth well under way. If you are having twins, they are separate entities before they reach your uterus. Muscular contractions in the tube nudge the fertilized egg (blastocyst) along the way to the uterus, where it implants in the blood-rich endometrium.

When fertilization does not occur, the egg simply passes out of the uterus through the cervical canal completely unnoticed. It is no bigger than the period at the end of this sentence.

The functions of the fallopian tubes are to provide a favorable milieu for conception, to maintain continuous waves of contractions to move the fertilized egg down the tube toward the uterus, and to provide a fluid current to orient sperm so that they will swim in the right direction as they move out of the uterus into the tube.

OVARIES

Ovaries look like miniature, firm, slightly flattened hard-boiled eggs, appropriately enough. There are two ovaries, one on each side of the uterus near the open end of each fallopian tube. The ovaries are covered with a tough, almost gristly white membrane and usually measure about 1 by 1½ inches (see Illustration 2). They may be quite smooth, or there may be rounded lumps on the surface where egg follicles, clusters of cells that enclose a developing egg, have enlarged. Each ovary lies in

Illustration 2 Ovary—actual size.

a shapeless fold of uterine suspensory ligament. Ligaments also supply blood to the ovaries.

Ovaries produce eggs and reproductive hormones, including estrogen and progesterone. Each cycle about 20 of the roughly 300,000 egg follicles in your ovaries enlarge, secrete estrogen, and begin to ripen an egg in response to hormone signals from your pituitary gland. As development progresses one follicle predominates, while the others stop growing, shrink, and disappear into the ovarian tissue. (If two follicles predominate, fraternal twins may be conceived from two different eggs.) The dominant egg follicle continues to enlarge until the ovary's outer membrane gives way and the ripe egg spills out inside a transparent, gelatinous cloud (zona pellucida).

While the fimbria draw the egg into the fallopian tube passageway, the empty follicle undergoes a dramatic transformation. Follicle cells reassemble into a small, yellow, hormone-producing lump right on the surface of the ovary called the *corpus luteum.* The corpus luteum produces progesterone on a hormone signal from the pituitary gland. After about 14 days it stops releasing progesterone and regresses, leaving only a smooth bump on the surface of the ovary. The 14-day lifespan of the corpus luteum is the most consistent, predictable interval in the entire hormone cycle.

When your clinician manipulates an ovary during your pelvic exam, you may notice a unique twinge, somewhere between pain and a tickle. You may also feel ovarian pain at the time of ovulation or if you develop an ovarian cyst. You will be able to pinpoint pain very low in your abdomen, slightly to one side or the other of your uterus.

VAGINA

The vagina is a muscular tube 4 to 5 inches long that connects the uterus with the outside of the body. When it is empty, it has no inner space at all, like an empty shirt sleeve. The pale pink vaginal lining is slippery and rippled. Glands in the lining continuously produce a small amount of thin mucus to keep the area moist. During sexual arousal these mucus-secreting glands increase their output, and you may notice a distinctly wet sensation.

Except for the tiny cervical canal opening, your vagina is a dead-end passageway. There is absolutely no way tampons can get lost, for example. The opening to the outside of your body (introitus) is ringed with strong, elastic muscles that are capable of expanding to accommodate a baby during delivery.

The vagina is an exit passageway for menstrual discharge and babies, a favorable environment for the survival of freshly ejaculated sperm, and half the equipment necessary for penis-vagina intercourse.

The vagina has few nerve endings. An ice water douche wouldn't feel cold, for example, and you can't feel a tampon once it is in place. Most sensations deep in the vagina feel like pressure. Nerve endings are concentrated near the introitus where skin begins, and that is where you perceive sensations of heat, cold, irritation, pain, or itching.

NEIGHBORS

All the internal reproductive organs lie within the abdominal cavity, closed off from air and surrounded by the large and small intes-

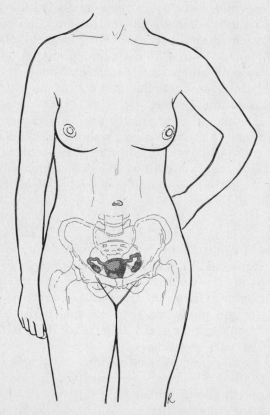

Illustration 3 The internal reproductive organs are surrounded and protected by pelvic bones.

tines, the tough, pink, glistening bladder, two ureters, and many blood vessels and nerves. All the organs in the pelvis are enclosed and protected by the large bones of the pelvic girdle (see Illustration 3). To reach your pelvic organs, a surgeon must penetrate a 1/16-inch-thick layer of abdominal skin, an ivory-colored layer of fat, a tough white layer of connective tissue (fascia), red, fibrous muscle, another layer of fascia, and the peritoneum, a thin, strong, translucent membrane that lines the entire abdominal cavity.

EXTERNAL STRUCTURES

All the external structures of the reproductive system together are called the **perineum** or **vulva** (see Illustration 4). The skin-colored outer lips (*labia majora*) and brown or pink inner lips (*labia minora*) shield and protect the vaginal introitus, urinary opening (urethral meatus), and clitoris. Both the inner and outer lips are responsive to pleasurable and painful tactile sensations. **Pubic hair**, much like eyebrows and underarm hair, serves to absorb and divert moisture. Pubic hair can be thick or scant; it can be confined to the skin areas covered by

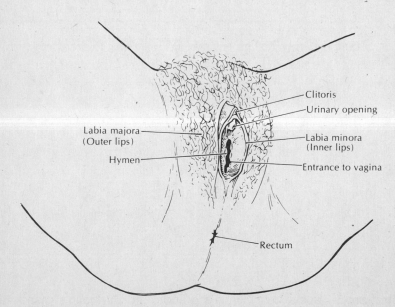

Illustration 4   All the external reproductive tract structures together are called the vulva or perineum.

the briefest bikini, or spread up the abdomen toward the navel and down the inner thighs. The **mons pubis** is a fatty cushion over the frontal pelvic bones. It is the soft, hairy triangle you see when you are standing up.

The **clitoris** is a ¼- to 1-inch-long, somewhat cylindrical mass of pink or brown erectile tissue. It lies protected beneath the clitoral hood (prepuce) just above the urinary opening. The clitoris is richly innervated and highly responsive to tactile sensations. It swells with blood during sexual arousal and is a woman's primary orgasmic focus. The sole function of the clitoris is sexual responsiveness.

Two **Skene's glands** are located near the urinary opening, one on either side (see Illustration 5). They serve no known function and may be vestigial glands originally intended to lubricate the urinary opening and protect it from bacterial invasion.

Two **Bartholin's glands** open into the vagina near the introitus, one on either side. They produce a thin mucus that lubricates the vagina and vulva to some degree. Most women aren't even aware of Bartholin's glands unless they become infected. Infections can be extremely painful.

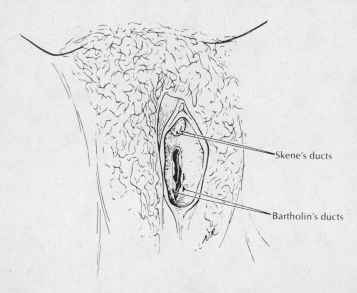

Skene's ducts

Bartholin's ducts

Illustration 5   Ducts from Skene's glands and Bartholin's glands are practically impossible to see with the naked eye.

BREASTS

A woman's two breasts are outposts of the reproductive system that develop at puberty. Fatty tissue protects the myriad milk-producing glands, and an intricate duct system channels milk into the nipple (see Illustration 6). Ligaments on the chest wall support the breast; the breast itself contains no muscles.

Nipples are erectile tissue and are quite responsive to tactile sensations. Each nipple is surrounded by a pink or brown circle of skin (areola) that is also responsive to tactile sensations. The areola may be ringed with sparse hair.

Some women have erect nipples all the time; other women find that nipple erection only occurs in response to touch, cold weather, or a sneeze. Nipples are always almost erect at the moment of orgasm. In never-pregnant women, the entire breast may swell during sexual arousal.

Breasts are responsive to cyclic hormone changes. Many women have enlarged, tender breasts just before a menstrual period. Nipple and areola color often darkens in early pregnancy.

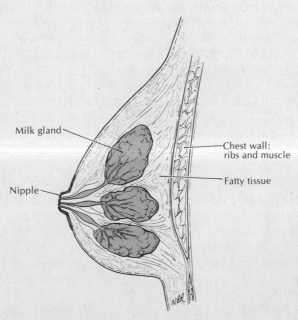

Illustration 6   The breast is composed almost entirely of fatty tissue and glands.

The two breast functions are milk production and sexual responsiveness.

Hormone Coordination of the Reproductive System

- Why are my periods so light when I take birth control Pills?
- My doctor says I have a hormone imbalance, but he isn't sure exactly what kind. Why can't he tell?
- Why do I seem to run a fever the last two weeks of every cycle?
- Why did my doctor order skull x-rays when my periods stopped?

All these questions have hormone answers. Two reproductive hormones, estrogen and progesterone, are famous, but the complex hormonal coordination of your reproductive system began three steps back and requires the participation of at least five or six other, less famous hormones, as well as input from your brain, your pituitary gland, your thyroid gland, and your adrenal glands.

Your body has two major ways to convey information from one organ or cell to another: the nervous system and the endocrine system.

The endocrine system uses hormones—chemical messengers—that are carried in the bloodstream. Hormones are produced by specialized glands such as the thyroid, the ovaries, and the adrenals. Some hormones act primarily on one specific target organ, and others have effects on a wide range of organs and cells.

A hormone's effect depends on the target organ's sensitivity to the specific hormone chemical. Target organs often have cells richly endowed with receptors for their specific hormones; the tiniest trace of hormone can cause profound changes in target cells. Hormones exert their influence by altering the chemical process within a cell, influencing a cell to grow more rapidly or to produce a specific chemical product, for example.

To the endocrinologist, your reproductive system looks like Illustration 7. Clearly, it is complex! Chances are your clinician would not be able to draw this chart from memory, and you can certainly under-

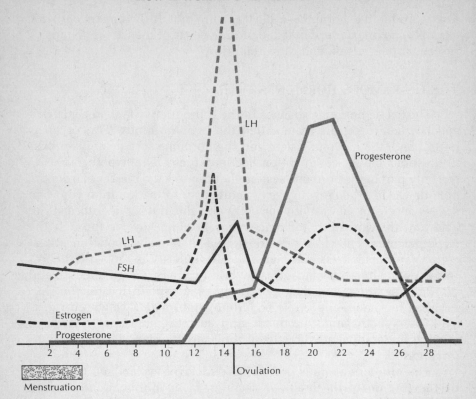

Illustration 7   Hormone activity in a normal 28-day reproductive cycle. (L Speroff, RH Glass, N Kase: *Clinical Gynecologic Endocrinology and Infertility*, ed. 2, Baltimore, Williams and Wilkins, 1978. Used with permission.)

stand the important facts about your reproductive hormones without memorizing all its details. Note that the normal level for each hormone changes continuously throughout the menstrual cycle. A normal estrogen level on cycle day 12 may be seven times higher than a normal estrogen level on cycle day 4 so **there is no one simple blood or urine test** that can determine whether your hormone levels are too high, too low, or normal.

When you read the description of hormone events in this chapter, it may be hard to believe it, but this is only part of the story. This description covers only the highlights. There are still many aspects of the reproductive hormone cycle that are not fully understood; for example, no one understands the precise cause of menstrual cramps or premenstrual tension and fluid retention.

THE UN-FAMOUS HORMONES

The cyclic hormone changes in the reproductive system begin in a specialized area of the brain called the *hypothalamus.* This organ is part of both the nervous system and the hormone system and is probably responsible for coordination between them. The hypothalamus is the only part of the hormone system that can react to messages from the outside world. The nervous system collects information from your five senses and from the rest of your body and integrates this information. The outside world can influence your hormone cycles through the hypothalamus. The clearly demonstrated relationship between physical or emotional stress and menstrual irregularity is probably orchestrated by the hypothalamus. Nearby brain centers govern appetite and body temperature, and their proximity may explain the relationship between hormones and cyclic body temperature and weight changes.

The hypothalamus produces and secretes hormones called *releasing factors* that act directly on their target organ, the nearby *pituitary gland.*

The pituitary gland is part of the endocrine system and is located in the middle of the brain. It secretes many hormones, including stimulating hormones that affect the ovaries, thyroid gland, and adrenal glands. The pituitary also produces *prolactin,* the hormone that governs breast milk production.

Disturbances in the pituitary gland can cause changes in many hormone patterns at once. Reproductive hormone problems might be accompanied by thyroid problems or by abnormal secretion of breast milk, for example. Pituitary gland enlargement from a tumor might cause headache or vision problems because the gland is in the middle of the brain and very near the optic nerves. That is why your clinician may recommend precise measurement of your field of vision and skull x-rays if she/he suspects that a pituitary tumor is causing your menstrual irregularity.

The two pituitary gland hormones that regulate reproductive function are *FSH (follicle stimulating hormone)* and *LH (luteinizing hormone).* The primary targets of both FSH and LH are the ovaries, which in turn produce the two famous hormones, estrogen and progesterone. Pituitary FSH and LH release is governed by the hypothalamus releasing factors and by the levels of estrogen and progesterone in the bloodstream.

FSH is responsible for development and maturation of the **egg follicle(s)** on the ovary. As the follicle cells develop they begin to release **estrogen.** The first half of your cycle—before ovulation—is dominated by estrogen and is called the follicular phase. As ovulation nears, estrogen production reaches a fairly high level and the pituitary is stimulated to release a burst of LH. LH triggers ovulation, release of a ripe egg from its follicle; and LH also transforms the empty follicle into a gland called the **corpus luteum.** The corpus luteum, a regrouping of the cells that formerly lined the egg follicle, produces and releases **progesterone,** the hallmark of the last half of the cycle. The corpus luteum produces estrogen during the last half of the cycle as well. Progesterone is produced only after ovulation. The second half of the cycle is called the luteal phase.

THE FAMOUS HORMONE: ESTROGEN

If there is a female hormone, it is estrogen. Actually a woman's body produces several slightly different estrogens. The primary sources of estrogen are the follicle cells of the ovaries. Fatty tissue throughout the body also manufactures estrogen by converting similar hormones (including androgens, male sex hormones that are *normally* produced in small quantities by the adrenal glands in women as well as men) into estrogen. Even after menopause, when the ovaries have stopped producing estrogen, fatty tissue production of estrogen continues, and may provide enough estrogen to cause an episode of menstruation-like bleeding following unusually high adrenal hormone production such as might occur during a stressful situation.

Your body's own estrogens are similar but not identical to the synthetic estrogens in birth control Pills and estrogen replacement therapy pills for menopausal women. Each estrogen has its own particular side effects and potency. Estrogens are carried in the bloodstream until they are deactivated by the liver and filtered by the kidneys into the urine. A woman with serious liver disease may not be able to use estrogen medication, because her estrogen may be poorly deactivated and may rise to an abnormally high level.

Estrogen can enter any body cell and has a very wide range of effects. The reproductive system is the primary target for estrogen, but alterations in other body processes do occur and may account for some of the side effects that women using estrogen may experience.

The list of known *normal* estrogen effects is very long and includes the following:

- Growth and development of the breasts, uterus, fallopian tubes, and vagina during fetal development and puberty
- Cyclic thickening of the lining of the uterus
- Production of thin, stringy, profuse cervical mucus at the time of ovulation
- Thickening of vaginal lining and production of vaginal mucus
- Promotion of vaginal acidity
- Promotion of feminine fat distribution patterns for body shape; increased thickness of fatty layers
- Increased water content and thickness of skin
- Decreased oil gland activity and oil secretion by skin
- Slows and stops growth of long bones—especially in arms and legs
- Increased protein metabolism rate
- Altered blood calcium and phosphate balance
- Increased blood level of certain plasma proteins; thyroid binding protein, cortisone binding protein
- Increased blood cholesterol levels
- Increased fluid retention
- Feedback to the brain to regulate the cyclic release pattern for FSH and LH

Clearly, too much or too little estrogen might cause a wide range of symptoms. The symptoms of too much estrogen are most often associated with the use of estrogen medication such as birth control Pills. Women undergoing menopause may experience symptoms of too little estrogen.

THE OTHER FAMOUS HORMONE: PROGESTERONE

Progesterone is manufactured by the ovary *only* after ovulation. It is released in small amounts from the adrenal glands as well, but it does not have any other significant sources. Progesterone is produced at very high levels during pregnancy and was first isolated and identified in pregnant women; so it was named pro ("supporting") gestation ("pregnancy").

Natural progesterone has a chemical structure very much like that of estrogen. Several synthetic progesterones, called *progestins,* are used in birth control Pills and for treatment of hormone disorders. Synthetic progestins often have side effects because of their structural similarity to estrogen and other hormones. A synthetic progestin may have its primary effect as a progestin, and additional effects as if it were a weak estrogen or weak androgen: a woman using a specific synthetic progestin in a birth control Pill may notice improvement (estrogen effect) or worsening (androgen effect) in her acne. Sensitivity to these effects varies from woman to woman and differs for each of the synthetic progestins. Changing to a different type of Pill may be helpful.

Deactivation of progesterone occurs at numerous sites within the body, and deactivation is not solely dependent on the liver, as is the case with estrogen. The effects of progesterone seem to be more limited than the effects of estrogen.

Known *normal* progesterone effects include the following:

- Maturation of the estrogen-primed uterine lining to promote the formation of glands, blood vessels, and distinct layers in the lining
- Decreased tendency for the uterus to contract
- Thick, sticky cervical mucus
- Maturation of the breast glands after estrogen priming
- Feedback to the ovary, pituitary gland, and hypothalamus for regulating cyclic hormone release
- Increased protein formation
- Altered liver and gallbladder function
- Increased tolerance to the presence of foreign protein, such as a fetus
- Elevation of body temperature (about 0.5 to 0.8 degrees Fahrenheit)

In early pregnancy, progesterone-induced maturation of the uterine lining allows the placenta to attach itself to the uterus properly and is essential for successful pregnancy. During the first three months of pregnancy, progesterone (and some estrogen) is produced by the corpus luteum. After three months, the placenta itself is able to produce both of these hormones and the corpus luteum wanes.

The maturation of the uterine lining is important for normal menstrual blood loss: the mature lining is able to shed its entire surface layer in a relatively short, predictable time period, with heaviest bleeding during the first 24 to 48 hours, followed by lighter bleeding and complete cessation of bleeding in five to seven days. If the lining is not matured, good separation between layers and efficient shedding of the whole lining is not likely; hence, a deficiency of progesterone can account for the prolonged or intermittent bleeding pattern that often occurs when a woman doesn't ovulate and her uterus has been exposed to estrogen stimulation alone.

OTHER HORMONES

Androgen. The ovary normally produces small amounts of male hormone (androgen), in addition to estrogen and progesterone. Ordinarily the amount of androgen is not significant enough to cause noticeable effects. When a woman's normal cyclic hormone patterns are disrupted, however, excessive androgen production can cause masculine hair growth, skin problems such as acne, scalp hair loss (balding), and deepening of the voice. Such symptoms require prompt evaluation, because similar symptoms can occur with tumors of the adrenal gland or ovary.

Prolactin. Prolactin is the hormone that regulates breast milk production (pro means "supports"; lactin means "lactation"). In the normal woman who is not breast feeding, levels of prolactin are low because its release is inhibited by the hypothalamus. Several problems can cause excessive production of prolactin and may cause you to develop breast milk. Tumors of the pituitary gland may cause excessive prolactin, or excessive amounts of synthetic estrogen can interfere with prolactin regulation and result in breast milk. Breast milk is fairly common among women using birth control Pills. Severe emotional or physical stress can affect the hypothalamus and may stop menstrual periods at the same time abnormal breast milk production starts.

Drugs, including tranquilizers (phenothiazines), amphetamines, and blood pressure medications, can cause breast milk production because they mimic the effect of high estrogen levels. *Abnormal breast milk production demands thorough investigation to be certain that a pituitary tumor is not present.* Your clinician will probably check your prolactin levels if your menstrual periods cease inexplicably.

Prostaglandins. The prostaglandins are a family of hormones whose role in reproduction is under intensive investigation. They are present in semen, the uterine lining, and in many body tissues. Each member of the prostaglandin family has its own distinct effects.

The normal role of prostaglandins is not yet fully understood. They can affect blood pressure, body temperature, kidney fluid balance, activity of the gastrointestinal tract, constriction of lung air passageways, and uterine contractions. Researchers suspect that prosta-glandin released by the uterus may play a role in menstrual cramps, for when the drug is given experimentally to normal women, it can cause cramps. It is also suspected that prostaglandin may play a role in initiating labor at the end of pregnancy. The presence of prostaglandin in semen may facilitate sperm transport or enable the sperm to unite with the egg in some way.

The only approved medical use for prostaglandins so far is termi-nation of pregnancy. The drug is most often used for abortions per-formed after the 15th week of pregnancy (see Chapter 20).

CHANGES IN THE OVARY AND UTERUS DURING THE HORMONE CYCLE

The menstrual cycle days are traditionally numbered *using the first day of a menstrual period as the first cycle day.* This scheme makes sense because menstrual bleeding is the most obvious external sign of internal cyclic changes. The first day of a menstrual period also turns out to be a logical starting point in relation to internal events. The menstrual bleeding phase is the time in the cycle when hormone levels are at their lowest point. As the production of estrogen and proges-terone drops, the hormone support to the uterine lining is lost, the lining sloughs off, and menstrual bleeding begins.

The length of a normal cycle varies from woman to woman, and from month to month in the same woman. Ninety percent of normal cycles fall between 23 and 35 days in length. Although the total number of days in the cycle may vary, the number of days between ovulation and the next menstrual period is *very consistent—about 13, 14, or 15 days.* The variations in normal cycles almost always occur in the first half of the cycle, *before* ovulation. Descriptions of the normal cycle traditionally assume that the cycle length is an average 28 days and that ovulation occurs on cycle day 14. You can adjust the descrip-tion to fit your own cycle by mentally adding or subtracting days from the *first half* of your cycle.

During the first few days of the cycle—the menstrual period itself—the falling level of estrogen triggers secretion of FSH to stimu-late growth of ovarian follicles. Initial growth occurs in 20 or so folli-cles. The cells lining the follicle soon begin to produce estrogen. One or two follicles assume dominance and continue to grow and produce estrogen, while the remaining follicles subside and shrink away (see Illustration 8).

As the follicle cells multiply and grow, estrogen production rises

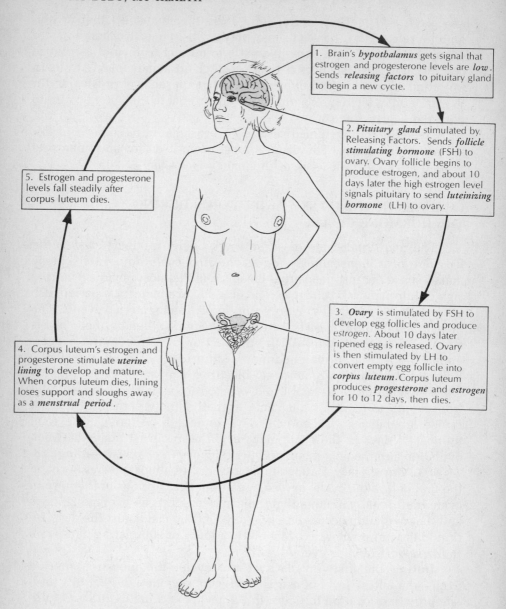

Illustration 8   Reproductive hormone cycle.

dramatically toward the middle of the cycle (days 11, 12, 13); estrogen rises to a critical peak and triggers the release of LH from the pituitary gland. The sudden burst of LH is the stimulus for ovulation: the release of the mature egg cell from inside the follicle (see Illustration 9).

After ovulation, the cells that line the fluid-filled egg follicle rearrange themselves into a cluster. LH changes follicular cell chemistry,

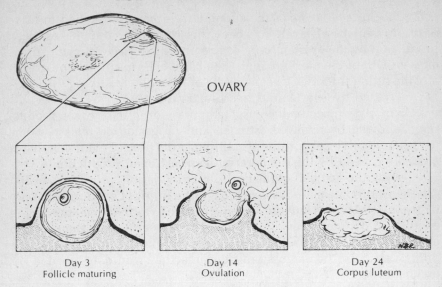

OVARY

| Day 3 | Day 14 | Day 24 |
| Follicle maturing | Ovulation | Corpus luteum |

Illustration 9   Changes in the ovary during the menstrual cycle.

and a yellow pigment called lutein accumulates within the cells (hence the name corpus luteum—yellow body). The cells resume production of estrogen and under the LH influence begin to produce progesterone as well. Both estrogen and progesterone are released during the last half of the cycle.

The LH level gradually decreases during the last half of the cycle. By cycle days 22 to 24, the LH level is so low that corpus luteum function is no longer supported and production of estrogen and progesterone declines rapidly. This drop results in menstrual bleeding and brings to an end one full cycle. The low estrogen level will soon serve as a trigger for pituitary production of FSH to begin the next cycle.

Some women notice cramping pain on one side of the lower abdomen at the time of ovulation. Fluid or blood released from the ruptured egg follicle may irritate the abdominal lining, or perhaps stretching of the surface of the ovary by follicle growth causes pain. Ovulation pain usually lasts only a few hours.

Except for ovulation pain, all the cyclic changes described so far are silent: they occur without noticeable symptoms. The *external* evidence of the reproductive cycle (bleeding) is the last step in the chain of hormone events and involves the effects of decreased estrogen and progesterone on the uterus and cervix.

The first few days of the new cycle set the stage for changes in the uterine lining (endometrium). As menstrual flow stops (on day 4, 5, 6, or 7), the surface layers of the endometrium have been shed to leave only the thin basal layer. At about this time (day 7 or 8), estrogen production by the ovarian follicle is beginning to rise. Estrogen stimulates growth of the uterine lining. The basal cells multiply, and gradually the lining thickens. By the middle of the cycle the lining thickness has increased five- to tenfold (see Illustration 10).

As ovulation occurs there is a temporary drop in estrogen production, followed by renewed estrogen and progesterone release. Some women notice a brief episode of spotting at the time of ovulation that is probably caused by the temporary lull in estrogen production.

During the last half of the cycle, after ovulation, progesterone and estrogen stimulate maturation of the uterine lining. The lining does not increase in thickness, but the cells reorganize to form mucus-producing glands and distinct layers. Small blood vessels grow into the lining to nourish it and to be available in case a fertilized egg implants. The lining cells also begin to store nutrients that would be needed for pregnancy.

At the conclusion of the cycle, estrogen and progesterone levels drop and the stimulus to the mature lining is lost. Decreasing blood flow into its tiny arteries causes shrinking and deterioration of the

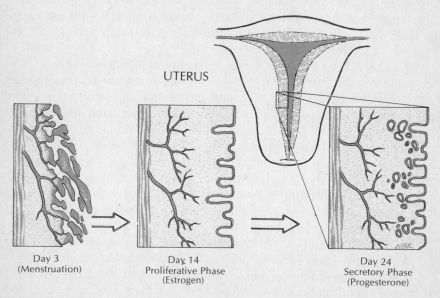

UTERUS

Day 3
(Menstruation)

Day 14
Proliferative Phase
(Estrogen)

Day 24
Secretory Phase
(Progesterone)

Illustration 10 Changes in the uterine lining during the menstrual cycle.

surface layers. Most of the endometrium separates from the uterine wall and is shed as menstrual blood.

Cyclic changes in estrogen and progesterone also produce changes in mucus production by the cervix. During the initial low-estrogen days of the cycle, there is very little mucus. As estrogen rises, mucus production increases and reaches a peak that coincides with ovulation. Mucus at the time of ovulation is characteristically fluid, stringy, elastic, and abundant.

Immediately after ovulation, as estrogen drops and progesterone appears, the cervical mucus becomes thick, sticky, and much less profuse. Mucus remains scant throughout the rest of the cycle, although some women do notice a second increase in mucus a few days before menstruation that is probably the result of renewed estrogen production during the last half of the cycle.

WHEN PREGNANCY OCCURS

If fertilization occurs, the hormone patterns of the last half of the menstrual cycle are altered. Assuming that you ovulate on cycle day 14, your egg can be fertilized on day 14 or 15 and implantation of the embryo in the uterine lining will occur on day 21 or 22. Soon after implantation, the production of pregnancy hormone (HCG—human chorionic gonadotropin) by the developing placenta reaches detectable levels. HCG hormone closely resembles LH hormone and takes over the declining LH role as a continuing stimulus to the corpus luteum. The corpus luteum, in turn, continues with its production of progesterone throughout the first three months of pregnancy. After the third month, progesterone production by the placenta itself completely replaces progesterone production by the corpus luteum. HCG *interrupts* the repetitive cycle of hormone changes and prevents menstrual loss of the uterine lining by maintaining progesterone production.

Puberty

by Geraldine Oliva, M.D.

Puberty is the phase of the life cycle during which a young woman's reproductive tract organs mature in size and function. Every female child is born with the organs and hormones described in the first sections of this chapter. During childhood, the hormone-producing thermostat of the hypothalamus is turned off, and no matter how low the level of estrogen or progesterone circulating in the child's blood, the hormonal thermostat in the brain does not switch on, as it would in a mature woman. No one knows just why or how this hormone system begins to function at puberty, but we do know that there is some relationship between body weight and the onset of puberty; most young women begin puberty at about 92 pounds.

The first changes of puberty are invisible. The hypothalamus becomes sensitive to the reproductive hormone levels, and the thermostat turns on. The hypothalamus gives the pituitary gland a signal to produce follicle stimulating hormone (FSH), and FSH travels to the immature ovary and causes it to grow and to secrete estrogen.

OUTWARD SIGNS OF PUBERTY

As the body's level of estrogen rises, a young woman's sex organs grow and mature and the first signs of puberty become apparent. The first outward sign of puberty in the young woman is usually budding of the **breast nipple** (see Illustration 11). Her nipple begins to grow and stand away from the chest wall, and later the breast itself begins to

STAGES OF BREAST DEVELOPMENT

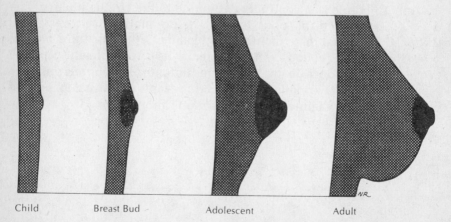

Child   Breast Bud   Adolescent   Adult

Illustration 11   The breast bud usually appears at about age 11; the nipple enlarges, and a **firm mound** of breast tissue develops under the skin. The adolescent breast often has a prominent, puffy areola.

grow. In 95% of young women, breast bud development occurs between ages 8½ and 13 (see Illustration 12). At the same time, the young woman begins her growth spurt, a period of rapid growth that ends when adult height has been reached. Meanwhile, estrogen causes the vagina and uterus to grow, and the lining of the uterus begins to thicken. Estrogen is also responsible for fat deposits over the hips and thighs that give her body a female contour.

Next the adrenal glands start to produce male sex hormones (androgen), which play an essential role in a young woman's pubertal development. No one knows why the adrenal glands begin making more of these hormones, but we do know that it happens as the estrogen level rises in the blood. The male hormones cause the growth of pubic hair and underarm hair and further stimulate the growth spurt. In

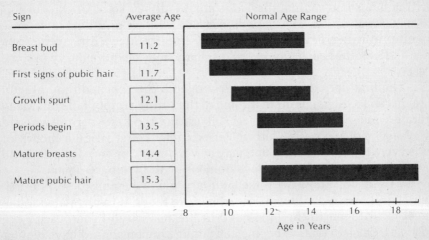

Sign	Average Age	Normal Age Range
Breast bud	11.2	
First signs of pubic hair	11.7	
Growth spurt	12.1	
Periods begin	13.5	
Mature breasts	14.4	
Mature pubic hair	15.3	

Age in Years

Illustration 12 Normal age ranges for each phase of pubertal development as documented in a 1972 study. The average age for puberty has steadily declined over the last several decades. A 1976 study of menstrual period onset found that young women in Britain began menstrual periods at about 12.8 years of age with an average range of 10.4 to 15.2 years. Average ages for other development signs may be shifting downward as well. Source: WA Marshall and J Tanner: in Albert Altchek (ed): *The Pediatric Clinics of North America* 19(3), August 1972; and L Zacharias, WM Rand, and R Wurtman: *Obstetric and Gynecologic Survey* 31:325–337, 1976.

95% of young women, hair appears between ages 9 and 14. The male hormones may also cause acne; for most young people the level of male hormones falls once puberty is completed, and the skin clears up.

When breast development is further along and the young woman has probably purchased her first bra, she will probably have a triangle of pubic hair and some hair under her arms, and her growth will have slowed down. She can now expect her first menstrual period.

MENSTRUATION

Menstruation usually begins between ages 10 and 16. The first period usually occurs about two years after the first signs of breast development. It is normal for periods to begin as early as six months or as late as five years after breasts begin to grow. Often a young woman will notice some vaginal discharge six months or so before she begins to menstruate. This discharge is clear or whitish and does not cause itching, burning, or foul odor. She may simply notice a little wetness on her underclothes each day, or the discharge may be quite heavy in some cases.

The first periods occur when estrogen has thickened the lining of the uterus to such a point that some of the lining simply falls off. Many young women have irregular periods during the first year or two, and they may not yet be ovulating. Periods may come twice a month or every two to three months, and may be very heavy or very light and still be normal for the stage of development of the young woman.

We do not know why the pituitary gland begins to secrete LH, which initiates ovulation. These events are thought to be related to the level of estrogen in the blood and to the maturity of the ovary's egg follicles. Once ovulation begins, the young woman should have regular periods every four weeks or so. Ovulation is necessary for pregnancy to occur, and many young women think that they are safe because their periods are irregular or infrequent. *Remember that there is no way of telling when ovulation will start* and that irregular periods will not necessarily protect a young woman from pregnancy.

FIRST PELVIC EXAMINATION

There are no hard and fast rules about when a young woman should begin having regular pelvic exams. If she has normal development for her age and no medical problems, she might consider having her first exam about two years after her periods begin. Her clinician can teach her how to do self breast examination, how to use tampons, and how her own body works. The pelvic exam can be performed comfortably on most young women in this age group. The single most important advantage of a pelvic exam for a normal, healthy young woman is that she will learn what a clinician's care can offer her. When she becomes sexually active or when she develops a problem in her reproductive organs, she will have some understanding of her body and will be less fearful about having an exam.

Any young woman who develops a heavy vaginal discharge that itches, burns, or has a foul odor needs an exam. Vaginal bleeding in a young woman before breast or pubic hair development requires a pelvic exam. Severe lower abdominal pain in a young woman with breast development and pubic hair but no periods requires an exam. Any sexually active young woman should have regular exams. Although periods may *normally* be irregular for the first year or two, there are certain circumstances that require an exam:

- No signs of puberty by age 14 or no periods by age 16
- No periods for several months in a sexually active young woman, even if her periods have been irregular
- Regular periods for four to six months and then no periods for more than four months
- Menstrual cramps so severe that the young woman misses school
- Heavy vaginal bleeding that might cause anemia
- Vaginal bleeding lasting more than ten days
- Known or suspected exposure to DES (Diethylstilbestrol) during fetal development (DES daughter)

The period of sexual maturation and growth is exciting but sometimes frightening for a young woman. Parents can make it a comprehensible and positive experience if they are comfortable themselves and carefully prepare the young woman for the changes that will occur, and if they are ready to deal with questions and concerns as they arise. It is probably best if parents can anticipate pubertal changes and discuss them with their children ahead of time. A young woman who knows in advance what puberty is all about is much less likely to be frightened or bewildered.

Emerging Sexuality in the Teenage Years

by Geraldine Oliva, M.D.

We are bombarded daily with references to the "sexual revolution," and each report is likely to bring pangs of fear, alarm, and sometimes outrage to parents of teenagers. Just how real this revolution is, how parents can prepare themselves and their teenage daughter or son for the realities of the liberated world, are subjects that occupy the minds of many parents. There are no easy answers. It may be best to concentrate on facts and options; the ultimate decision making about these issues falls to the individual parents and teenagers themselves.

A number of recent nationwide studies have described patterns of teenage sexual activity and have elucidated the trends that are occurring in the 1980s. Between 1971 and 1976 there was an increase in the percentage of teenagers who were having intercourse. In 1976, about 55% of teenage women had had at least one sexual experience by age 19; this was true of young women in all social and economic groups (1). Another way of looking at this, of course, is that 45% of teenage women **have not** had intercourse. Almost half of the teenage women have decided not to participate in the sexual revolution—yet. This fact certainly contradicts the media picture of an entire population of sexually active teenagers.

These studies have also demonstrated that only about 27% of sexually active teenage women regularly use a method of birth control and that there are about 780,000 premarital pregnancies among teens each year (2). Studies in family planning clinics that serve teens have found that the average lag time between beginning intercourse and using birth control is one year. Some 70% of teens who seek family planning clinic services do so because they think they might be pregnant (3).

These facts put to rest the myth that teens become sexually active earlier when birth control methods and services are available to them. Even when they use birth control, most teens choose over-the-counter products such as condoms or foam, or they rely on withdrawal or douching. At least 25% of young women surveyed for these studies **did not understand the menstrual cycle** and did not know when in their cycle they were most likely to become pregnant. Teenagers seem to get most of their information about sex from other teens or the media and get very little from parents or health professionals, according to these studies.

Sex education is an extremely controversial issue. Many parents fear that knowledge about sex will lead teenagers to begin sexual activity. It is apparent from recent studies, however, that with or without access to reliable information, teens are choosing to experiment with sex in increasing numbers.

SUGGESTIONS FOR PARENTS

Parents themselves are often uncertain about their own sexual knowledge so they are uncomfortable about discussing sex with their own children. They may put off discussions that ideally should begin in early childhood. When parents delay discussion of sexual issues, the young person may get the message that sex is a taboo subject. The teenager either remains ignorant or goes to friends for information, and the parent has no idea what her/his child's level of curiosity is and loses the opportunity to be helpful and constructive during the child's formative years. The teenager, in turn, has no resources for coping with pressure to experiment with sex and may be totally incapable of handling the tremendous amount of sexual emphasis and stimulation in the environment. When parents think ahead and fill in the gaps in their own sexual information, and even seek help from health professionals or educators to learn when and how to begin sex education, everyone benefits.

Young children begin to have sexual feelings and questions early. All parents notice masturbatory activities of infants and young children and witness the emergence of a toddler's sexual identity. It is never too early for a child to know the parts of her/his body and to name them accurately. Body exploration is a normal part of child development. In the beginning this is a fairly public activity, but by age 4 or 5 almost all children understand that this is a private issue and public genital exploration will be uncommon, *provided* parents have not overreacted.

Four- and five-year-olds begin to wonder where babies come from. Simple, straightforward answers geared to the child's age usually satisfy a child. It is hard to give inappropriate information, since children will absorb and remember only what they can comprehend.

As a child reaches puberty she/he begins to hear a lot of talk about sex from friends. There is no way to "protect" a child from sex-related information. Good preparation for the changes of puberty will take the fear and "dirtiness" out of sexuality, and a matter-of-fact approach will strengthen the teenager's ability to cope with emerging body changes and feelings. If a parent feels uneasy about acquiring or providing sex information, help is available. A PTA group can invite a sex education speaker, or a parent can, get help and advice from a pediatrician or family planning specialist.

A child will know if her/his parents are reluctant to talk about sex; so the best approach for the parents is to be open about their own discomfort. Nobody knows everything about sex, and many people are embarrassed by some aspects of sexuality. Giving a teenager a book to read is not bad, but a book is not enough. A teenager needs someone to talk to about the feelings and questions that books elicit. Some parents go with a teenage child to a sex education program at a Planned Parenthood clinic or other health facility, and they learn together. A sex education program is often a very good experience for both parents and teens, and it helps them to learn to talk to each other.

TALKING TO TEENAGERS

It is never too late to start talking to your teenager about reproductive health. A 14-year-old will be aware that parents may be uncomfortable talking about sex; she/he is embarrassed, too, and is beginning to rely more and more on information from friends. Push on! You might read a book together for a start. Begin with very factual information that both of you can feel comfortable with, such as basic anatomy and menstruation. Then go on to pregnancy. At this point you can begin to discuss feelings and decision making about sex. If you don't get into this area, the game is lost. Very few teens will simply accept blanket statements such as, "it's immoral unless you're married," or, "our religion prohibits it." Teens are at a point in their lives when they **question everything,** and if you can participate in their questioning, you have a chance to be truly helpful.

It helps when parents can recall the feelings they had in their own teenage days and can remember how they felt about parents, how they wanted to be accepted by the "in" group at school, how they wanted to be popular with the opposite sex, how they liked to take risks and do crazy things. It is especially important to remember the sexual pressures all of us have experienced at whatever age—how hard it was to say "no," especially when you liked someone or had sexual feelings yourself. Imagine what it must be like in the 1970s to be a newly emerging person in a world of changing values, bombarded by hundreds of sexual stimuli every day!

Before you try to discuss sexual behavior with your teenager, remember that there are a number of crucial psychological tasks that a young person must master on the journey to adulthood. Separation from parents and efforts to attain a separate identity are major struggles that often seem like totally uncalled-for recalcitrance, at least to parents. It often seems that your teenager meets any sort of request with objections. Your teenager may spend most of the time in her/his room, and may refuse to participate in family activities and outings. This can be a very difficult time for everyone, but it is essential for your child's developmental process. Many teens even manage to sail through adolescence smoothly. Teens begin to focus on friends as they search for identity. Utmost in the mind of your teenager is being acceptable to friends, and many teens will go to any lengths to be accepted. Your teen is acquiring skills and competence and beginning to think of the future in more concrete terms. The more solid an opinion she/he has of her/himself as a competent individual, the more capable she/he is of dealing with the tasks of emerging adulthood.

The older teen begins to emerge as a truly separate and distinct person, apart from family or friends. This young person is developing a sense of competence and self-esteem and is for the first time capable of truly intimate relationships with others. Her/his sexuality is reaching an adult level as well. Teenagers vary in when and how they deal with these developmental tasks, but all teenagers struggle with them sooner or later.

You have just had a crash course in child and adolescent psychology, and much of it may be overwhelming. Relax! You know your child, and the love and support you have given in the childhood years will carry all of you through the tumult of adolescence. The most difficult part for most parents is dealing with the adolescent's need for separation, privacy, and the right to make her/his own mistakes. All parents go through it. There is no way to shelter a teenager but there *are* ways to provide guidance and support. She/he will grow 10,000-fold in an environment that fosters her/his individuality. Self-esteem and a strong sense of a positive future are likely to lead to a happy, peaceful, and satisfying adult life. Furthermore, teenagers with self-esteem are likely to use contraception well and to avoid the pitfalls of early unwanted pregnancy.

In initiating discussions of sex, it helps if you have confidence in your teenager and are prepared for her/him to make important decisions independently. Given the same set of facts, different individuals make different decisions. Your teenager's values may be different from yours, and nothing will change that.

Hit the subject head-on. Allow your teen to back away on the first approach. She/he may not be ready to talk about sex with you. Most teens can't even imagine their parents having intercourse! Try to open the door. Sometimes it helps to talk about sex in terms of teenage friends or relatives. You might talk about a young woman at school who got pregnant and had the baby or had an abortion. This approach gives you room to discuss a major pitfall of sex—unprotected intercourse that leads to pregnancy. Moralizing about sex rarely helps, but discussing sex in realistic terms does help. Raise questions such as, "What will Jane do after the baby is born? Who will take care of it if she wants to stay in school? How will she support it? Will the father take any responsibility for the child?" If Jane has had an abortion, how does she feel about it? How does your teenager feel about it? What does your teenager think about giving up a child for adoption? Share your feelings. What would you want for your daughter if she became pregnant?

Discuss the pros and cons of teenage pregnancy. You may see only negative facts, but your teenager may think that it would be nice to grow up with a baby; or that it would be nice to have someone to love and who loves her; or that it would be fun to play with a baby. These ideas may sound silly to anyone who has raised a child, but these are common feelings among teenagers. If your teenager seems to feel the need for love from a baby, work on other ways of providing love yourself.

Some teens answer questions about the financial responsibilities of parenthood with, "I could go on welfare," or "We could live here." It is important for your teenager to understand the financial realities of childbearing, the inadequacies of the welfare system, *your* financial limitations, and how willing you would be to raise another child.

Sexually transmitted infections are commonly covered in high school sex education programs. The subject, however, is usually presented in outdated movies of deformed people in the final stages of syphilis. The fact is that people in the final stages of syphilis are very rare today. The most common infection we see in teenagers is gonorrhea. There are usually no lasting effects if gonorrhea is treated promptly, but gonorrhea can scar a young woman's fallopian tubes and cause sterility if treatment is delayed or inadequate. *Any teenage woman who is having intercourse needs to know the symptoms of gonorrhea, how to avoid it, and where to go for treatment.*

It helps young people to know that sexual feelings are normal and to have some idea about how to deal with sexual feelings. Sometimes touching feels good, and if touching happens in an affectionate relationship, it can lead to sexual exploration. Let the young person know that you recognize this possibility, and then allow for her/his expression of feelings. It may be helpful to discuss the issue in terms of other people and to ask what the teenager's friends are saying. "Do you have friends who are having intercourse? What do they say about it? What do you think about their behavior? What are the pluses and minuses?"

If your teen is starting to date, she/he needs to know how to handle sexual advances. You might ask, "What would you say if your date wanted to experiment with sex? Suppose you want to participate? Suppose you don't? What are your choices? Can you say no and still keep the relationship? If you say no, then what?"

A parent who wants an open and honest relationship with a teen needs to *be prepared for any answers the teen may give.* If it looks as though your teen is likely to start having intercourse, she/he needs to know how and where to get birth control information. You may be opposed, but your opposition may not deter your teen, who is trying to define her/his identity. Express your opinion, but consider your teen's feelings too. You might say, "I think you're too young, but if you do decide to have intercourse, make sure that you use some birth control." Some parents prefer to know when their teens start having intercourse, and others prefer that their teen seek advice elsewhere. *Your teen needs to know where you stand.*

TEENS AND BIRTH CONTROL

Studies show that teens in general aren't very good birth control users for a number of reasons:

- Teens may feel guilty about having sex and may deny their intentions. Getting a method of birth control would be an admission that they are doing "something wrong."
- Teens may not know where to go for confidential birth control services. In most states it is legal for teens to seek birth control services without parental consent. Planned Parenthood, county, and state family planning clinics may provide free services to teens.
- Teens may enjoy taking risks and may be at the stage of development where they have not learned to make decisions based on careful judgments.
- Teens may be rebelling against family or society.

Talking about all these issues will help your teen make responsible choices so that she/he can avoid an experience that could cause lasting harm.

A young person who is armed with good information and who has some practice in decision making is unlikely to find her/himself in an unexpected situation such as an unplanned pregnancy. And a parent can feel confident that a teenager is a *competent* individual making *competent* choices: maybe not the parent's choices, but good choices just the same.

Menopause

If you grew up in Pakistan, China, or Africa, you would probably believe that the good life begins at menopause. In many cultures, women past the childbearing years are respected and revered for their wisdom; younger women take over child care (at last), and relatives look to older women for advice on all important family matters. Older American women aren't always so fortunate. In our youth-worshiping culture, some women even dread menopause.

Most female mammals bear young until they die, and reproduction is often the cause of death. Ours is an unusual species in that female reproductive function ceases before the end of life. If indeed evolutionary changes happen for a reason, then we can assume that nature intends for postmenopausal women to have a significant role in our cultures; we Americans may have some important lessons to learn from other cultures.

> I only had hot flashes for a few months. Our sex life was fine once I started using vaginal lubricant so I wouldn't be so dry. I think you have to be philosophical about getting older. What was it Maurice Chevalier said? "It isn't so bad when you consider the alternatives"? That's really true, I think.
>
> If you enjoy being alive—and I do—it *is* a little saddening to look in the mirror and realize you are *aging*. But since *nothing* is going to turn back the clock I concentrate on the good things: more time for my own projects now that the children are grown; a sense of my own hard-won wisdom. The last few years I have felt quite peaceful and contented. I think life's unavoidable changes are much harder when you resist them.
>
> —*Woman, 62*

Physical and Hormone Changes with Aging

The transition from the reproductive phase of a woman's life cycle into the postreproductive phase is called the *climacteric.* Menopause, the cessation of menstrual periods, is the most obvious event, but many other changes occur as well. Most women are able to cope with this transition without difficulty. For some women, however, the physical and hormonal changes that accompany the climacteric can be quite distressing and disabling.

Approximately 50% of women undergo menopause at or before 50 years of age, although the normal range is fairly wide, 45 to 55. The timing of menopause is not predictable. You may follow the same pattern that your mother and sisters experienced, or your menopause may be earlier or later. Climacteric changes begin considerably before menopause. A significant decline in fertility occurs in the mid-40s. The reason for this decline is not known, but a decrease in the number of maturing ovary follicles and in ovarian estrogen production occurs at about this time.

The rate of ovarian changes varies from individual to individual. Some women seem to experience a gradual decrease in hormone production over a period of several years that is associated with irregular menstrual cycles or prolonged intervals between periods. For other women, the changes may be more abrupt, with a normal cycle one month and a complete cessation of bleeding two or three months later. Women who undergo premature menopause because of surgical removal of the ovaries have extremely abrupt hormone changes, and symptoms related to menopause are often quite severe.

As the climacteric nears completion, ovarian estrogen production declines to extremely low levels. The ovary is no longer responsive to the stimulating hormones produced by the brain. The pituitary FSH and LH output rises to high levels because their release is triggered by low levels of estrogen.

As estrogen production by the ovary declines, the importance of *other* estrogen production increases. Fatty tissue is able to convert other hormones to estrogen; hence, estrogen levels do not drop to zero. In some women, a significant estrogen level is maintained into old age.

The relationship between the known hormone changes and the various symptoms that occur during the climacteric, however, is not well understood.

COMMON SYMPTOMS AND PROBLEMS

Physicians used to identify low estrogen levels as the cause of a host of problems, ranging from hot flashes to irrationality and decrepitude. Research in the last decade, however, has concluded that estrogen drop can be unequivocally blamed for only a few problems. Problems that are clearly improved by estrogen replacement therapy include hot flashes; vaginal dryness; muscle tone loss in the urinary tract; and bone density loss caused by osteoporosis. The use of estrogen replacement therapy and alternatives for nonhormonal management of menopause symptoms are discussed in Chapter 36.

Hot Flashes. The occurrence of hot flashes (flushes) is an almost universal symptom of the climacteric. A flush usually begins as a sudden, unprovoked wave of heat in the trunk or chest that radiates to the head, arms, and legs. Perspiration and red flushing of neck and facial skin may accompany the heat wave. For some women, flushes are brief and infrequent and occur once a week or less. For other women, hot flashes can be severe enough and frequent enough to be disabling, interrupting sleep at night or interfering with work and normal daytime activities.

Flushes are usually most bothersome immediatety before and after menstrual periods stop. They tend to subside in frequency and severity over a 6- to 12-month period as the body adjusts to decreased hormone levels. Occasional flushes may occur over longer periods, but it is very unusual for women to report serious problems with flushes for longer than a year or so.

Vaginal Dryness and Urethral Changes. The lining of the vagina is a specialized mucus membrane similar to the lining of the mouth. It is very elastic and has a rich supply of mucus-secreting glands that produce lubrication during sexual arousal. The vaginal walls and the skin of the vulva and urinary opening (urethra) respond directly to estrogen stimulation. When estrogen is low, therefore, the vaginal lining becomes thinner and loses some of its elasticity and mucus-producing capability. These changes, called atrophy, often result in vaginal dryness that is especially noticeable during intercourse. Dryness can result in greater susceptibility to injury, vaginal irritation, and infection.

Similar changes in the lining of the urethra may result in irritation and loss of elastic support of the urethral muscles. Poor muscle support can aggravate problems with bladder control, such as involuntary urine loss with coughing or sneezing.

Unlike hot flashes, the vaginal and urethral changes usually occur gradually and often persist, becoming more severe throughout the menopausal years.

Bone Density Loss. Osteoporosis due to estrogen deficiency is one specific form of bone density loss that occurs in about 25% of white women after menopause. (Black women rarely develop osteoporosis.) Since there are many other causes of bone density loss, this problem requires careful evaluation to determine whether or not estrogen deficiency is a significant factor in your case.

Loss of bone density results in fragile bones and an increased risk of fracture. Fractures commonly occur in the spine (vertebrae), and they may be the cause of decreasing height and gradual vertebral deformity, the "dowager's hump." Fractures of the wrist are very common. An increased risk for hip fracture is especially important because of the serious or even fatal complications that are linked to hip fracture. Routine height measurements and careful evaluation if a bone fracture occurs may help your clinician identify this problem. See Chapter 36 for routine care recommendations after menopause.

Psychological Problems. It is not known whether nervousness, loss of sex drive, depression, headache, anxiety, skin changes, and memory loss result from decreased hormone levels. Treating these problems with estrogen has produced no better results than has treatment with a placebo (sugar pills that contain no drugs); therefore, estrogen deficiency per se probably is not the cause of these problems. It is not known whether other hormone changes may contribute to these problems. Hormone changes that occur at puberty and recur cyclically throughout the reproductive years are known to influence emotional equilibrium. Stress at home or at work or difficulties resulting from a partner's adjustment to transitions in his own life cycle can also profoundly affect emotional well-being. Cultural values about aging likewise have an influence on emotional well-being.

A reasonable conclusion is that the emotional problems attributed to hormone deficiency probably stem from a *combination* of factors: hormonal, personal, and cultural. Most women feel the effects of at least some of these factors, but the majority are able to cope smoothly with the transition to the postreproductive years and require little or no assistance. It is extremely rare to encounter serious psychiatric disability associated with menopause in a person who has not had previous psychiatric disease.

REFERENCES

1. Zelnick M, Kantner JF: Sexual and contraceptive experience of young un-married women in the United States, 1976 and 1971. *Family Planning Perspectives* 9(2):55–71, 1977. Statistics for teenage sexual experience and contraceptive practice cited in this chapter are all found in *Eleven Million Teenagers: What Can Be Done About the Epidemic of Adolescent Pregnancies in the United States?* Prepared and published by The Alan Guttmacher Institute, The Research and Development Division of Planned Parenthood Federation of America, New York, 1976. Copies of the monograph are available from The Alan Guttmacher Institute, 360 Park Avenue South (at 26th), New York, New York 10010.
2. Zelnick M, Kantner JF: Contraceptive patterns and premarital pregnancy among women aged 15–19 in 1976. *Family Planning Perspectives* 10(3):135–142, 1978.
3. San Francisco-Alameda Planned Parenthood Association: Unpublished survey of new patients registering for services, 1977.

2 | How to Examine Your Own Breasts

Any clinician will tell you that women find their own breast lumps most of the time. It is rare for a clinician to find a lump that a woman has not first discovered herself. You are the best person to examine your breasts because you know your own breast tissue much better than your clinician does if you examine yourself regularly. And you are the only person you know who will certainly be around once a month when it is time for your breast examination.

Almost all clinicians recommend that women do a breast self-examination (BSE) once each cycle, and for most women that means about once every four weeks.

The best time to do your exam is right after your menstrual period when your estrogen levels are low. A high level of estrogen sometimes causes breast swelling and tenderness that can make it difficult for you to do a careful, accurate exam. If your period begins on Monday, for example, mark your calendar to do your exam the following Monday. If your periods are very irregular or if you do not have periods for some reason (hysterectomy or menopause, for example), pick a date for your exam each month. Use your birthday, the first day of the month, or any day that is easy to remember.

Overcoming Natural Resistance

Few women enjoy examining their own breasts. After all, you might find something, and that is a completely understandable worry.

> I've examined my breasts each and every month for at least ten years, and I still have to *make* myself do it every time! I always do it *in the morning of a weekday;* so I know I can call my doctor *immediately* if I find anything. I don't think I could do it at night.
>
> —*Woman, 33*

It would be less frightening to find a lump that wasn't there a month ago than to find a lump that wasn't there a year ago. Two recent breast cancer studies estimate that there may be a 15% to 24% increase in survival after breast cancer for women who do monthly breast self-exams compared to women who do not (1). Investigators believe that regular breast self-exams clearly helped women find breast cancer at an earlier, more treatable stage.

Breast cancer is most common in women over 35 but can occur in young women as well. If you begin examining your breasts as a teen-ager, you will be an absolute expert on your own breast tissue by the time you reach the age when breast cancer is a significant risk. Most clinicians advise young women to begin BSE as soon as they begin having menstrual periods.

Breast lumps are fairly common, and about eight out of ten lumps are **not cancer.** See your clinician at once if you find a lump. You may avoid anxious, worrying nights. There is absolutely nothing to be gained by waiting to see if your lump goes away. You need an exam, and you need your clinician's advice immediately. Read Chapter 32 to learn how your clinician will evaluate and treat you should you find a lump.

How to Examine Your Own Breasts

A thorough breast exam has three stages: (1) observing your breasts in a mirror; (2) examining your breasts while you are lying down; and (3) examining your breasts while you are sitting or standing.

OBSERVING YOUR BREASTS IN A MIRROR

Stand in front of a mirror that has good lighting and let your arms hang relaxed at your sides. Is there any change in the direction your nipples are pointing? Does either nipple seem unusually drawn up into the breast? Do you see any skin areas that are dimpled or reddened? Is there an area of skin with enlarged, coarse pores, skin that looks somewhat like an orange peel? Report any of these changes to your clinician promptly.

Put both hands on your hips and push down. Do your chest muscles contract about the same amount? (They should.) Does any skin area dimple when you press down? (It shouldn't.) *Put your hands in front of your chest at about heart level and press your palms together. Then raise your arms straight above your head.* Check each time for muscle contraction and dimpling.

Squeeze each nipple gently. Is there any discharge at all? It is not uncommon to have some nipple secretions after delivery, miscarriage, or abortion, or if you take birth control Pills. Women whose sexual patterns include a great deal of breast stimulation may develop a nipple discharge. Not all nipple discharges indicate illness, but you should *discuss any nipple discharge with your clinician.*

BREAST EXAM—LYING DOWN

When you lie flat on your back, your breast tissue spreads out over your rib cage and it is easier to feel deep tissue layers with your fingers.

Lie down and put one arm behind your head. You will first examine the breast on the same side as your raised arm. (Putting your arm behind your head stretches chest muscles so that you will have a firmer surface to press downward on.) *Feel every part of your breast by pressing the flat part of your fingertips on a spot and then moving your whole hand in a small circle so that the breast tissue slides back and forth under the skin* (see Illustration 1). You can move your hand around in any pattern you like as long as you examine all parts of your breast. Go all the way to the middle of your chest and all the way under your arm. Be sure to check directly under your nipple.

You may notice that glands are a little more prominent in the outer half of your breast than the inner half (see Illustration 2). This is normal. *Examine your armpit carefully for enlarged lymph nodes.* An enlarged node would feel like a rounded, firm bump. If you find an enlarged node in your armpit, talk to your clinician promptly.

If your breasts are large, it may be hard to feel all the way down to your chest wall, especially when you are checking the lower half of

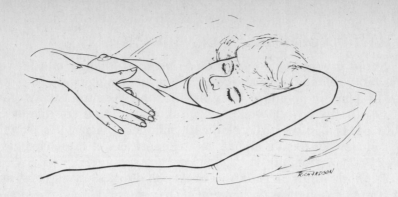

Illustration 1 Use the flat part of your fingertips to feel each area of the breast. Repeat your exam in a standing or sitting position.

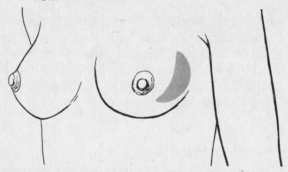

Illustration 2 Glands can be quite prominent in the outer half of your breast.

your breasts. Use your other hand to shift your breast around so that you can check each part.

Repeat the entire procedure for your other breast. Your behind-the-head arm becomes your examining arm, and vice versa.

BREAST EXAM—SITTING OR STANDING

It is important to repeat exactly the same examination steps while you are sitting or standing, because a sitting or standing position creates a different distribution of breast tissue. Some lumps are easier to find while you are lying down, and other lumps are more apparent when you are sitting or standing.

40

What You Can Learn from Your Breast Exam

You examine your breasts in order **to detect a change** since your exam four weeks ago. Certainly you will feel more confident about your ability to spot a change when you've done 40 exams than when you've done three.

> The first time I examined myself I didn't know *what* I was doing! I felt about 20 places I thought were lumps! I thought everything was supposed to feel smooth, and I sure didn't feel smooth.
> So I went to my doctor; she checked me, and said my breasts were normal.
> After about ten months I got the hang of it, finally. I learned where I'm smooth and where I'm kind of grainy. Now I think I would spot something different without much trouble.
>
> *—Woman, 19*

If you feel uncertain about your first few exams, forge ahead. You **will** get good at it. If you're worried, you can ask your clinician to examine your breasts first to verify that you really are normal.

Lumps can be round and smooth, or quite irregular. They can be movable or fixed. There may not be a true lump at all, but rather a place that feels thicker or stringier than usual. **Report any change to your clinician.**

REFERENCE

1. Foster RS, Lang SP, et al: Breast self examination practices and breast cancer prognosis. *New England Journal of Medicine* 299:265–271, 1978; and Greenwald P, Nasca PC, Lawrence CE, et al: Effect of breast self-examination and routine physician examinations on breast-cancer mortality. *New England Journal of Medicine* 299:271–273, 1978.

3 | Vaginal Hygiene

Until 1979, toxic shock syndrome was a little known and very rare disease of interest only to a handful of medical specialists. Tampons were a well-accepted, uncontroversial product. In 1980, researchers confirmed a link between tampon use and the occurrence of toxic shock syndrome, and discovered new vaginal ulcer problems caused by some tampons. Suddenly, the choice of menstrual protection has become a very serious medical issue. Women and their clinicians are concerned, and justifiably so.

Toxic Shock Syndrome

Researchers believe that toxic shock syndrome (TSS) is caused by a toxin (poison) released by *Staphylococcus aureus* bacteria. (This bacterial family produces many different toxins—including the "poison" responsible for common food poisoning.)

Almost all the TSS victims reported so far have been women, and almost all of the women were menstruating (1). Typically, the disease begins with sudden high fever, diarrhea, vomiting, muscle ache, inflamed eyes, and widespread rash that looks like sunburn. In severe cases there may be kidney, heart, liver, and blood-clotting problems, and severe low blood pressure (shock). The disease can be fatal—about 10% of patients hospitalized with TSS in 1980 died of its complications (2)—but more commonly, it occurs in a mild or moderate form that resolves completely when toxin exposure is ended.

The national Center for Disease Control, which is actively investigating TSS, has found a definite statistical link involving tampon use, *Staphylococcus*, and TSS. The precise role that tampons play, however, is not known. Stagnant blood in or behind a tampon would make an ideal site for bacterial growth. Tampons, however, have been used for many years while TSS is a new problem. What has changed? Some researchers believe that genetic mutation in *Staphylococcus* has evolved a new, hardier, or more toxic strain of this bacterium. Other researchers point to recent changes in tampons themselves.

Several tampon manufacturers have introduced synthetic "superabsorbent" fibers in their products in the last two years. Rely tampon, recently withdrawn from sale by Procter & Gamble, was one of the most popular of the many superabsorbent brands on the market. How new tampon technology might be linked to TSS is not known. TSS cases have been reported among users of all the major tampon brands, old and new, and even among women who use natural sponges for menstrual hygiene.

MINIMIZING YOUR RISK OF TOXIC SHOCK SYNDROME

TSS could occur after *Staphylococcus* infection anywhere in the body (with serious injury, for example). For more than 95% of women TSS victims, however, silent infection in the vagina has been the source of the problem.

Your risk for TSS is almost entirely eliminated if you use sanitary pads instead of tampons. Even if you choose to use tampons, your risk for TSS is quite low. The Center for Disease Control estimates that for every 100,000 women between 15 and 50 years of age, about 3 require hospital treatment for severe TSS each year (2).

Women who want to use tampons can take steps to reduce their TSS risks:

Don't use any Rely tampons left over.
Avoid all tampons with superabsorbent fibers.
Don't leave a tampon in place more than 8 hours (change to a fresh one).

Wash your hands before inserting a tampon, and insert the tampon carefully to avoid carrying bacteria from your skin or rectum into your vagina.

Allow a tampon-free interval every day (for example, use pads at night).

If you think you may have had mild TTS symptoms in the past (one or more of the danger signs below), see your clinician. A culture to find out whether you have *Staphylococcus* in your vagina may be reasonable.

If you have had TSS, stop using tampons, at least until you are sure you no longer have Staph in your vagina.

Watch the newspaper for new recommendations from the Center for Disease Control and the Food and Drug Administration as the TSS story continues to unfold.

WATCH FOR DANGER SIGNS during your period:
- Fever (temperature of 101 degrees F. or more)
- Diarrhea
- Vomiting
- Muscle aches
- Rash (like sunburn)

If one or more danger signs occur, *stop using tampons and see your clinician immediately.* Be sure your case is reported to the Center for Disease Control, Special Pathogens Branch, 1600 Clifton Road, N.E., Atlanta, Georgia 30333.

Vaginal Ulcers

Ulceration (a raw area where the normal vaginal mucous membrane surface is missing) is not a common problem, but many clinicians have noticed a recent increase in the number of ulcers they are seeing. One 1980 study (3) reported 10 cases of vaginal ulcer—all associated with prolonged (19 consecutive days or longer) use of tampons. At least 8 of the 10 women had used superabsorbent tampon brands, and in 4 cases, microscopic examination revealed synthetic fibers adhering to ulcerated areas. In another 1980 study, researchers in Milwaukee carefully examined healthy women before and after use of traditional and superabsorbent tampons. They found that microscopic damage to the vaginal lining could occur with both types of tampons but was more likely with use of a superabsorbent brand (4).

In itself, a vaginal ulcer is not a serious problem—with treatment and a vacation from tampon exposure all the reported patients had good healing. These cases do seem to show, however, that tampons, especially superabsorbent ones, can damage the vaginal lining. It is possible that a damaged vaginal surface is somehow more vulnerable to bacterial invasion or more readily absorbs toxin from bacteria. This finding may provide an important clue to the link between TSS and tampon use.

Additional recommendations for tampon users who want to avoid vaginal ulcers and other tampon problems include:

Avoid prolonged use of tampons (more than 7 to 10 consecutive days).

Don't use tampons when your flow is so light that your vagina is dry, or when you are not bleeding.

Avoid perfumed or deodorized tampons and pads. The chemical agents they contain may be irritating to mucous membranes in and around the vagina in some women.

Remove the last tampon at the end of your period. A forgotten tampon can cause terrible vaginal discharge and a very foul odor.

Vaginal Douches and Sprays

The normal, healthy vagina cleanses itself every day. Slight discharge from the cervix and vaginal walls keeps the vagina moist, and the downward flow of moisture carries old cells, menstrual blood, and other matter out of the vagina quite effectively. Normal vaginal discharge is scant, sticky, and clear or white on most days. For several days around the time of ovulation in each cycle, discharge becomes abundant, clear, and slippery. A normal discharge has a characteristic mild odor and dries to a yellowish color on underclothes.

Almost all clinicians agree that *there are no health benefits whatsoever to be gained from douching or using vaginal hygiene sprays.* (In some cases, clinicians do recommend douching as a temporary adjunct to treatment for certain vaginal infections.) In fact, douching and hygiene sprays may even be harmful, especially if you use these products incorrectly.

Some researchers suspect that douching may encourage the spread of infection from the vagina up into the uterus and tubes. The force of the douching liquid may actually push infection-contaminated liquid up into the uterus. Or perhaps douching washes away the protective mucous plug in the cervical canal, and so makes it easier for bacteria and other organisms to travel up the cervical canal into the uterus. If you choose to douche, follow these suggestions for using douche products safely and effectively.

Do not rely on douching as a method of birth control. Even if you douche immediately after intercourse, some sperm will still have time to enter the cervical canal where they won't be washed away by the douching liquid.

Use gentle water pressure. If you use a bulb syringe, squeeze gently. If you use a hanging bag, don't hang it more than two or three feet above your body.

Use plain warm water only and don't douche more often than once a week. Water cleans just about as well as commercial douching products and is less likely to be irritating. If you choose to use commercial products, use half the strength recommended on the label. If you use vinegar and water douches, use only 1 or 2 tablespoons of vinegar to each quart of water.

Avoid douching if you suspect you have an infection. Don't risk spreading infection up into your uterus. Also, your clinician cannot diagnose an infection if all the evidence has been washed away.

Avoid douching and tampons for three days before a pelvic exam. Pap test results may be less accurate if your cervix has recently been rinsed or rubbed, and your clinician will want to see your typical discharge.

Vaginal sprays are no more necessary for good hygiene than is douching. If you do choose to use a vaginal deodorant spray, follow label instructions carefully. Don't spray more frequently than the manufacturer recommends, and hold the can at least 6 inches away from your skin. Most important, don't spread your labia apart to spray directly into the entrance to your vagina. Stop using sprays if you develop signs of irritation, such as itching, swelling, redness, or tenderness.

REFERENCES

1. American College of Obstetricians and Gynecologists: "Toxic shock syndrome and tampon use: Recommendations offered by American College of Obstetricians and Gynecologists." News release, October 8, 1980.
2. Center for Disease Control: Epidemiologic notes and reports: Follow-up on toxic shock syndrome. *Morbidity and Mortality Weekly Report* 29(37):441-445, 1980. Personal communicator: Stephen Von Allmen, Toxic Shock Syndrome Surveillance Coordinator, Center for Disease Control, Atlanta, Georgia, December 8, 1980.
3. Jimerson SD, Becker JD: Vaginal ulcers associated with tampon usage. *Obstetrics and Gynecology* 56(1):97–99, 1980.
4. Friedrich EG, Siegesmund KA: Tampon-associated vaginal ulcerations. *Obstetrics and Gynecology* 55:149–156, 1980.

4 | Recognizing the Early Signs of Pregnancy

Early diagnosis gives us the chance to have a filling instead of a tooth extraction, or hypertension pills instead of kidney failure. With pregnancy the benefits of early diagnosis are incalculable. When pregnancy is welcome news, good prenatal care can begin immediately, and you can protect the embryo during early pregnancy when it is most vulnerable to countless physical and chemical agents. When pregnancy is not welcome news, you can have an early, safe abortion procedure.

And yet many pregnancies progress utterly unacknowledged until they are a third over, or even more. We are all risk takers, and we exempt ourselves from the law of averages. If 100 average couples have intercourse without birth control for a year, about 80 women will become pregnant. Pregnancies occur at all times of the cycle, with or without birth control, even when risk-taking worked last month and the month before. It is embarrassing to get caught with risky behavior showing, and it is very easy to wait. "Maybe my period will start tomorrow."

Some women wait because they fear being told that they are not pregnant. When a period is late after months of trying to conceive, it is natural to hold tight to hope and excitement. "I'll go in next week."

Waiting doesn't make pregnancy happen, and it doesn't make pregnancy go away. It just gives risks a toehold. Early diagnosis of pregnancy benefits every single woman, and each sexually active woman needs to know the early signs of pregnancy and how to get medical confirmation of pregnancy.

47

Almost all pregnancy tests are accurate when your period is about two weeks late. When you wait longer than that to see your clinician, you are stalling, and the stakes are simply too high for that. "Am I pregnant?" Surely this is one of the most important, life-changing questions a woman ever asks. Promise yourself to ask it promptly.

Early Signs of Pregnancy

The more attuned you are to your body and to your cycle, the earlier you are likely to notice pregnancy changes. Symptoms that often occur during the first 6 to 12 weeks are:

- Missed period(s)
- Breast tenderness and swelling
- Fatigue
- Queasiness or nausea; sensitivity to smells; vomiting and/or gagging
- Urinary frequency; waking up at night to urinate
- Slightly elevated body temperature; 99 to 100 degrees (Fahrenheit) by mouth
- Mood swings; possibly increased sex drive
- Weight gain
- "Glowing countenance"; happiness gets a boost from extra-active facial oil glands
- Unusual food cravings; clinicians call this "pica" (the Latin word for magpie, a bird that eats anything). Unusual cravings for ice, clay, or cornstarch may be a warning that your body is deficient in iron or other important nutrients. Talk to your clinician about your cravings so that she/he can check you for anemia.

Most women begin to have pregnancy symptoms two or three weeks after conception: the week after a period should have started. You may develop all the above symptoms, or one, or none of them. You may feel exactly as you did during a previous pregnancy, or the pattern may be entirely different. These changes are caused by the hormones that your reproductive system is churning out. Within a few days after conception, the tiny placenta begins to produce human chorionic gonadotropin (HCG), the pregnancy hormone. In addition, the ovary that released your newly fertilized egg continues to produce large amounts of progesterone.

An overdue period is usually the first clear-cut sign of pregnancy, but not always. Some women have "false" periods and bleed even though they are pregnant. Sometimes a period arrives but is not quite normal—perhaps light, or late. It is not unheard of for a woman to have two or even three periods in early pregnancy. These periods usually occur at about the time you would expect a normal period.

There are many reasons for missed periods other than pregnancy. Women on strict weight-loss diets occasionally miss periods, as do women who failed to ovulate in the previous cycle. Travel, emotional upset, or illness can temporarily interrupt your cycle. It is fairly common for a woman using birth control Pills to miss a period. Most clinicians advise you to continue your regular Pill schedule for the next cycle if you haven't missed any Pills (see Chapter 11). If you may have missed a Pill or two or have other pregnancy symptoms, however, *stop your Pills,* use another method of birth control, and have a pregnancy test and exam promptly.

In sum, *pregnant women don't always miss periods, and missed periods don't always signal pregnancy.* The presence or absence of the other pregnancy signs and a consultation with your clinician are necessary for a definite diagnosis—yes or no—regarding pregnancy.

SIGNS OF PREGNANCY AFTER THE 12TH WEEK

By week 12, some of the early signs of pregnancy may subside; others may persist. They are joined by a whole new constellation of signs:

- Breasts increase in size; bras don't fit
- Nipples darken
- Chloasma; spotty darkening appears on the forehead, on the cheekbones under the eyes, and on the upper lip
- Lower abdomen protrudes; waistbands are tight; pants are too short to fasten comfortably at the waist
- Weight gain increases
- Vaginal discharge increases; greater susceptibility to yeast infections (see Chapter 22 for treatment)
- Fetal movement begins about weeks 18 to 20; first noticeable as an intermittent flutter, then graduates to serious kicking

Some of these signs reflect the physical impact of an enlarging uterus, and others reflect the continuing high hormone production.

EVERY WOMAN KNOWS

The old saw has it that "every woman knows" when she is pregnant. Some women do, especially those who have been pregnant before, but some women don't. Some simply don't spot the signs, or ignore them, or are misled. For example:

Some women ignore early signs of pregnancy because they believe that they can't become pregnant. Perhaps you didn't become pregnant in the past when you had intercourse without birth control, or perhaps you were misled by something your clinician said.

> I had gonorrhea two years ago, and the doctor I went to said my tubes were infected. He went on and on about how I wasn't going to be able to have children later on if I wasn't careful. I just figured he meant I was sterile, but I had to have an abortion last summer.
>
> —Woman, 20

> When our son was born, we were told we couldn't have any more children because of my tilted uterus. We accepted the fact, I got my degree, and taught one year. Then I found out I was pregnant. Our life style that had been so free changed drastically with the birth of our daughter.
>
> —Woman, 38

Some women assume that a tipped uterus means impaired fertility, but it does not. Clinicians' warnings can be taken more literally than they are intended and lead a woman to assume that intercourse without birth control will be safe. No clinician can determine with certainty that you *are* fertile, and similarly it is almost impossible for a clinician to be certain that you *are not* fertile unless you have had a hysterectomy.

Women who stop birth control Pills may misinterpret a missed period and other signs of pregnancy as the body's readjustment to being off Pills. The error can be compounded when Pill users wrongly assume that Pill protection extends for some vague period of time after they stop Pills. Most women resume normal cycles within a few days after taking their last Pill, and ovulation usually occurs within two weeks. (See Chapter 11 for advice on planning pregnancy after Pills.)

Some women fail to recognize pregnancy because they had intercourse only on "safe" days. It is impossible to be absolutely accurate in calculating your safe days unless you live in a research lab. Ovulation can occur earlier or later than you expected if your cycle is disrupted for some reason. You may not have any hint of the change until pregnancy occurs.

> My niece was so sure she was "safe" that she told everybody she had an abdominal tumor! She believed that until the baby started kicking!
> —*Woman, 50*

Pregnancy Testing

When your period is about two weeks late or when you have other early signs of pregnancy, it is time for pregnancy confirmation. Confirming pregnancy is a two-step procedure that includes both a pregnancy test and a pelvic exam to verify the pregnancy test result and to estimate how far along in pregnancy you are. Neither step alone gives a conclusive answer. Uterine enlargement can be caused by conditions other than pregnancy, and pregnancy test results can be incorrect. Only when the results of your test and your exam confirm each other is your clinician able to give you a definite yes or no diagnosis. During the first 12 weeks of pregnancy an experienced clinician should be able to determine the length of your pregnancy accurately. She/he will judge from the size of your uterus and the dates of your recent menstrual periods.

Accurate, specific diagnosis of how far along you are is important, whether you plan to continue your pregnancy or are thinking about abortion. If your clinician is not able to give you a definite diagnosis *in number of weeks,* arrange an examination with another clinician as soon as possible.

DATING FROM LMP

One bit of inside information you need in any discussion of pregnancy has to do with the all-important LMP. LMP means "last menstrual period," *the date your last normal menstrual period started.* More than likely it will be one of the first questions your clinician will ask you. It is medical tradition to date the beginning of pregnancy from LMP because LMP is the most recent provable and recordable event in your reproductive life.

> *Example:* Your period began January 1st. It was normal. You had intercourse once in January, on the 14th. Your period, due around the 1st of February, was late. You had a positive pregnancy test on Valentine's Day.
>
> Your clinician will tell you on Valentine's Day that you have a pregnancy of six week's size. In medical language, your pregnancy "began" January 1st.

Now, *you* know and your clinician knows that your pregnancy actually began with intercourse on January 14, but everything and everybody in the medical world consistently uses the LMP system of dating, so you may as well get used to it. (In your heart of hearts you can secretly subtract two weeks for the true age of your developing embryo.)

PREGNANCY TESTING METHODS

Human chorionic gonadotropin (HCG), the pregnancy hormone, is easily detectable in your blood serum and urine for about the first five months of pregnancy. All pregnancy tests use chemical procedures to demonstrate the presence of HCG. Rabbit tests have not been used in years. Illustration 1 shows how HCG levels rise during the first few weeks of pregnancy, and when the common pregnancy tests will be accurate (counting from your last menstrual period).

A simple **two-minute urine slide test** can accurately detect pregnancy 42 days after your last normal period started: in other words, when your period is about two weeks late if you normally menstruate once a month. The great majority of pregnancy testing is done with the two-minute urine slide test (see Illustration 2).

A **two-hour urine tube test** can be accurate when your period is only about one to one and a half weeks late. Tube tests are now available in many drugstores, without a prescription, to use at home yourself (see Illustration 3). Take-home tests are simple to use. The only problem is that there is no such thing as a do-it-yourself pelvic exam to verify your urine test results; and you have no way of steering clear of some uncommon kinds of pregnancy test errors. If you use a do-it-yourself kit, be careful to buy a type that measures HCG. Some tests have been marketed in the past that measure estrogen and other hormone levels in the urine, and they may be less reliable (1).

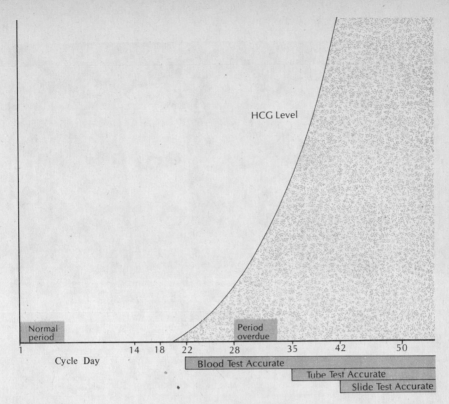

HCG Level

Normal period

Period overdue

Cycle Day

1   14 18 22   28   35   42   50

Blood Test Accurate

Tube Test Accurate

Slide Test Accurate

Illustration 1   Blood pregnancy tests are accurate as early as 22 days after the beginning of your last normal period. Routine, two-minute urine slide tests are accurate about 42 days after your last period.

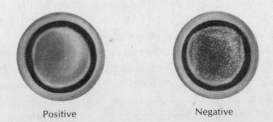

Positive   Negative

Illustration 2   This type of urine slide test will show clumping if you aren't pregnant (negative). Liquid remains smooth at the end of two minutes if you are pregnant (positive).

Illustration 3   A do-it-yourself two-hour urine tube test for pregnancy. (Photograph by Rita R. Harris, Medical Photographer.)

All types of urine pregnancy tests are most reliable if you use your first morning urine. Since early morning urine is the most concentrated, the concentration of HCG will be highest, and easier to detect than in urine samples taken later in the day.

New, highly sensitive **blood serum tests** can give you an accurate verdict as early as one week after conception, a week before your period is due. The original pregnancy blood test, radioimmunoassay, is a very expensive laboratory process. A newer test, **radioreceptor assay,** is more reasonably priced and is becoming widely available. Women who have had a tubal (ectopic) pregnancy in the past or who have diabetes, hypertension, heart disease, kidney disease, or other health problems that can be adversely affected by pregnancy are good candidates for the earliest possible pregnancy diagnosis with blood serum tests.

Table 1   PREGNANCY TESTS

Cost	Type of Test	Specimen Needed	Approx- imate Time to Perform	Number of Days After LMP the Test Will Become Accurate
$3–5	Slide	Urine[a]	2 minutes	42
$9–13	Test tube	Urine[a]	2 hours	31–38
$10–15	Do-it-yourself tube test	Urine[a]	2 hours	34–37
$5–25	Radioreceptor assay	Blood	1½ hours	21–28

[a]First morning urine will provide most accurate results.

Common pregnancy tests are described in Table 1.

GETTING A PREGNANCY TEST

See your regular clinician, or go to a family planning clinic or an abortion clinic for a pregnancy test. Pregnancy testing is available without an appointment at some clinics. It is best to call first for instructions, because you may be advised to bring in a specimen of your first morning urine for your test. Put your specimen (half a cup is plenty) in a clean glass jar, cover it, and store it in the refrigerator to prevent growth of bacteria until you leave for the clinic or doctor's office.

Take your menstrual calendar with you. You will be asked about your recent periods, recent sexual activity, and birth control methods. Think through the last two or three months and mark down all the dates you can reconstruct, especially the first day of your last two normal periods.

INCONCLUSIVE OR INCORRECT PREGNANCY TEST RESULTS

Chemical pregnancy tests are not infallible and pelvic examination may be inconclusive, especially very early in pregnancy when the HCG level is too low to be detected and your uterus has not yet become noticeably enlarged. If your urine test is negative and your pelvic exam is inconclusive, then you can either have a blood pregnancy test or simply wait one more week and repeat the urine test and pelvic exam. Blood tests are subject to few errors and are quite sensitive early in pregnancy.

There are a number of reasons, however, for incorrect **urine** pregnancy test results: (1) *Negative* test result even though you **are** pregnant (clinicians call this a "false" negative): test performed incorrectly; test performed too early or too late in pregnancy; urine too dilute; urine stored too long at room temperature; tubal (ectopic) pregnancy; threatened miscarriage (spontaneous abortion) or incomplete spontaneous abortion. (2) *Positive* test result even though you are **not** pregnant (clinicians call this a "false" positive): test performed on the day of ovulation; blood or protein in the urine sample; normal or premature menopause; aspirin in large doses; detergent residue on glass urine container; thyroid disorder; marijuana or methadone; psychotropic drugs such as antidepressants; antiparkinsonian drugs, and anticonvulsants; hypertension drugs such as Aldomet (alpha-methyl dopa); test performed within ten days after a full-term pregnancy, abortion, or miscarriage; certain uncommon diseases and infections; or test performed incorrectly.

Your urine contains a high level of LH (luteinizing hormone) for about 24 hours at the time you ovulate each cycle. The chemical structure of LH is very similar to that of HCG, and urine pregnancy tests cannot distinguish between LH and HCG in your urine. Either hormone can cause a positive test result. If LH caused your positive test result, then another test one week later will be negative and you can expect a menstrual period to start in about a week. Blood pregnancy tests are more accurate, and LH will not cause a positive test result.

SPECIAL WARNING—PILLS OR SHOTS TO BRING ON A PERIOD

In the past, clinicians sometimes tested for pregnancy with a "progesterone challenge" test. In this procedure, a woman takes a progestin shot or pills for five consecutive days; the synthetic progestin will trigger bleeding if you are not pregnant. If you are pregnant, no bleeding will occur. Progestin does not stop the pregnancy but merely demonstrates whether pregnancy has occurred.

Several investigators have recently reported that exposure to progestin early in fetal life may cause fetal abnormalities. If your clinician should suggest such a test (it is unlikely that she/he would if she/he suspects that you might be pregnant), **decline the procedure if there is any chance that you would want to continue the pregnancy.** Hormone drugs, including estrogen and progestin, may harm your developing fetus.

Signs of Trouble in Early Pregnancy

ECTOPIC PREGNANCY

Ectopic pregnancy is a significant hazard for women in the early months of pregnancy, and early diagnosis may save your life. An ectopic pregnancy is one that implants and begins to grow outside the uterine cavity. Ectopic implantation occurs in about 1 in 50 to 200 pregnancies. Most ectopic pregnancies occur inside one of the fallopian tubes, as shown in Illustration 4. As tubal pregnancy advances, it stretches the tube and can cause tearing or tubal rupture. Symptoms of ectopic pregnancy usually begin at about the seventh or eighth week. Tubal rupture can cause sudden, massive internal bleeding, and is a serious complication. Ectopic pregnancy hemorrhage is a leading cause of pregnancy-related death.

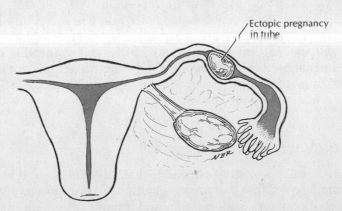

Ectopic pregnancy in tube

Illustration 4   This ectopic pregnancy implanted in a fallopian tube. Urine pregnancy test results in this case may be positive **or** negative.

A woman who has an ectopic pregnancy often has a positive pregnancy test, but not always. Your clinician may find that your uterus is smaller than it should be according to your menstrual dates, and sometimes it is possible to feel an enlarged tube. Ectopic pregnancy may also cause intermittent bleeding or spotting during early pregnancy. Many times, however, early ectopic pregnancy occurs with no symptoms, or with symptoms that are very subtle.

Think about ectopic pregnancy any time you suspect you could be pregnant and develop any of these danger signs:

- Sudden intense pain or persistent pain or cramping in the lower abdomen, usually localized to one side or the other
- Irregular bleeding or spotting with abdominal pain when your period is late or after an abnormally light period
- Fainting or dizziness persisting more than a few seconds may be a sign of internal bleeding. You will not necessarily have any bleeding from your vagina if you have internal bleeding.

Call your clinician or go to an emergency room at once if you develop any of these signs. You could have a real medical emergency on your hands, and will very likely need emergency abdominal surgery. Tell anyone you talk to that you think you could be pregnant.

Suspect ectopic pregnancy especially if you have had pelvic infections (PID) such as gonorrhea in the past. Scarring from infection can partially block your fallopian tubes and prevent a fertilized egg from reaching your uterus. Suspect ectopic pregnancy if you are pregnant with an IUD in place or have conceived while you are taking Pills or Minipills. IUDs prevent uterine pregnancy, but they do not effectively protect you against tubal pregnancy. Pills and Minipills prevent uterine pregnancy more effectively than they do ectopic pregnancy. The likelihood of ectopic pregnancy is also increased if you have previously had an ectopic pregnancy.

PREGNANCY WITH AN IUD IN PLACE

Pregnancy can sometimes occur with an IUD in place. If you have an IUD and suspect that you are pregnant, call your clinician without delay. Early pregnancy confirmation and a pelvic exam are important because of the risk of ectopic pregnancy and because your clinician will want to remove your IUD if possible.

The presence of an IUD does not necessarily interfere with pregnancy, but leaving the IUD in place does increase your risk of miscarriage (spontaneous abortion). About 50% of IUD pregnancies end in miscarriage if the IUD is left in place, and the risk is reduced to 30% if the IUD is removed (2). If you delay getting care, your IUD strings can disappear up into your uterus as it enlarges. If the strings are not visible, your clinician probably will be unable to remove your IUD.

If you plan to have an abortion, your IUD can be removed at the time of your abortion procedure. If you haven't made a decision about abortion or continuing your pregnancy, and your IUD strings are still visible, be sure that your clinician removes your IUD at the time your pregnancy is diagnosed.

Infection. If you have an IUD in place and are pregnant, you face a significant risk both of miscarriage and of uterine infection. This problem is particularly serious because illness can have a very rapid onset and develop literally overnight into a life-threatening, massive infection. It is infection risk that leads many clinicians to advise that you seriously consider abortion if you become pregnant with an IUD in place.

If you have an IUD, be alert not only to the early signs of pregnancy but also to the following danger signs of pelvic infection. Danger signs of infection are:

* Pain in your lower abdomen or pain during intercourse
* Bleeding or spotting between periods or when your period is late
* Chills, fever (a temperature of more than 100.4 degrees Fahrenheit by mouth), headache, or other "flu"-like symptoms. Be sure that your exam for "flu" includes a pelvic exam.
* Unusual vaginal discharge

See your clinician at once if you develop these signs of infection any time you have an IUD. And if you suspect that you could be pregnant as well, run don't walk. You may need to be admitted to a hospital for antibiotic therapy.

MISCARRIAGE (SPONTANEOUS ABORTION)

About 15% of all pregnancies end in miscarriage (spontaneous abortion). The vast majority occur between the 4th and 12th weeks of pregnancy (3). Something goes wrong, and your body has the good sense to call everything off before the going gets worse. *You need prompt medical care for a miscarriage.* Call your clinician or go to an emergency room if you develop any of these danger signs:

- Your last period was late, and bleeding is now heavy, possibly with clots or clumps of tissue; cramping is more severe than usual
- Your period is prolonged and heavy; five to seven days of "heaviest" days
- You have abdominal pain and fever

Even if your miscarriage is complete, you need to see your clinician to have your blood Rh type determined. If you are Rh negative, you will need treatment within 72 hours with Rh_o (D antigen) immune globulin to prevent Rh problems in future pregnancies (see Chapter 20). Common brand names for this drug are RhoGAM, Gamulin Rh and HypRho D. Your clinician will also want to be sure that all the fetal and placental tissue has been expelled from your uterus; uterine infection is much more likely if tissue remains in your uterus.

Importance of Early Diagnosis

If you plan to continue your pregnancy, early diagnosis gives you an opportunity to avoid the multitude of physical and chemical agents that can harm a developing embryo. Embryos are most vulnerable in the first three months of pregnancy, the organ-forming stage. Avoid x-rays, alcohol, smoking, aspirin, caffeine, hormones (including birth control Pills), tranquilizers, antihistamines, narcotics, tetracycline, and large doses of vitamins, especially A and C. When you need drugs in pregnancy, you must weigh their usefulness to you against their possible harm to the embryo. Your clinician can help you assess the pros and cons. The basic rule is to avoid any drugs—licit or illicit—that you don't absolutely need.

Ideally, your special precautions and excellent diet should begin even before you are sure you are pregnant. Think of yourself as pregnant as soon as you stop using birth control or begin trying to conceive. You may want to take a multivitamin and iron supplement as well. One study in England (4) found a lower rate of spina bifida and other neural tube birth defects when pregnant women took routine multivitamins and iron three times a day for at least 28 days before conceiving and during the first two months of pregnancy.*

---

*The vitamin used contained Vitamin A, 4000 International Units (I.U.); Vitamin D, 400 I.U.; Thiamine, 1.5 Milligrams (mg); Riboflavin, 1.5 mg; Pyridoxine, 1 mg; Nicotinamide, 15 mg; Ascorbic acid, 40 mg; Folic acid, 0.36 mg; Ferrous sulphate equivalent to 75.6 mg Fe (Iron); and Calcium phosphate, 480 mg.

If you are pregnant and don't want to be, legal abortion is both safe and widely available in early pregnancy. If you are not clear in your mind whether abortion is the right choice for you, your local Planned Parenthood agency can probably refer you to pregnancy counselors who can help you evaluate the pros and cons. Remember that abortion is safer and cheaper early in pregnancy; so try to make your decision as quickly as you can. (See Chapters 18 and 20 for a complete discussion of pregnancy decision making and how to find reputable abortion services.)

If you are not pregnant and would like to be, talk with your clinician or with the staff at your family planning clinic. They can give you advice and refer you to specialists who treat fertility problems, if necessary. Many of the problems that cause infertility can be resolved, and sometimes counseling alone does the job. (See Chapter 34 for a discussion of common fertility problems.)

If you are not pregnant and you breathe a sigh of relief, reevaluate your birth control status, especially if you have been relying on luck or on one of the less reliable methods of birth control. This may be an ideal time to make some new contraceptive resolutions. Ask yourself whether you might be better off with another method, or a more effective one. Chapters 5 to 17 provide a complete description of the most popular methods of birth control. Ask your clinician or ask at your family planning clinic for advice. If you and your partner don't have a method you trust and feel comfortable with, it could be pregnancy testing time again in a couple of months, and no one enjoys the sweaty palms and sleepless nights of a pregnancy scare.

REFERENCES

1. Hunt W II: Pregnancy tests—the current status. *Population Reports*, Ser J, No 7, 1975, p J-121. Washington, DC, The George Washington University Medical Center.
2. Alvior G: Pregnancy outcome with removal of intrauterine device. *Obstetrics and Gynecology* 41:894–896, 1973.
3. Hellman L, Pritchard J (eds): *Williams' Obstetrics*, ed 14. New York, Appleton-Century-Crofts, 1971.
4. Smithells RW, Sheppard S, Seller MJ, et al: Possible prevention of neural-tube defects by periconceptional vitamin supplementation. *Lancet* 1:339–340, 1980.

5 | Choosing a Method of Birth Control

If there were a perfect method of birth control, we wouldn't need this chapter. A perfect contraceptive would be 100% effective, totally safe, available to everyone, inexpensive, completely without side effects, instantly reversible, and easy to use. It would not interfere with love-making in any way, and would require a minimum of advice and care from a clinician. There is no such method. It doesn't exist today, and according to research experts there are no likely prospects for the near future.

What we do have today is an assortment of at least nine good methods, each with advantages and disadvantages. Your task is to discover which method or combination of methods comes closest to meeting your own needs. Your first concerns will probably be safety and reliability, and rightly so. Many other factors also influence how well you do with birth control: your health status, your life style, and the patterns in your sex life.

Choosing a method of birth control is not a totally rational process; romance isn't rational, and sexual feelings may be even less so. Your feelings, your fears, and your unadorned instincts and hunches are valid considerations.

Remember that you can always change your mind about your method, unless you choose sterilization. Most people use several different methods over the years.

Basic Birth Control Assumptions

Start with six basic assumptions as you consider your own choices about birth control:

1. ***There are at least ten methods of birth control*** that have proved to be at least 98% effective (2 pregnancies per 100 women per year) in studies of couples who used the methods exactly according to instructions all the time. They are:

   The Pill (combined estrogen and progestin)
   Minipills (progestin alone)
   IUDs
   Diaphragms
   Condoms and foam in combination
   Condoms
   Foam
   Foaming tablets and suppositories
   Fertility awareness (basal body temperature method with intercourse after ovulation only)*
   Sterilization

   These are the most effective popular methods. The group does not include methods that fall into a lower average range of effectiveness, such as withdrawal and calendar rhythm.

2. ***The effectiveness of your method of birth control depends on how carefully and consistently you use it.***

3. ***Two methods are better than one:*** you need a primary method and a backup method. IUD strings disappear, Pills are forgotten, or you are snowed in with no diaphragm jelly. Think of condoms or foam as your birth control first-aid kit. Some couples use two methods all the time for extra protection.†

---

*Limited studies show high effectiveness rates for other Fertility Awareness techniques as well. See Chapter 8.

†Using two methods at once will give you an extremely high level of effectiveness. You can figure combined rates for yourself. **Subtract** the effectiveness rate from 100 to get the failure rate for each of the methods you want to combine, then **multiply** the two failure rates to get a **combined failure rate.** Foam (15% failure) used with condoms (10% failure) gives a combined failure rate of 1.5% ($0.15 \times 0.10 = 0.015$) or an effectiveness rate of 98.5%. An IUD (5%) with foam (15%) gives a 0.75% failure rate, or an effectiveness rate of 99.25%.

4. ***Most women in the United States have all the children they want by their late 20s,*** and may have as many as 20 to 25 more years of fertility. Sterilization procedures for both men and women can be performed safely without overnight hospital stays and are very close to 100% effective. (See Chapters 14, 15, and 16 for a full discussion of sterilization.)

5. ***There is no "best method" of birth control.*** The best method for you is the one you and your partner trust and feel most comfortable about using.

6. ***There are danger times when birth control is often abandoned or forgotten:***
   At the end of a relationship
   At the beginning of a relationship
   After a pregnancy scare or abortion when a woman says, "Never again. Sex isn't worth it."
   During major life changes: divorce, new job, new school, a move, or serious illness in the family

Effectiveness Rates: What Do the Numbers Mean?

I was sitting in my doctor's office flipping through magazines. One article said diaphragms were 98% effective, and another one said 87%. I asked my doctor which was right, and she said, "Take your pick, they're both right." That's no way to comfort a woman who still has one in diapers!

—Woman, 26

Investigators calculate effectiveness rates for methods of birth control by following a group of couples who use the method for a certain length of time and counting the pregnancies that occur. In general, the larger the study group and the longer the study time, the more reliable the results. For example, you can have more confidence in a Pill study that follows 2,000 users for three years than in a study that follows 500 users for one year, all other factors being equal. You can have more confidence in results reported for a group of women close to you in age, cultural background, and socioeconomic status. If you are a 26-year-old single American female, for example, you can't really put a lot of stock in a foam study that investigated only teenage married women in Bora Bora.

Effectiveness rates are sometimes calculated in terms of "pregnancies per 100 women per year of use." An *effectiveness* rate of 97% means a *failure rate* of 3%; in other words, 3 pregnancies per 100 women per year studied.

Manufacturers of contraceptives want their products to sell well, of course, so they tend to advertise the very best study results they can find, such as studies of well-motivated, well-counseled couples who come through like champs. These rates tell you how well you and your partner could do if you use the method *exactly right, all the time, no mistakes.*

But loving couples are human and don't do things perfectly all the time. An "average" effectiveness rate takes into account the couples who don't use their method perfectly all the time. Average effectiveness rates are lower than the highest effectiveness rates, of course; *how much lower tells you what the margin of error is for using that particular method.* Foam, for example, has a "highest reported" effectiveness rate of 98% and an "average" effectiveness rate of 85.1%. These two figures tell you that plenty of people found plenty of ways to use foam incorrectly, or not at all. Table 1 lists high, average, and low effectiveness rates for the major methods of birth control.

CLINICIAN BIAS

None of us is free of biases. Clinicians tend to quote from the high rates column for methods they like and trust and from the average rates column for methods they don't like (1). For example, your Pill-loving clinician may say, "Pills are better than 99% effective, and diaphragms are only 87% effective." On the other hand, if your clinician is a diaphragm fan, she/he may say, "Diaphragms are 98% effective, just as good as Pills." It isn't sound logic to quote a *high* effectiveness rate for one method and compare it with an *average* effectiveness rate for other methods.

WHAT EFFECTIVENESS RATES MEAN TO YOU

At best, effectiveness rates can give you a general idea of how successful other couples have been who used your method in the past.

Table 1 BIRTH CONTROL EFFECTIVENESS

Percent of Women Who Use Method for One Year Without Pregnancy	Reported Rate Excellent Use[a]	Reported Rate Typical Use[b]
Sterilization surgery	99+	99+
Pills	99+	98
IUD	97–99	96
Minipills[c]	98	97
Condoms[d]	98	90
Diaphragm with cream or jelly	98	87
Foam	98	85
Foaming tablets/suppositories[e]	98	(85)?
Spermicidal cream alone[e]	96	(85)?
Cervical cap[f]	92 (?)	?
Fertility awareness[g]	86–99	76–80
Withdrawal[h]	90	84
Douche[i]	?	60
No method	20	15

SOURCES:

[a]FDA-approved product labeling for oral contraceptives, May 1980. Manufacturer's information for physicians as well as the text of product labeling for patients appear in *Physician's Desk Reference* (ed. 34), Medical Economics Co., Oradell, NJ, 1980.

[b]B Vaughn, J Trussell, et al: Contraceptive failure among married women in the United States, 1970–1973. *Family Planning Perspectives* 9:251–258, 1977.

[c]Both rates are from FDA-approved product labeling for oral contraceptives, see footnote *a* above.

[d]Excellent rate is from J Peel: The Hull family survey. II. Family planning in the first 5 years of marriage. *Journal of Biosocial Science* 4(3):333–346, 1972.

[e]S Coleman and PT Piotrow: Spermicides—simplicity and safety are major assets. *Population Reports,* Ser H, No 5, September 1979. Baltimore, The Johns Hopkins University. No studies of "Typical Use" comparable to those cited for the other methods have been published. Many family planning researchers feel these products are roughly comparable to foam for typical users.

[f]C Tietze, H Lehfeldt and H Liebmann: The effectiveness of the cervical cap as a contraceptive method. *American Journal of Obstetrics and Gynecology* 66:904–908, 1953. Caps used in this study are no longer manufactured; newer caps differ somewhat in mode of use and construction. There are, as yet, no published effectiveness rates for the newer caps.

[g]Rates depend on whether couples used calendar, basal body temperature, mucus signs, or a combination (symptothermal). Highest rates (99) are achieved when intercourse is permitted only after ovulation has been documented.

[h]Excellent rate is from CF Westoff, LF Herrera and PK Whelpton: Social and psychological

factors affecting fertility; the use, effectiveness, and acceptability of various methods of fertility control. *Milbank Memorial Fund Quarterly* 31:291–357, 1953. Typical rate is from CF Westoff, RG Potter, PC Sagi, et al: *Family Growth in Metropolitan America.* Princeton, Princeton University Press, 1961.

¹Typical rate is from NB Ryder: Contraceptive failure in the United States. *Family Planning Perspectives* 5:133–144, 1973. No "Excellent Use" studies of douche have been published. Most family planning researchers do not consider douching to be effective enough to warrant effectiveness studies.

Table prepared by Reproductive Health Resources, Inc, a nonprofit corporation. Used with permission.

Remember that someone else's high rate of effectiveness cannot protect you if you are careless; someone else's low success rate need not deter you from using a method if you believe that you can use it correctly.

The doctor was right who told her patient that diaphragms are both 87 and 98% effective; 98% is about the maximum protection a woman can expect if she is careful about following instructions each and every time. And if she is not so careful, she can expect about 87% effectiveness. Whether she spends the next year at the 87% or the 98% level is entirely up to her and her partner. Diligence is all.

Risks: What Are Your Odds?

If women think first about birth control effectiveness, they think second about risks. "What are the chances I'll have a serious medical problem or be hospitalized? What are the chances I will die?" Morbidity (illness) and mortality (death), the statisticians call it. Some risks are caused directly by the birth control method. Pills, for example, do cause blood-clotting disorders that result in about 2 to 14 deaths for about every 100,000 users each year (2). Other risks are indirect; when your method fails, you are vulnerable to the medical risks of pregnancy or abortion. For every 100,000 full-term pregnancies, some 14.9 women die each year as a direct result of pregnancy (3). If you should choose abortion in the first two months of pregnancy after a method fails, your risk of death is less than 1 per 100,000 procedures (3).

Risks vary from method to method and are spelled out in great detail in the following chapters. Birth control risks may be best understood in relation to your overall risk of death during the reproductive years. Table 2 shows rates for all causes of death for American women aged 15 to 44.

Some of the deaths in Table 2 represent the small number of women who die each year as a direct result of birth control method

BIRTH CONTROL AND RISK OF DEATH

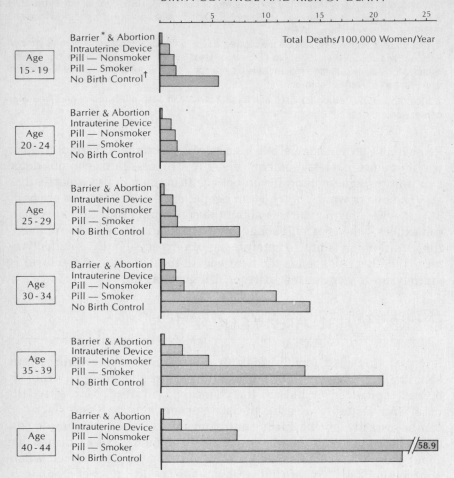

*Barrier = Diaphragm or Condom
†Deaths in women not using birth control = Deaths from pregnancy complications

Illustration 1 Birth control-related deaths are very rare. You are far more likely to die as a result of a traffic accident than as a result of a birth control complication (see Table 2 for comparison), unless you are a Pill user over 40 who smokes. You are more likely to die as a result of a traffic accident than as a result of pregnancy complications, unless you are over 35. Note that a diaphragm or condoms with abortion in the event of pregnancy is the

Table 2   LEADING CAUSES OF DEATH: AMERICAN WOMEN AGED 15
TO 44 YEARS

Cause	Deaths per 100,000 Women per Year
All causes	93.95
Cancer	20.31
Motor vehicle accidents	14.44
Heart disease	7.91
Suicide	7.20
All other accidents	5.94
Homicide	5.50
Stroke	3.45
All other causes	24.86

SOURCE: Mortality Statistics Branch, Division of Vital Statistics, National Center for Health
Statistics, US Department of Health and Human Services. Unpublished table, 1978 data.

complications. Illustration 1 shows birth control and pregnancy death
risks in detail. For example, if you are a 19-year-old Pill user who does
not smoke, your risk of death from Pill complications is 1.3 per 100,000
users per year. If you are 35 years old, use Pills, and smoke, your risk of
death is 13.4 per 100,000 users per year. If you are 30 years old and
have an IUD, your risk of death from IUD complications is 1.4 per
100,000 users per year.

LONG-TERM RISKS

Diaphragms, foam, and condoms are unlikely to carry any long-

safest method of birth control for all age groups. Pill
users who smoke have higher risks than Pill users who
don't smoke, and after age 29, risks increase dramatically for Pill users who smoke. Birth control is safer than
full-term pregnancy for all method users except Pill
users over 40 who smoke. For all age groups, there is
very little difference in the risk of death for IUD users, Pill
users who don't smoke, and diaphragm or condom users
who don't choose abortion (not shown). (Adapted from C
Tietze: Induced abortion: 1977 supplement, *Reports on
Population-Family Planning* No 14 (ed 2), suppl, December 1977. Used with permission.)

term risks that we don't yet know about. The chemicals in spermicidal foam and in diaphragm jelly and cream are almost entirely noninvasive and have been studied extensively for many years.

Whether Pills and IUDs have long-term risks is still **unknown.** The first Pill user swallowed her first Pill about 20 years ago, and IUDs have been marketed in the United States since 1959. We cannot yet be certain what will happen, if anything, to these women in their menopausal years and after.

> I can handle a nice clear-cut blood clot risk a lot better than I can handle *not knowing* what might happen to me in 20 years! I have a vivid imagination, for one thing. I would lie awake and imagine all the diseases I was going to get. And for another thing, why should I be a guinea pig? I quit Pills four years ago.
>
> —*Woman, 29*

Some people are bothered less than others by unknown risks. Many Pill and IUD users can accept the notion that unknown risks may exist, and others cannot.

CONTRAINDICATIONS

Some women are more likely to encounter problems with birth control than others, and contraindications to the methods are an important element to consider as you make your birth control choice. *A contraindication is a medical condition that renders a course of treatment inadvisable or unsafe that might otherwise be recommended.* For example, a history of thrombophlebitis, inflammation of the veins that can produce blood clots, is a contraindication to Pill use; a woman with a history of thrombophlebitis is more likely than average to develop a blood-clotting disorder on Pills, and she should never use Pills. Knowing—and respecting—the contraindications for your method may be the single most important way to avoid problems.

Clinicians usually rank contraindications on three levels:

- *Absolute* contraindications: you *must not* try to use the method.
- *Strong relative* contraindications: you will be *strongly advised* not to use the method.
- *Relative* contraindications: you may be able to try the method if you are willing to be followed very carefully by your clinician so that she/he can watch for early signs of trouble.

Review your own medical history and the contraindications for methods you are considering before you adopt a method. There is nothing to be gained by hiding a contraindication from your clinician; you may fool her or him, but you won't fool your body. Be alert to contraindications after you start using your method as well. If you develop a condition that you know is a contraindication, talk to your clinician at once.

CONSENT FORMS

Many clinicians ask you to sign a consent form before you begin using a method, and drug manufacturers are now required by the Food and Drug Administration to provide Pill and IUD users with a pamphlet that spells out the risks and benefits to be expected. Risks are serious business to your clinician, and it is important for you to take risks seriously, too. Be sure that you understand any consent form completely before you sign, and remember that you have a right to have all your questions answered.

You *can* put risks and benefits in perspective for yourself and make your own decision about a method. The birth control chapters in this book may be a good place to begin. They are designed to give you a complete picture of what we know about each method, both the comforting facts and the disquieting ones. If these chapters contain more bad news than you are accustomed to reading, you will know why.

Living in Harmony with Your Method

When do you want to become pregnant?

Never? Sterilization may be an option to consider, or one of the most effective temporary methods, or, better yet, two methods in combination. Avoid IUD types that must be replaced on a regular basis.

Three years from now? Think about the most effective temporary methods.

Some time this year? Use anything you like. Remember to stop Pills for at least three cycles or have your IUD removed one cycle before you try to become pregnant.

How do you feel about abortion? If you would not choose abortion, and an unplanned pregnancy would be a disaster for you, consider sterilization or a combination of two good methods, such as foam and condoms, IUD and condoms, or a diaphragm and condoms.

How often are you having intercourse? If you have intercourse frequently, you might get tired of foam, condoms, or a diaphragm. If you have intercourse infrequently, you may feel frustrated about exposing yourself to Pill or IUD risks 30 days a month in order to be protected two or three days.

How many partners do you have? If you have two or more partners, you will probably want effective contraception and infection protection as well. The more partners you have, the greater your risk of infection. Foam or a diaphragm will protect you from infection to some degree, but a condom with spermicide will give you the best protection against sexually transmitted infections, and excellent contraception as well.

How good is your access to medical care? Avoid Pills and IUDs if it would be hard for you to get quick, competent medical care in an emergency.

How old are you?

If you are a young teenager and have difficulty getting birth control services, condoms and foam may be your best choice, and you can even order them by mail (see Chapter 6 for details).

If you are over 30, smoke, and use Pills, your risk of cardiovascular problems such as heart attack and stroke is significant; if you are over 35, your risk is significant, even if you don't smoke.

How much money can you afford to spend for birth control? Good birth control protection can cost as little as 50 cents for one condom and one foam application, but doctor visits for prescription methods can be expensive. If money is a factor for you, try to find a family planning clinic that offers supplies free or on a sliding scale based on your income. Keep birth control expenses in perspective: it now costs between $100,000 and $140,000 to raise a child to age 18 and put him or her through a four-year public college (4).

Matters of the Heart

Why is it so hard to talk about sex? I talk for a living, for heaven's sake! I've slept with Roger for three years, and I still don't really know what he thinks about our sex life. We make love under some kind of self-imposed vow of silence that by now is habit more than anything else. Could *you* say, "Well, Roger, tell me what you've thought about me as a lover for the last three years"?

—Woman, 29

As you think about a method of birth control, think about the patterns in your sex life. Intimacy flowers in different ways for different couples, and birth control is a less obtrusive visitor to the bedroom when it is compatible with your own particular lovemaking style. Here are some questions to ask yourself:

How much cooperation can you expect from your partner? Methods such as a diaphragm, foam, or condoms are more likely to succeed if contraception is a joint undertaking. If you have a topnotch, stable relationship with plenty of trust, natural family planning may be an option.

How do you feel about touching yourself? Using a diaphragm or foam calls for an easy familiarity with your vagina. Checking for an IUD string on a regular basis requires putting a finger deep inside your vagina. (Your partner might check the strings for you.)

Are you afraid of any of the methods? You may have a sister who had an IUD-related infection, a friend who was hospitalized with a Pill complication, or a co-worker with two "diaphragm babies." It would be hard to use a method consistently that scares you. "Life is too short to be scared when you don't have to be," one woman said.

What methods have you had difficulties with in the past? If you couldn't remember Pills on time three years ago, or if you found yourself risking unprotected intercourse from time to time after you decided on a diaphragm, foam, or condoms, chances are you might still be vulnerable to the same mistakes.

Do you like a lot of spontaneity in your sex life? Unanticipated sex has enormous appeal for many people, and if you fit into that category, you may not enjoy calling Time Out for foam, condoms, or a diaphragm.

Making up Your Mind

When the time comes to choose a method, start with a list of all your options. Go through the contraindications first and eliminate methods that are unsafe for you. As the list gets shorter and you discard some methods for concrete, objective reasons, begin to consider your feelings and your partner's feelings. Your goal is to choose the safest, most effective method you will feel comfortable about using.

Remember to select two methods, your primary method and a backup method as well. Unexpected problems happen often enough to warrant a second line of defense for all birth control users.

You can always change your mind. There is no reason to stay with a method if you don't like it or if your contraceptive needs change. If your clinician is reluctant to have you switch methods, try another clinician or go to a family planning clinic.

Unreliable Methods

You may know of birth control methods that haven't been discussed in this chapter. Many less reliable methods do exist, but you would probably be wise to avoid them. These methods are at the low end of the effectiveness scale as far as we can tell.

> My cousin's wife used Norforms faithfully for years, and she *never* got pregnant. Then when they *wanted* a baby, they found out that both her tubes were blocked from an old infection. I hope she hadn't talked any of her friends into using Norforms for birth control!
>
> —Woman, 35

The birth control methods that don't work well (or perhaps even at all) are douching; avoiding orgasm; pseudo-barriers inserted in the vagina such as lemon slices, plastic wrap, Vaseline, and tampons; pseudo-sperm killers such as Norforms and other hygiene suppositories, hygiene sprays, hot baths (for men), and jockey shorts (for men); breast feeding; variations of rhythm such as astrological birth control and lunaception; and standing up after intercourse. You probably know of others, and no doubt more methods will appear in the future.

A significant problem with the methods on this list is that they have not been thoroughly evaluated. No one has ever determined the exact effectiveness rates for astrological birth control or any of these other methods, because researchers do not have any promising evidence that would encourage them to undertake such studies. It would be unethical (and costly) for them to ask couples to participate in a study without some reasonable expectation that the couples could avoid unplanned pregnancy.

BREAST FEEDING

Breast feeding (lactation) does delay your return to fertility after giving birth, but it is impossible to predict how long. Since ovulation may occur before menstrual periods return, nursing women have no advance warning of their return to fertility. *Begin using reliable birth control as soon as you resume intercourse after delivery.*

One study found that 50% of women who did not nurse were ovulating three months after delivery; 50% of the women who did nurse were ovulating four and a half months after delivery. Clearly, nursing does not delay a return to fertility very much. In fact, one investigator found that more than half of nursing women who did not use birth control conceived within nine months after delivery, and that can mean two in diapers (5).

REFERENCES

1. Trussell T, Faden R, Hatcher R: Efficacy information in contraceptive counseling: Those little white lies. *American Journal of Public Health* 66(8):761–767, 1976.
2. FDA-approved product labeling for oral contraceptives. May 1980. Manufacturers of oral contraceptives are required to provide a leaflet explaining the benefits, risks and possible complications of Pills for each patient who fills a Pill prescription. You should be able to obtain a copy of the leaflet, entitled "What You Should Know About Oral Contraceptives," from your physician or pharmacist. Manufacturer's information for physicians as well as the text of the patient leaflet appear in *Physician's Desk Reference* (ed. 34), Medical Economics Co., Oradell, N.J., 1980.
3. Cates W, Tietze C: Standardized mortality rates associated with legal abortions: U.S. 1972–75. *Family Planning Perspectives* 10:109–112, 1978.
4. Espenshade TJ: as quoted in the *Wall Street Journal*, October 2, 1980, P. 33; from the Population Reference Bureau, Inc.
5. Vorherr H: Contraception after abortion and postpartum. *American Journal of Obstetrics and Gynecology* 117:1002–1025, 1973.

6 | Condoms

For a long time, condoms were **the** modern birth control method. Venerable. Effective. Simple. Inexpensive. Virtually free of medical risks.

Men, too, care about contraception. Unwanted pregnancy is often a joint experience, with sadness, turmoil, and expense for both partners. It is entirely reasonable that a man would want to protect himself from this situation, and many do. Most men are also genuinely concerned about the health risks that their partners face with birth control, and are quite willing to share birth control responsibility.

Discussions of foam and condoms are presented in separate chapters, but many couples use the two in combination as one method: the foam-condom method. Either one alone does provide first-rate effectiveness and is a rational birth control option, but together foam and condoms provide unexcelled protection from both pregnancy and infection. The fail-safe principle means that using foam (as high as 98% effective) with condoms (as high as 97% effective) offers a combined effectiveness of about 99.94%. Even if you use average effectiveness rates to make your calculation, the combined rate is still high: 98.5%. No temporary contraceptive method is better.

The earliest condoms were probably linen sheaths, which Falloppio described in Italy as early as 1564. Condoms from animal intestines soon followed.

Ten months ago I would have called this an invention of the
devil, but now I find that its inventor must have been a man of
good will.

—*Casanova, 1758*

The Great Womanizer had his first bout with venereal disease
before he was 20; no wonder he thought condoms were a godsend.
Condoms were originally designed to protect men from contracting
venereal disease in brothels, and their birth control effect was no more
than a handy side effect.

Today there is an array of latex condoms to select from: transparent
or a whole rainbow of colors, plain end or reservoir-tipped, ribbed or
smooth, dry or lubricated. Illustration 1 shows some of the condom
brands available. All latex condoms meet United States standards for
quality control (length between 16 and 22 cm; width unstretched between 4.9 and 5.6 cm; thickness at least 0.08 mm; and weight no more
than 1.7 gm) (1), and they are tested for holes, strength, and aging. The
dozens of latex condom brands are essentially the same, and no one
brand is better than any other. In fact, practically all condoms in this
country are manufactured by three companies.

Illustration 1   A condom sampler. (Photograph by Rita R. Harris, Medical Photographer.)

Some men consider natural skin condoms to be exquisitely sensitive. They comprise about 2 to 4% of all condom sales in the United States. Skin condoms aren't regulated the way latex condoms are, and size and thickness may vary (1). No study has ever compared the effectiveness of latex and skin condoms, so we don't know whether skin condoms are as effective as the latex products.

How Condoms Work

Condoms protect against pregnancy because they fit snugly along the entire length of the penis and prevent semen from being ejaculated in or near the vagina. They protect against infection because they prevent contact between mucous membranes of the vagina and the skin of the penis. Germs that carry sexually transmitted infection usually require direct mucous membrane contact in order to be contagious.

Effectiveness

If 100 fertile couples used condoms *exactly according to instructions each time they had intercourse,* about 3 women would become pregnant in a year's time (2). Highest reported success rates for condoms very nearly equal those for IUDs and diaphragms. Even if condoms are used perfectly, however, failures might be caused by defective condoms that rupture or have pinhole faults (no product quality control is perfect).

Studies of average couples who use condoms show that if 100 couples use condoms for a year about 10 women might become pregnant (3). There are several possible reasons for these pregnancies:

• The condom slipped off during intercourse.
• The condom slipped off as the man withdrew his penis, spilling semen at the entrance to his partner's vagina.
• The couple used an old, brittle condom that ruptured. (Perhaps it had been in his wallet for a couple of years.)

- The couple decided to have intercourse without protection "just this once."
- The man was unwilling to use condoms regularly because he felt that they decreased sensitivity.

Many couples use condoms for years without any unplanned pregnancies. A survey of 287 British couples married for five years who used condoms exclusively revealed only 4 pregnancies per 100 women per year (1).

Problems and Risks

There are virtually no health risks associated with condoms. A few people are allergic to latex and experience sensitivity reactions to condoms. Switching to skin condoms obviates the risk. Some women find that the added friction of a condom causes irritation at the entrance to the vagina or on the vaginal walls themselves. Lubricated condoms or extra lubrication such as contraceptive foam or a water-soluble lubricant such as K-Y Jelly may be helpful.

Condoms cause significant health problems only when they are defective or are not used correctly and pregnancy follows. These are the risks any woman faces with pregnancy or abortion. See Chapter 5 for the comparative death risks of condoms and other birth control options.

Most problems with condoms are nonmedical. Some couples can't fully enjoy intercourse if they use condoms. Some men are unable to maintain an erection when they use condoms. Some couples dislike interrupting lovemaking to put on the condom. Some people dislike the way condoms smell or feel.

Contraindications

None. A contraindication is a medical condition that renders a course of treatment inadvisable or unsafe that might otherwise be recommended.

Advantages

The condom has a number of obvious advantages, and some that are not so well known. Condoms can be extremely reliable if they are used conscientiously; they provide better protection against sexually transmitted infection than any other contraceptive method. Condoms are less expensive than other temporary methods, except for couples who have intercourse very frequently (more than 30 to 40 times a month); they aren't bulky (tuck them right in your backpack); they are disposable; and they have essentially no health risks or side effects. Women whose partners use condoms have little or no postintercourse drippiness; couples can buy and use condoms without seeing a clinician; condoms permit men to take an active role in birth control; and they provide users with instant visible proof—after intercourse—of how well they worked.

Sex therapists may recommend condoms as an adjunct to treatment for premature ejaculation, because condoms may reduce sensitivity and help prolong intercourse. Condoms may have esthetic value for those who find penis-vagina contact distasteful or for a woman who dislikes having semen in her vagina. The silicone lubrication on prelubricated condoms can reduce friction during intercourse and reduce the risk of vaginal or penile irritation. Men who are older or have had lower abdominal surgery may have trouble maintaining an erection long enough to achieve orgasm, and the slight tourniquet effect of the condom rim may help them maintain a satisfactory erection.

Condoms can be valuable in the treatment of fertility problems. A few couples are unable to become pregnant because the woman's body is allergic to her partner's sperm. If they use condoms regularly for several months, her allergic response may decrease so that intercourse *without* condoms can lead to pregnancy.

Most clinicians recommend that couples use condoms during and after treatment for reproductive tract infections to protect against immediate reinfection.

One of the most important advantages of condoms is their convenience and reliability as a backup contraceptive. Many couples who rely on Pills or IUDs as primary contraceptives use condoms on occasion. Pill users can rely on condoms during the initial 7 to 14 days when they first begin to use Pills; when the Pill-taking schedule gets interrupted; and for several months after stopping Pills before planning to become pregnant. Couples who choose the IUD often rely on condoms during the first 6 to 12 weeks after the IUD is inserted when pregnancy risk is highest; when the woman is unable to find her IUD strings; or during the seven or so fertile days each month when she is most likely to conceive.

CONDOMS AND CANCER

There is no evidence that condom use causes cancer. In fact, condoms may have a protective effect against cancer in that they protect against the transmission of genital herpes virus. Researchers suspect that herpes virus may play some role in the development of cervical and penile cancer.

Where to Get Condoms

Many thousands of condoms are dispensed in medical settings such as family planning clinics and venereal disease clinics—eloquent testimony to the high regard that specialists in family planning and venereal disease have for condoms. Most clinics dispense condoms free or sell them at low cost.

Many people buy condoms in drugstores, from vending machines, or by mail order. In drugstores, condoms may be behind the counter or openly displayed. A survey of pharmacists in 22 states revealed that sales went up an average of 72% when condoms were placed in open displays. Some stores reported sales increases of 500% (4).

> The first time I bought them in a drugstore I went all the way over to the other side of town. I asked the guy behind the counter for "a box of condoms." He pulls out this crate about the size of a shoebox. Not exactly something to slip into your jacket pocket! They usually come 3 or 12 to a little flat box, I found out, and so did all the other people who were hanging around the counter.
>
> —Man, 17

Women are buying condoms too. "I'm the only one in our house who's organized enough to keep us stocked; that's why I buy them," one woman said.

Vending machines are legal in only about half the states. Machine sales have both advantages and disadvantages. Distribution timetables can be uneven, and the customer runs the risk of buying an aged condom that is about as supple as parchment. Condoms last two to three years from date of manufacture if stored under ideal conditions, but it makes sense to avoid vending machines unless it's an emergency and there's no 24-hour drugstore around.

Many national magazines regularly feature ads for mail-order condoms. Apparently many people appreciate the convenience of browsing through a catalog and then mailing in a check. (Where else can you order a "Surprise Assortment" and "Father's Day Specials"?) And no doubt it spares many couples lots of wear and tear on their nerves.

> I know it's silly to be embarrassed. But you do have to *ask* for them, and the store owner plays golf with my father-in-law. It's easier to order them.
>
> —Man, 24

Using Condoms Correctly

When condom-using couples have unplanned pregnancies, it's almost always because they haven't used condoms correctly each time they have intercourse.

Rule One is **use condoms every time.** Commitment and discipline are called for, and it is hard to get out of a cozy bed and hunt around in the bathroom when you're feeling amorous. It helps to keep a supply of condoms in a bedside table drawer, or wherever you're most likely to need them. Unless both partners are willing to be diligent about using condoms, they may need to choose another method.

Put the condom on before the penis comes anywhere near the entrance to the vagina. The clear lubricating fluid that collects at the tip of the erect penis may contain living sperm, especially after a recent ejaculation. If you have intercourse for a while and then stop in the middle to put on the condom, you expose the cervix to those sperm.

Leave room at the tip of the condom for the semen. Some condoms are made with receptacles at the end to catch semen, but others

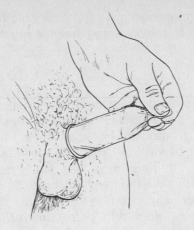

Illustration 2 When putting on a condom without a reservoir end, pinch the tip to leave a little space for semen.

aren't. If you use condoms without a reservoir end, allow for a little space at the end by pinching the very tip of the condom as you roll it on (see Illustration 2). A condom stretched very tightly across the head of the penis is more likely to rupture; or semen may be pushed back along the length of the penis and out into freedom (and the vagina). There's no reason a woman can't help her partner put on the condom. It's not difficult, and besides, as one writer says, "It makes it more of a treat than a treatment."

Hold on to the rim of the condom as the penis is withdrawn from the vagina. The penis begins to lose its erection soon after ejaculation, and a form-fitting condom will quickly become baggy. If it slips off, semen can spill in or near the vagina. (If that ever happens, a quick dose of contraceptive foam is better than just worrying. Try to keep foam and a foam applicator handy if you use condoms. You might also consider "morning-after" birth control. See Chapter 13.)

Withdraw the penis before erection completely subsides. Here again, you're guarding against semen slipping out of a baggy condom. Prompt withdrawal also guards against semen leaking out of an undetected pinhole.

Check the condom before you throw it away. A quick look tells you whether it's intact; a telltale leak means rush for the foam.

There's no more satisfying feeling than holding up a full condom. And there's nothing worse than the sight of tattered remnants.

—Man, 34

Store condoms away from heat. Condoms are good for two to three years from date of manufacture if they are stored properly. Most condoms, especially lubricated ones, are sealed in individual packets to keep them from drying out. Heat deteriorates latex and makes it brittle. Don't store condoms near heat vents or radiators, in glove compartments, or in a wallet—even body heat can deteriorate condoms. Purses, on the other hand, are fine for carrying condoms.

Don't lubricate condoms with petroleum jellies such as Vaseline. Lubrication is important because well-lubricated condoms are less likely to tear. But petroleum jelly may weaken latex, and condoms are only 0.08 mm thick to start with. If you need extra lubrication, try contraceptive foam, lubricated condoms, or a sterile water-soluble lubricant such as K-Y Jelly, available in drugstores without a prescription.

Use a condom only once, then throw it away. In a pinch you could wash, dry, lubricate, and reroll a condom, but it's best to use a new condom each time you have intercourse.

Always have a backup method available. A time may come when you just don't want to use a condom; so be prepared with foam or a diaphragm.

I thought John would *hate* condoms, but he doesn't. We started using them after I had *had it* with four years of headaches on Pills. I got a diaphragm last year in case he changed his mind, but I haven't used it yet.

—Woman, 27

Try to talk about your feelings. Problems with condoms can sometimes be solved by talking about what you like and what you don't like. Your partner may not be able to guess how you are feeling. You may find that a special signal for the right time to put on the condom helps, for example. Some couples find that variety makes a big difference—condoms on Monday, Wednesday, and Friday; a diaphragm on Tuesday, Thursday, and Saturday.

Share the responsibility for cost and for keeping the bedside table supplied.

If a condom breaks, slips off inside the vagina, or you suspect a leak, then think about emergency measures. You can use contraceptive foam, jelly or cream to fill the vagina immediately. If you don't have any one of these contraceptives on hand then a thorough douche (see Chapter 3) with plain warm water is reasonable. Also, you may want to consider morning after treatment (see Chapter 13); if so, plan to see your clinician within 24 hours if possible.

Both new and experienced condom users will find excellent information in the *Consumer Reports* study of condoms published in October, 1979 (5). Researchers tested available condom brands for defects and tabulated users' comments and preferences.

Starting to Use Condoms: The Moment of Truth

The beginning of a new relationship is one of the most risky times for unwanted pregnancy because so many couples find it difficult—or at least uncomfortable—to talk about birth control beforehand. Probably both partners are quietly worried about it. Condoms were the solution 20 years ago, and they can be today as well. A woman may feel *good* if a new partner reaches for a condom, even if she does have an IUD. He is saying, "I care about us and about you, and I am willing to bear some of the birth control burden; I don't want a pregnancy scare to jeopardize the beginning of our relationship." It is very unlikely that a woman will protest or even say a word if a man reaches for a condom. If she does, a comment like, "A little extra protection never hurts," or, "No method is perfect," is absolutely in order.

For a woman, being prepared with a condom certainly makes as much sense as being prepared with Pills or a diaphragm. He probably won't say a word, but if he does, "I didn't think I would—you know—be needing anything; so I quit Pills six months ago," should do it. As you hand him the condom or put it on him yourself you don't have to say anything, but maybe you could think of something loving and funny: "I know it's your favorite color." "Do you think this will fit?" "I got these on sale at a flea market." "My brother left these here last weekend." It isn't easy, but it does make sense. Mostly it takes courage.

REFERENCES

1. Dumm JJ, Piotrow PT, Dalsimer IA: The modern condom—a quality product for effective contraception. *Population Reports*, Ser H, No 2, May 1974. Washington, DC, The George Washington University Medical Center.
2. FDA-approved product labeling for oral contraceptives, May 1980. Manufacturers of oral contraceptives are required to provide a leaflet explaining the benefits, risks and possible complications of Pills for each patient who fills a Pill prescription. You should be able to obtain a copy of the leaflet, entitled "What You Should Know About Oral Contraceptives," from your physician or pharmacist. Manufacturer's information for physicians as well as the text of the patient leaflet appear in *Physician's Desk Reference* (ed. 34), Medical Economics Co., Oradell, NJ, 1980.
3. Vaughan B, Trussell J, Menken J, et al: Contraceptive failure among married women in the United States, 1970–1973. *Family Planning Perspectives* 9:251–258, 1977.
4. Dalsimer IA, Piotrow PT, Dumm JJ: Condom—an old method meets a new social need. *Population Reports*, Ser H, No 1, December 1973. Washington, DC, The George Washington University Medical Center.
5. Condoms, a report based on laboratory tests and on detailed questionnaires filled out by nearly 1900 readers. *Consumer Reports*, October 1979, pp 583–589.

7 | Vaginal Spermicides

About 4 million American women use vaginal spermicides. These products can be used alone or in combination with condoms or a diaphragm. Family planning specialists usually recommend foam over other vaginal spermicides when the spermicide is to be used as the only method of birth control. Foam is more effective than the other types of spermicide, and it seems to be a more reliable product; it disperses quickly and evenly, and product quality seems to be consistent. Foam is also the most popular spermicide. Because it corners the market, foam is discussed first in this chapter. Sections on other vaginal contraceptives follow.

With foam, there is a wide gap between average effectiveness rates (85%) and high effectiveness rates (98%). Any woman considering foam is clearly justified in wondering how effective it is likely to be for her. The answer is not clear. Both rates are based on quite reliable research reports. One fact that may account for some of the low effectiveness rates reported is that foam is often a last-resort recommendation for a woman who is not enthusiastic about any method of birth control. She may accept foam knowing full well that she doesn't want to use it, simply to escape a zealous clinician or counselor.

If effectiveness is your concern, remember that a combination method such as foam with condoms offers somewhat better effectiveness and with many of the same advantages as foam alone: safety, low cost, and easy availability.

About 2 million women in the United States use foam, and they follow in a tradition as old as time. More than 2,000 years ago, Egyptian women used a recipe of sodium carbonate, honey, and crocodile dung for a contraceptive paste. Aristotle's concoction was probably more savory; he recommended frankincense, oil of cedar, and olive oil. In the Middle Ages, rock salt was popular. The perseverance and inventiveness of these early birth control users are remarkable, and it is comforting to know that their efforts probably did prevent unwanted pregnancy to some degree. Pastes *will* seal off the cervix, and anything very acidic or very alkaline *will* kill some sperm. Today's products have powerful sperm-killing chemicals, are easy to use, aren't abrasive (can you imagine having intercourse with rock salt inside your vagina?), and don't smell like crocodile dung.

Foam

HOW FOAM WORKS

When you insert a dose of foam deep inside your vagina, two contraceptive actions are ready to work for you. First, the foam spreads over the surface of your cervix and vagina and serves as a mechanical barrier between your cervical opening and sperm. Second, the spermicidal chemical in foam (nonoxynol-9, a surfactant*) coats and breaks down the surface of sperm cells on contact. The sperm-killing action is probably a more important contraceptive effect than the mechanical barrier.

To use foam effectively, timing must be right and placement must be right. After 30 minutes or longer, foam will begin to drip out of your vagina, away from the cervix where it is needed. And if foam isn't inserted deep enough to begin with, it won't reach the cervix and won't be effective. Masters and Johnson studied the dispersal characteristics of several types of vaginal spermicides, and foam won out over jellies, suppositories, and tablets. They found that foam dispersed rapidly and formed an effective barrier (1). (How do they know, you may well be asking yourself. Women volunteers had simulated intercourse with a

---

*Nonoxynol-9 is the active ingredient in all brands of foam now distributed in the United States. Mercury-based spermicides were sold in the past and may still be marketed in other countries. Mercury may be harmful, so avoid products that contain phenylmercuric acetate or other mercury compounds.

see-through plastic penis. The penis had a little camera inside it. Honest.)

EFFECTIVENESS

If 100 fertile couples used foam *exactly according to instructions* each time they had intercourse, about 2 women would become pregnant in a year's time (2). The two failures might be caused by the foam's inability to kill all the sperm or by the foam's inability to stay on and near the cervix long enough to work, even when placed properly.

Studies of average couples who use foam show that if 100 couples use foam for a year, about 15 women might become pregnant (3). There are many possible reasons for these pregnancies:

- The couple decided to have intercourse without protection "just this once."
- Foam was not inserted deep enough into the vagina.
- The couple inserted foam more than 30 minutes before intercourse, and it began to lose its effectiveness.
- The couple had intercourse a second time without adding more foam.
- The woman douched within six to eight hours after intercourse and washed away foam while living sperm were still in her vagina.
- The couple wanted to have intercourse, discovered the foam can was empty, and didn't have a backup method.
- The couple chose not to use foam because it irritated her vagina or his penis, or because they didn't like the taste of foam during oral sex.
- The couple failed to shake the foam can vigorously enough to get a good mix of bubbles and spermicide.
- The couple didn't use as much foam as the manufacturer recommends for each insertion.

Many couples use foam very effectively for years, despite these pitfalls. Foam's effectiveness is largely dependent on the foam user's motivation to do the job correctly. The higher the motivation, the higher the effectiveness rate.

I haven't been pregnant since I was 18, and my husband and I have *never* used anything but foam. It works for us.

—*Woman, 33*

PROBLEMS AND RISKS

There are virtually no serious health risks associated with foam. A few people are irritated by the chemicals in foam, but just changing brands often clears up the problem. Different brands use different perfuming agents, and a switch may eliminate the offending chemical.

There is some evidence that nonoxynol-9, and possibly other chemical ingredients in a spermicide, can be absorbed through the walls of the vagina and into a woman's circulation. So far, however, there have been no reports of serious side effects among spermicide users, nor any evidence in long-term studies that women exposed to spermicide (diaphragm, foam, and vaginal spermicide users) have any higher incidence of cancer, serious illness, or death than do women using no contraception (4).

Foam causes significant health problems only when it fails and pregnancy follows. These are the risks any woman faces with pregnancy or abortion. See Chapter 5 for a discussion of birth control risks and a statistical comparison of foam risks with other birth control options.

Most problems with foam are nonmedical. Some couples find it unpleasantly messy. Some dislike interrupting lovemaking to insert the foam. Some dislike the way it tastes and smells. Some women find inserting foam an unpleasant experience. Some couples who have intercourse several times in one lovemaking session find multiple doses of foam a little overwhelming. Switching to condoms may help.

CONTRAINDICATIONS

A contraindication is a health condition that renders a course of treatment inadvisable or unsafe that might otherwise be recommended. There are no medical problems that would make it inadvisable for a couple to use foam, other than a history of allergy to foam or other spermicides.

ADVANTAGES

Foam works immediately. After inserting it, you can have intercourse without waiting for it to melt or fizz, as you must when you use suppositories and foaming tablets. Many women like foam because it is noninvasive: no hormones in your bloodstream, no foreign bodies in your uterus, and no surgery. Foam is a good method for people who have intercourse infrequently or unpredictably. It's a good choice for the first 6 to 12 weeks you have a new IUD, the first 7 to 14 days on Pills, or any time you need a backup method. Foam adds lubrication, which many women find helpful. It is convenient and slips nicely into a pocketbook or suitcase.

Foam, like condoms, the diaphragm, and other vaginal spermicides, provides some protection against sexually transmitted infection. Precisely how effective foam is as a germ-killer is still under study. One study of nonoxynol-9, the spermicidal agent in foam, showed an almost tenfold decrease in the rate of gonorrhea among foam users (5). Laboratory studies also show that spermicidal agents may protect users against yeast and trichomonas infections, and even against the herpes virus.

Foam can also be used as an emergency measure when a condom breaks or you have intercourse without any birth control at all. If you insert foam after intercourse, you'll kill lots of sperm, but there are no guarantees. Sperm released into an unprotected vagina can enter the cervical canal in seconds, and then they are safely out of harm's way, even if you do add foam. (That's why douching isn't effective birth control.) Foam after-the-fact may help some, but it's impossible to say how much.

FOAM AND CANCER

There is no evidence that foam causes any form of cancer. In fact, foam may have a protective effect against cancer in that it may help prevent the transmission of genital herpes virus. Researchers suspect that herpes virus may play some role in the development of cervical and penile cancer.

HOW TO GET FOAM

Many family planning clinics dispense foam free or at low cost. For a wider selection of brands, shop at the drugstore or even at some enlightened supermarkets. Foams are dispensed in metal aerosol cans, and the ecology-conscious can be reassured that the propellants are not flurocarbons. Foams are commonly sold in single-dose, 6-dose, 20-dose, and 34-dose containers. The key word on the label is "contraceptive." Don't be misled by deodorants, hygiene sprays, or fancy shaving creams. Make sure that the box you select has a plastic applicator tube enclosed if you buy multiple-dose cans. Illustration 1 shows some of the widely marketed foam products.

Some mail-order houses specializing in condoms also sell foams. If you prefer catalog shopping, check the ads in some national magazines.

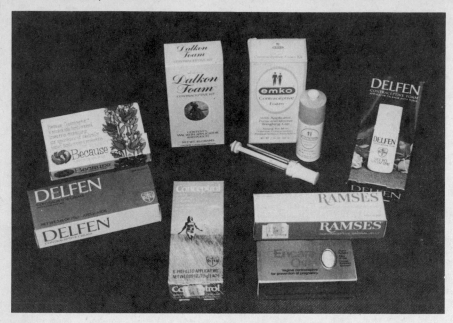

Illustration 1   A sample of vaginal spermicide brands. (Photograph by Rita R. Harris, Medical Photographer.)

INSTRUCTIONS

You can insert foam in less than a minute, but it is crucial that you do it correctly. First, shake the can vigorously 20 or 30 times to mix the spermicide with the bubbles. Fill the applicator either once or twice, according to label instructions (see Illustration 2). (If it will make you feel better, use an extra applicator full. They say you can't be too rich or too thin, and there probably is no such thing as too much foam.) Insert the foam applicator the same way you insert a tampon, and take care to place it as deep inside your vagina as possible. Push the plunger and remove the applicator. If you don't have any experience using tampons, practice inserting foam a few times before you use it with a partner. Illustrations 3 and 4 show correct and incorrect foam placement.

You are protected for half an hour. If more time elapses, insert another dose of foam before you have intercourse. Use another full dose of foam beforehand each time you have intercourse, even if it means more foam every 15 minutes. (There are new legions of sperm.) Do not douche until at least six to eight hours after the last time you have

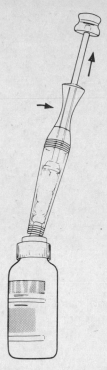

Illustration 2 Tilt the applicator to one side, and foam will fill applicator automatically.

intercourse. Give your spermicide plenty of time to work. (Generally, clinicians say douching is not necessary except in the treatment of certain infections.)

Rinse the applicator in warm water after each use, and store it in a dry place so that the inside has a chance to dry out. Applicators need no special soaps or disinfectants. A full can is no good without an applicator, so keep them together at all times.

Tips for Success. Keep foam handy so that you can reach it without getting up.

Some cans of foam have indicators that show when your supply is running low, and others don't. If you use a brand without an indicator, keep at least two cans on hand at all times. (It's almost impossible to shake and jiggle a can and tell how much you have left. They're all deceptively heavy.) Store foam away from heat. If you buy multiple-

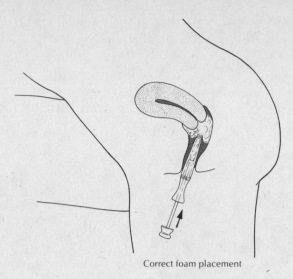

Correct foam placement

Illustration 3 Insert the applicator deep in your vagina so that foam will cover your cervix.

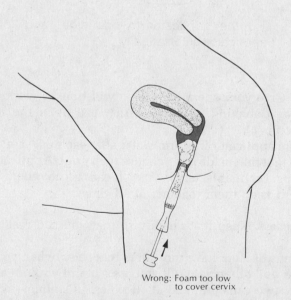

Wrong: Foam too low
to cover cervix

Illustration 4 *Incorrect* foam placement. Foam is too near the vaginal entrance and has not covered the cervix.

dose cans, it is especially important to have more than one on hand. One nice thing about prefilled single-dose applicators is that you always know exactly how much foam you have, but they are more expensive.

If you are bothered by dripping foam after intercourse, you can use a tampon or pad.

If oral sex is frequently part of lovemaking for you and your partner, there's no reason to abandon it just because you think foam tastes terrible. Insert your foam after oral sex and before intercourse. If that doesn't fit in with your lovemaking patterns, you might switch to condoms.

Creams, Jellies, Suppositories, and Foaming Tablets

Most clinicians recommend foam over creams, jellies, suppositories, or foaming tablets because the effectiveness rates with foam are generally higher than those with other vaginal spermicides.

On the other hand, it is one of the eternal verities of birth control practice that couples are likely to be successful with the methods they like to use, and many people use creams, jellies, and other spermicides very effectively. It is unlikely that a clinician would try to convince a happy and successful cream user to switch to foam, for example. All the vaginal spermicides have much in common with foam. They all provide spermicidal chemicals in an inert base, and all of them act by killing sperm and by blocking the cervical opening to protect it from sperm. The risks are the same, and so are the advantages, contraindications, and basic instructions. **Read the foam section first,** even though you're reading this section to learn about cream, jelly, suppositories, or tablets. What follows is a description of what's **different** about the other vaginal spermicides.

CONTRACEPTIVE CREAMS AND JELLIES

Masters and Johnson ranked creams right along with foam in their study of dispersal characteristics. Cream disperses quickly and evenly. They found, on the other hand, that jellies are quite watery and do not disperse evenly or quickly. Masters and Johnson also noted that jelly tends to remain exactly where it is inserted. Since these products are similar, it makes sense to choose cream rather than jelly.

Creams are packaged in tubes like toothpaste; you have the advantage of always knowing how much you have on hand. They are inserted with an applicator much like the foam applicator. With most brands, both the end of the applicator and the end of the tube are threaded; to fill the applicator you simply screw off the cap of the tube, screw on the applicator, and squeeze the tube. Manufacturers generally instruct you to wait two to three minutes after insertion before you begin intercourse to allow time for the cream to disperse. Add more cream if you haven't begun intercourse within an hour. Another dose is required for each subsequent time you have intercourse.

Be careful when you buy spermicidal cream. On drugstore shelves it is likely to be right alongside other creams and jellies designed for use with a diaphragm, and noncontraceptive vaginal products as well. Read the labels carefully. You will probably have to buy these products in drugstores. Most family planning clinics do not stock them.

Investigators have reported cream failure rates from 3.9 to 9.06 pregnancies per 100 women per year. Rates for users of spermicidal jelly have ranged from 7.75 to 36.09 pregnancies per 100 women per year (6). The largest studies reported, however, give cream (6.19 failures per 100 women per year) a better rating than jelly (23.1) and show that neither cream nor jelly compares favorably with foam (3.98) (6). Using condoms along with cream or jelly will increase your protection dramatically.

BIRTH CONTROL SUPPOSITORIES AND FOAMING TABLETS

Suppositories melt on contact with the vagina and release a spermicidal chemical. Foaming tablets fizz. At least that's what they are supposed to do. The major problem with both of these vaginal contraceptives is that suppositories *don't* always melt and foaming tablets *don't* always fizz.

> I decided to quit using suppositories the morning I got up and one fell out *intact* that I inserted the night before. It's a good thing Larry fell asleep watching Johnny Carson!
>
> —Woman, 20

Effectiveness rates for suppositories and foaming tablets are not yet accurately known. Pregnancy rates as low as 1 or 2 pregnancies per 100 women per year, and as high as 38 pregnancies have been reported (7). There are several special problems with vaginal tablets and suppositories that may explain why research findings on effectiveness vary so widely.

Proper placement of the suppository, along with faithful use, is important. Women who do not understand how to insert the suppository deeply in the vagina, or who have difficulty doing so, may not achieve maximum effectiveness. A woman whose cervix is in an unusual position, perhaps because of a severely retroflexed (tipped) uterus, might have less adequate spermicidal coverage.

Suppositories melt because of body heat, and foaming tablets depend on vaginal moisture to effervesce. If the vaginal environment is not suitable, less than complete melting or fizzing could occur. A woman who has vaginal dryness, or has recently used tampons that absorbed part of the moisture normally present, might theoretically have less complete, or slower, effervescence if she tries to use a foaming product.

A special word of warning: When Encare, the first of these products, was initially marketed in the United States, a very high effectiveness rate (99%) from a study in West Germany was publicized. This study and several smaller studies published since that time that seemed to show surprisingly high effectiveness rates for vaginal suppositories have been carefully reviewed by researchers. Unfortunately, each of the studies has had flaws in design or methods significant enough that accurate conclusions about effectiveness are not yet possible (7). Because many women, and clinicians as well, might have been misled by the "documented" 99% effectiveness rate statistics for Encare, federal officials were concerned.

The Food and Drug Administration (FDA) Over-the-Counter Contraceptives and Other Vaginal Drug Products Review Panel urged that the FDA officially review Encare. The panel stated in a February 9, 1978, memorandum to FDA Commissioner Donald Kennedy, "the Panel believes that the way in which the survey was designed and the manner in which the various incentives were offered would clearly make the data resulting from the survey unacceptable to any scientific group or regulatory agency" (8).

For the time being, it seems reasonable to assume that the effectiveness rates for Encare and for the other vaginal suppositories and tablets are not likely to be better than for foam. In other words, if 100 couples used suppositories or foaming tablets exactly according to instructions each time they had intercourse, at least 2 women would become pregnant in a year's time. If 100 average couples use these products in an average way for one year, about 15 women would become pregnant.

Safety issues with suppositories are the same as those for foam (see Foam, Problems and Risks). There are no known serious side effects.

The germicidal properties of nonoxynol-9 (and possibly also the inert base) can be a major incidental benefit for users of spermicides. These products offer at least some protection against gonorrhea, syphilis, herpes, yeast, and trichomonas infection.

INSTRUCTIONS

For maximum effectiveness, follow package instructions carefully; notice that instructions differ slightly for different products (see Table 1). The active ingredient in all the currently–marketed products is nonoxynol-9. The other chemical components of the products, however, differ. If you or your partner find that one product causes irritation, you might try another brand.

Insert the tablet or suppository deeply into the very back of your vagina just below the cervix. Check the position of your cervix with your finger to be sure that the tablet or suppository rests close to it.

Allow time for the spermicide to be released before you begin intercourse. Follow the recommendation on the package—10 or 15 minutes, depending on your brand.

If more than 1 hour elapses before intercourse, insert a new tablet or suppository (2 hours in the case of S'Positive).

Each time you have intercourse use a new tablet or suppository; don't guess about "safe" and "unsafe" days. If you want to use fertility awareness to determine your most fertile time, by all means do so, but this means careful, precise record-keeping—not guessing.

Do not douche or rinse your vagina until at least six hours after intercourse. (Douching is not necessary even then.)

If you suspect or are sure that your tablet or suppository hasn't fully fizzed or melted, then allow more time and insert a fresh one—or consider changing to another method of birth control such as foam, condoms, or a combination.

Condoms used along with a suppository tablet make a very reliable birth control method. You might want to consider using them together, especially during the most fertile part of your cycle. (See Chapter 8 for precise instructions on locating your most fertile days.)

Table 1 VAGINAL FOAMING TABLETS AND SUPPOSITORIES

	Encare	Intercept	Semicid	S'Positive
Spermicide content (nonoxynol-9)	75 mg	100 mg	100 mg	81 mg
Waiting time before intercourse	10 min	10 min	15 min	15 min
Time limit for effectiveness	1 hr	1 hr	1 hr	2hr

SOURCES: S Coleman, PT Piotrow: Spermicides—simplicity and safety are major assets. *Population Reports*, Ser H, No 5, September 1979. Baltimore, Md, The Johns Hopkins University, and product labeling.

REFERENCES

1. Johnson VE, Masters WH, Lewis KC: The physiology of intravaginal contraceptive failure, in Calderone MS (ed): *Manual of Family Planning Contraceptive Practice*, ed. 2. Baltimore, Williams and Wilkins, 1970, pp 232–245.
2. FDA-approved product labeling for oral contraceptives, May 1980. Manufacturers of oral contraceptives are required to provide a leaflet explaining the benefits, risks and possible complications of Pills for each patient who fills a Pill prescription. You should be able to obtain a copy of the leaflet, entitled "What You Should Know About Oral Contraceptives," from your physician or pharmacist. Manufacturer's information for physicians as well as the text of the patient leaflet appear in *Physician's Desk Reference* (ed. 34), Medical Economics Co., Oradell, NJ, 1980.
3. Vaughan B, Trussell J, Menken J, et al: Contraceptive failure among married women in the United States, 1970–1973. *Family Planning Perspectives* 9:251–258, 1977.
4. Coleman S, Piotrow PT: Spermicides—simplicity and safety are major assets. *Population Reports*, Ser H, No 5, September 1979. Baltimore, The Johns Hopkins University.
5. Cutler JC, Singh B, Carpenter U, et al: Vaginal contraceptives as a prophylaxis against gonorrhea and other sexually transmitted diseases. *Advances in Planned Parenthood* 12(1):45–56, 1977.
6. Belsky R: Vaginal contraceptives: A time for reappraisal? *Population Reports*, Ser H, No 3, January 1975. Washington, DC, The George Washington University Medical Center.
7. Edelman DA: Barrier contraception—an update. *Advances in Planned Parenthood* 14(4):144–148, 1980.
8. Over-The-Counter Contraceptives and Other Vaginal Drug Products Review Panel (Elizabeth B. Connell, Chairman): Unpublished memorandum, "Encare Oval," February 9, 1978, to Food and Drug Administration Commissioner Donald Kennedy.

8 Fertility Awareness, Abstinence, and Withdrawal

Abstinence and withdrawal probably rank at the top of the birth control list from a historical or worldwide perspective. Abstinence, particularly, is a cornerstone, and very strong abstinence rules in most cultures insure that the society's childbearing goals are protected. Cultural values set the proper marriage age and proper abstinence interval after a baby is born, for example. Historians credit withdrawal for the dramatic decline in the birth rate in the United States during the Great Depression, and probably this practice accounted for earlier birth rate declines as well. Many cultures have attempted to use fertility awareness with abstinence from intercourse during fertile days to prevent pregnancy. Real success with this method, however, is a very recent phenomenon. The timing of human ovulation, approximately 14 days before the onset of each menstrual period, was not understood until just 50 years ago.

These methods certainly are valid approaches to birth control. They are often omitted from the family planning specialist's "recommended list," however, because each relies heavily on user commitment and significant willpower, and because effectiveness rates for these methods, even among motivated couples, are not consistently as high as rates for other approaches to birth control.

Nevertheless, almost everyone relies upon one of these three birth control techniques at some time in her/his life.

100

Abstinence

Abstinence means no intercourse at all. Many couples who are highly motivated to prevent pregnancy simply don't have intercourse. It is one of the most commonly used forms of birth control, especially among young people. Only about half the women in the United States, for example, have had intercourse by age 20. And abstinence is everybody's first method of birth control.

Willpower is all. Abstinence is 100% effective only if you use it. Many people resolve to use abstinence, saying, "Never again—it isn't worth it," after a disastrous relationship, or a bad scare on Pills, or an abortion. But it is easy to underestimate powerful needs for affection; and abstinence, indeed, may make the heart grow fonder.

Remember that abstinence as a form of birth control means only that you abstain from penis-in-vagina intercourse; it doesn't mean abstaining from sex. Many couples use abstinence for birth control by substituting oral sex, mutual masturbation, or any number of other pleasurable activities for intercourse. It's important to know yourself and your partner well enough to be confident that you can resist intercourse when the going gets passionate—and no cheating: no putting the penis in the vagina "just a little," and no penis hovering near the vagina when ejaculation occurs. If you can resist intercourse and still enjoy sex, you have a terrific method of birth control: free, safe, highly effective, and always available.

Many people, however, find that they are not reliable abstainers. If you have decided on abstinence, it may help if you try to minimize temptations. Most people find it extremely hard to resist intercourse when the mood, scene, and opportunity converge.

> Tom and I did go all the way one time. We were *panicked* till my period started. We went back to his father's cabin once after that, but it certainly is easier just to go out with a group of other kids. Sex is really hard to resist out there by the lake, even though we both try as hard as we can.
>
> —*Woman, 17*

Withdrawal

You remember Onan, of course. He's the Biblical family planning hero who "spilled his seed on the ground" in the 38th chapter of Genesis. (Dorothy Parker had a canary named Onan because he spilled his seed on the ground, too.) Withdrawal or coitus interruptus—interrupting intercourse before the man's ejaculation—is a method of birth control as old as recorded history. As soon as people figured out that semen had something to do with pregnancy, they figured out withdrawal.

HOW WITHDRAWAL WORKS

A couple using withdrawal has intercourse until the man feels that ejaculation is imminent. At that point he withdraws his penis, taking care to ejaculate well away from the entrance to his partner's vagina. Since sperm theoretically do not enter the vagina, they cannot travel through the cervix, uterus, and tube to meet an egg, and pregnancy cannot occur.

EFFECTIVENESS

If 100 fertile couples used withdrawal each time they had intercourse for a year *without any mistakes,* about 9 women would become pregnant. In studies of average couples who use withdrawal, 20 to 25 women out of 100 become pregnant in a year's time (1). Withdrawal can fail either because the man is unable to withdraw his penis in time or because some sperm are deposited in his partner's vagina *before* he ejaculates. Using withdrawal in combination with another method such as foam increases your protection dramatically.

PROBLEMS AND RISKS

There are no medical risks associated with withdrawal, other than those associated with pregnancy or abortion should withdrawal fail to work and a woman becomes pregnant. The effectiveness rate for withdrawal is fairly low because it is difficult for a man to know precisely when ejaculation will occur, and it is difficult to stop intercourse in the middle.

Like most men, I guess, I think of intercourse as something that isn't over till I come. And coming in mid-air isn't half as satisfying as coming in my wife's vagina. And the worst part is, when you have to pull out, you really can't get lost in sex; you can't let yourself get blissed out. It must be even worse for women—like having intercourse with a time bomb.

—Man, 34

Some men, hard as they try, simply can't pull out in time; the momentum toward orgasm is too great. If you and your partner have a failure, use a full dose of birth control foam immediately and call your clinician if you want to discuss "morning-after" options (see Chapter 13).

Withdrawal can fail even if a man pulls out in time. If sperm are deposited near the entrance to the vagina, pregnancy is possible. Even if a man withdraws his penis and ejaculates in the next county, withdrawal can still fail. A drop of clear lubrication fluid normally collects on the tip of the penis during sexual arousal, and this fluid can contain thousands of living sperm. If a man has had a recent ejaculation, the sperm count in that drop of fluid will be even higher. These sperm enter the vagina as soon as the penis does. You can decrease your pregnancy risk by wiping away the fluid just before the man inserts his penis, and by using another method of birth control such as condoms for repeated acts of intercourse.

Most of the problems associated with withdrawal are psychological. Some couples may feel sexually short-changed, and withdrawal can be rough on the nerves, as well.

It was a weird feeling, lying there having intercourse with a man I've loved and lived with for years, and suddenly asking myself, "Can I trust this guy to pull out?" I think using withdrawal causes a lot of deep-seated doubts, and it gives me the hoo-hahs. Who needs that, especially when you're making love?

—Woman, 28

One aspect of using withdrawal that bothers many sex therapists is that withdrawal tends to promote sexual "spectatoring," an ungainly word that means shifting your concentration from pleasure to performance. When both you and your partner concentrate on his pulling out in time, it is hard to concentrate on bliss.

CONTRAINDICATIONS

A contraindication is a health problem that renders a procedure or course of treatment inadvisable or unsafe that might otherwise be recommended. There are no true contraindications to withdrawal. Men who do not have normal ejaculatory control and men who have problems with premature ejaculation probably should not attempt to use withdrawal.

ADVANTAGES

Withdrawal is medically safe, always available, and the price is right. It is certainly better than no birth control at all, since it offers a fair degree of protection.

Part of my luggage got lost in Italy, and it was two weeks before my diaphragm caught up with me. Chuck and I used withdrawal that whole time. I wouldn't want to use it all the time, and I *know* Chuck wouldn't, but it worked for us in a pinch.

—*Woman, 19*

Some couples find that withdrawal is an effective, comfortable method for long periods of time. It can be a reasonable, satisfactory choice as a primary method of birth control for couples who can live with a moderate pregnancy risk. It is an excellent backup along with other methods such as foam; and it is quite handy in emergency situations. It certainly makes sense for couples to explore the full range of satisfying sexual communications; there is a lot more to sex than ejaculation in the vagina.

INSTRUCTIONS

Be sure that the man withdraws his penis well before his orgasm, and take care that he ejaculates well away from the entrance to the vagina. Try to have a supply of birth control foam handy to use immediately in case of an accident. Wipe off the tip of the penis just before intercourse. Avoid using withdrawal for repeated acts of intercourse, because it is likely that the lubricating fluid at the tip of the penis will contain large numbers of living sperm the second time around.

A man may be more comfortable using withdrawal if his partner takes his penis in her hands and stimulates him to orgasm as soon as he withdraws, so he doesn't feel so lost in space.

Have intercourse in positions you can extricate yourself from quickly.

Don't try to use withdrawal when one or both of you might be a little short on willpower—after drinking, for example. Switch to another mode of sexual pleasuring, or use condoms, foam, or a diaphragm.

Fertility Awareness (Rhythm, Periodic Abstinence, Natural Family Planning)

The basis of fertility awareness is heightened awareness of your fertility cycle. Your body temperature, your vaginal discharge, and your menstrual period calendar can all alert you to internal events in your cyclic patterns of fertility. You can use fertility awareness either to prevent pregnancy or to maximize your chance of conception when you are trying to become pregnant. For simplicity, this chapter assumes that you are using fertility awareness for birth control.

Couples who use fertility awareness for birth control either avoid intercourse or use another method of birth control on the fertile days in each cycle; they have intercourse without protection on the remaining days.

Step One is a conscious, cooperative decision between man and woman to abide by this agreement. It helps to remember that abstaining from intercourse does not necessarily mean abstaining from sex. Oral sex, mutual masturbation, and other forms of sexual pleasuring need not be avoided on fertile days. Once you and your partner have agreed that intercourse will be off limits on fertile days, the next step is to calculate your own particular fertile days for your present cycle. That used to be impossible; today it is only extremely difficult; in the future, it may be only moderately difficult.

HOW FERTILITY AWARENESS WORKS

Women are fertile, as a general rule, for a week or so during each cycle, and that week usually falls about halfway between two menstrual periods. For all of history before the 1930s, it was commonly believed that women were fertile immediately after menstruation. (Not such a dumb conclusion, because bleeding is associated with estrus and mating in other mammals.) Finally in the 1930s, scientists on opposite sides of the world, Ogino in Japan and Knaus in Austria, demonstrated the crucial facts about the timing of human ovulation: ***Ovulation occurs quite consistently 14 days*** (plus or minus two days) ***before your next menstrual period begins,*** whether your cycles are 20 days long, 28 days long, or 35 days long (see Illustration 1). (Read that sentence again, because that simple fact is the keystone of human reproductive physiology.) Their information was used to devise calendar-based formulas for calculating and predicting fertile days for women—the early "rhythm" charts.

Another piece of the puzzle fell into place in the 1940s when Ferin in Belgium first recommended that women using calendar rhythm double-check the reliability of their calculations by taking their temperature each day. Body temperature is related to the hormonal fertility cycle and is normally higher after ovulation than during the first half of the cycle.

The quantity and quality of a woman's normal cervical mucus and vaginal discharge also undergo cyclic changes. During fertile days, women usually have a profuse, clear, slippery discharge, and at other times discharge is normally thick, cloudy, and scant.

Calendar Method. The theory of the calendar method is that a record of your past cycles can be used to predict your future cycles. Women are usually instructed to keep careful records of their menstrual periods for at least eight months before attempting to predict fertile days in future cycles. Count your first day of bleeding as day 1 of each cycle. After keeping records for several months you may find that your shortest cycle, for example, was 22 days long and your longest was 28 days.

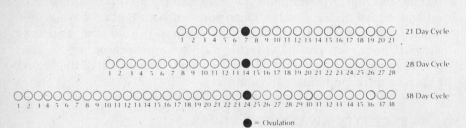

Illustration 1   When your cycle length varies, it is the phase *before* ovulation that changes. The number of cycle days *after* ovulation remains the same—usually about 14 days.

Consult the fertile days chart (see Illustration 2B) and you learn that your first fertile day is day 4, and your last fertile day is day 17; hence, you can either avoid intercourse or use another method of birth control for those 14 days. Always use the most recent eight cycles when you make your calculations, and recheck them with each cycle.

Temperature Method. Your goal using the temperature method is to identify the drop and subsequent rise in your basal body temperature (bbt) that signals ovulation. (Basal body temperature is the lowest temperature reached by a healthy person during waking hours.) A drop in temperature sometimes precedes ovulation by about 12 to 24 hours, and a sustained rise follows for at least three days. Intercourse may be risky in the first half of your cycle. Your temperature may not give you enough advance warning of ovulation to protect yourself. Avoid intercourse or use another method of birth control throughout the first half of your cycle, or at least as soon as bbt drops, and until it has been elevated for at least three days in a row.

Cervical Mucus Method. In order to use the cervical mucus method, you must become familiar with your own discharge patterns so that you can spot the changes that herald ovulation. After menstruation and before ovulation, normal vaginal discharge is white, cloudy, or yellowish in color, thick, and sticky. A few days before ovulation, the volume of discharge increases and discharge becomes clear and quite slippery, much like raw egg white. Intercourse may be risky in the first half of your cycle. Your mucus changes may not give you enough advance warning of ovulation to protect yourself. Avoid intercourse or use another method of birth control throughout the first half of your cycle, or at least as soon as you notice any discharge and until four days after your peak day of slippery discharge. Most women use a calendar to record mucus changes so that they can compare patterns from cycle to cycle.

EFFECTIVENESS

Effectiveness rates approaching 99% have been reported in two studies of fertility awareness method users. A large German study of couples who used basal body temperature charts, and who had intercourse only *after clear indication of ovulation,* showed 99.7% effectiveness (2); and a study of 135 couples who relied on mucus changes demonstrated an effectiveness of 98.7% for the first year of use (3). Most studies have not been so encouraging. A more recent study comparing couples using cervical mucus signs with couples using a combination of calendar, cervical mucus, and basal body temperature signs found an effectiveness rate of 76.2% for the cervical mucus method and 91.6% for the combined approach (4). In these groups, about two-thirds of the couples discontinued the method within 12 months. In another study, couples who chose to use a combination of basal body temperature and mucus signs, and a barrier method of birth control during fertile days (88% of the group), were more satisfied with their method—less than one-third dropped out during the first year (5). Their overall effectiveness rate, however, was similar: 91.1%.

Effectiveness rates from studies of couples using basal body temperature have ranged from 80 to 93%. Two large studies of couples who used the calendar method found effectiveness rates of 70% and 85.6% (2).

Most family planning specialists do not consider fertility awareness a highly effective method, in general, because many women simply don't have clear bbt patterns, regular periods, and clearly differentiated discharge changes.

PROBLEMS AND RISKS

No matter how fertile days are determined—calendar method, temperature changes, mucus changes—fertility awareness can be burdensome. Sexual spontaneity is pretty seriously restricted, and frustration is no doubt the most common problem. Some 31% of couples in one British study found abstinence "frequently difficult" (2). Some people dislike a feast-or-famine sex life.

Fertility awareness is not a method that you can use halfway, either; it does no good to "sort of" keep a bbt chart. And all that work can be useless when temperature charts are equivocal and discharge changes maddeningly elude description.

There is one chilling possibility with all forms of fertility awareness for birth control: If pregnancy does occur, the risk is somewhat greater than average that an *old egg* will be fertilized because the couple has either avoided intercourse or used another method of birth control until they believed that fertile days were over. It has been well documented in animal studies that the fetal abnormality rate is higher than average when pregnancies result from old eggs (2). What work has been done with human subjects indicates that the same risks may be present.

Here is a summary of a Netherlands study from 1971 that revealed an abnormality rate of 69%:

Working with Catholic parents of institutionalized mentally deficient children, Jongbloet found that *the greatest number of disturbed progeny occurred as a result of accidental conception by couples using rhythm where intercourse was limited to the post-ovulatory period only.* Among these families 35 couples produced 59 pregnancies, 41 (69 percent) of which were abnormal: 8 of these resulted in spontaneous abortions (13 percent) and 33 in abnormal progeny (56 percent). Careful review of these cases revealed no age-related factors and no family histories indicative of hereditary disease. Furthermore, when these same couples conceived intentionally, without use of rhythm, the ratio of normal to abnormal pregnancies was reversed: out of 100 pregnancies, 74 percent resulted in normal offspring and 26 percent in either spontaneous abortion (14 pregnancies) or abnormal progeny (12 pregnancies) (6).

Old eggs may be the biggest concern. Other factors may be old sperm, the pregnant woman's age, and her history of miscarriages and abnormalities. Some couples faced with an accidental postovulatory pregnancy might choose abortion, but for many couples who use fertility awareness, abortion is not a comfortable option.

Calendar Method—Problems. Menstrual patterns vary from month to month, and from year to year. In the teen years and premenopausal years, especially, cycles are often irregular. Women who have markedly irregular cycles find it hard to use calendar prediction. Cycles that fluctuate widely may mean you have only four or five "safe" days a month, and there goes romance.

Another major problem with the calendar method is that you must accumulate eight months of good menstrual records before you can begin relying on your calculations to predict fertile days, and you must continue faithfully to record your days of bleeding as long as you use the calendar method.

Temperature Method—Problems. Not all women have easily identifiable "drop, then rise" bbt patterns. One study found that 6 out of 30 women had no identifiable bbt pattern in a cycle when hormone tests clearly documented ovulation (7), and even women who can usually identify the pattern may be thwarted by a cold, an early morning nightmare, flu, jet lag, or a 6 A.M. diaper change. Days go by, and you wait for The Pattern to materialize.

The temperature method may not be very effective if you have intercourse without birth control in the first half of your cycle. However, it can be quite effective, in the 93 to 99% range (2), if you have intercourse *only after* a temperature pattern has clearly indicated ovulation. If you delay intercourse until 4 days after ovulation, you may have only 10 to 12 days for intercourse without birth control in each cycle. (Add more days if you and your partner have intercourse during your period.) Some women dislike having to take and record a temperature each and every morning.

Cervical Mucus Method—Problems. The cervical mucus method may not be very effective if you have intercourse without birth control during the first half of your cycle. Checking for changes in vaginal discharges may be unpleasant for some women. Douching makes it practically impossible to notice discharge changes, and sometimes it is difficult to tell semen from a slippery discharge. Abnormal discharges that result from infections can mask normal discharge changes, and medications such as creams and suppositories can throw you off the track as well. Lubrication—natural or store-bought—can also mask the nature of the discharge.

CONTRAINDICATIONS—ALL METHODS

A contraindication is a medical condition that renders a course of treatment inadvisable or unsafe that might otherwise be recommended. Women whose cycles are quite irregular may find it hard to use fertility awareness ("Quite irregular" is a variance in cycle length of more than two to three weeks or so over the course of a few months. There is no specific, arbitrary definition.)

A couple whose idea of great sex is to park the car on a deserted stretch of roadside, or to take a quick lunch break now and then, would probably be unhappy using fertility awareness. There isn't much room for spontaneity when you use this approach to birth control correctly.

Women who don't ovulate regularly may have difficulty using this method. Your temperature charts may look more like Arabic than the familiar "drop, then rise" pattern.

ADVANTAGES—ALL METHODS

Fertility awareness is completely safe, and either free or very inexpensive; you need only buy a thermometer and charts for recording your temperature. It is acceptable to the Catholic Church and some other religious groups that oppose other contraceptive methods. It gives you an opportunity to tune in on and understand your cyclic patterns, and it may open up new areas of sexual pleasuring for you and your partner. Fertility awareness can be extremely helpful when you are trying to become pregnant (see Chapter 34 for additional suggestions).

SUPPLIES

Most drugstores carry bbt thermometers, and they are often packaged with charts for record keeping. Most family planning clinics provide printed instructions and blank calendars, but you really need some good face-to-face counseling as well. Talk to your clinician or another family planning specialist.

INSTRUCTIONS

This section gives you detailed instructions for using the calendar method, basal body temperature method, and cervical mucus method. The instructions are followed by our recommendation for the most reliable combination of methods; a combination is preferable because *your calendar helps you set your first fertile day, while your bbt and discharge changes help you pinpoint ovulation and your last fertile day.*

Calendar Method. Recalculate your fertile days each cycle, as soon as your menstrual period starts. Consult your calendar and find the shortest and longest cycles you have had in the most recent eight months. (Your first day of menstrual bleeding is the first day of a cycle. The last day before a period is the last day of a cycle.) Use the fertile days chart to predict your first and last fertile days for the present cycle. Begin counting from the day your present period started, and mark your calendar with your predicted fertile days. A sample calendar calculation is explained on page 113.

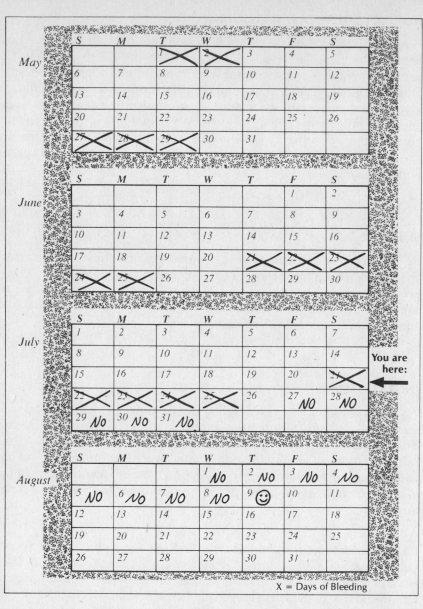

Illustration 2A How to record your fertile days on a calendar.

HOW TO CALCULATE FERTILE DAYS

If your shortest cycle has been:	Your first fertile day is:	If your longest cycle has been:	Your last fertile day is:
21	3rd Day	21	10th Day
22	4th	22	11th
23	5th	23	12th
24	6th	24	13th
25	7th	25	14th
26	8th	26	15th
27	9th	27	16th
28	10th	28	17th
29	11th	29	18th
30	12th	30	19th
31	13th	31	20th
32	14th	32	21st
33	15th	33	22nd
34	16th	34	23rd
35	17th	35	24th

Day 1 = First day of menstrual bleeding

Illustration 2B   Fertile days chart.

On July 21 this woman's period started; so she sat down to calculate and predict her next fertile period. She looked back at her calendar (see Illustration 2A) to find the shortest and longest cycles in the most recent eight cycles. Her May 27 to June 20 cycle is shortest: 25 days. Her June 21 to July 20 cycle is longest: 30 days. Next she consulted her fertile days chart (see Illustration 2B). She learned that her first fertile day is day 7; her last fertile day is day 19. Then, beginning with July 21, the first day of her present cycle, she counted forward to day 7 and marked her first fertile day, July 27. She counted on to day 19 and marked her last fertile day, August 8. All the days from July 27 through August 8 will be fertile days. She and her partner will avoid intercourse or use another method of birth control July 27 through August 8.

The calendar method gives you your best clue for the beginning of fertile days, so keep your records carefully.

Temperature Method. Take your temperature each morning before you get out of bed. You can take either oral or rectal temperatures, but be consistent. If possible use a special basal temperature thermometer rather than a standard fever thermometer. A bbt thermometer registers a maximum of 100 degrees so each degree is larger and easier to read. You can purchase a bbt thermometer without a prescription. Take a reading after five full minutes and record your temperature on a chart (see Illustration 3). Charts are available in family planning clinics and are sold along with bbt thermometers in drugstores.

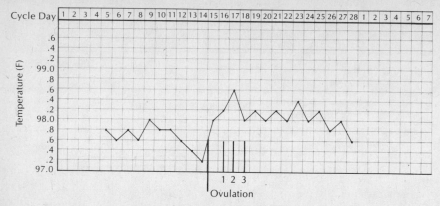

Illustration 3   A textbook example of basal body temperature changes during a normal menstrual cycle. Most women's patterns are not this clear and easy to interpret.

Your temperature may drop about 24 hours before you ovulate. Then it will rise and remain elevated for at least three days following ovulation. Abstain from intercourse or use another method of birth control throughout the first half of your cycle, or at least as soon as your temperature drops and until it has been elevated three full days. For example, see the bbt record in Illustration 4:

This woman could probably tell by Tuesday, July 6, that her temperature was dropping regularly. On Thursday it rose almost a whole degree, and remained at about 98.0 degrees for three full days. Her fertile days are Tuesday through Saturday. Illustration 5 shows a typical bbt record for three months.

July

S	M	T	W	T	F	S
4th	5th	6th	7th	8th	9th	10th
97.8	97.6	? NO · 97.4	NO 97.2	NO 98.0	NO 98.2	NO 98.6

11th	12th	13th	14th	15th	16th	17th
98.0 ☺	98.2	98.0	98.2	98.4	98.4	98.0

Illustration 4   Two weeks of basal body temperature readings.

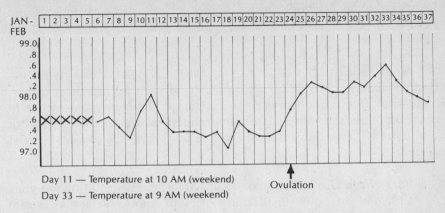

JAN-FEB

Day 11 — Temperature at 10 AM (weekend)
Day 33 — Temperature at 9 AM (weekend)

Ovulation

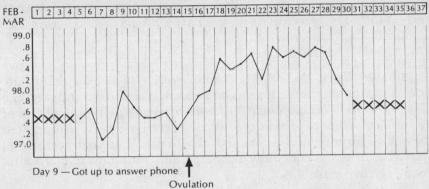

FEB-MAR

Day 9 — Got up to answer phone

Ovulation

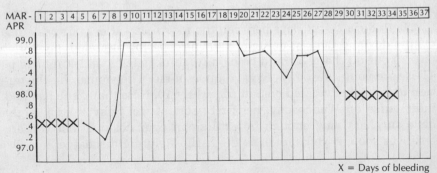

MAR-APR

X = Days of bleeding

Illustration 5 Temperature readings reflect this woman's bout of flu early in her March-April cycle. Fever totally obscured her "drop, then rise" temperature pattern.

Cervical Mucus Method. Keep a record of the quality and quantity of your vaginal discharge each day as you pass through these four cyclic phases:

    Menstruation: Ovulation can occasionally occur during your period, especially if you have long menstrual periods and short cycles. Menstrual blood would mask the discharge changes you look for to pinpoint ovulation. Abstain from intercourse or use another method of birth control, especially during the last few days of a long menstrual period.

    Early Safe Days: These are relatively "dry" days following your period, when you notice no discharge around your vulva. It may be safe to have intercourse. Women with very short cycles may not have *any* early safe days; preovulatory discharge changes may begin immediately after menstruation.

    Unsafe Days: As your estrogen levels rise and ovulation approaches, your discharge appears and becomes abundant, slippery, and clear. *Ovulation occurs about 24 hours after the peak or last day of abundant, slippery discharge.* Avoid intercourse or use another method of birth control throughout the first half of your cycle, or at least as soon as you notice any discharge, and until three full days after your peak discharge day.

    Late Safe Days: Days between the fourth day after your peak discharge day and the beginning of your next period are relatively "dry" days. Your discharge should be cloudy, thick, sticky, and scant again. These are your safest days to have intercourse. The woman in Illustration 6 probably ovulated on Saturday, July 10. Note that if she had had intercourse on Wednesday, her first "sort of wet" day, sperm might have survived long enough to fertilize an egg. Assume that you are fertile as soon as you spot even the earliest sign of discharge.

Warning About the Temperature and Cervical Mucus Methods. Remember that sperm can live inside a woman's reproductive tract 48 hours or even longer. Even when you abstain from intercourse as soon as your temperature drops or you notice a discharge, it may be too late to prevent fertilization. For example, had the woman whose bbt record is shown in Illustration 4 had intercourse Monday, July 5, sperm

July

S	M	T	W	T	F	S
4th	5th	6th	7th	8th	9th	10th
Dry	Dry	Dry	Sort of wet *NO*	Wet *NO*	Wet *NO*	Dry *NO*

11th	12th	13th	14th	15th	16th	17th
Dry *NO*	Dry *NO*	Dry ☺	Dry	Dry	Dry	Dry

Illustration 6   Two weeks of vaginal discharge changes.

possibly could have fertilized the egg she ovulated on Wednesday or Thursday. Your bbt and mucus changes do not predict ovulation far enough ahead of time to protect you on the first couple of fertile days. But both techniques give you a very good idea of when your fertile time has **ended.**

How to Combine Your Calendar, Temperature, and Discharge Changes. Pick a nice big calendar on which to record all your cyclic events, one that is yours alone and not cluttered with dentist appointments, and carpool schedules.

Use the fertile days chart (Illustration 2B) to set your first fertile day each cycle. Remember that calendar calculations usually give you *earlier* warning than other methods.

Meanwhile, keep an eye on your discharge changes and check your bbt. Use these two calculations together (peak discharge day and "drop, then rise" temperature) to pinpoint ovulation. Wait three full days to make sure that your temperature remains elevated and that you have identified your peak discharge day accurately. If you think your bbt and discharge signals are definite and clear, it is safe to ignore your chart-calculated "last fertile day" and assume that your fertile days are over beginning three full days after ovulation as documented by bbt and discharge changes. If you don't have clear bbt and discharge signs, however, assume that you are fertile until after your last chart-calculated fertile day.

If illness, travel, or life's general chaos obscures your patterns, don't guess. Abstain from intercourse or use another method of birth control. Remember that most accidental pregnancies occur in the first half of the cycle, when couples have intercourse just before ovulation.

Fertility awareness will be much more effective if you limit intercourse to after-ovulation safe days only.

If your signs do not all agree, then your best bet is to abstain or use another birth control method. Changes in your temperature and mucus should make sense with the calendar, and with each other. If they don't, it is not reasonable to assume that you are "safe."

The grand combination of signs you are watching for is shown in Illustration 7.

Tips for Success. Pull out all the stops, if you can. If you have noticed that you feel especially amorous around midcycle (some women do), start making a note of it on a calendar. Record any changes at all that you think may be related to ovulation.

Some women have dark red or brownish spotting when they ovulate. Make a note of spotting on your calendar.

The luckiest women of all—perhaps about a fifth of women—can feel ovulation. It's a distinct pain, low in the abdomen on one side or the other, that lasts for a few minutes or even up to 24 hours. It can be

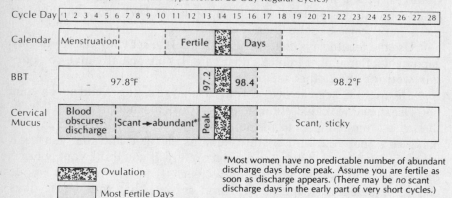

COMBINING ALL TECHNIQUES FOR FERTILITY AWARENESS
(Cyclic Events: Hypothetical 28-Day Regular Cycles)

*Most women have no predictable number of abundant discharge days before peak. Assume you are fertile as soon as discharge appears. (There may be *no* scant discharge days in the early part of very short cycles.)

Mucus cycle description after Dr. John Billings, Natural Family Planning: The Ovulation Method, Liturgical Press, Collegeville, Minn (1972)

Illustration 7   Use all three techniques—calendar, basal body temperature, and discharge changes—for the best results, whether you are planning pregnancy or avoiding pregnancy. (Source: Reproductive Health Resources, Inc. Used with permission.)

on one side one month and then switch, or appear on the same side for several months in a row. The technical word for it is Mittelschmerz, German for midcycle pain, and it is great for identifying, **but not predicting,** ovulation.

> I always know when I'm ovulating. I'm kind of tender on one side, and it hurts for about half a day. When Jack and I were first married, we had intercourse one night and the next morning I had my ovulation pain. I told him right then I was pregnant, and I was right!
>
> —Woman, 30

Some women are able to examine a discharge sample carefully and determine whether ovulation signs are present. Try stretching a discharge sample, either between your thumb and index finger or between two hands as you would a rubber band. You may be able to stretch fertile days discharge 3 inches or more before it breaks. If discharge is stretchable and elastic, it is a clear sign of ovulation. (Clinicians call this stretching phenomenon Spinnbarkeit. It probably enables sperm to swim into the uterus more easily.)

If you have a microscope around the house (a child's model is fine), try spreading discharge thinly on a glass slide. Let it dry, then look at it under low or medium magnification. If you can spot *ferning* patterns

Illustration 8   Cervical mucus dries in a ferning pattern at the time of ovulation.

you have another clear signal that ovulatory discharge is present. A ferning pattern as seen under the microscope is shown in Illustration 8.

Ovulatory discharge is thinner (less viscous) than discharge at other times in the cycle. It may well be that in the near future you and your clinician will be able to buy simple instruments that test a discharge sample for its thickness so that you can know immediately whether or not you are fertile. If these devices are as accurate as some developers claim, days of abstinence or birth control may be considerably shortened each cycle. (Of course, infection and certain medical conditions may render instrument readings inaccurate.) Ask your clinician, and watch for announcements that mucus viscosity testers have become available.

REFERENCES

1. Hatcher RA, Stewart GK, Stewart FH, et al: *Contraceptive Technology, 1980–1981.* New York, Irvington, 1980.
2. Ross MA, Piotrow PT: Birth control without contraceptives. *Population Reports,* Ser I, No 1, June 1974. Washington, DC, The George Washington University Medical Center.
3. Klaus H, Goebel J, Woods R, et al: Use-effectiveness and analysis of satisfaction levels with the Billings ovulation method: Two-year pilot study. *Fertility and Sterility* 28:1038–1043, 1977.
4. Wade ME, McCarthy P, Abernathy JR, et al: A randomized prospective study of the use-effectiveness of two methods of natural family planning: an interim report. *American Journal of Obstetrics and Gynecology* 134:628–631, 1979.
5. Rogow D, Rintoul EJ, Greenwood S: A year's experience with a fertility awareness program: a report. *Advances in Planned Parenthood* Vol. XV, No. 1:27–33, 1980.
6. Jongbloet PH: Mental and physical handicaps in connection with overripeness ovopathy. Quoted in Ross MA, Piotrow PT: Birth control without contraceptives. *Population Reports,* Ser I, No 1, June 1974. Washington, DC, The George Washington University Medical Center.
7. Moghissi KS: Accuracy of basal body temperature for ovulation detection. *Fertility and Sterility* 27:1415–1421, 1976.

9 | The Diaphragm

We are in the midst of a renaissance in diaphragm popularity. Manufacturers have been hard pressed to meet the demand for diaphragms as sales have increased dramatically. Increasing concern about the safety of Pills and IUDs has brought many women into the diaphragm fold. When used correctly, the diaphragm is as effective as the IUD and very nearly as effective as the Pill, and it carries a lower risk of serious complications. Renewed enthusiasm for the diaphragm seems well justified, and reflects increasing consumer sophistication about health care. Diaphragm users are willing to trade off a little convenience in return for a high level of safety.

The diaphragm was invented in 1838 by a German physician, Dr. Frederic Wilde. Birth control pioneer Margaret Sanger introduced the diaphragm to the United States, but because of the "Comstock laws" prohibiting the import of contraceptives she was unable to distribute the diaphragm. In the 1920s the Holland-Rantos Company began manufacturing diaphragms in the United States, and diaphragms became widely available for the first time.

121

How the Diaphragm Works

The diaphragm is a dome-shaped latex cup rimmed with a firm, flexible metal band or spring. The diaphragm is first coated with sperm-killing cream or jelly and then inserted in the vagina before intercourse. The latex dome covers the cervix and holds the spermicidal cream or jelly directly against the cervix. The diaphragm is a physical barrier between your partner's penis and your cervix, but it does not remain perfectly stationary or create a tight seal against the walls of your vagina. Sperm can travel around the rim of your diaphragm and come into contact with your cervix, but spermicidal cream or jelly inside the diaphragm dome will immobilize sperm before they have a chance to enter your cervical canal. The primary function of the diaphragm is to hold spermicidal jelly or cream directly against your cervix.

Effectiveness

Diaphragm effectiveness depends in part on medical factors such as proper fit, but effectiveness depends mostly on how careful—or careless—the diaphragm user is herself.

Effectiveness rates in the range of 86 to 87% (86 to 87 out of 100 couples able to use the diaphragm for one year without an unwanted pregnancy) have been reported for average diaphragm users (1). A five-year study of 4,000 couples in Great Britain who were experienced diaphragm users reported an effectiveness rate of 97.6% (2).

The largest study of diaphragm effectiveness in the United States followed 2,000 users for two years and reported a 98% effectiveness rate among this group of young, unmarried women with no previous diaphragm experience (3).

> I don't know if Allen worries about pregnancy as much as I do or not; why would he? He isn't going to get pregnant! But he *acts* as if he cares as much as I do. He never complains about my diaphragm, and is as conscientious about using it right as I am. That kind of empathy means more to me than I could ever tell him. He's a prince.
>
> —*Woman, 31*

The diaphragm can be as effective as the IUD and very nearly as effective as Pills if you are careful to use it correctly and conscientiously. If you get tired of your diaphragm, you might try condoms some of the time—say a diaphragm for weekdays and condoms for the weekend.

If you find yourself risking unprotected intercourse "just this once," and "just this once" happens over and over, you probably need to change to another method of birth control. Your diaphragm can't protect you if it stays in the bathroom (unless, of course, you have intercourse in the bathroom).

Problems and Risks

There are no known life-threatening risks directly related to the diaphragm other than the health risks of pregnancy or abortion should you become pregnant.

ALLERGY TO LATEX OR SPERMICIDE

Some diaphragm users develop vaginal irritation, swelling, or blistering, which most often is an allergic reaction to spermicidal jelly or cream. Partners occasionally develop allergic reactions as well. Changing brands in order to change the perfuming agent will often solve the problem, but if you are allergic to the spermicidal chemical itself, you may not be able to use a diaphragm. Allergy to latex is possible, but very rare.

PRESSURE FROM THE DIAPHRAGM RIM

Some diaphragm users experience bladder pressure, rectal pressure, or cramps when the diaphragm is left in place six to eight hours after intercourse as recommended. You might talk to your clinician and try a smaller diaphragm or a different rim type. If the problem persists, you may need to use another method of birth control.

REPEATED BLADDER INFECTIONS

There is some evidence that diaphragm users develop cystitis (bladder infection) and urethritis (inflammation of the urinary opening) more frequently than women who use other birth control methods (4). There is no definite proof that diaphragm use causes infection, however; it may be that in some women the diaphragm rim exerts enough pressure against the lower part of the bladder or the urethra to increase susceptibility to infection. A different diaphragm size or type might help.

VAGINAL INFECTION

Your diaphragm may cause a vaginal infection if you leave it in place more than 24 hours, just as a forgotten tampon can cause infection. These infections cause a foul-smelling discharge, but usually are not serious and clear up quickly once you remove the diaphragm.

PARTNER COMPLAINTS

Most diaphragm users and their partners are not even aware of the diaphragm during intercourse. Occasionally, however, a partner may complain about "bumping something" or may have some discomfort during deep penetration. Recheck your diaphragm position to be sure you have inserted it properly. Your partner's penis is likely to bump the rim of a small diaphragm; so you might see your clinician and find out if you can use a larger diaphragm.

TASTE

Many couples object to the taste of spermicidal cream or jelly. If oral sex is frequently a part of lovemaking for you, wait and insert your diaphragm and cream after oral sex and just before intercourse.

Contraindications

A contraindication is a medical condition that renders a course of treatment inadvisable or unsafe that might otherwise be recommended.

ALLERGY

Women who are allergic to latex or spermicide, or whose partners are allergic, may not be able to use a diaphragm.

VAGINAL ABNORMALITY

Women who have had many pregnancies or difficult deliveries may have poor muscular support in and around the vagina, with the result that a diaphragm won't stay in place properly. A woman born with an abnormal vaginal shape may not be able to use a diaphragm.

INABILITY TO INSERT DIAPHRAGM

A woman who is not able to insert a diaphragm and cannot rely on her partner to do so will not be able to use a diaphragm.

Advantages

The diaphragm does not cause any physical, chemical, or hormone changes in your body, and there are no life-threatening complications directly related to the diaphragm. Less serious medical problems are extremely uncommon, and involve only a small percentage of diaphragm users. A diaphragm backed up by early abortion in the event of accidental pregnancy is one of the safest methods of birth control available. In this situation, the risk of death with the diaphragm is no more than 0.3 per 100,000 users per year; see Chapter 5, Illustration 1, to compare diaphragm safety with the safety of other methods of birth control.

Diaphragm effectiveness comes very close to that of Pills, and equals the protection afforded by Minipills, an IUD, or the condom-foam combination. Effectiveness rates as high as 98% have been reported (3).

The diaphragm can be inserted several hours before intercourse and need not interrupt lovemaking. The spermicidal cream or jelly has some bacteria-killing effect and decreases your risk of sexually transmitted infection (5). The diaphragm can be especially appealing to women who have intercourse infrequently or sporadically, for you use the diaphragm only when you need it. The diaphragm does not interfere with breast milk production or cause any alteration in the chemical or hormone content of the milk. You can use your diaphragm for tidier lovemaking during your menstrual period. The diaphragm will contain menstrual flow for about 6 to 12 hours. The diaphragm does not alter your normal fertility.

CANCER AND THE DIAPHRAGM

There is no evidence that the diaphragm causes any increased cancer risk. In fact, the diaphragm may have a protective effect against cancer because it decreases the likelihood that you will develop vaginal and cervical infections, including herpes viral infections. (See Chapter 22 for details on herpes.) Researchers suspect that herpes virus may play a role in the development of cervical cancer (6,7).

Using a Diaphragm

Diaphragms come in several sizes and types, and you need a good fit for good contraceptive protection. You will need to see your clinician for an examination and fitting. Fitting is not difficult or painful for you, but it does require training and experience on the part of your clinician. It is not unusual to encounter physicians who have not been trained in fitting diaphragms, especially if they had their medical training during the 1960s and early 1970s—the "antidiaphragm" era. If your clinician seems to be opposed to the diaphragm or tries to persuade you to select another method, it may simply mean she/he does not often do diaphragm fittings. Your local Planned Parenthood clinic may be able to refer you to clinicians who have the necessary knowledge and experience.

DIAPHRAGM TYPES

There are three types of diaphragms: flat spring, coil spring, and arcing spring. They differ slightly in rim construction only. The differences are most evident when the diaphragm is folded for insertion: each of the three asumes a slightly different shape. Most women could use all three types with equal success, but in certain circumstances one rim type may prove to be better than the others.

Many clinicians recommend the arcing spring as a first choice for most patients; it is well tolerated by most women, and it is difficult to insert incorrectly. Some women find the coil spring more comfortable. The flat spring type is primarily recommended for women with poor muscle tone in the wall of the bladder or rectum (cystocele or rectocele).

Diaphragm sizes range from 50 to 105—the rim diameter is expressed in millimeters. Your clinician's goal is to select the *largest size that is comfortable for you.* The most common fitting error is selecting too small a size.

Two factors will determine the size of the diaphragm you need: the depth and width of your vagina and the strength of your vaginal muscle tone. Two women with the same vaginal depth in millimeters may need different diaphragm sizes because of a difference in muscle tone. *The importance of a snug fit cannot be overemphasized.* Masters and Johnson have demonstrated that during sexual excitement the vaginal depth increases as much as several inches (8). Using the largest comfortable fit will help insure that your diaphragm remains in position and covers your cervix during sexual excitement.

The most common diaphragm sizes are 75 to 85. The 90 to 100 sizes are fairly common, and 50 to 70 sizes are fairly uncommon.

Your clinician may fit you with sample diaphragms, or she/he may use fitting rings (see Illustration 1). Do not be confused by the rings, which are the latex-covered rims alone, without the latex dome. Your diaphragm will have a dome. It needs a dome to cover your cervix.

Be sure that you have a chance to practice inserting and removing

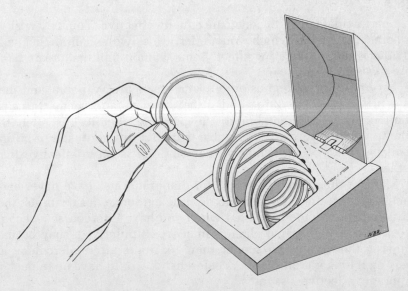

Illustration 1   Your clinician uses graduated fitting rings to determine your correct diaphragm diameter. Sample diaphragms can also be used for fitting.

your diaphragm before you leave your doctor's office or clinic. Have your clinician check to be sure you are inserting it correctly. Some clinicians ask that you return in a week or two wearing your diaphragm to have your fit checked and to make sure you are inserting it properly. Be sure to use another method of birth control, such as condoms or foam, until you have had your fit and your insertion technique checked. It is a good idea to take your diaphragm with you whenever you visit your clinician so that you can have your fit checked as part of your regular exams.

If you go to a family planning clinic for a diaphragm, you will probably pick up your diaphragm at the clinic. If you see a private physician for your fitting, she/he may give you a diaphragm or a prescription for buying your diaphragm at a drugstore. In either case, be sure to pick up all the supplies that you will need:

- a diaphragm in a plastic case
- one or two tubes of spermicidal jelly or cream
- a plastic applicator tube for inserting extra jelly or cream

INSTRUCTIONS

Spermicidal jelly and cream are equally effective. You may wish to try both and decide which you prefer. Most women find that jelly provides a more lubricating effect. Some women find that cream has a more pleasant smell.

Several different brands of jelly and cream are available, and they differ primarily in perfume and price. If one brand seems to cause irritation, try a different brand; the perfume chemical is often the irritant. Although brands do have slightly different sperm-killing chemicals, there is no evidence that any one is more effective than another.

Many of the accepted "rules" for diaphragm use have never been conclusively studied. There is no definite evidence, for example, that additional spermicide is needed when you have intercourse a second time with the diaphragm already in place. Similarly, it may be that removing the diaphragm sooner than six hours after intercourse, or inserting it longer than six hours beforehand, would have no impact on diaphragm effectiveness rates.

Although further study is needed to determine actual effectiveness of the diaphragm method when more flexible rules are used, it is certainly clear that leaving the diaphragm in place with spermicide is

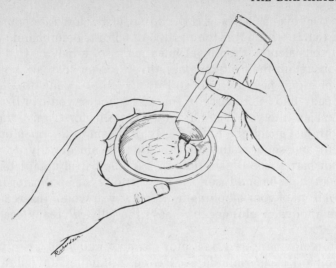

Illustration 2   Sperm-killing cream or jelly goes *inside* the dome of the diaphragm.

worthwhile even if the time limits are exceeded a little. In other words, if you find it difficult or impossible to meet your time limits precisely, it is better to bend the limits than to leave your diaphragm in the drawer. If you need to put in your diaphragm way ahead of time, or remove it early, do so. You will be much better protected than if you decide not to use your diaphragm at all!

The following instructions use accepted time limits for traditional diaphragm use. Some clinicians have used a two-hour limit for place-ment of the diaphragm prior to intercourse, and so do some diaphragm and spermicide package instructions. A limit of six hours is used here, however, because six hours was the interval permitted in the largest United States study of diaphragm effectiveness, and the success rate was excellent (98% effectiveness) (3).

Applying Jelly or Cream. To apply contraceptive jelly or cream, hold your diaphragm with the dome down, like a cup. Squeeze the jelly or cream from the tube into the dome (see Illustration 2). Be sure to use plenty, about a tablespoon, and spread a little around the rim of the diaphragm with your finger. The jelly or cream remains active for at least six hours; so you can insert your diaphragm with cream or jelly up to six hours before you have intercourse. If you haven't had intercourse within that time, you can remove the diaphragm to add the extra jelly or cream.

You can insert your diaphragm, of course, just before intercourse, but if you find that inserting it as long as 4, 5 or 6 hours beforehand helps you to use it consistently, then by all means do so. It may be that the jelly and cream retain their effectiveness even longer than six hours.

If you don't have an opportunity to remove your diaphragm, or have already had intercourse in the last 6 hours, you can insert extra jelly or cream into your vagina with an applicator. To use the plastic applicator, just attach the tube of jelly or cream to the open end of the applicator and squeeze the tube to force cream or jelly up into the applicator barrel (see Illustration 3). Fill the barrel completely. Then disconnect the tube and insert the open end of the applicator into your vagina in front of your diaphragm, much as you would insert a tampon. Push the applicator plunger to release the jelly or cream (see Illustration 4).

If you have intercourse more than once, use an additional applicator full of spermicide each time, no matter how short a time your diaphragm has been in place. *Do not remove or dislodge your diaphragm to add cream or jelly if you have already had intercourse.*

Some women find that extra applications of jelly or cream are messy. Use condoms for a second or third act of intercourse instead of more jelly or cream if you prefer.

Inserting the Diaphragm. You can insert your diaphragm while you are standing with one foot propped up, or while you are squatting or lying down. To insert your diaphragm, hold it dome down (with spermicide inside the dome) in one hand and press the opposite sides of the rim together so that the diaphragm folds (see Illustration 5). Spread the lips of your vagina with your other hand and insert the folded diaphragm into your vagina. Push the diaphragm downward and back along the back wall of your vagina as far as it will go (see Illustration 6). Then tuck the nearest rim up behind the firm bulge in the roof of your vagina

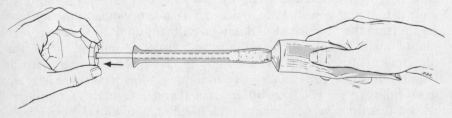

Illustration 3   Add more jelly or cream with a plastic applicator tube.

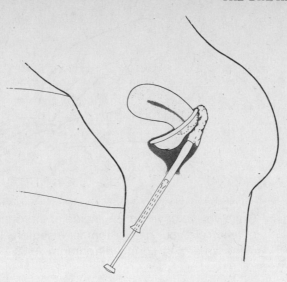

Illustration 4   Insert more cream or jelly for repeat intercourse without removing or dislodging your diaphragm.

that covers the pubic bone. Once your diaphragm is in proper place, you should not be able to feel it except with your fingers. If it is uncomfortable, it may be incorrectly placed; so take it out and insert it again.

You can use a plastic inserter with a coil spring diaphragm if you prefer. Some women find insertion easier with an inserter, but all types of diaphragms can be inserted by hand easily enough. To use the inserter, apply spermicidal jelly or cream, fold the diaphragm, and place it on the inserter. Gently push the inserter and diaphragm into your vagina, aiming downward and back. When you reach the deepest part of your vagina, gently twist the inserter to release the diaphragm in place. Finally, check the placement of the diaphragm with your finger.

Double-checking the Position of the Diaphragm. Always check the position of your diaphragm before you have intercourse. The back rim should be below and behind your cervix, and the front (nearest) rim tucked up behind your pubic bone. Often it is impossible to feel the back rim with your finger. Check to be sure that you can feel your cervix through the soft rubber dome of the diaphragm (see Illustration 7), and check to be sure that the front rim is snugly in place behind the

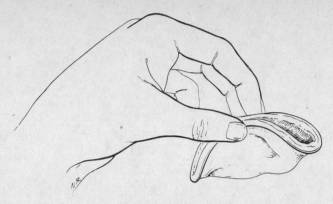

Illustration 5 Once you've covered the inside of the dome with cream or jelly, fold your diaphragm for insertion. This woman is using an arcing spring diaphragm.

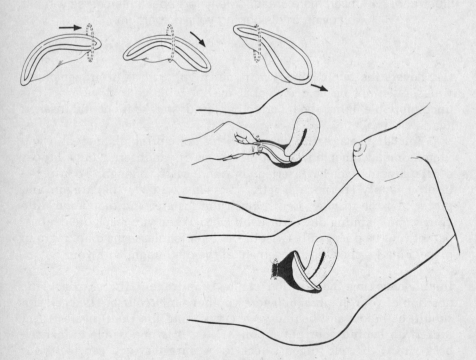

Illustration 6 Use your fingers to guide the diaphragm along the back wall of your vagina.

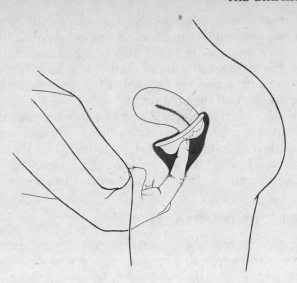

Illustration 7   Check for proper diaphragm placement. You should be able to feel your cervix *through* the dome of your diaphragm.

pubic bone. The jelly or cream should be on the inside, in contact with your cervix.

Finding your cervix often takes practice. You might try to find it first without your diaphragm. Use two fingers rather than one, and try a squatting position. Your cervix will feel like a firm, round bump, somewhat like the tip of your nose.

Check your diaphragm again after intercourse. If it seems to be dislodged, add more jelly or cream with your applicator and talk to your clinician if you want to consider "morning-after" emergency birth control (see Chapter 13). You might also want to see your clinician to check for proper fitting and insertion techniques.

The position of your diaphragm should not be affected by either urination or bowel movement, but you can check afterwards to be sure. Urination will not wash away the cream or jelly. An ordinary shower or tub bath won't interfere with your diaphragm either—but douching will wash away jelly or cream.

When to Remove the Diaphragm. Leave the diaphragm in place for six to eight hours after intercourse, and do not douche during that time. You can remove your diaphragm any time after the six-hour minimum.

If you anticipate intercourse again, simply wash and dry it, add more jelly or cream, and reinsert it. Remove and wash your diaphragm at least once every 24 hours to avoid infection and an unpleasant odor, but stick to the six-hour minimum after intercourse for leaving your diaphragm in place. It may take six hours for spermicidal chemicals to immobilize and kill all the sperm.

To remove your diaphragm, reach inside with your index finger, hook your finger behind the front rim of the diaphragm, and pull down and out (see Illustration 8). Be careful not to tear your diaphragm with a fingernail. If you find it hard to hook your finger behind the rim, try a squatting position and push downward with your abdominal muscles.

CARING FOR THE DIAPHRAGM

Wash your diaphragm with plain soap (Ivory is recommended by manufacturers) and water, rinse it thoroughly, and dry it with a towel. Store it in its plastic container, well away from radiators and other heat sources. You can dust it with cornstarch if you wish, but do not use talcum powder or perfumed powder; talc may be a cancer-causing agent and perfume may deteriorate the latex.

Inspect your diaphragm for defects or holes each time you use it.

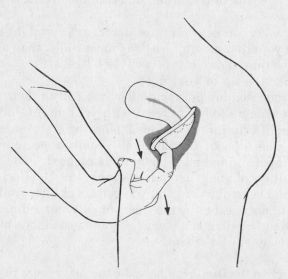

Illustration 8   To remove your diaphragm, hook one finger underneath the rim and pull downward.

Do not use petroleum jelly such as Vaseline with your diaphragm, because it can cause deterioration of the latex. If you use extra lubrication, try a water-soluble lubricant such as K-Y Jelly, which you can buy in a drugstore without a prescription.

The latex part of your diaphragm will discolor and turn darker brown or mottled brown in time, but even so, your diaphragm will last for about two years if you care for it properly.

If you have had a vaginal infection of any kind, be especially thorough as you wash your diaphragm. Wash and dry your plastic storage case and plastic spermicide applicator carefully as well. Common infection organisms will be killed by thorough washing and drying.

WHEN TO SEE YOUR CLINICIAN

Your diaphragm size may not always remain the same. Vaginal depth and muscle tone are usually altered by full-term pregnancy, and they can also change after you first begin to have intercourse regularly. Have your diaphragm fit checked as part of your routine annual examination. Be sure to take your diaphragm with you any time you visit your clinician.

Be sure to see your clinician promptly for a check on your diaphragm fit:

- Any time you believe for any reason that your diaphragm is not fitting you properly or if you have any doubt about whether you are inserting it correctly
- If you have discomfort, pain, or recurring bladder infections
- After you have been pregnant
- After you have had surgery involving your reproductive organs

Tips for Success

Practice inserting your diaphragm by yourself several times when you first get it until you are confident about your technique. If you have intercourse before you feel sure that you are inserting it correctly, protect yourself with a backup method such as condoms or foam.

Some women find it convenient to have two diaphragms, one for home and one for travel or to permit each one to dry thoroughly after use. Be sure to keep an extra tube of jelly or cream on hand.

Check the fit of your diaphragm yourself. The diaphragm rim should be a snug fit. When it is in proper place, there should be only a small gap between the front edge of the rim and your pubic bone, about half an inch or so. If the gap seems large to you and you can insert more than one fingertip between the bone and the rim, then you may need a larger diaphragm size.

Pay attention to the position of your diaphragm in case it should slip during intercourse, for it is occasionally possible for the diaphragm to be dislodged. Masters and Johnson found that the diaphragm could be dislodged during initial penetration of the penis, but was most likely to be dislodged with rapid, repeated penetration. You may want to help guide your partner's penis along the back vaginal wall during entry. Masters and Johnson found that the woman-on-top position was especially risky for dislodging the diaphragm at the time of penis entry. Avoid this position, or be careful to guide your partner's penis away from the front diaphragm rim (8).

Your diaphragm will not interfere with your own natural lubrication during lovemaking. The normal lubrication response to arousal is secreted or "sweated" directly from the walls of the vagina and is not blocked by the diaphragm.

Most suppositories, tablets, and creams for vaginal infections do not interfere with your diaphragm, or the jelly or cream, and you can use them safely at the same time you use your diaphragm.

Any substance containing petroleum such as Vaseline and certain medications, however, may deteriorate the latex of your diaphragm. Common vaginal medications that contain petroleum are Candeptin (candicidin) ointment, Candeptin capsules, and Vanobid ointment, another brand of candicidin. Some common vaginal medications that do not contain petroleum are AVC Cream, ACI-JEL, Monistat cream, Mycostatin (nystatin) tablets, Nilstat (nystatin) tablets, Premarin cream, Sultrin cream, Vagitrol cream, and Vanobid tablets.

Read the medication label, or check with your clinician or pharmacist to determine whether your medication does contain petroleum. Ask your clinician whether to abstain from intercourse during treatment for infection. Some kinds of vaginal infection are contagious; and in some cases intercourse might interfere with your own recovery.

REFERENCES

1. Vaughan B, Trussell J, Menken J, et al: Contraceptive failure among married women in the United States, 1970–1973. *Family Planning Perspectives* 9:251–258, 1977.

2. Vessey M, Wiggins P: Use-effectiveness of the diaphragm in a selected family planning clinic population in the United Kingdom. *Contraception* 9(1):15–21, 1974.

3. Lane M, Arleo R, Sobrero A: Successful use of the diaphragm and jelly by a young population: Report of a clinical study. *Family Planning Perspectives* 8(2):81–86, 1976.

4. *Family Planning Perspectives Digest*: Seven-year prospective study of 17,000 women using the Pill, IUD, and diaphragm. *Family Planning Perspectives* 8(5):241–248, 1976.

5. Cutler J, Singh B, Carpenter U, et al: Vaginal contraceptives as prophylaxis against gonorrhea and other sexually transmitted diseases. *Advances in Planned Parenthood* 12:45–56, 1977.

6. Melamed M, Koss L, Flehinger B, et al: Prevalence rates of uterine cervical carcinoma in situ for women using the diaphragm or contraceptive oral steroids. *British Medical Journal* 3(5664):195–200, 1969.

7. Stern E, Shankman P, Coffelt C, et al: Contraceptive choice and dysplasia: changes following the 1970 Senate hearings. *Contraception* 7(5):435–441, 1973.

8. Johnson V, Masters W: Intravaginal contraceptive study Phase I: Anatomy. *Western Journal of Surgical Obstetrics and Gynecology* 70(4):202–207, 1962.

10 Intrauterine Device (IUD)

Medical opinions about the IUD are divided, and there are strong feelings in both camps. Some clinicians point out the tragedy of hysterectomy or infertility for a young woman who develops an IUD-related infection. Others point out that the overall death rate from IUD-related complications is lower than that for Pills, and remind us that studies show that IUD users are more likely to be using their method at the end of one year than Pill users are.

Remember that with the IUD, you yourself play a major role in determining how safe and effective the IUD is for you. Serious complication statistics in this chapter are for average women, and you may be able to minimize risks for yourself dramatically. From a risk and safety perspective, the ideal IUD user is a woman who:

- Has one permanent partner
- Has no risk of gonorrhea exposure
- Has had one or more previous pregnancies
- Does not plan any future pregnancies
- Would plan early abortion if she became pregnant while using her IUD
- Is comfortable using foam, condoms, or a diaphragm during her fertile days each cycle
- Has a clinician who is experienced with the IUD and who is readily available should any problem occur
- Is over age 25

138

If you choose the IUD, the single most important fact to remember is that early danger signs of IUD problems can be subtle. If you have any problems at all, medical evaluation must be your first priority. Don't let other obligations delay you in seeing your clinician. Early treatment for IUD problems can almost always prevent really serious complications.

The presence of a foreign object inside a woman's uterus tends to prevent pregnancy. Although this concept has been understood for decades, the intrauterine device (IUD) has been in widespread use for less than 20 years. IUDs simply were not acceptable in preantibiotic days when IUD-related infection loomed as a potentially catastrophic illness.

IUD popularity has fluctuated considerably in the last 20 years. About 15 million women worldwide were using the IUD in 1974, including 3 to 4 million American women (1). IUD popularity peaked in 1971, but subsequently declined somewhat as problems with the Dalkon Shield (see Chapter 17) brought widespread attention to potential IUD complications.

The five types of IUDs now approved for use in the United States are shown in Illustration 1. All five are made of inert plastic that is infused with a small amount of barium to make the IUD visible in an x-ray. All other IUD types are experimental and cannot be marketed until Food and Drug Administration (FDA) approval is applied for and granted.

All five IUD types are delicate and lightweight to minimize bleeding and cramping problems. Copper wire on the Copper-7 and Copper-T, and progesterone hormone in the Progestasert-T, enhance their effectiveness. All the IUDs have nylon strings that trail out of the uterus through the cervix and into the vagina so that an IUD user can check to be sure that her device is in place.

How the IUD Works

The presence of an IUD inside the uterus alters a number of factors necessary for pregnancy, but most experts believe that the primary birth control effect is the uterine inflammatory response its presence

COMMON IUD's

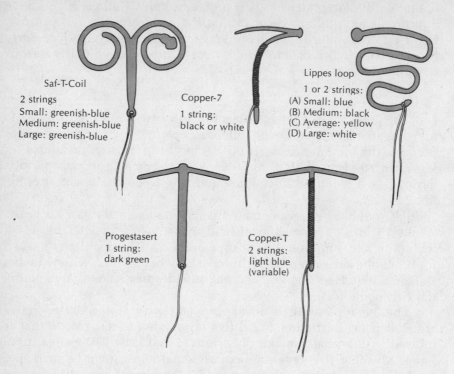

Saf-T-Coil
2 strings
Small: greenish-blue
Medium: greenish-blue
Large: greenish-blue

Copper-7
1 string:
black or white

Lippes loop
1 or 2 strings:
(A) Small: blue
(B) Medium: black
(C) Average: yellow
(D) Large: white

Progestasert
1 string:
dark green

Copper-T
2 strings:
light blue
(variable)

Illustration 1　Five IUDs that are currently available in the United States.

causes—the same kind of foreign body reaction your body produces when you get a splinter in your finger, for example.

UTERINE INFLAMMATORY RESPONSE

The IUD is a foreign body, and the uterus responds to its presence just as it would to any other foreign material. Infection-fighting white blood cells and inflammatory cells (macrophages) gather in the lining of the uterus and disrupt the normal structure of the uterine lining with the result that implantation of a fertilized egg is unlikely to occur. The copper on the Copper-7 and Copper-T devices appears to enhance the inflammatory effect.

ALTERED UTERINE AND FALLOPIAN TUBE CONTRACTIONS

The presence of an IUD may accelerate the normal rhythmic contractions of the fallopian tubes and may disrupt the timing of implantation. An IUD may also stimulate the uterus to produce excess amounts of prostaglandin hormone. Prostaglandin causes uterine contractions that could also interfere with implantation. The physical presence of an IUD may even dislodge a pregnancy as it first implants if uterine contractions cause the IUD to brush against the implantation site.

CHEMICAL CELL CHANGES

Copper and progesterone IUDs provide a continuous release of copper or progesterone into the uterine cavity. These substances add to the contraceptive effects of the IUD because they are at least partially absorbed by the uterine lining cells. Researchers suspect that copper may alter chemical processes within lining cells by altering enzyme function. The progesterone absorbed from a Progestasert affects fertility much as do Minipills. See Chapter 12 for a full description of the birth control effects of low-dose progestins; these include partial suppression of ovulation; hostile cervical mucus, inadequate corpus luteum function, and unsuitable uterine lining.

Effectiveness

Effectiveness rates as high as 99% have been documented for some IUD users (1) but are generally between 95 and 96% (2). If 100 women use the IUD for one year, about 4 or 5 will become pregnant.

It is impossible to cite one precise IUD effectiveness rate because at least eight factors influence IUD effectiveness:

- How long your IUD has been in place
- Your age and previous pregnancy history
- The size of your uterus
- The size and type of IUD

- The size of your IUD in relation to the size of your uterus. (An IUD that is too small for your uterus won't be as effective as one of the proper size.)
- The experience and skill of the clinician who inserts your IUD
- The care with which you check your strings
- Whether or not you use a backup method during your fertile days each cycle

Pregnancies are most common in the first few months after an IUD is inserted. For plain plastic IUDs the effectiveness rate improves steadily from year to year. For example, effectiveness rates for the Lippes Loop D are 96.8% in the first year; 97.9% in the second year; 98.7% in the third year; and 99.1% after six years (1).

Effectiveness of the copper IUDs and the Progestasert depends partly on the effect of the copper or progesterone that is released from the IUD. For this reason, the effectiveness rate for these IUDs should improve initially and then later decline as the release of copper or progesterone from the IUD declines. Studies of the copper IUDs indicate that effectiveness is maintained for at least three to four years; the FDA and manufacturers, however, recommend replacement of copper IUDs after three years of use. The Progestasert is designed to maintain drug release for a shorter period—18 to 24 months. After that time its effectiveness may be expected to decline. The FDA and Progestasert manufacturer recommend replacement once every 12 months.

Some pregnancies occur because a woman expels her IUD and isn't aware of it. Partial or complete expulsion can cause cramps or unusual bleeding that would alert you to check for your IUD strings, but expulsion can also occur with no symptoms at all. If your IUD is not inside your uterus, it cannot work.

> After my IUD was inserted I had some cramps for the first day, but not a *twinge* after that. I was astounded when my clinician checked me out two weeks later and told me it was coming out. I hadn't checked it myself for a few days because I wasn't having sex; thank goodness.
>
> —*Woman, 22*

Problems and Risks

Infection, pregnancy, ectopic pregnancy, and perforation are the most serious complications that can occur with an IUD. IUD complications are serious enough to require hospitalization for 1 out of every 100 to 300 IUD users each year (3). The rate of hospitalization for IUD-related problems is probably higher than the hospitalization rate for Pill-related problems, but the likelihood of death is lower (4). See Chapter 5, Illustration 1, for a comparison of overall death risks for the common methods of birth control.

INFECTION OF THE UTERUS, TUBES AND OVARIES (PELVIC INFECTION)

The presence of an IUD may cause an infection, may make an existing infection worse, or may interfere with your body's infection-fighting defenses and increase your susceptibility to pelvic infection. A woman who uses an IUD appears to have a risk of pelvic infection that is about three to nine times higher than the risk for a woman who uses another birth control method (5). A typical woman whose risk for pelvic infection might normally be 1.6 in 100 has an increased risk of infection with an IUD, and chances are between 5 and 14 in 100 that she will require treatment for infection. Researchers estimate that for about 1 IUD user in every 300 to 1,000 each year, infection is serious enough to require hospitalization (1).

Most IUD-related infections are diagnosed and treated at an early stage when they are not life-threatening and can be cured with anti-biotic pills and rest at home. Infection can be severe, however. Infection that spreads to the uterus and tubes can have a serious impact on a woman's health and future fertility. Read Chapter 25 for a full description of pelvic infection treatment and consequences. Untreated infection can cause permanent scarring of the fallopian tubes and can lead to infertility. Severe infection can also spread to the entire abdomen (peritonitis), or may spread to the liver and cause liver damage and jaundice. You may need surgery to drain an abscess or even to remove your uterus, tubes, and ovaries. Spread of infectious bacteria through the bloodstream can even be fatal.

Obviously, it is important to see your clinician immediately if you have any of the danger signs of infection so that treatment can be started promptly. Watch for:

- Abdominal pain or tenderness, or pain during intercourse
- Fever or chills
- Unusual vaginal bleeding or discharge
- Flu-like symptoms: muscles aches, fatigue, headaches

If you have an infection, your clinician will probably recommend that your IUD be removed—especially if you plan to become pregnant in the future—for the presence of the IUD may hinder the healing process. If you are not concerned about future pregnancy, your infection is mild, and you want to keep your IUD, your clinician may believe that it is safe to leave your IUD in place, begin treatment with antibiotics, and evaluate your progress after 24 to 36 hours. If your infection is improving satisfactorily, you may be able to keep your IUD. If your infection isn't improving after 24 to 36 hours, your clinician will definitely remove your IUD.

Treatment for IUD-related infection includes antibiotics, bed rest, and tests to determine, if possible, what kind of bacteria is causing your infection. The gonorrhea organism is a frequent cause of IUD-related infection, but other kinds of bacteria can cause infection as well.

Infection is most likely to occur within the first few weeks after insertion, because the insertion procedure itself may transport bacteria from the vagina and cervix up into your uterus. Infection can occur, however, months or years after you get your IUD. Pelvic infection caused by *Actinomyces* organisms is a rare disease that may be specifically associated with prolonged IUD use (6). Some clinicians recommend that plain plastic IUDs be removed and replaced periodically, just as the copper and progesterone-bearing IUDs are, in hopes of decreasing the risk of *Actinomyces* problems.

INFECTION DURING PREGNANCY

The combination of infection and pregnancy is potentially fatal for an IUD user. The likelihood that you will become pregnant with your IUD in place is small, about 4 to 5% per year; but when pregnancy does occur and infection follows, the presence of the IUD can result in extremely serious life-threatening illness. You are much more likely to have a miscarriage (spontaneous abortion) with an IUD than you would ordinarily be, and a uterus that contains remnants of a miscarried pregnancy is a perfect growth site for bacteria. As a result, a *massive infection can develop in a very short period of time.* You might feel entirely well one morning and have an infection so severe that you are gravely ill 12 hours later.

Your symptoms may be subtle as infection begins. You may suspect that you have flu because of headache, muscle aches, chills, and fever. Even your clinician may fail to recognize that you have an IUD-related infection. If you have an IUD and you ever have *any* signs of early pregnancy (see Chapter 4), such as a menstrual period that is late, too short, or too light, breast tenderness, nausea, or fatigue, *be sure to let your clinician know that you think you could be pregnant.* If you have signs of early pregnancy combined with infection danger signs, *run, don't walk,* to your clinician.

If you are pregnant, your clinician will want to remove your IUD in order to decrease your infection risk. Your risk of death from infected spontaneous abortion is about 50 times higher if you have an IUD than it would be during a normal pregnancy (7). Between 1972 and 1974, a total of 17 deaths from infected spontaneous abortion was reported for IUD users in the United States. Two deaths were reported for the period 1974 to 1977. Most clinicians and IUD users now understand the importance of recognizing infection and pregnancy early and treating them promptly.

PREGNANCY

Pregnancy itself can cause serious problems for an IUD user even without infection. If you become pregnant with an IUD in place, your likelihood of miscarriage (spontaneous abortion) is high. Miscarriage most often occurs during the first three months of pregnancy, but with an IUD in place late miscarriage can also occur even after six or more months of pregnancy. About 50% of IUD pregnancies end in spontaneous abortion, compared with about 15% of other pregnancies (1). The risk of miscarriage is slightly lower, about 30%, if your IUD is removed as soon as you are aware of the pregnancy (8).

A miscarriage very early in pregnancy may involve little more than an extra-heavy period with stronger than average cramps. Later in pregnancy, spontaneous abortion can cause prolonged, severe cramps and considerable bleeding. You need to see your clinician in either case. She/he will test your blood Rh type to determine whether you need Rh protection (see Chapter 20) and will examine you carefully to be certain that all the fetal and placental tissue has been expelled. Retained tissue or clots will increase your risk of infection, so if there is any question, your clinician will recommend a vacuum procedure (see Chapter 20) or a D&C (see Chapter 40) to be sure that your uterus is empty.

If you are pregnant but have no evidence of infection or miscarriage, you will want to consider several factors as you decide whether to continue the pregnancy or to terminate it. Unless you are absolutely certain that you will terminate the pregnancy, your clinician will try to remove your IUD when she/he first confirms that you are pregnant.

If you are certain that you will have an abortion, your IUD can be removed during your abortion procedure. Remember that abortion is safest when done early in pregnancy; so decide what you want to do as quickly as you can.

Removing the IUD decreases your risk of infection and miscarriage if you continue the pregnancy. It may be impossible, however, for your clinician to remove your IUD without disturbing the pregnancy if your IUD strings have drawn up inside your enlarging uterus. If the IUD cannot be removed, your risk of serious infection is high enough that your clinician will probably advise that you seriously consider terminating the pregnancy.

Whether or not the IUD has any effect on a developing fetus is not known. Many women have delivered babies with an IUD in place. With plain plastic IUDs or with copper IUDs, so far, there is no documented increase in fetal deformities (1,9). The total number of fetuses exposed to copper is quite small. Whether or not fetal exposure to progesterone from a Progestasert will cause the same birth defects that oral progestin can cause (see Chapter 11) is not known.

ECTOPIC PREGNANCY

A tubal (ectopic) pregnancy is a pregnancy that develops anywhere outside the uterus. Ectopic pregnancy most often develops in one of the fallopian tubes. It is an extremely dangerous problem because growth of the pregnancy can cause the tube to rupture, and massive internal bleeding or even death can result. An IUD user who becomes pregnant is more likely to have an ectopic pregnancy than is a woman who becomes pregnant using foam, condoms, or a diaphragm. Ectopic pregnancies account for about 1 out of every 5 pregnancies that occur with a Progestasert in place; with the plain plastic IUDs the proportion is lower: 1 out of 20, and with the copper IUDs the proportion is 1 out of 60 (10). The percentage of ectopic pregnancies is higher for IUD users because the IUD protects against uterine pregnancy more effectively than it protects against ectopic pregnancy. Researchers estimate that about 1 or 2 ectopic pregnancies occur among every 1,000 IUD users each year (11).

Read Chapter 4 for a description of ectopic pregnancy, and watch for these danger signs:

- Sudden intense or persistent pain in the lower abdomen, usually on one side or the other
- Irregular bleeding or spotting when your period is late or after an abnormally light period
- Dizziness or fainting (possible signs of internal bleeding) that persists more than a few seconds. *Massive internal bleeding can occur without any bleeding from your vagina.*

If you have an IUD in place and these signs occur, *see your clinician immediately or go to an emergency room.* Be sure to explain that you think you might be pregnant and that you have an IUD.

PERFORATION OF THE UTERUS

The muscle wall of the uterus is about ½ inch thick, and it is possible for an IUD to puncture (perforate) the uterine wall partially or completely. This rare complication is most likely to occur during IUD insertion and is probably more likely if your clinician is not experienced with IUD insertion techniques. Reported rates for perforation vary from less than 1 to about 9 in 1,000 IUD users (1). Perforation may not be immediately apparent. You might not find out about perforation until several days or weeks later when your IUD strings disappear and your clinician discovers that your IUD is not inside your uterus as she/he attempts to retrieve the strings. If you do not routinely check for your strings, pregnancy may be what tips you off to perforation; an IUD cannot work if it isn't in your uterus.

Spontaneous puncture or gradual migration of an IUD through the uterine wall is uncommon but has been documented for the Copper-T, Progestasert, and Copper-7, three IUDs with a straight, rigid stem (10) (see Illustration 1). Muscular contractions of the uterus may help push the IUD through the cervix itself. Partial perforation or embedding of an IUD within the muscle wall of the uterus also occasionally occurs.

Perforation may cause pain when it occurs, but unless infection develops or the IUD entangles a loop of intestines, your are apt to have few symptoms. The all-plastic IUDs may not cause any problems even if they stay inside your abdomen. However, the presence of an IUD in your abdomen, especially a copper device, can cause an inflammation response and can trigger scar tissue formation. Most clinicians recommend that a lost IUD be removed.

Removal of an IUD that has perforated the uterus is done in a hospital or surgical center, and you need general anesthesia for the procedure. The clinician may be able to use a laparoscope, a lighted tube inserted through a 1-inch incision below your navel, or you may need a full 5-inch incision across your lower abdomen.

SPONTANEOUS EXPULSION

Between 5 and 20% of IUD users spontaneously expel the device within the first year of IUD use (1). The likelihood of expulsion is higher for women who have never been pregnant, women who have a relatively small uterus, and women who are using small IUDs. Clinician skill may also be a factor. Expulsion may cause cramping and bleeding, or it may be completely painless. You can expel your IUD without even knowing it; it could fall into the toilet and get flushed away unnoticed, for example. Expulsion is most likely to occur during a menstrual period within the first few weeks after insertion but can also occur after months or years of problem-free IUD use. Signs that would alert you to the possibility of expulsion are:

- Unusual vaginal discharge
- Bleeding or spotting
- Cramps or abdominal pain
- Your IUD strings seem longer
- Your IUD strings disappear
- You feel the IUD itself protruding from your cervix
- Your partner feels the IUD with his finger or during intercourse
- Your menstrual period is overdue, or other symptoms indicate pregnancy

If your IUD is partially or completely expelled, it cannot prevent pregnancy. Check your strings regularly to detect expulsion and avoid pregnancy.

If you expel an IUD, your clinician will probably be willing to insert another one just like it, or perhaps another IUD type if you want her/him to do so. Some clinicians prefer to wait one month before inserting another IUD. If you expel an IUD more than once, it may mean that your uterus does not tolerate the IUD for some reason; it may be that your uterine cavity has an abnormal shape, for example.

INCREASED BLEEDING AND CRAMPING

Many IUD users have heavy menstrual periods, and about 15% of women who try IUDs have them removed because of bleeding and cramping problems (1). You are likely to notice at least some change in your menstrual periods after you get an IUD. Many women find that the total amount of menstrual blood loss increases and also that the number of days of bleeding increases. You might have light bleeding or spotting for a day or two before your period begins in earnest, and then spotting for several additional days at the end of a regular period. Increased cramping and bleeding problems tend to improve with time; so it may be worth while to see how your second and third periods go before you decide whether to have your IUD removed.

Unlike all the other IUD types, the Progestasert may reduce cramping and bleeding during menstrual periods because of the effect of progesterone hormone on the uterine lining.

It may be hard for you to distinguish between abnormal bleeding and cramps due to infection and those due simply to a typically heavy menstrual period. Menstrual cramps are almost always intermittent, with episodes of real pain lasting only a few hours, then subsiding, and possibly returning again. If you have cramps or pain that is *continuous* and persists for *longer than 12 to 24 hours,* think seriously about the possibility of infection. Remember that infection is most likely to develop within the first few weeks of IUD use and that it often begins with menstrual bleeding or causes abnormal bleeding. If your pain is severe or persistent or if you have other symptoms of infection, see your clinician promptly.

Overall blood loss because of heavy menstrual periods is usually not a serious medical problem unless you are anemic in the first place or your nutritional iron intake is inadequate. Some clinicians recommend iron supplements for IUD users, such as nonprescription ferrous sulfate tablets once or twice a day. Your clinician can check your blood count to determine whether you are anemic if there is any doubt.

It is common for IUD users to have bleeding or spotting between periods. You may notice spotting especially around the time of ovulation, or you may have some spotting throughout your cycle. Be sure to discuss this problem with your clinician, for you may need further evaluation to be sure that the bleeding is not caused by infection, tumor, or another serious problem. Your clinician may also recommend that you try vitamin C for spotting. One study showed significant improvement in heavy spotting after treatment with 200 mg of vitamin C (ascorbic acid) three times a day (12).

An episode of sudden, heavy bleeding is a problem some IUD users encounter. The IUD may rub against the uterine wall, erode a spot, and trigger sudden, massive bleeding. Your clinician will probably remove the IUD, and you will probably find that bleeding stops immediately.

Cramps, pain, and backache are common during the first 24 hours after IUD insertion. Pain that is severe, that is not relieved by aspirin, or that persists longer than 24 hours merits a call to your clinician.

Many IUD users notice cramps or pelvic pain whenever uterine contractions are stimulated, such as during intercourse, during orgasm, or during breast feeding. Backache, leg pain, and soreness can also be associated with contraction cramps. You may also find that ovulation pain is more noticeable after you get an IUD. Remember that pain can be a sign of serious problems. See your clinician promptly if you have any questions.

CERVICITIS

Infection on the surface of the cervix or in the cervical canal is more frequent among IUD users than it is among women who use other birth control methods. The presence of the IUD string inside the cervical canal may cause infection in some way, or may decrease the cervix's normal resistance to bacterial invasion. The most common sign of IUD-related cervical infection is a discharge with a strong fishy odor when you have no evidence of vaginal or even cervical infection. This troublesome problem is very common, but it does not seem to be medically hazardous. Vaginal creams or suppositories usually do not help, but treatment with oral antibiotics such as tetracycline or ampicillin for 10 to 14 days is usually effective (13). It is common for this problem to recur. Remember that abnormal discharge can also mean *serious uterine infection.* An examination is essential to determine what treatment you need and whether it is safe to leave your IUD in place.

INSERTION AND REMOVAL PROBLEMS

Some women become quite weak and faint immediately after IUD insertion. The stimulation of nerves in your cervix during insertion can trigger an autonomic nervous system reaction that causes a drop in blood pressure and marked slowing of your heartbeat. These reactions cause a sudden decrease in blood circulation; consequently, you feel dizzy, faint, nauseated, and extremely weak. Decreased circulation can even cause convulsions or heart stop (cardiac arrest). Most reactions are fairly mild and subside spontaneously within 15 to 30 minutes. The likelihood of severe reaction is minimized when your clinician uses local anesthesia to block cervical pain nerves before IUD insertion. If you do have a severe reaction, your clinician may try using a local anesthetic or another drug called atropine after insertion to stop the reaction, or she/he may recommend that your IUD be removed. Symptoms are likely to subside immediately once your IUD is removed.

IUD removal is usually quick, uncomplicated, and less painful than insertion, but in some cases removal is difficult. If your IUD strings are not visible, if the IUD has become embedded, if it has been in your uterus for several years, if the IUD strings break off, or the IUD has become fragmented, then removal may be tricky. Your clinician may need to use special grasping instruments to retrieve the IUD and may need to dilate or widen your cervical opening slightly to make removal easier. Occasionally, removal requires local anesthesia or even general anesthesia in a hospital or surgery center.

STRING DISAPPEARANCE

IUD strings can spontaneously draw up inside your cervix or uterus, and when this happens, you have no way to be sure that your IUD is in its proper position. This problem has been especially common for the Copper-7 device; the Copper-7 string bends upward when it is stored in its inserter, and the string seems to retain an upward-bend tendency once it is in the uterus. (Copper-7 string position is illustrated later in this chapter.) Your clinician will first try to retrieve your strings with a narrow clamp. If this is not successful, she/he may have to remove the IUD entirely. A new IUD can be inserted immediately if you wish, but some clinicians do recommend waiting one month before inserting a new device to minimize infection risk.

ALLERGIC REACTIONS

Allergy to copper is rare, but if you are allergic to copper, you may develop a skin rash or other allergic reaction with a copper IUD. The potential for allergic reaction also exists with the Progestasert IUD. Women who have Wilson's disease, a very rare condition that causes abnormal retention of copper in body tissues, may react adversely to a copper IUD. The actual amount of copper released by the copper IUDs is very small, however: about 1/30 of the normal adult requirement for copper in the daily diet (1).

OTHER PROBLEMS

Partners of IUD users occasionally report discomfort during intercourse or irritation of the penis after intercourse. Check to be sure your IUD has not been completely or partially expelled. Most often, penile irritation is caused by a short, bristly IUD string protruding from the cervix: thrusting during intercourse pushes the penis against the end of the string. Trimming the string may aggravate the problem rather than solve it. Occasionally, penile irritation is caused by a knot in the string or by a clump of material adhering to the string. You may be able to reposition the end of your string so that the string tip is pointing toward the back of your vagina, or your clinician may be able to help you with these problems by heating the tip of the string with cautery so that a smooth ball forms on the tip.

A number of other problems have been reported among IUD users, such as weight loss or weight gain, nervousness, bladder inflammation, and cysts on the ovaries and fallopian tubes. It is not clear whether there is any real link between the IUD and these problems, or how the IUD might cause them.

THE IUD AND CANCER

Many women and their clinicians have expressed concern that the mechanical irritation and the uterine inflammatory response that the IUD causes might increase the risk of uterine or cervical cancer. Exposure of the uterus to copper or progesterone in the medicated IUDs raises similar concerns. (Current research information regarding hormones and cancer is summarized in Chapter 11.) So far, there is no evidence that IUD use increases your risk for any type of cancer. It is possible that a cancer association might not become apparent until many years after IUD exposure, but after 20 years of evaluation there are no worrisome research findings.

Contraindications

A contraindication is a medical condition that renders a treatment or procedure inadvisable or unsafe that might otherwise be recommended.

ABSOLUTE CONTRAINDICATIONS

A woman who is *pregnant* or has *active pelvic infection* must not have an IUD inserted under any circumstances. Active pelvic infection involving your tubes (salpingitis) or uterus (endometritis) can become much worse if you have an IUD inserted. If you have *gonorrhea* or even suspect that you may have been exposed to gonorrhea, have a gonorrhea test and treatment; and have your cure confirmed by a repeat test before you get an IUD. IUD insertion during pregnancy can lead to miscarriage or to the very dangerous problem of infection in pregnancy.

STRONG RELATIVE CONTRAINDICATIONS

The following conditions mean that your clinician will probably advise you not to use an IUD. You may be vulnerable to serious health risks.

1. Pelvic infection within the last two to six months
2. Repeated pelvic infections in the past
3. Abnormal (inflammatory, Class II) Pap smear, or active cervical infection (cervicitis). Infection should be treated before an IUD is inserted.
4. Ectopic pregnancy in the past. Your risk for a second ectopic pregnancy is high.
5. Abnormal thickening of uterine lining (endometrial hyperplasia)
6. Rheumatic heart disease or other heart-valve abnormalities. An IUD-related infection could spread through your bloodstream to the heart valves and could be potentially catastrophic.
7. Diabetes or other disease or medications that result in lowered resistance to infection, such as cortisone therapy for asthma or arthritis
8. Abnormal blood clotting due to blood-thinning (anticoagulant) drugs or blood disorders. Diminished clotting may cause very heavy bleeding with an IUD.
9. Copper intolerance (Wilson's disease) or copper allergy. Avoid copper-bearing IUDs only.
10. Lack of access to emergency care. Immediate attention from a clinician who could remove your IUD and initiate proper treatment for infection could save your life should you develop a serious complication.

OTHER RELATIVE CONTRAINDICATIONS

Some of the following conditions mean that you may be able to use the IUD if you are willing to be followed very carefully by your clinician so that she/he can watch for early signs of trouble. Other conditions mean that your clinician may not be able to insert an IUD at all.

1. Abnormal uterus size or shape; abnormally narrow cervical canal; or previous uterine surgery
2. Previous problems with IUD expulsion
3. Severe menstrual problems, such as heavy bleeding or severe cramps during natural cycles or when you had an IUD in the past
4. Severe anemia
5. Active vaginal infection or abnormal vaginal discharge. You may have an increased infection risk.
6. Abnormal vaginal bleeding, spotting, or bleeding between periods. Bleeding from any cause may be aggravated by an IUD.
7. Unexplained vaginal bleeding, or cancer of the reproductive organs. IUD-related bleeding may be confused with bleeding caused by other serious problems.
8. Recent pregnancy (abortion, miscarriage, or full-term delivery within the past 10 to 14 days). Infection risk may be increased.
9. Frequent fainting attacks. You may be more likely to have a severe reaction to IUD insertion.
10. Fibroid tumors of the uterus or endometriosis. An IUD may aggravate bleeding problems that can occur with these conditions.
11. Inability to check for IUD strings
12. Concern for future fertility

Many clinicians believe that *your future fertility should be a primary consideration as you evaluate the pros and cons of IUDs.* If you intend to become pregnant in the future, it may make sense for you to consider as additional relative contraindications these factors:

* *Any* episode of pelvic infection any time in the past
* Gonorrhea infection any time in the past
* More than one sexual partner
* Age under 25 years (5)

Each of these factors can mean that your risk of IUD-related infection is increased, and infection can cause scarring and infertility.

Minimizing Your Risks of IUD Complications

Serious IUD infections usually develop gradually and have warning signs that you will notice if you are alert. Prompt treatment can often make the difference between a fairly simple problem and a serious problem.

The following are suggestions for using the IUD as safely as possible based on what is known about IUDs so far. Don't be surprised if your clinician doesn't mention these suggestions to you: *these are not routine instructions.* You may or may not decide to pay attention to all these recommendations; you can use them to help you keep your IUD risks at a minimum.

- Do everything you can to avoid exposure to gonorrhea: If you can't talk to your partner about your concerns, leave quietly by the back door or do anything you have to. Avoid intercourse if your partner has a discharge from his penis, and pay attention to your intuitions. See Chapter 22 for more on gonorrhea symptoms.
- Memorize the IUD danger signs, and get treatment immediately, even if your symptoms are not severe (see Illustration 2).

IUD DANGER SIGNS

* PELVIC PAIN,
  painful intercourse
* UNUSUAL BLEEDING or
  discharge
* exposure to GONORRHEA
* missed period or other
  signs of PREGNANCY
* FEVER or chills
* missing string

Illustration 2   See your clinician right away if you develop a danger sign. (Reproductive Health Resources, Inc. Used with permission.)

- Rely on condoms routinely for the first three months with a new sexual partner, or any time you have more than one partner, or if you ever suspect that your partner has an infection.

- Use foam, condoms, or a diaphragm for the first three months you have your IUD and during your fertile days in the middle of each cycle. (See Chapter 8 for information on determining your fertile days.) Using a backup method along with your IUD means that your chance of pregnancy is less than 0.1%, even lower than the chance for Pill users. Infection complications during pregnancy with an IUD in place are responsible for most of the IUD-related deaths, and if you avoid pregnancy by using a backup method during your fertile days, you can reduce this death risk to almost zero.

- Consider delaying IUD insertion if you have recently been pregnant. After abortion or miscarriage, wait 2 weeks. After full-term delivery, wait 8 to 12 weeks. After cesarean section delivery, wait 12 weeks. Use another method of birth control in the meantime.

- Consider waiting one month after your IUD is removed before you have a new one inserted.

- If you move, find a new clinician immediately so that you can minimize any delay in getting care if you develop a danger sign.

- Check your strings regularly. Frequent string checks may help you to prevent pregnancy that can occur if your IUD is partially or completely expelled.

- Be sure that you know what kind of IUD you have. If you have a copper or progesterone IUD, know when you will need to have it replaced and make your replacement appointment on schedule.

- Choose a clinician who is experienced with IUDs. Some clinicians do not insert IUDs very frequently and do not have extensive experience with recognizing and treating IUD problems.

Advantages of the IUD

Overall effectiveness rates for the IUD range from 95 to 99%, and effectiveness exceeding 99% has been documented for some long-term users of plain plastic IUDs. Using an IUD does not interrupt lovemaking and requires no extra equipment or supplies (except on the days you use a backup method). There is nothing to remember except paying attention to danger signs and being diligent about your routine string checks. The IUD provides continuous protection as long as it remains in place. It does not interfere with breast milk production and plain plastic IUD's do not alter the chemical or hormone content of your breast milk. The IUD does not affect your normal cyclic hormone patterns.

> I decided to get an IUD after my daughter was born. Bob and I really didn't think we wanted a third child, but neither of us felt ready for a permanent decision yet. I didn't want to use Pills again because I was close to 35; and we had tried the diaphragm before, but frankly I just didn't like it. My doctor explained about infections with an IUD, but I felt that *for me* the risk would be small. Bob and I have an old-fashioned relationship; so there isn't much chance I am going to get gonorrhea, and we feel okay about using condoms once or twice a month when we have sex during my fertile days. Overall I have liked my IUD. I certainly don't worry about getting pregnant, and the only thing I really have had to get used to is long periods.
>
> —*Woman, 39*

An IUD can help reestablish normal menstrual periods that have stopped because of uterine scar tissue (Asherman's syndrome). The IUD physically separates the two walls of your uterus so that uterine lining tissue can grow and develop normally.

The IUD can be an effective "morning-after" emergency birth control measure if you have it inserted within five days after unprotected intercourse. See Chapter 13 for details.

Getting an IUD

If you want to use an IUD, you will need to see your clinician or go to a family planning clinic. Your clinician will review your medical history for any factors that might increase the risks of an IUD for you, and perform a routine physical examination and Pap test. Make sure that you also have a gonorrhea test. Some clinicians strongly recommend that the IUD insertion itself be delayed at least a few days after your exam so that your clinician will know the results of your gonorrhea test beforehand.

WHEN TO HAVE YOUR IUD INSERTED

An IUD can be inserted safely at any time in your menstrual cycle before implantation of a new pregnancy could have already occurred. For a woman whose normal cycle is 28 days long, this means any time during the first 16 to 20 days, counting the first day of a normal period as day 1. This policy protects you from IUD insertion during early pregnancy. Some clinicians prefer to schedule insertion during menstrual bleeding to be certain you are not pregnant. A careful study of 9,000 copper IUD insertions found, however, that insertions later in the cycle (after day 11) were somewhat preferable. In the study, medical problems after insertion were similar enough throughout the cycle that the authors concluded there was no reason to place strict limits on the timing of insertion (14).

PREPARING FOR INSERTION

Arrange for someone to accompany you to the office or clinic when you go for your IUD insertion. If you feel queasy, shaky, or weak after the insertion, you will be glad you don't have to travel home alone.

> I've been using my Loop for two years now. I haven't had any real problems, but it sure hurt the first 24 hours. I stayed home from work and took aspirin and a good stiff drink. Every woman getting an IUD should have a friend come along with her to the doctor's office. Driving home was miserable, and I would love to have had my husband do that for me.
>
> —*Woman, 26*

You may want to take two or three aspirin tablets about an hour before your insertion. Aspirin is a good pain medication; also it theoretically blocks release of prostaglandin hormone and may decrease uterine contractions and cramps after insertion.

CHOOSING WHICH IUD TO USE

You and your clinician will want to consider several factors as you choose the best IUD for you: the size and depth of your uterus; your previous pregnancy history; your future pregnancy plans; previous problems you may have had with IUD expulsion; your clinician's special expertise with one or several types of IUDs; and any known allergy to copper.

If you have had one or more full-term pregnancies in the past, you are likely to have a relatively large uterus and can probably use one of the larger IUDs, such as the Lippes Loop D, the large Saf-T-Coil, or a copper or progesterone IUD. Smaller all-plastic IUDs would probably be less effective for you. The Lippes Loop D and large Saf-T-Coil have some advantage in this situation; you do not have to replace them on a regular basis, as you do with copper and progesterone IUDs, and they are less expensive.

If you have never been pregnant, you are likely to have a relatively small uterus. Expulsion, cramps, and bleeding are more likely if you use Lippes Loops B, C, or D, or a large Saf-T-Coil. A copper IUD, the Progestasert, or the small Saf-T-Coil is likely to be a better choice. Some clinicians favor the copper IUDs in this situation because they may offer better effectiveness in an average-size uterus than the small Saf-T-Coil and because the copper IUDs need to be replaced only once every three years. The Progestasert may be less attractive, because it must be replaced every 12 months, although it may be a good choice for you if you have severe menstrual cramps and bleeding and also want to use an IUD.

If your uterus is quite small, with a depth of less than 2¾ inches (7 cm), the likelihood of spontaneous expulsion is high for the copper and progesterone IUDs; the small Saf-T-Coil may be a better choice (15) because it is about ½ inch shorter than any of the other IUDs (see Illustration 3). If your uterus is less than 1¾ inches deep (4.5 cm), it is unlikely that you will be able to use any IUD (15).

If you have preferences about your IUD type, plan to discuss them with your clinician beforehand. Your clinician will try to give you the IUD you want, but she/he can't really make a final recommendation until the insertion procedure has begun and she/he has measured the depth of your uterus.

INSERTION

IUD insertion usually takes about five minutes. Most women say that insertion does hurt, but that the pain isn't unbearable. Some women have no pain at all.

After a pelvic exam (see Chapter 21) to confirm the position of your uterus, your clinician will place a speculum in your vagina and wash

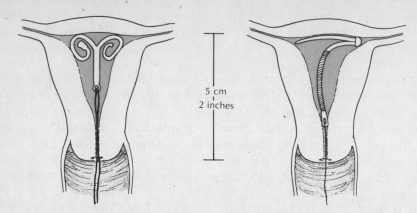

5 cm
2 inches

Illustration 3 This uterus is not big enough for a Copper-7 IUD (right). The tip of the Copper-7 is down in the cervical canal, and expulsion is likely. The Saf-T-Coil (left) is a good fit.

your cervix with disinfectant. You will probably have fairly intense but brief cramps when your clinician grasps your cervix with a clamp (tenaculum) to hold it steady during insertion, and more cramping as she/he inserts a blunt rod through your cervical canal all the way to the top of your uterus to measure your uterine depth. Next your clinician will gently push the IUD inserter through the cervical canal into your uterus. The IUD inserter is a hollow plastic tube with the IUD folded inside. The IUD is released once the inserter is inside your uterus (see Illustration 4). It is common to have cramping as the IUD is released, because the procedure stimulates uterine contractions; contractions may continue off and on for the first 12 to 24 hours after insertion. After the IUD is in position, your clinician removes the inserter tube, trims the IUD string with scissors, and the procedure is completed. Most women feel able to leave within a few minutes after IUD insertion. Adverse reactions to IUD insertion (see "Problems and Risks" section) do occasionally occur and may cause faintness, nausea, vomiting, weakness, and a cold, clammy sensation.

Some clinicians use local anesthetic to decrease discomfort during the insertion. Injection of the local anesthetic into your cervix is unlikely to cause much discomfort, and you may not even be able to tell when it is being done. Some women do find the anesthetic injection fairly painful, however.

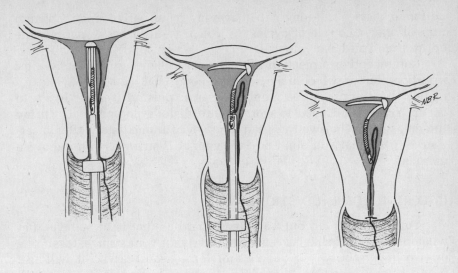

Illustration 4   IUD insertion usually takes less than five minutes.

AFTER INSERTION

You may have cramps and/or bleeding for several days, or even several weeks after IUD insertion. Be sure to read the "Problems and Risks" section to assess whether your cramps might be caused by infection. *If you have any doubt about your cramps, pain, or bleeding symptoms, don't hesitate to call your clinician.*

Your risk for IUD infection is highest in the first few weeks after insertion. You can minimize infection risk if you will:

- Avoid intercourse for the first two to four weeks
- Use condoms for the first three months
- Be alert for infection signs such as persistent cramps or pelvic pain, pain during intercourse, abnormal vaginal discharge, general aches and pains, fever, or chills
- Have a followup examination two to four weeks after insertion so that your clinician can check for uterine tenderness that might indicate infection. She/he will also check for partial or complete IUD expulsion.

You can expect your next period at about its regular time, or perhaps a few days early. You will probably find that your first IUD period is heavier and longer than average. Your periods may return to normal after a couple of cycles, or you may have heavy periods the entire time you have your IUD.

Contraceptive protection with the IUD begins immediately after insertion, but most clinicians recommend that you use a backup method for the first three months when expulsion is most likely to occur. You do not need to worry about dislodging your IUD during intercourse or when you use tampons, even immediately after insertion. Be sure that you don't pull on your IUD string as you remove a tampon.

CHECKING YOUR IUD STRINGS

Your IUD can fall out unnoticed (hard as that is to believe after what insertion feels like); so check regularly for your strings. Insert one or two fingers into your vagina and locate your cervix. It will feel round, smooth, and firm, like the tip of your nose. Your IUD strings will feel like nylon fishing line extending from your cervix about 2 inches or so. Press your fingertip against the opening in the middle of your cervix to be sure that you don't feel any firm plastic in the opening. Your cervical opening should feel like a dimple or indentation at the center of your cervix.

If you have difficulty locating your strings or your cervix, you can use two fingers (index and third finger) in your vagina to reach deeper inside. Move your finger in a circular motion around the top of your cervix several times. The IUD string is thin and may not be obvious until you feel your finger pass over it as it curves out of your cervical canal over the rim of your cervix. It is sometimes helpful to change your position as you check for IUD strings. Try squatting down, then bear down with your abdominal muscles (just as you would for a bowel movement) to bring your cervix closer to your vaginal opening; or try lying on your back with your knees bent. You can also ask your partner to check for you.

Instructions for IUD Users

Reread the section "Minimizing Your Risks of IUD Complications" to assess which suggestions make sense for you and your particular life style. There is very little that you will have to do to use your IUD, but *there is a great deal you can do to use it as safely as possible.* Instructions that are essential for safe IUD use are:

- Be sure that you know what kind of IUD you have. If it is a medicated IUD, you will be responsible for arranging to replace it at the proper time. The Copper-7 and Copper-T must be replaced after three years; the Progestasert must be replaced after one year.

- Check your strings regularly. Many women routinely check for their IUD strings before intercourse each time. At a minimum, you need to check your IUD strings once a week for the first three months and then at least once a month after each menstrual period and after any episode of bleeding or cramping. If you cannot feel your strings, if you do feel firm plastic, or if you have any questions about proper placement, see your clinician as soon as you can and rely on foam, condoms, or a diaphragm until she/he can examine you.

- Use a backup method for the first three months you have your IUD.

- If you have any IUD danger signs, see your clinician immediately. Watch for signs of infection, prolonged or abnormal vaginal bleeding, or signs of pregnancy.

- If you become pregnant while you have your IUD, have it removed as soon as possible, preferably before seven weeks of pregnancy.

- See your clinician for regular checkups once every six months, or more often if you are having any problems.

- Do not try to remove your IUD yourself, and do not let your partner try. See your clinician to have your IUD removed because she/he is able to see what she/he is doing and will be able to deal effectively with any removal problems that might occur.

- Do not take medical heat treatments (diathermy using microwave or shortwave) for your back or pelvis if you have a copper IUD. Heat transmitted through the copper might injure your uterus. Ultrasound or sonogram examinations (see Chapter 21) or using a microwave oven, however, should not present a problem.

HAVING YOUR IUD REMOVED

It is possible for your clinician to remove your IUD at any time, but many clinicians prefer to schedule IUD removal during the first 10 days or so of your cycle. If your IUD is to be removed during the middle of your cycle, avoid intercourse or use a backup method for at least seven days before removal. ***Removing the IUD after conception but before implantation could lead to pregnancy.*** Some clinicians believe that removal is easiest during menstrual bleeding.

Your clinician will first examine you to determine the position of your uterus and cervix and the angle of your cervical canal. Next a speculum will be placed in your vagina so that she/he can see your cervix and IUD string. Your clinician will grasp the string with a clamp and remove the IUD by pulling on it with steady, gentle traction. You will probably have brief cramps as the IUD travels through the cervical canal, but removal is almost always faster and less painful than insertion.

If your IUD is difficult to remove, your clinician may use local anesthesia to block pain nerves in your cervix. She/he can then widen your cervical canal slightly or use other instruments to make removal easier. See the "Problems and Risks" section for further discussion of difficulties with removal.

PLANNING PREGNANCY AFTER AN IUD

The birth control effect of your IUD stops as soon as it is removed. For optimal pregnancy planning, however, it makes sense to use condoms, foam, or a diaphragm for at least one month after your IUD is removed to allow some time for your uterine lining to return to normal.

REFERENCES

1. Huber SC: IUDs reassessed—a decade of experience. *Population Reports,* Ser B, No 2, January 1975. Washington, DC, The George Washington University Medical Center.
2. Vaughan B, Trussell J, Menken J, et al: Contraceptive failure among married women in the United States, 1970–1973. *Family Planning Perspectives* 9:251–258, 1977.
3. Kahn H, Tyler C: IUD-related hospitalizations: United States and Puerto Rico, 1973. *Journal of the American Medical Association* 234:53–56, 1975.
4. IUD safety: Report of a nationwide physician survey. *Morbidity and Mortality Weekly Report* 23(26):226–231, July 5, 1974. US Department of Health, Education and Welfare, Center for Disease Control.

5. Ory H: A review of the association between intrauterine devices and acute pelvic inflammatory disease. *Journal of Reproductive Medicine* 20:200–204, 1978.

6. Aubert JM, Goveaux-Castadot MJ, Boria MJ: Actinomyces in the endometrium of IUD users. *Contraception* 21:577–583, 1980.

7. Cates W, Ory H, Rochat R, et al: The intrauterine device and deaths from spontaneous abortion. *New England Journal of Medicine* 295:1155–1159, 1976.

8. Lewit S: Outcome of pregnancy with intrauterine devices. *Contraception* 2:47–57, 1970.

9. Orlans FB: Copper IUDs: Performance to date. *Population Reports*, Ser B, No 1, December 1973. Washington, DC, The George Washington University Medical Center.

10. Progestasert IUD and Ectopic Pregnancy. *FDA Drug Bulletin*, 8:6, December 1978–January 1979.

11. Vessey MP, Yeates D, Flavel R: Risk of ectopic pregnancy and duration of use of an intrauterine device. *Lancet* 2:501–502, 1979.

12. Margolis AJ, Jones GF, Doyle LL: Control of intermenstrual bleeding after IUCD insertion. *Excerpta Medica*, International Congress Series No 86. Proceedings of the Second International Conference on Intrauterine Contraception, New York, October 1964.

13. Goldsmith, S: Personal communication, 1976.

14. White MK, Ory HW, Rooks JB, et al: Intrauterine device termination rates and the menstrual cycle day of insertion. *Obstetrics and Gynecology* 55:220–224, 1980.

15. Hatcher RA, Stewart GK, Stewart FH, et al: *Contraceptive Technology, 1980–1981.* New York, Irvington, 1980.

11 Birth Control Pills

American health care entered a new era in the late 1970s when for the very first time the Food and Drug Administration (FDA) required that each user of certain hormone drugs be given an FDA-approved leaflet explaining the drug's benefits and risks in detail. This information requirement may represent one of the most important, far-reaching changes in our health care system in many decades. It is encouraging to know that the FDA acknowledges the fact that consumers can and should understand complex personal medical issues. Perhaps detailed consumer information on a wide range of drugs and procedures will follow in the future.

Birth control Pills are among the drugs that must be accompanied by FDA-required consumer information, and all 6 to 7 million American Pill users now receive an FDA-approved leaflet with each new supply of Pills. Credit should go to the concerned and persevering women and men who worked for many years to bring about this revolution in consumer education; it drew widespread media attention with the FDA Pill Safety Hearings in the 1960s.

Many Pill users have read and learned a great deal about Pill-related risks, but other Pill users may find the FDA-approved leaflet a real eye-opener. One important characteristic of the FDA-approved leaflet is that **unknown** risks are included along with well-known risks. As most Pill users are aware, they face a well-documented increased risk of blood-clotting disorders (thrombophlebitis, heart attack, stroke) with Pills, especially if they are older than 30 and smoke. Many

Pill users, however, are not aware that the effect, if any, of Pills on a woman's risk for problems such as cancer or miscarriage is not well understood and is still under intensive investigation. Whether or not Pill hormones in breast milk have any harmful effects on a nursing infant is also unknown. It may turn out that these risks are real; or it may turn out that Pills don't increase your risk for these problems at all. For now, no one knows the answers.

It is difficult to know what to make of these possible but so far unsubstantiated risks. Do the best you can to base your decision about Pills on your own careful, thoughtful appraisal of the facts, and watch for new facts as they come to light.

It isn't easy for physicians to weigh the benefits of Pills against the risks, and it may not be easy for you either. You yourself are the person who cares most about your well-being, and ultimately you have the responsibility for your own health. Also, you are the only person who can evaluate your own particular problems, feelings, and philosophy as you decide about Pills.

The Pill era began in April 1956 in San Juan, Puerto Rico, with the first large clinical trial of combined estrogen and progestin oral contraceptives. Four years later, the Food and Drug Administration approved birth control Pills* for use in the United States. Pills achieved worldwide popularity almost immediately. In the United States the number of Pill users peaked at about 8 million in 1974 and 1975, when almost 20% of all women between ages 15 and 44 took Pills (1). Illustration 1 shows the estimated number of Pill users in the United States.

The first Pills contained 150 micrograms (mcg) of estrogen and 10 milligrams (mg) of progestin. Today's Pills contain about one-third as much estrogen and one-tenth as much progestin as the earliest products, for many studies have shown that lower doses are just as effective and are less likely to cause side effects.

---

*The authors use the term "birth control Pills" and "Pills" for regular, **combined** estrogen and progestin oral contraceptives, no matter what the dose level. The term does not encompass progestin-only pills which we consistently call "Minipills" or "progestin-only pills."

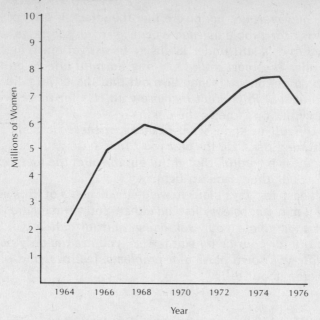

Illustration 1   Pill users in the United States. (Adapted from chart prepared by the Population Information Program, The George Washington University Medical Center, for the Office of Population, US Agency for International Development, using data supplied by IMS America Ltd., Ambler, Pennsylvania.)

How Pills Work

Both estrogen and progestin contribute to the Pill's birth control effects. When you take Pills, the synthetic hormones in the tablet are absorbed through your digestive system into your bloodstream. The synthetic Pill hormones mimic the effects of natural estrogen and progesterone that your ovaries ordinarily produce, and your brain does not distinguish these synthetic hormones from natural ones. Because there is a steady synthetic hormone level day after day, your pituitary gland does not produce its normal cyclic pattern of FSH and LH, the hormones that stimulate your ovaries (see Chapter 1). Your ovaries, therefore, do not produce their cyclic pattern of estrogen and progesterone. *As long as you take Pills, your own reproductive hormone cycle is suppressed and the Pill's synthetic estrogen and progestin take the place of*

*natural hormones produced by your ovary. You do not have your
own cycles. Instead, you have a Pill cycle* (see Illustration 2).

SUPPRESSION OF OVULATION

Without your brain's signal for cyclic FSH and LH release, the
ovary egg follicle cannot mature and ovulation will not occur. Suppression of ovulation is a primary reason Pills work as a contraceptive.

A steady level of estrogen is extremely effective in suppressing
ovulation. A steady level of progestin also blocks ovulation, but somewhat less reliably. In case ovulation does occur, which can happen
once in a while on Pills, several additional contraceptive effects of Pills
nevertheless prevent pregnancy.

ALTERED CERVICAL MUCUS

Cervical mucus remains thick, sticky, and scant throughout the Pill
cycle. The profuse, slippery mucus of ovulation does not occur. Thick
cervical mucus impedes sperm travel through the cervical canal and
inhibits chemical changes in sperm cells that allow them to penetrate
the egg's outer covering.

ALTERED UTERINE LINING

In a natural cycle, the uterine lining thickens under the influence
of estrogen during the first part of the cycle, and then matures under the

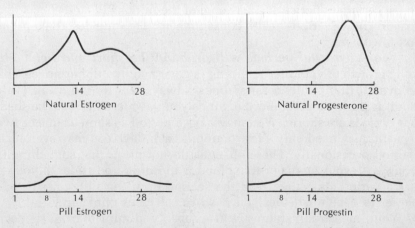

Illustration 2   Pill users have low, steady hormone levels throughout
the cycle.

influence of both progesterone and estrogen after ovulation. This development sequence is not possible during a Pill cycle because both progestin and estrogen are present throughout the cycle. Even if ovulation and conception did occur, successful implantation would be unlikely.

ALTERED CONTRACTILITY

Estrogen and progestin may also alter the pattern of muscle contractions in the tubes and uterus. This may interfere with implantation by altering the fertilized egg's travel time so that it reaches the uterus at the wrong time to implant.

MINOR SIDE EFFECTS OF BIRTH CONTROL PILLS

Pills have many effects that are unrelated to birth control. Some of these effects involve the reproductive organs, but others involve organs as remote as the liver and kidney. Pills can affect blood vessels, the circulatory system, and chemical processes within individual cells. These changes are called "side effects" because they have nothing to do with birth control, the primary reason for using Pills. Some of the changes occur in every woman who uses Pills; others occur only in a small number of Pill users; some side effects are beneficial; others can cause serious medical problems or even death.

Harmful side effects of Pills are uncommon and are discussed in the section on Pill risks and complications later in this chapter. You are almost certain to notice at least some of the minor Pill side effects that have no known serious health consequences. They are described in the next few pages.

Your menstrual periods will probably be short and light. The cyclic growth of your uterine lining is governed by Pill hormones, and the overall lining thickness is almost always less during a Pill cycle than it is during a natural cycle. Since you have less lining to be shed, your periods are shorter. You may have a period as short as one or two days and may need only a few tampons each day. You may even miss a period occasionally. These changes do not mean that something is wrong with your uterus or that blood is building up inside. (If you do miss a period altogether, read the section on using Pills later in this chapter to decide whether you need to call your clinician.)

Your menstrual cramps will probably diminish or disappear. Cramps seem to be linked to ovulation in some way, and it is rare for a woman to have cramps when she is not ovulating. Pill users almost never ovulate; therefore, they are very unlikely to have cramps.

Some women notice mood changes when they take Pills. Pill hormones may have a direct chemical effect on emotions in some women; other women may be affected indirectly because of their own psychological reaction to taking Pills. For example, when you have no worries about unwanted pregnancy, you may be less anxious, and that can cause an increased sex drive (libido). Other Pill users experience a decreased sex drive. Some women also report depression, irritability, or irrational mood swings when they use Pills. These mood changes are similar to those some women experience during the premenstrual phase in a natural cycle or during pregnancy. They may be directly caused by the Pill hormones or perhaps by hormone-induced alterations in your vitamin levels. Vitamin B_6 (20 mg a day) has been used successfully to treat Pill-related depression in some cases (2).

You will not experience midcycle ovulation pain (Mittelschmerz), except possibly in rare cycles when ovulation occurs despite Pills. *Ovary cysts are unlikely to occur,* for most cysts arise from mature egg follicles and follicles usually do not mature while you are using Pills.

Your premenstrual symptoms probably will be diminished. Although some women do experience breast tenderness, fluid retention, irritability, lower abdominal bloating, or a crampy stomach on Pills, these problems tend to be milder and more uniform throughout a Pill cycle and can sometimes be improved by changing to a different Pill.

You may have spotting or bleeding between periods. Low or dropping estrogen will often trigger uterine bleeding, and the level of synthetic estrogen during a Pill cycle is often lower than the level of natural estrogen that your ovaries produce during a natural cycle. This is called *breakthrough bleeding*: uterine bleeding that breaks through (occurs despite) the hormones in Pills. If you forget a Pill or are late taking a Pill, you may find that even a short interruption in your estrogen supply is enough to start an episode of breakthrough bleeding. Breakthrough bleeding is not harmful in and of itself. It can be annoying, and it can cause confusion, because irregular bleeding can also be a danger sign for serious problems such as uterine cancer. Report unusual bleeding to your clinician; you may need evaluation to be certain that your irregular bleeding is not caused by an unrelated problem. If your clinician finds that Pills are probably responsible for your bleeding, she/he may be able to correct the problem by giving you a different type of Pill.

The Pill hormone pattern with progestin present throughout the cycle may make you *more susceptible to vaginal yeast infections.*

You are less likely to develop breast cysts when you take Pills, because Pills create a more stable pattern for your breast tissue, with fewer hormone-induced changes each cycle. You may have a noticeable increase in overall breast size (as much as one bra cup size) that persists as long as you use Pills. It is possible to develop breast milk (galactorrhea). *Get in touch with your clinician if you develop breast milk when you are not nursing.* Breast milk is not directly harmful but can occasionally be a symptom of a pituitary gland tumor. Your clinician will probably suggest laboratory tests to be sure that Pills are actually responsible for the breast milk.

Nausea was a very common problem when Pills were first introduced, because of the high estrogen content in early Pills; today's Pills contain a much smaller amount of estrogen, and nausea is quite uncommon. Nausea is not medically hazardous, but it can be very unpleasant. If you have nausea, try taking your Pill in the evening with dinner. You may find that nausea subsides after the first cycle or two, or that it occurs only on the first few days of a new cycle. Changing your Pill brand sometimes eliminates this problem.

Pills can influence weight in two ways. First, you may notice a gain each month while you take hormone Pills, followed by a loss during the seven no-hormone days. This weight gain is caused by fluid retention and rarely amounts to more than 5 pounds. Second, you may find that taking Pills influences your appetite. Some women have a decreased appetite on Pills and lose weight, but some have an increased appetite and gain weight. Pill progestin probably causes this change, because of its influence on the brain center that controls appetite. Weight gain was a fairly common problem with the early Pills that contained high levels of progestin but is not common today.

Most women who have acne notice significant improvement when they take Pills. Less frequently, Pills may make acne worse. It is often helpful to change to a different type of Pill.

Pills may cause chloasma, darkening of skin pigment on the upper lip, under the eyes, and on the forehead (see Illustration 3). Chloasma is fairly common (perhaps 5%) among Pill users. It is not hazardous and will usually fade after you stop Pills. It can be permanent in some cases. Loss of scalp hair (alopecia) can occur as a result of Pill use. It can begin while you are taking Pills or after you stop them. Do not despair if regrowth seems slow; hair grows slowly.

Women occasionally notice increased hair growth or the appearance of darker hair on the body and face. This can be a result of male

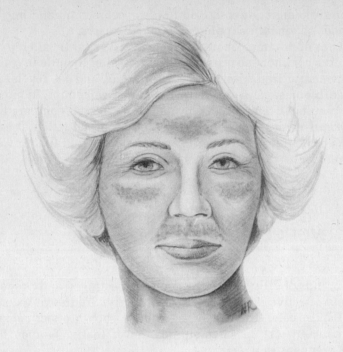

Illustration 3   Chloasma usually fades away once you stop Pills.

hormone (androgen) effects that some progestins cause, and may improve if you change to a Pill with a different progestin.

SILENT CHEMICAL CHANGES CAUSED BY PILLS

Pills cause many changes in body chemistry that you will probably not detect and that have only recently become a subject of research interest. Levels of vitamins B_2 (riboflavin), B_6 (pyridoxine), B_{12} (cyanocobalamine), vitamin C (ascorbic acid), and folic acid are lower in Pill users than in women who do not take Pills; vitamin A (retinol) levels are elevated, as are iron and copper levels (3). Folic acid deficiency and resulting anemia have been reported among women who have low folic acid intake and use Pills. Vitamin B_6 (pyridoxine) deficiency may lead to depression (2). It is not known whether the other vitamin and mineral alterations can lead to medical problems, and most family planning experts do not, as yet, recommend any routine nutritional or vitamin supplements for Pill users.

Dozens of different laboratory tests may be slightly altered by Pills. Some of the common lab tests that Pills may alter include thyroid level, liver chemistry, iron level, blood cholesterol and fat levels, glucose tolerance, blood sugar level, and white blood cell count. In most cases, the test results—even though elevated or depressed compared to your own *normal* values—do remain within the normal range. It is important for your clinician to know that you are taking Pills, however, so that your results can be interpreted correctly.

Effectiveness

All the brands of Pills containing combined estrogen and progestin are extremely effective if you take them properly. Studies of women who take Pills consistently and correctly have shown effectiveness rates better than 99% (1); in some studies, fewer than 2 women in 1,000 became pregnant in a year.

When less careful, less consistent Pill users are studied, rates of about 98% are more typical (4), and rates as low as 89% have been reported for very young women (5).

No matter which 50-mcg Pill brand is prescribed, you can expect effectiveness of 99% or better *if you take them correctly.* "Low-dose" Pills containing less than 35 mcg of estrogen may be slightly less effective, about 98 to 99% (6). Pills containing more than 50 mcg, which are no longer commonly used for routine contraception, are no more effective than the 50-mcg brands.

Consistent use is important because Pills have their contraceptive effect, not day by day, but cycle by cycle. Ovulation is suppressed because of the prolonged, steady level of synthetic hormone you have when you take Pills. When you miss a Pill or two, the level drops, and if you miss Pills, *especially* in the first two weeks of a cycle, you may ovulate. Clearly, taking Pills for a few days, or once in a while, or even several Pills a day once in a while does not provide reliable contraception.

Some studies have found that as many as 25 to 60% of women who choose Pills do not continue using them even for one year (7,8). Therefore, *it is essential to have a backup method on hand.* Turning immediately to foam, condoms, or a diaphragm any time your Pill schedule is interrupted is the best way to protect yourself from unwanted pregnancy.

> Occasionally we see a woman who is *sure* she has not missed any Pills—and I believe her.
>
> One of the most common situations, though, is a woman who stopped taking Pills—maybe because her doctor told her to—and didn't get started right away with something else.

> —*Abortion clinic counselor*

Pill Risks and Complications

Dozens of clinical studies on Pill risks and complications have been published in the last 20 years. Many different groups of women have been studied, and no two studies find exactly the same rate for Pill complications. This discussion relies on rates that seem to be representative, or are from the best, most careful studies.

A very large number of women must be studied for a long period of time in order to determine whether rare health risks are truly increased by Pills or whether the same number of problems would have occurred among Pill users anyway because of random chance. For example, researchers estimate that they would have to study 125,000 women for a full year in order to document a 100% increase in the risk of lung blood clots. Rare problems can only be evaluated accurately in very large studies.

Not many larger, long-term Pill studies have been undertaken. Studies still being conducted in Great Britain are the source for many of the complication rates cited in this chapter. Preliminary data from a large study of Walnut Creek, California, Pill users confirm the links involving smoking, Pill use, hemorrhagic stroke, and certain blood-clotting disorders also found in Britain (9). This is the first long-term United States Pill study. Just as in the British studies, very few women in the California study died (0.7% over the first 7 years) for any reason.

Most of the statistics used in this chapter are taken directly from the

FDA-approved Pill leaflet, which includes complete reference citations, and these statistics appear without any reference citation here. In some cases, when we felt that additional information would be helpful, statistics from other sources are cited.

BLOOD-CLOTTING DISORDERS

Blood-clotting disorders are the most important cause of serious and fatal Pill complications.

The hormones in Pills increase your risk of blood-clotting disorders. Hormones can alter the normal body chemicals that are responsible for blood clotting, and in some women, these alterations may increase abnormal, inappropriate clotting, and clots occur more readily than is normal. Abnormal blood clot formation can occur in any blood vessel in the body. A clot is especially serious if a vital organ such as the brain, heart, or lungs is involved, or if a large clot forms in the veins of the leg or abdomen and then travels to the lung where it can block blood circulation through the lung. Table 1 shows the most common blood-clotting disorders.

Table 1 BLOOD-CLOTTING DISORDERS

Medical Name	Location of Clot	Symptoms
Thrombophlebitis	Lower leg	Calf pain, swelling, heat, or "knot"
Thrombophlebitis	Thigh	Pain, heat, or redness
Pulmonary embolism	Lung	Chest pain, cough, shortness of breath
Myocardial infarction (heart attack)	Heart	Chest pain, left arm and shoulder pain, difficulty breathing, weakness
Cerebral infarction (stroke)	Brain	Headache, weakness, or numbness, visual problems, sudden intellect impairment
Retinal vein thrombosis	Eye	Loss of vision, headache
Mesenteric vein thrombosis	Intestine	Abdominal pain, vomiting, weakness
Pelvic vein thrombosis	Pelvis	Lower abdominal pain, cramps

Table 2 RISK OF DEATH FROM PILL-RELATED BLOOD-CLOTTING DISORDER

Age	Pill Users Who Smoke	Pill Users Who Don't Smoke
	Deaths per 100,000 Users	
15–19	1.5	1.3
20–24	1.6	1.4
25–29	1.6	1.4
30–34	10.8	2.2
35–39	13.4	4.5
40–44	58.9	7.1

SOURCE: C Tietze: Induced abortion: 1977 supplement, *Reports on Population-Family Planning*, No 14 (ed 2), suppl, December 1977. New York, The Population Council.

All these disorders can occur in women who do not use Pills, and in men, and they are strongly associated with smoking, high blood pressure, diabetes, and obesity. These disorders are very rare in young people, but many careful research studies clearly show that Pills increase your risk of blood-clotting disorders. The increased risk is higher if your Pill contains more than 50 mcg of estrogen, if you use Pills for longer than five years (10), if you smoke, and if you are over 35 years old. Table 2 indicates your risk of death from a blood-clotting disorder.

By about age 40, the death risk of Pills is higher than the death risk of full-term pregnancy, and ***Pills are not a good birth control method for women over 40.*** Many clinicians discourage Pill use even for 35-year-old women. Blood-clotting disorders account for most Pill-related deaths. The risk continues as long as you use Pills and may extend even after you stop Pills (11). Pill death rates for smokers and nonsmokers are shown in Illustration 1 of Chapter 5, along with death risks for other birth control methods.

A woman who has had a stroke, thrombophlebitis, a heart attack, or clots in her legs, lungs, or any part of her body should never take Pills or any other form of estrogen hormone. Her risk of a clotting disorder with Pills is high.

LIVER PROBLEMS

Researchers have recently confirmed that Pill users have an increased risk of developing a liver tumor. These tumors are extremely rare but can be serious. Most of the Pill-associated tumors occurred among women who had used Pills for several years. The tumors were benign (not cancer), but some nevertheless caused serious or even fatal problems because of internal bleeding. The risk of liver tumors among long-term Pill users is about 3.4 per 100,000 per year (12). In addition, a small number of cancerous liver tumors among Pill users have been reported (6). Symptoms of liver tumor might include severe abdominal pain, swelling in the upper right abdomen, and dizziness and weakness from internal bleeding.

Pills can also cause jaundice, a liver problem that leads to the accumulation of yellow pigments so that the skin and eyes take on a yellow tinge. Jaundice is probably related to the progestin in Pills and is quite rare: about 1 Pill user in 10,000 (13). Jaundice is serious enough that you should stop Pills. Women who have had jaundice during pregnancy should not take Pills, because the problem is likely to recur.

Other liver problems such as hepatitis and mononucleosis can also cause jaundice. Don't use Pills if you have evidence of liver damage, because your liver's ability to deactivate and break down estrogen may be impaired and high levels of estrogen could accumulate in your body.

SKIN CANCER

A recent study in California found that women who had used Pills were almost twice as likely to develop malignant melanoma—a very serious cancer involving skin pigment cells—than were women who never used Pills (14). It is possible that the statistical relationship reported in this study is merely coincidental, but Pills are known to stimulate skin pigment cells in at least some women. Chloasma, increased pigmentation on the facial skin, is a fairly common Pill side effect. The reported link between Pills and skin cancer is therefore worrisome. Another worrisome finding is an overall increase in the rate of malignant melanoma among women in general. Between 1970 and 1975, the San Francisco Bay Area reports an increase in the incidence of malignant melanoma from 6.4 to 10.7 per 100,000 females per year (15). Environmental factors such as exposure to sunlight are known to be linked to skin cancer, but an increase in the use of Pills may also be a factor.

Malignant melanoma usually occurs as an enlarging mole—a dark (black or brown), flat spot or raised lump on the skin. In some cases, however, the tumor is not dark and does not show noticeable growth.

The tumor may be surrounded by a slightly red skin area, and may develop ulceration or nearby small satellite tumors. Behavior of malignant melanoma varies greatly. In some cases it is a very malignant tumor with rapid spread to vital, internal organs. In other cases it is slow growing and is cured by surgery to remove the tumor, adjacent skin and nearby lymph nodes. Be sure to see your clinician about any suspicious-looking growth or moles.

GALLBLADDER DISEASE

A woman who uses Pills for two years or more has twice the risk of gallbladder disease as a woman who doesn't use Pills. Gallbladder disease is fairly common among Pill users (2 in 1,000 users per year) and among other women (1 in 1,000) and usually is not life-threatening, although surgery may be required to remove the gallbladder. The risk of gallbladder disease is increased by obesity, previous pregnancies, and age for Pill users and other women alike. Don't use Pills if you have had gallbladder attacks or previous gallbladder surgery, because you may develop similar problems such as gallstones in your liver ducts even if your gallbladder has been removed.

HIGH BLOOD PRESSURE (HYPERTENSION)

About 1% of Pill users develop elevated blood pressure. Hypertension is three times as likely after five years on Pills as it is after one year, and your risk increases with age. Pill-related hypertension usually is not severe and is unlikely to be life-threatening. High blood pressure is a contributing cause in heart disease and stroke; so you should stop Pills in any event, even if your blood pressure isn't seriously elevated. Pill-related high blood pressure usually subsides within a few weeks after you stop Pills, but there is some evidence that potentially harmful cardiovascular changes may persist, at least in some women (11).

Pills may or may not influence your blood pressure if it is already high. Your risks for extreme blood pressure elevation are higher, however, and most clinicians would advise you not to try Pills. Women who have previously experienced hormone-related blood pressure elevation, during pregnancy, for example, are more likely to develop hypertension with Pills. *All women who use Pills should have a blood pressure check at least once every 6 to 12 months, as long as they use Pills.*

PROLONGED HORMONE SUPPRESSION AND FUTURE FERTILITY

For about 1 to 2% of Pill users, there is a significant delay in the return of normal periods and normal cyclic hormone patterns after they stop Pills. Your clinician may call this "post-Pill amenorrhea." A delay is more likely if you had irregular periods or long intervals between periods before you took Pills than if your periods were fairly regular. Prolonged hormone suppression may be more likely to occur among very young Pill users who began Pills before their natural cyclic patterns were well established. (Incidentally, there is no evidence that Pills will stunt the growth of a young teenager, provided she has already begun having normal periods.) When a woman has "post-Pill amenorrhea," her pituitary hormones remain suppressed, as they were on Pills: ovary follicles fail to mature, ovulation does not occur, and menstrual periods may be light, infrequent, or entirely absent. As long as your natural hormone cycle is suppressed, it is extremely unlikely that you would be able to conceive. Hormone suppression can continue for months or even years, but *in most cases menstrual periods return spontaneously within three months.* Be sure to report this problem to your clinician; if your periods have not resumed within 6 months, evaluation of the problem probably will be recommended (see Chapter 26 for discussion of Amenorrhea).

One recent study has suggested that Pill users who have had no previous pregnancies may have impaired fertility—with 5% fewer full-term pregnancies at the end of 30 months off Pills than women who had recently used other methods of birth control (11). After 40 months, however, there was no difference in fertility rates between former Pill users and women who had used other methods.

PILLS AND CANCER

It is not yet possible to be certain what all the long-term effects of Pill use will be, for there can be a delay of years between exposure to a cancer-causing agent and the actual appearance of a tumor. Except for the very rare liver tumors and the statistical findings on skin cancers just described, there is no evidence to date that Pill users have an increased risk of cancer. There is even some evidence that Pill use may protect against cancer of the ovary and uterus. (16) There are, however, disquieting facts that link other reproductive hormones with increased cancer risk:

- A link between estrogen and increased rates of breast, cervix, vagina, and liver cancer in animals is well documented.

- A possible link between synthetic progestin and cancer has been suggested by the occurrence of breast cancer in beagle dogs treated with high doses of two similar synthetic progestins, medroxy-progesterone acetate and chlormadinone acetate. Beagle dogs are especially susceptible to breast tumors.

- An association between sequential birth control Pills and increased rates of uterine cancer in women has been found. This finding led the manufacturers to remove sequential Pills from the market in 1975. Sequentials contained an 80- to 100-mcg estrogen dose for the first part of each cycle, followed by estrogen-progestin combination Pills for the last part of each cycle (see Chapter 17).

- An association between estrogen used for menopause symptoms and an increased risk of uterine cancer has been reported (see Chapter 36).

- One study cited in the Pill leaflet has suggested an increased risk of breast cancer in women who already had noncancerous breast disease and then took Pills.

- Several studies have documented an increased rate of cervical dysplasia, abnormal growth of cells on the surface of the cervix, among Pill users when compared to diaphragm users. Another large study showed that a Pill user's risk for developing cervical dysplasia increases the longer she uses Pills and appears to be three to five times higher after four years or more than for a woman who has never used Pills (17). Dysplasia is known to precede the development of cervical cancer in some women (see Chapter 27), but so far research has not shown an increased rate of cervical cancer among women who have used Pills.

- One study of women who took diethylstilbestrol (DES, a synthetic estrogen) during pregnancy to prevent miscarriage suggests that these women (DES mothers) have a three times higher rate of breast cancer than a group of women who didn't use DES. The study also suggested that DES mothers may have an increase in cervical and ovarian cancer rates as well, but further study will be required to document this for certain (18) (see Chapter 37).

The FDA-approved patient leaflet for Pills includes a discussion of the cancer issue and stresses the importance of careful routine exams, including breast examination, liver examination, and Pap tests for all Pill users. *It is clearly essential that an abnormal Pap smear, a breast lump, abnormal vaginal bleeding, or other cancer danger signs be thoroughly investigated.* The FDA-approved leaflet further recommends that a woman with a strong family history of breast cancer or who herself has had previous lumps, fibrocystic disease, abnormal mammograms, or diethylstilbestrol (DES) exposure be followed with special care if she chooses to use Pills. Many investigators are suspicious enough about the possible Pills-cancer link that it is under intensive scrutiny in a number of studies.

EYE PROBLEMS

On rare occasions, Pills may cause inflammation of the optic nerve, with loss of vision, double vision, swelling, or pain in one or both eyes.

Women who wear contact lenses may find that lenses don't fit well when they take Pills. Pill-related fluid retention can alter cornea contour, and you may need a new lens fitting. Some Pill users find that they can't wear contact lenses at all.

HEADACHE

Some women develop severe, recurrent, or persistent headaches on Pills, and others notice an increase in the frequency or severity of migraine headaches. Headaches could be a direct Pill effect, or they may be caused by Pill-related fluid retention. Severe headaches may be a danger sign of stroke or other serious blood-clotting disorders. Stop Pills if you develop severe headaches, and discuss the problem with your clinician.

BLADDER, KIDNEY, AND OTHER INFECTIONS

Women who use Pills have a slightly higher incidence of bladder and kidney infections (5.6% per year versus 4.5%), bronchitis, viral illness (9), cervical erosion, and vaginal discharges. The cause of these increased rates is not known. Progestin causes mild relaxation of bladder muscles and the tubes (ureters) that carry urine from the kidney to the bladder, and this might delay urine transport and allow more time for bacteria to multiply. Pills also decrease the level of infection-fighting gamma globulin protein in the blood, so susceptibility to infection could be generally increased. Women who use Pills tend to have intercourse more frequently than do women who use other methods, and this increased intimate contact may be the reason urinary tract infection, upper respiratory illness, flu, and other viral illness rates are high. Pill users may simply be exposed to more germs more often than other women.

ECTOPIC PREGNANCY

The likelihood of tubal (ectopic) pregnancy is higher if you become pregnant while you are using Pills. Ectopic pregnancy can be a life-threatening problem; arrange for an examination and pregnancy test as soon as possible if you suspect pregnancy. It is essential that ectopic pregnancy be detected and treated early. A routine pregnancy test alone may not reveal ectopic pregnancy. Since urine pregnancy tests may be negative when you have an ectopic pregnancy, a pelvic exam is crucial. Blood pregnancy tests are more likely to detect the low levels of pregnancy hormone produced by ectopic pregnancy than are urine slide tests (see Chapter 4).

FETAL DEVELOPMENT

Never use Pills during pregnancy or when you think you might be pregnant.

Pills may have harmful effects on a developing fetus, especially during the first few weeks of pregnancy. Researchers suspect that Pills increase the risk of congenital heart defects, arm and leg defects, and abnormal female reproductive tract development. About 1 to 4 out of every 1,000 fetuses exposed to Pills shows evidence of such defects. The defects appear to be related to the Pill's progestin, for the same problems occur when women take progestin alone during pregnancy.

Estrogen, too, may have harmful effects that have been well documented for both women and men exposed to diethylstilbestrol during fetal life (see Chapter 37). Whether similar problems will occur after exposure to Pills during fetal life is not yet known.

There is some evidence that severe fetal genetic (chromosome) abnormalities occur more frequently when pregnancy begins during or immediately after Pill use. These pregnancies are almost sure to end in miscarriage (spontaneous abortion).

BREAST FEEDING

Pills may cause a significant decrease in the amount and quality of milk you produce while you are breast feeding. Pill hormones do appear in breast milk in minute quantities. It is not known whether or how exposure to Pill hormones might affect a breast-fed infant. The FDA-approved Pill information recommends that Pill use begin only after your infant has been weaned if at all possible.

MEDICAL PROBLEMS THAT MAY BE AGGRAVATED BY PILLS

Pills alter insulin and blood sugar balance. Women with diabetes may find that they must adjust their medication and diet if they use Pills.

Pills can cause an elevation in cholesterol and triglyceride levels that would be especially significant for a woman with hereditary lipid elevation.

Pills can stimulate growth of uterine fibroid tumors. If you have fibroids and choose Pills, be sure to have frequent pelvic examinations so that your clinician can determine if your fibroids are increasing in size. (Read more about managing fibroids in Chapter 30.)

Pills can cause depression or aggravate preexisting depression. (Some women find that Pills actually improve depression.) If you have been seriously depressed or have attempted suicide in the past, your clinician will want to follow you carefully if you choose to use Pills. One British study has suggested that suicide rates may be higher than average among Pill users (9). Stop your Pills if depression recurs.

Epilepsy, seizure disorders, migraine headaches, asthma, heart disease, and kidney disease can all worsen under the influence of Pill-related fluid retention. You must be careful to see your clinician regularly if you choose Pills.

RARE PROBLEMS

True allergy to Pills is very rare but could cause skin rash or bleeding sores. Painful red bumps or blotches (erythema nodosum) have occasionally been reported. Several rare problems that have been reported among Pill users but that have not yet been definitely linked to Pills include chorea (abnormal movements of the trunk and limbs), dizziness, and porphyria (abnormal pigments in the urine).

PILL INTERACTION WITH OTHER DRUGS

Two drugs can interact with each other if you take them at the same time, and some interactions can be harmful. Pills are known to interact with insulin, anticoagulants (blood-thinning medications), certain tranquilizers (promazine), Demerol pain medication (meperidine), and tuberculin skin tests (19). *Tell every clinician who cares for you that you are taking Pills even if your medical problem has no apparent relationship to birth control.*

The effectiveness of birth control Pills may be decreased by drugs that alter liver function such as ampicillin, sulfa drugs, antihistamines (including over-the-counter brands), tranquilizers such as Librium (chlordiazepoxide) and meprobamate, some antidepressants, blood pressure medications, sedatives (including phenobarbital), diphenylhydantoin (Dilantin) (for epilepsy), rifampin (for tuberculosis), and phenylbutazone (for arthritis) (19). *Use a backup method of birth control in addition to Pills if you use any of these drugs.*

MAJOR PILL RISKS IN PERSPECTIVE

The list of possible Pill complications and risks is long and overwhelming. The reason that so many well-informed women do choose Pills and that responsible and knowledgeable clinicians continue to prescribe Pills for patients who want them is that Pill risks are acceptable to many women, especially when they compare Pill risks with the risks of pregnancy and many other common, accepted activities of daily living. See Illustration 1 and Table 2 of Chapter 5 for a comparison of death risks of various birth control methods and death rates for common accidents and illnesses and other causes of death in the childbearing years.

There are many different kinds of Pill complications, but in total the serious complications are *rare.* Blood-clotting disorders account for nearly all the deaths and serious complications. Table 3 lists all deaths that occurred among 46,000 British women who took part in a long-term study of contraceptive risks.

Very few of the women died for any reason during the study period (a total of 99 deaths occurred among the 46,000 participants). This table shows, however, that Pill users had 20 more circulatory problem deaths per 100,000 than users of other birth control methods, and that Pill-related circulatory problems were the leading cause of death for all the women, that is, were responsible for about one-third of all the deaths. Most of the circulatory disease deaths occurred in older Pill users, and in Pill users who smoked.

Another way of looking at Pill risks is to calculate your risk as one individual for developing a specific complication. Table 4, for example, shows the Pill user's average risk of developing a circulatory disease.

If you take into consideration only the known Pill risks, statistics in the FDA-approved pill leaflet show that Pills are not as safe as a diaphragm, foam, or condoms backed up by abortion in the event of pregnancy. Safety, however, is not the only valid factor to consider as you choose a birth control method. Effectiveness is uppermost for many

Table 3   ALL CAUSES OF 'DEATH AMONG 23,000 WOMEN USING PILLS AND 23,000 USING OTHER METHODS OF BIRTH CONTROL (1968–1974, GREAT BRITAIN)

Cause of Death	Pill Users	Other Method Users	True Increased Risk?
	Deaths per 100,000 Women per Year		
Circulatory problems, including blood-clotting disorders	25.8	5.5	YES: Pill user risk is 4.7 times higher
All cancers	15.8	21.1	Not known
Accidents	9.5	7.6	Not known
Suicide	5.3	2.2	Not known
All other causes	7.2	9.6	Not known
TOTAL DEATH RATE[a]	63.6	46.0	

SOURCE: V Beral: Mortality among oral contraceptive users, *Lancet* 2:727–731, 1977.
[a]There were 99 deaths among 46,000 women studied.

women, especially those for whom abortion is not an acceptable option. When known Pill risks are weighed against risks of (unplanned) full-term pregnancy associated with less effective methods, Pills may be safer than less effective methods. If one assumes that no additional serious health risks of Pills are documented in the future, Pills may be approximately equal in safety to, or even safer than, other methods of birth control for a woman who considers abortion unacceptable; a woman who has medical problems that would make her health risks with pregnancy higher than average and who considers abortion unacceptable; or a couple who finds other birth control methods unacceptable and also finds abortion unacceptable.

Minimizing Your Risks of Pill Complications

Serious Pill complications sometimes occur suddenly with no warning, but many times complications have danger signs—early warnings of potential trouble.

Table 4 AVERAGE RISK OF DEVELOPING PILL-RELATED CIRCULA-
TORY DISEASE

	Risk in One Year
Hospitalized for blood-clotting disorder	
Pill user aged 20–44	1 in 2,000
Other method user aged 20–44	1 in 20,000
Death from circulatory disease (including blood-clotting disorders)	
Pill user aged 15–34	1 in 12,000
Other method user aged 15–34	1 in 50,000
Pill user aged 35–44	1 in 2,500
Other method user aged 35–44	1 in 10,000
Death from heart attack	
Pill user who smokes aged 30–39	1 in 10,000
Pill user who doesn't smoke aged 30–39	1 in 50,000
Other method user who doesn't smoke aged 30–39	1 in 100,000
Pill user who smokes aged 40–44	1 in 1,700
Pill user who doesn't smoke aged 40–44	1 in 10,000
Other method user who doesn't smoke aged 40–44	1 in 14,000

SOURCE: FDA-approved product labeling for oral contraceptives, May 1980.
Manufacturers of oral contraceptives are required to provide a leaflet explaining the benefits, risks and possible complications of Pills for each patient who fills a Pill prescription.
You should be able to obtain a copy of the leaflet, entitled "What You Should Know About
Oral Contraceptives," from your physician or pharmacist. Manufacturer's information for
physicians as well as the text of the patient leaflet appear in *Physician's Desk Reference*
(ed. 34) Medical Economics Co., Oradell, NJ, 1980.

Always pay attention to Pill danger signs. Remember this list:

- Chest pain
- Pain in calf (leg)
- Severe headache
- Vision changes
- Breast lump
- Severe depression

- Yellowing of the skin (jaundice)
- Abdominal pain

Don't ignore these symptoms or wait to see if they go away. Stop taking Pills and see your clinician immediately.

Early symptoms of blood-clotting disorders are not necessarily severe. If you have mild chest pain, your clinician will ask about coughing and breathing difficulty. Even an examination and a chest x-ray may not reveal a lung clot. Your clinician may have to arrange for a heart tracing (electrocardiogram) and a lung scan to be certain. Be sure you have a thorough evaluation, and don't be content with superficial reassurance.

> About three weeks after I started taking Pills I noticed a little dull ache in my chest. It didn't hurt much, and stayed in one spot. It kept on for a couple of days; so I called my doctor, because she told me to if I had chest pain.
>
> She examined me that same afternoon but couldn't tell whether anything was the matter. When she asked me about it, I remembered I had been coughing more than usual. She had my chest x-rayed, and the x-ray doctor thought I had a little pneumonia.
>
> My doctor was surprised; she said I should have a fever and *feel* sick if I had pneumonia; so she sent me to the hospital for more tests. When they did the lung scan and electrocardiogram, they found out I had *blood clots* in my lung. I had to stay in the hospital for about a week for blood-thinning medicine, and I took medicine for another month after I went home. I didn't have any more trouble after that. They never did find out where the blood clots started.
>
> *—Former Pill user, age 15*

The following paragraphs summarize the authors' suggestions for using Pills as safely as possible, based on what is known so far. Don't be surprised if your clinician doesn't mention these suggestions to you: *these are not routine instructions.* You may or may not decide to pay attention to all these recommendations; but you can use them to help keep your Pill risks at a minimum.

Stop your Pills if you develop a contraindication. Read the FDA-required Pill pamphlet or leaflet each time you receive your Pill refill to double-check the list of contraindications. Ask your clinician if you are not certain about any illnesses or problems you have had. (Read more about Pill contraindications in the following section.)

Be faithful about routine checkups as long as you take Pills. Have your blood pressure checked every 6 to 12 months, and make sure your exam includes your breasts, abdomen (for enlarged liver), and a pelvic exam. Be sure to examine your breasts yourself once a month and to watch for new or suspicious moles. See your clinician promptly if you have any question about your own exams.

Avoid using Pills that contain more than 50 mcg of estrogen if possible. Look up your Pill in Table 5 later in this chapter, or look on your package insert. The estrogen will be either mestranol or ethinyl estradiol. The amount should be 50 micrograms or less, which can be written 50 μg, 0.05 mg, or 50 mcg.

Don't think of Pills as your permanent answer to birth control. Some Pill complications, including circulatory disease, liver tumors, and gallbladder disease, are more likely after several years on Pills.

Be sure that any clinician who takes care of you for any problem is aware that you are taking Pills. If your clinician prescribes other drugs, ask if the other drugs will interact with Pills.

Stop Pills if you have a serious injury, such as a broken leg, or if you stay in bed longer than a day or two at home or in a hospital. *Stop Pills one month before any major elective surgery.*

If you are over 30, begin to think about changing to another birth control method, and plan to make the change before you are 35.

Remember that smoking increases pill risks: one more good reason to stop smoking.

Assess your own risks by comparing yourself with this hypothetical woman who has the lowest possible risk for Pill complications:

Age: 15 to 30
Weight: Normal
Smoking: None
Blood Pressure: Normal or low, and remained normal during pregnancy
Varicose Veins: None
Contraindications: None

Contraindications

A contraindication is a medical condition that renders a treatment or procedure inadvisable or unsafe that might otherwise be recommended. *Contraindications are extremely important for safe Pill use.* The list of contraindications for Pills is long, but most of the medical conditions on the list are rare, especially among young women. Nevertheless, this list means that there are many women who should never use Pills, even if they would very much like to.

ABSOLUTE CONTRAINDICATIONS

A woman with any of the following conditions *must not take Pills under any circumstances, with no exception.* If you develop any of these conditions while taking Pills, you must stop your Pills at once.

1. Blood-clotting disorder now or in the past, such as thrombophlebitis, pulmonary embolism (clots in the lung), heart attack or stroke, or angina (heart pain)
2. Impaired liver function, including active or recent hepatitis, alcohol liver damage, severe mononucleosis, or liver tumor in the past
3. Known or suspected cancer of the breast, cervix, uterus, ovaries, or vagina, or malignant melanoma, now or in the past, or abnormal vaginal bleeding whose cause has not yet been determined
4. Current pregnancy or current suspected pregnancy

STRONG RELATIVE CONTRAINDICATIONS

The following conditions mean that your clinician will strongly advise you not to use Pills. You may be vulnerable to serious health risks.

1. High blood pressure now, or elevated blood pressure during pregnancy in the past*
2. Diabetes or strong family history of diabetes*
3. Gallbladder disease now or in the past, or gallbladder surgery in the past
4. Pregnancy jaundice (cholestasis) in the past
5. Mononucleosis now or in the recent past
6. Sickle cell disease*

---

*Increased risk of blood-clotting disorders and circulatory disease, including heart attack.

7. Leg cast, body cast, or serious leg injury*

8. Fibrocystic breast disease or fibrous breast lumps (fibroadenoma), abnormal breast x-rays in the past, or close family history of breast cancer

9. Precancerous Pap smear (sometimes called CIN, severe dysplasia, or Class III or IV; see Chapter 27)

10. Major surgery scheduled within the next month*

11. Recent pregnancy (delivery, abortion, or miscarriage within the last 10 to 14 days)*

12. Heavy smoking (more than 15 cigarettes a day)*

13. Severe migraine (vascular) headaches*

14. Age over 35 to 40*

RELATIVE CONTRAINDICATIONS

The following conditions mean that you may be able to use Pills if you are willing to be followed very carefully by your clinician so that she/he can watch for early signs of trouble.

1. Serious heart or kidney disease

2. Serious depression or suicidal feelings now or in the past (depression may worsen or improve on Pills)

3. Epilepsy or other seizure disorders

4. Severe asthma

5. Severe varicose veins

6. History of chloasma (darkening of facial skin) or hair loss during pregnancy or during previous Pill use

7. Uterine fibroids (may worsen or improve on Pills)

8. Acne (may worsen or improve on Pills)

9. Very irregular menstrual periods or long delays between periods

10. Menstrual periods recently begun and not yet regular (young teens)

11. Breast feeding

12. Previous Pill use for five years or more*

13. Past exposure to diethylstilbestrol during pregnancy (DES daughter or DES mother)

---

*Increased risk of blood-clotting disorders and circulatory disease, including heart attack.

14.   Compromised ability to use Pills safely (no access to emergency care for Pill problems; emotional or intellectual impairment that would make it difficult to follow Pill schedule or recognize danger signs)

Some clinicians do not agree that all these conditions should be treated as relative contraindications, and some would add factors to the list, such as high cholesterol levels, recurrent urinary tract infections, and sickle cell trait.

Advantages of Pills

Pills provide the best contraceptive protection possible with a temporary birth control method—99% or better—when you use them consistently and correctly. They do not interrupt lovemaking and require mininal paraphernalia. Pills provide continuous protection throughout the Pill cycle and during the one-week interval when you are off hormones, no matter how frequently you have intercourse.

For many women the greatest advantage of Pills is freedom from debilitating cramps and heavy bleeding.

> I never would have made it through my medical training without Pills. I couldn't have endured 48 hours on call with cramps like the ones I used to have every month! I *also* needed really good contraceptive protection, because when you're pushed to your physical and emotional limit all the time, you *don't* want pregnancy scares or the stress of an unplanned pregnancy.
>
> —*Woman physician, 29*

Your periods are almost always regular, predictable, light, and painless. You can reschedule your periods to avoid having periods during important events. Pill users are less likely to have premenstrual symptoms than are other women.

Iron deficiency anemia is less common among Pill users than among women who do not use Pills, because the amount of blood you lose during a period on Pills is about half the amount you would normally lose, so your body's iron supply is less likely to become depleted. The likelihood of developing the common types of ovarian cysts is reduced for Pill users. Some 38 out of 100,000 women are admitted to hospitals because of ovarian cysts each year, but only 3 per 100,000 Pill users are admitted for cysts (20). Ovulation pain (Mittelschmerz) is very unlikely to occur while you take Pills. Most women find that acne improves on Pills.

Other Uses of Pills

Pills have been used in the past to treat severe cramps or acne, and to regulate periods for women who have irregular menstrual cycles. Most clinicians no longer recommend Pills in such situations unless a woman also wants the birth control effect of Pills. Safer treatments are available for cramps and acne. If your natural cycle is irregular, you will almost surely have regular periods on Pills, but Pills do not correct your underlying problem. Instead you may increase your risk of developing prolonged hormone suppression after you stop Pills, and you may have difficulty becoming pregnant.

Pills are sometimes used as hormone replacement for women with premature menopause, a chromosomal sexual abnormality, or surgically removed ovaries. Milder hormone doses are usually effective and may be preferable to Pills in these instances.

Clinicians occasionally prescribe Pills for women with medical problems such as endometriosis, polycystic ovaries (Stein Leventhal syndrome), and deficient blood-clotting factors (idiopathic thrombocytopenic purpura or ITP), and to control extremely heavy menstrual bleeding.

Using Pills

Your clinician will review your medical history for any factors that might increase the risk of Pills for you and will perform a physical examination. Your exam will include blood pressure and weight, a breast exam, an abdominal exam, inspection of your cervix, a Pap test, and a bimanual exam to be sure your uterus and ovaries feel normal. Some clinicians also include a gonorrhea test, routine blood count, and urine test as part of your initial exam. (Read Chapter 21 for more details.)

CHOOSING WHICH PILL TO USE

There are about 25 different Pill brands. In some cases, different brands are identical except for packaging; in other cases, brands have different hormones in slightly differing amounts.

Each of the synthetic Pill hormones has unique properties. The two synthetic estrogens used in the United States are *mestranol* and *ethinyl estradiol.* Ethinyl estradiol is somewhat more potent than mestranol: 100 mcg of ethinyl estradiol has about the same effect as 170 to 200 mcg of mestranol (21). Progestins vary in potency and in the degree to which they cause additional estrogen-like or androgen-like effects. Table 5 lists the hormone content of all Pills available in mid-1980. Illustration 4 ranks Pills in order of potency.

Most clinicians consider estrogen dose the single most important factor in choosing a Pill. The risk of serious Pill complications is higher among women who take more than 50 mcg of estrogen. Some researchers also suspect that higher progestin potency, as well as higher estrogen potency, may increase your risk for blood clotting complications (22). It makes sense to try to choose a Pill with the lowest estrogen and progestin potency that is effective in preventing pregnancy. Pills that contain less than 50 mcg of estrogen may be slightly less effective and somewhat more likely to cause spotting between periods than are Pills that contain 50 mcg of estrogen.

Most family planning specialists rely on two or three brands as standard initial choices and then are guided by each woman's individual response. Most women do well on any of the 50-mcg Pills. The lower potency of mestranol makes either Norinyl 1/50 or Ortho-Novum 1/50 (the two are chemically identical) a logical choice. Pills with 30 to 35 mcg of ethinyl estradiol (Brevicon, Norinyl 1/35, Lo-Estrin 1.5/30, Lo-Ovral, Ortho Novum 1/35), would provide a similar estrogen effect.

Chances are good that you will be able to use any of these brands with no difficulty. If side effects do occur, your clinician may recommend another brand. Some common Pill side effects and possible solutions are listed in Table 6. Remember that your estrogen dose ideally should not be increased above 50 micrograms without discussion and a good reason.

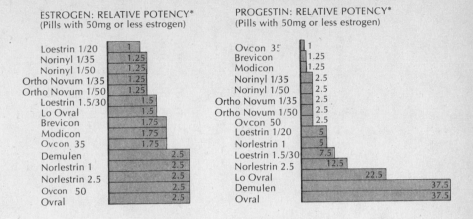

ESTROGEN: RELATIVE POTENCY*
(Pills with 50mg or less estrogen)

PROGESTIN: RELATIVE POTENCY*
(Pills with 50mg or less estrogen)

*Pills with the *lowest* potency are given the number 1.   Numbers for other pills
show *how many times more potent* they are than the first pill on each list.
For example, the progestin in Lo Ovral is 22.5 times *more* potent (stronger)
than the progestin in Ovcon.

Illustration 4   Hormone potency of the various Pill brands. (Reproductive Health Resources, Inc. Used with permission.)

GETTING STARTED ON PILLS

You can take the first Pill in your first Pill pack any time during the first seven days of a natural cycle. Counting the first day of a normal menstrual period as day 1, you can take your first Pill any day from day 2 through day 7. If you start Pills before day 8, chances are good that you will not ovulate during your very first Pill cycle; most clinicians recommend, however, that you rely on another method of birth control, such as foam, condoms, or a diaphragm, for the first 10 to 14 days you use Pills. You will also need to use another birth control method while you are waiting to start your first pack.

Do not start Pills if you think there is any chance you might be pregnant. For example, if your last menstrual period did not seem entirely normal (too light, early, or late), then consult your clinician to decide whether it would be safe for you to begin Pills.

One easy Pill-taking scheme is the *Start-on-Sunday* method. Begin your first pack of Pills on the first Sunday after a normal menstrual period begins. You will begin a new pack of Pills every fourth Sunday, and you can avoid having menstrual periods on weekends.

Once you have started your first Pill pack, your Pill cycle is set and you will always follow the same Pill schedule.

Table 5 PILL HORMONE CONTENT

Brand	Estrogen Dose (micrograms)	Type of Estrogen	Progestin Dose (milligrams)	Type of Progestin
50 micrograms of estrogen or less				
Brevicon	35	Ethinyl estradiol	0.5	Norethindrone
Demulen	50	Ethinyl estradiol	1.0	Ethnodiol diacetate
Lo Estrin 1/20	20	Ethinyl estradiol	1.0	Norethindrone acetate
Lo Estrin 1.5/30	30	Ethinyl estradiol	1.5	Norethindrone acetate
Lo-Ovral	30	Ethinyl estradiol	0.3	Norgestrel
Modicon	35	Ethinyl estradiol	0.5	Norethindrone
Norinyl 1/35	35	Ethinyl estradiol	1.0	Norethindrone
Norinyl 1/50	50	Mestranol	1.0	Norethindrone
Norlestrin 1	50	Ethinyl estradiol	1.0	Norethindrone acetate
Norlestrin 2.5	50	Ethinyl estradiol	2.5	Norethindrone acetate
Ortho-Novum 1/35	35	Ethinyl estradiol	1.0	Norethindrone
Ortho-Novum 1/50	50	Mestranol	1.0	Norethindrone

Ovcon 35	35	Ethinyl estradiol	0.4	Norethindrone
Ovcon 50	50	Ethinyl estradiol	1.0	Norethindrone
Ovral	50	Ethinyl estradiol	0.5	Norgestrel

More than 50 micrograms of estrogen

Enovid-5	75	Mestranol	5.0	Norethynodrel
Enovid-E	100	Mestranol	2.5	Norethynodrel
Norinyl 1/80	80	Mestranol	1.0	Norethindrone
Norinyl 2	100	Mestranol	2.0	Norethindrone
Ortho-Novum 1/80	80	Mestranol	1.0	Norethindrone
Ortho-Novum 2	100	Mestranol	2.0	Norethindrone
Ortho-Novum 10	60	Mestranol	10.0	Norethindrone
Ovulen	100	Mestranol	1.0	Ethnodiol diacetate

Table 6 COMMON PILL SIDE EFFECTS AND POSSIBLE SOLUTIONS

Side Effect	Possible Solution
Nausea	Reduce estrogen
Spotting	Increase estrogen and/or increase progestin
Missed menstrual periods	Increase estrogen and/or use progestin with estrogenic effect and/or reduce or increase progestin
Fluid retention, breast tenderness	Reduce estrogen and/or reduce progestin
Contact lenses don't fit	Reduce estrogen
Breast enlargement	Reduce progestin and/or reduce estrogen
Vaginal yeast infections	Reduce progestin
Weight gain	Reduce estrogen and/or reduce progestin
Irritability, depression	Reduce or increase estrogen and/or reduce progestin
Decreased sex drive	Reduce progestin and/or increase estrogen
Heavy menstrual periods	Increase progestin
Excessive vaginal discharge	Reduce estrogen and/or reduce progestin

Pill packs are available for three different Pill schedules; so check your pack to determine whether you have a 21-day pack, a 20-day pack, or a 28-day pack.

The most common is the 21-day pack that contains 21 hormone Pills. On 21-day Pills, your schedule will be 21 days of Pills, seven days off, 21 days of Pills, seven days off, and so on. Swallow one Pill a day for three weeks until the pack is empty. Wait one full week; then begin your second pack. If you are using the Start-on-Sunday method, your calendar will look like Illustration 5.

If you have a 20-day Pill package, you begin each new pack on the fifth day after your period starts (counting the first day of bleeding as day 1) or the eighth day after you took your last Pill, whichever occurs first.

The 28-day pack contains two different kinds of tablets: 21 hor-

S	M	T	W	T	F	S
X	X	X	X	X	X	X
X	X	X	X	X	X	X
X	X	X	X	X	X	X
— week	off	—		No Pills		

X = Pill Day

Illustration 5 The 21-day Pill schedule using the Start-on-Sunday method.

mone Pills and seven tablets of a different color that contain no hormone. (The blank tablets contain sugar or sugar plus iron.) Take the 21 hormone Pills first, and then the seven blank tablets. When you have taken all the tablets in your pack, you begin your next pack immediately, with no days off, starting with the 21 hormone Pills. On the 28-day schedule the seven blank tablets *are* your seven days without hormones.

No matter which type of pack you use, you can expect your menstrual period during the seven no-hormone days; bleeding usually begins about 48 hours after your last hormone Pill.

USING PILLS CORRECTLY

Try to take your Pill at about the same time each day. You may find it helpful to keep a calendar and mark off each day as you take your Pill.

Have a backup method of birth control on hand, such as a diaphragm, foam, or condoms. You will need your backup method until you have taken the first 14 Pills in your first pack, or if you stop Pills for any reason, or if you miss more than one Pill.

If you miss one Pill, take two the next day. Take a missed Pill as soon as you remember, and take your regular Pill for that day at the regular time. You do not need to call your clinician or use backup birth control.

If you miss two Pills in a row, take two each day for two days until you catch up. Take the first missed Pill as soon as you remember and the regular Pill for that day at the regular time. Take the second missed

Pill along with your regular Pill the following day. You may have some spotting. Use your backup method until you have your next period.

If you miss three Pills or more in a row, stop your Pills and wait until you have a period. Then start a new pack of Pills as you normally would after your period starts. Begin using your backup method as soon as you realize you have missed Pills, and continue using it until you have taken 14 Pills in your new pack. Call your clinician if you do not have a menstrual period.

If you do not have a menstrual period during your seven no-hormone days and are *sure* that you have taken all your Pills on schedule, you can begin a new pack on schedule. There is only a very small chance that you could be pregnant.

If you miss a period and are not sure you have taken all your Pills correctly, do not start a new pack. Stop Pills, begin using your backup method, and arrange for a pregnancy test and exam as soon as you can.

If you miss two periods in a row, even if you are sure that you have taken all your Pills on schedule, stop Pills. Begin using your backup method, and arrange to see your clinician.

If you have spotting or bleeding while you are taking Pills, stay on your regular Pill schedule. Bleeding usually subsides after a few days and is most likely during the first month or two on Pills. If your bleeding is heavier than on the heavy days of a natural period, if you soak more than three pads in an hour, or if spotting continues through more than one cycle, call your clinician. You may need evaluation to be certain that Pills are the cause of your unusual bleeding. *If you have cramps or fever along with bleeding, you need to see your clinician at once. You may have an infection.*

If you have nausea, try taking your Pill along with dinner or in the evening. If you vomit within an hour after taking a Pill, take an extra Pill from a separate pack to replace the Pill vomited up.

If you accidentally damage or lose your Pills or run out of Pills, call your clinician. An immediate telephone refill can almost always be arranged so that you won't have to interrupt your Pill schedule. Many family planning clinics are able to provide emergency refills for their own patients or for other women in emergency situations.

If you want to alter your Pill schedule and avoid having your menstrual period during final exams or a trip, for example, you will need to do a little advance planning. You can change your cycle length by taking as many as seven additional Pills added onto your regular pack or by discarding one or two Pills at the end of a regular pack. Your menstrual bleeding will begin about 48 hours after your last Pill—

either one or two days earlier than usual or up to seven days later than usual. Allow your usual seven no-hormone days between packs, and remember to set aside the pack you used for extra Pills; you may need "extra" pills again.

PILL EMERGENCIES

It is essential that you learn how to recognize a true Pill emergency. If you develop any of the Pill danger signs (see Illustration 6), stop Pills, contact your clinician at once, and use a backup method of birth control. Do not wait to see if the symptoms go away. If you can't see your clinician or get to your clinic, go to an emergency room.

STOPPING PILLS

You can stop Pills after you finish a Pill pack or any time in the middle. Nothing bad happens when you stop Pills, but you do need to begin using another method of birth control immediately. There is no carry-over birth control protection once you stop Pills. Most Pill users ovulate within two or three weeks after their last Pill (23). Whether you stop in the middle of a pack or at the end, your body quickly begins to reestablish its own cyclic patterns. You will probably have a menstrual

PILL DANGER SIGNS

* CHEST PAIN, shortness of breath, coughing
* PAIN IN CALF (leg)
* severe HEADACHE, vomiting, dizziness, faintness, muscle weakness or numbness, or speech disturbance
* VISION CHANGES or loss
* breast lump
* severe abdominal pain
* severe depression
* yellowing of the skin

Illustration 6   See your clinician right away if you develop a danger sign. (Reproductive Health Resources, Inc. Used with permission.)

period a day or two after your last Pill. Your first natural menstrual period will usually come four, five, or six weeks after that. Then you can expect natural cycles to be as regular—or as irregular—as they were before you started Pills.

"VACATIONS" FROM PILLS

In the earliest days of Pill use in this country, the FDA-approved package leaflet for Pills recommended that Pill users go off Pills for a cycle or two every year or so. However, so many women became pregnant during their "Pill vacations" that most clinicians stopped recommending a rest from Pills. Today some clinicians have come full circle and are again recommending that women go off Pills periodically so that suppression of the *natural* hormone cycle can be detected early should it occur.

PLANNING PREGNANCY AFTER PILLS

You need to plan ahead for pregnancy if you use Pills. Stop taking Pills at least three months before you would like to conceive, and switch to another method of birth control—condoms, foam, or a diaphragm. This Pill-free interval allows your body to return to normal and gives your natural cycle a chance to reestablish itself.

If you conceive before you have your first natural period, it may be difficult for you and your clinician to determine exactly when you became pregnant. It is important to be able to estimate the beginning of your pregnancy accurately in case you should need a cesarean section delivery or should need to have labor induced. Your clinician decides when to perform these procedures on the basis of your estimated length of pregnancy. If her/his estimate is wrong because pregnancy began when you weren't having normal periods, your baby could be born prematurely.

Studies have shown an increased risk of birth defects in infants conceived *during* Pill use, and abnormalities were seen in miscarried (spontaneously aborted) pregnancies that were conceived during or immediately after Pill use. (See the previous section on risks and complications.) There is as yet no evidence of increased risk of abnormality among full-term infants conceived immediately after Pill use. In light of these studies, however, it would seem prudent to wait at least three months after you stop Pills before you try to conceive.

REFERENCES

1. Rinehart W, Ravenholt RT: U.S. morbidity and mortality trends relative to oral contraceptive use, 1955–1975, and Danish morbidity trends, 1953–1972. *Population Reports*, Ser A, No 4, May 1977. Washington, DC, The George Washington University Medical Center.
2. Adams PW, Rose DP, Folkard J, et al: Effect of pyridoxine hydrochloride (vitamin B₆) upon depression associated with oral contraception. *Lancet* 1:897–904, 1973.
3. Wynn V: Vitamins and oral contraceptive use. *Lancet* 1:561–564, 1975.
4. Vaughan B, Trussell J, Menken J, et al: Contraceptive failure among married women in the United States, 1970–1973. *Family Planning Perspectives* 9:251–258, 1977.
5. Ryder NB: Contraceptive failure in the United States. *Family Planning Perspectives* 5(3):133–142, 1973.
6. FDA-approved product labeling for oral contraceptives, May 1980. Manufacturers of oral contraceptives are required to provide a leaflet explaining the benefits, risks and possible complications of Pills for each patient who fills a Pill prescription. You should be able to obtain a copy of the leaflet, entitled "What You Should Know About Oral Contraceptives," from your physician or pharmacist. Manufacturer's information for physicians as well as the text of the patient leaflet appear in *Physician's Desk Reference* (ed. 34), Medical Economics Co., Oradell, NJ, 1980.
7. Hatcher RA: Evaluation of the Columbus, Georgia, program. *Advances in Planned Parenthood* 5:24–42, 1969.
8. Tietze C, Lewit S: Use-effectiveness of oral and intrauterine contraception. *Fertility and Sterility* 22:508–513, 1971.
9. Pettiti DB, Wingerd J, Pellegrin F, et al: Risk of vascular diseases in women smoking, oral contraceptives, noncontraceptive estrogens, and other factors. *Journal of the American Medical Association* 242:1150–1154, 1979.
10. Beral V: Mortality among oral contraceptive users. *Lancet* 2:727–731, 1977.
11. Vessey MP, McPherson K, Johnson B: Mortality among women participating in the Oxford Family Planning Association contraceptive study. *Lancet* 2:731–733, 1977.
12. Rooks JB, Ory HW, Ishak KG, et al: Epidemiology of hepatocellular adenoma: the role of oral contraceptive use. *Journal of the American Medical Association* 242:644–648, 1979.
13. Metreau JM, Dhumeaux D, Perthelot P: Oral contraceptives and the liver. *Digestion* 7:318–335, 1972.
14. Beral V. Ramcharan S, Faris R: Malignant melanoma and oral contraceptive use among women in California. *British Journal of Cancer* 36:804–809, 1977.

15.   Interview with Dr. Donald Austin, Chief, California Tumor Registry, reported in the New York Times, November 12, 1978.

16.   Wiess NS, Sayvetz TA: Incidence of endometrial cancer in relation to the use of oral contraceptives. *New England Journal of Medicine* 302:551–554, 1980; and Casagrande JT, Pike ML, Ross RK, et al: "Incessant ovulation" and ovarian cancer. *Lancet* 2:170–172, 1979.

17.   Peritz E, Ramcharan S, Fran J, et al: The incidence of cervical cancer and duration of oral contraceptive use. *American Journal of Epidemiology* 106:462–469, 1977.

18.   DES and breast cancer. *FDA Drug Bulletin* 8:10, March-April 1978.

19.   Martin EW: *Hazards of Medication.* Philadelphia, Lippincott, 1971.

20.   Ory H: Functional ovarian cysts and oral contraceptives: negative association confirmed surgically, a cooperative study. *Journal of the American Medical Association* 228:68–69, 1974.

21.   Dickey RP, Chihal HJW, Peppler RD: Estrogen potencies of three new low-dose oral contraceptives. *American Journal of Obstetrics and Gynecology* 125:976–979, 1976.

22.   Shelton JD, Petitti D: Formulation-dependent effect of oral contraceptives on H.D.L.-Cholesterol. *Lancet* 2:677, 1978.

23.   Garcia CR, Rosenfeld DL: *Human Fertility: The Regulation of Reproduction.* Philadelphia, FA Davis, 1977.

12 | Minipills

Taking Minipills* is a method of birth control that many women would seriously consider if they only knew about them. Estrogen-free Minipills offer many of the benefits of regular Pills, with fewer side effects and a lower overall dose of hormone. Although Minipills are relatively new and detailed studies of Minipill safety are not yet completed, this method seems to deserve a more prominent place among contraceptive options than it now has. If manufacturers' marketing policies were altered to give Minipills the exposure that regular Pills now receive, it is likely that many women who now choose Pills might decide to try Minipills instead.

Minipills are estrogen-free contraceptive tablets that provide a continuous, low dose of progestin. They were approved for use in the United States in 1972 and 1973, 12 years after the approval of regular combined Pills containing both estrogen and progestin. The idea behind Minipills, however, is not new. The original research on hormone contraception started with progestin as the primary ingredient. Estrogen was added later to insure a more regular pattern of bleeding.

---

*The authors use the terms "regular Pills," "combined Pills," and "Pills" consistently to refer to oral contraceptives containing both estrogen and progestin. "Minipills" contain a lower dose of progestin than combined Pills, and no estrogen.

Research attention returned to the progestin-only concept again in the 1960s when complications of regular birth control Pills became apparent. Researchers hoped to develop a different but equally effective type of oral contraceptive that contained a lower dose of hormone and eliminated estrogen risks entirely.

Surprisingly, Minipills have not been widely used. Many clinicians are unfamiliar with them, and many women have not even heard of them. Whereas about 50 million women used the regular birth control Pill worldwide in 1975, only about 300,000 used Minipills (1). It is not clear why progestin-only pills have not lived up to the expectations of early researchers who saw them as the successor to combined Pills.

Commercial marketing policies may explain the limited acceptance. The Minipill has not been advertised or promoted aggressively by its manufacturers. All three brands sold in the United States are produced by companies that also produce successful, widely advertised combined Pills.

Another explanation may be the Minipill's short-comings. Minipills are slightly less effective than regular Pills and often cause irregular menstrual patterns: these drawbacks may keep Minipills from assuming an equal popularity with other methods of birth control. Also, the long-term research that will be necessary to determine whether Minipills are safer than regular combined Pills is not yet completed.

How Minipills Work

A low dose of progestin taken by mouth every day alters several different components of fertility. Contraceptive effectiveness may result from the sum of all these effects, or it may be that one specific effect is most important. Minipills cause the following changes:

PARTIAL SUPPRESSION OF OVULATION

The steady, continuous level of progestin from Minipills in the bloodstream distorts the normal pattern of pituitary hormone production. The pituitary hormone is not fully suppressed, as is the case with combined Pills; but the LH (luteinizing hormone, see Chapter 1) trigger for ovulation is blunted or absent, so that in 15 to 40% of the Minipill user's cycles the ovaries do not release an egg (1).

"HOSTILE" CERVICAL MUCUS

Cervical mucus remains scant, thick, and sticky throughout the cycle under the influence of the progestin in Minipills. Thick mucus decreases the likelihood that sperm will be able to penetrate the cervical canal and enter the uterus and tubes. Thick mucus may also inhibit chemical changes within sperm cells that permit them to fertilize an egg. Furthermore, the "hostile" mucus decreases sperm motility (swimming capacity), and may not provide the nutrients that sperm require for optimal survival.

INADEQUATE CORPUS LUTEUM FUNCTION

Continuous progestin may interfere with normal development of the corpus luteum from an egg follicle after ovulation (see Chapter 1). The high levels of progesterone normally produced by the corpus luteum are necessary for establishing and maintaining a healthy pregnancy.

UNSUITABLE UTERINE LINING

Normal development of the uterine lining (endometrium) requires an initial estrogen phase followed by a combined estrogen and progesterone phase after ovulation (see Chapter 1). Minipills provide progestin continuously throughout the cycle and thus interfere with endometrial development, so it is less likely that a fertilized egg could implant in the uterine lining.

ALTERED TUBAL CONTRACTIONS

Safe passage of a fertilized egg through the fallopian tube down to the uterus depends in part on rhythmic contractions of the tube itself. Minipill progestin may alter fallopian tube contractions, causing the fertilized ovum to reach the uterus at the wrong time to implant properly.

Despite all these alterations in the normal fertility cycle, Minipills do not totally suppress hormone production. Your normal hormone pattern is altered, but you will nevertheless have natural estrogen and progesterone production that is usually sufficient to trigger menstrual periods. Your own internal cycle will determine when your menstrual periods will occur, not the Minipill. In this respect, Minipills are completely different from regular combined Pills. (see Chapter 11).

Common Minipill Side Effects

The Minipill progestin hormone travels in the bloodstream and can potentially affect any organ in the body. Side effects of Minipills—effects unrelated to birth control—seem to be less numerous than side effects of regular Pills. But since experience with Minipills is much less extensive than experience with regular Pills, it is entirely possible that new side effects will be discovered in the future. Common side effects that are not believed to be dangerous are discussed in this section. Potentially harmful side effects are discussed in the section on Minipill complications and risks.

CHANGES IN MENSTRUAL PATTERNS

Most women who use Minipills find that they have less premenstrual tension and fewer annoying premenstrual symptoms, such as breast tenderness, than they do during a natural cycle. Your menstrual bleeding may be lighter and shorter, and you will probably have very mild cramps, or none at all.

The interval between your periods may remain the same, but it may become longer or shorter, and it may vary from cycle to cycle. *Menstrual periods tend to be less predictable when you use Minipills.* It is also common to have episodes of spotting or light bleeding between periods.

OTHER HORMONE SIDE EFFECTS

Some of the common side effects associated with regular combined Pills may also occur with Minipills, but they are somewhat less likely. Nausea, headache, breast tenderness, vaginal discharge, and depression have been reported but seem to be less common with Minipills than during a natural hormone cycle. Acne problems, increased appetite, and weight gain also can occur but are not common with Minipills, perhaps because Minipills contain only about one third as much progestin as regular combined Pills. Other possible side effects as yet not definitely linked with Minipills include dark patches on the face (chloasma) and changes in sex drive (libido).

Minipills do not decrease the amount of breast milk produced or alter milk content the way regular Pills do. Progestin from Minipills does appear in the breast milk, however; about 0.1% of the amount in the mother's bloodstream (1). Whether or not this trace of hormone has any harmful effect on the nursing infant is not known. Minipills would probably be a better birth control choice than regular Pills if you are nursing and choose not to use an IUD, diaphragm, foam, or condoms.

Some clinicians who would not prescribe regular Pills would approve Minipills for women with fibrocystic breast disease, for progestin alone may be less likely to aggravate this condition than an estrogen-progestin combination.

Studies of Minipill effects on vitamin levels, the body's chemical processes, and lab test results so far do not show the kind of major alterations that occur with regular, combined Pills (see Chapter 11 on problems and risks).

Effectiveness

One study of women who used Minipills consistently and correctly documented an effectiveness rate higher than 99% (1). Most studies, however, have reported rates ranging from 87 to 98% (1). The FDA-approved leaflet cites an average rate of 97% (2), which puts Minipills on a par with the IUD and the diaphragm. Fewer than 3 women in 100 would become pregnant in a year.

Like regular birth control Pills, Minipills have their contraceptive effect because of a continuous, steady level of hormone intake. Obviously, they are only effective if they are taken, and taken consistently.

One major difference between progestin-only pills and regular Pills is that there is little margin for error with Minipills. The likelihood of pregnancy increases substantially if you miss only one or two tablets, and contraceptive protection is almost entirely lost if you forget more than three consecutive pills. **It is essential to take Minipills every day without fail.**

To protect yourself against pregnancy, be sure that you and your partner have a backup method on hand. Begin using foam, condoms, or a diaphragm whenever you forget to take two or more Minipills, and continue using your backup method until your next period starts. Use your backup method immediately if you stop Minipills for any reason.

Complications and Risks

Even though Minipills contain only a low dose of one of the two hormones in regular combined Pills, the official FDA-approved Minipill leaflet provides the same risk warnings for Minipills as for regular Pills. Minipills have been used only a short time and have been used by a relatively small number of women; hence, the kind of long-term research involving tens of thousands of users that would be necessary to determine whether or not Minipill risks are the same as combined Pill risks is simply not available. In the absence of good information, the FDA has decided that for now the safest course is to presume that Minipill risks and combined Pill risks are the same. Major Pill risks are listed below. All these risks and complications are described in detail in Chapter 11, in relation to regular birth control Pills.

• Blood-clotting (thromboembolic) and circulatory disorders such as heart attack, stroke, and blood clots in the lungs
• Liver tumors and liver jaundice (yellow skin)
• Cancer risks associated with hormone exposure
• Gallbladder disease
• High blood pressure
• Bladder or kidney infections
• Headache
• Eye problems
• Delayed return to normal cycles after stopping Minipills, and possible effects on future fertility
• Ectopic pregnancy
• Birth defects when a fetus is exposed to Minipills
• Effects on breast milk
• Aggravation of diabetes, fibroids, epilepsy, depression, asthma, and kidney and heart disease
• Interactions with other drugs

Although official information brochures must be identical, *most family planning experts believe that Minipills are safer than combined Pills.* Estrogen is probably responsible for the most serious Pill-related risks. Estrogen is known to cause major alterations in blood-clotting factors. The progestin in regular birth control Pills does affect blood cholesterol and fat balance. Progestin, along with estrogen, may play a role in causing blood-clotting problems, especially when Pills with a high dose of progestin are used. The total dose of progestin in Minipills, however, is much lower than the dose of progestin in regular birth control Pills and it is not known whether the lower dose in Minipills has any adverse effect on clotting. If blood-clotting alterations are responsible for the increased incidence of heart attack, stroke, thrombophlebitis, and other circulatory problems among combined Pill users, then Minipills should carry a lower risk. But to date there is no conclusive evidence to pinpoint progestin and estrogen problems separately. Just as there have been no large studies of women using progestin alone, there have been no large studies of women using estrogen alone in doses comparable to those of regular Pills.

MENSTRUAL IRREGULARITY

One significant problem associated with Minipills is menstrual irregularity. Unpredictable bleeding is the single most common reason women stop taking Minipills. Menstrual problems are not in themselves medically harmful. Irregular bleeding can be a hazard, however, if it is falsely attributed to Minipills and there is a delay in recognizing a serious medical problem such as uterine or ovarian tumors.

ECTOPIC PREGNANCY

Another important Minipill problem is tubal (ectopic) pregnancy: pregnancy that implants in one of the fallopian tubes rather than in the uterus. If a woman using Pills or Minipills becomes pregnant, her risk of ectopic pregnancy is higher than it would be if she were using no birth control, or if she used foam, condoms, or a diaphragm. This risk is more important for Minipill users than for regular Pill users, because the overall pregnancy rate is a little higher with Minipills and therefore the ectopic pregnancy risk is higher as well. See Chapter 4 for danger signs of ectopic pregnancy.

Contraindications

A contraindication is a medical condition that renders a treatment or procedure unsafe or inadvisable that might otherwise be recommended. The official FDA-approved leaflet information for Minipills lists exactly the same contraindications for Minipills as it does for regular combined Pills. There is no evidence that Minipills will aggravate all the problems on the list of contraindications, but neither is there evidence that Minipills would be safe. Because these problems are so serious, even potentially fatal, it seems prudent to respect these absolute contraindications until further research clarifies Minipill safety.

ABSOLUTE CONTRAINDICATIONS

A woman with any of the following conditions must not take Minipills under any circumstances, with no exception. If you develop any of these conditions while taking Minipills, stop them at once.

1. Blood-clotting disorder now or in the past, such as thrombophlebitis, pulmonary embolism (clots in the lung), heart attack or stroke, or angina (heart pain)
2. Impaired liver function, including active or recent hepatitis, alcohol liver damage, severe mononucleosis, or liver tumor in the past
3. Known or suspected cancer of the breast, cervix, uterus, ovaries, vagina, or malignant melanoma, now or in the past, or abnormal vaginal bleeding whose cause has not yet been determined
4. Current pregnancy or current suspected pregnancy

RELATIVE CONTRAINDICATIONS

As with "Absolute Contraindications" there is no conclusive information on which to base "Relative Contraindications." Many clinicians feel that Minipills may be a reasonable birth control option for a woman who has had problems with regular combined Pills or has developed a relative contraindication such as headaches while taking Pills. She may be able to use Minipills safely and without problems.

Because there is no definite, accepted list of contraindications specifically for Minipills, however, it makes sense to review the contraindications for regular Pills and to discuss any factors that apply in your case with your clinician before you begin Minipills. The contraindications for regular combined Pills, discussed in Chapter 11, are listed below. Asterisks (*) indicate factors that may be especially important for a woman considering Minipills; these are conditions that are in theory probably related to progestin.

1. High blood pressure now, or elevated blood pressure during pregnancy in the past
*2. Diabetes or strong family history of diabetes
*3. Gallbladder disease now or in the past, or gallbladder surgery in the past
*4. Pregnancy jaundice (cholestasis) in the past
5. Mononucleosis now or in the recent past
6. Sickle cell disease
7. Leg cast, body cast, or serious leg injury
8. Fibrocystic breast disease or fibrous breast lumps (fibroadenoma), abnormal breat x-rays in the past, or close family history of breast cancer
9. Precancerous Pap smear (sometimes called CIN, severe dysplasia, or Class III or IV; see Chapter 27)
10. Major surgery scheduled within the next month
11. Recent pregnancy (delivery, abortion, or miscarriage within the last 10 to 14 days)
12. Heavy smoking (more than 15 cigarettes a day)
*13. Severe migraine (vascular) headaches
14. Age over 35 to 40
15. Serious heart or kidney disease
*16. Serious depression or suicidal feelings now or in the past (depression may worsen or improve)
*17. Epilepsy or other seizure disorders
18. Severe asthma
19. Severe varicose veins
20. History of chloasma (darkening of facial skin) or hair loss during pregnancy or during previous Pill or Minipill use

*Factors of special importance for Minipill use.

21. Uterine fibroids (may worsen or improve)
*22. Acne (may worsen or improve)
*23. Very irregular menstrual periods or long delays between periods
24. Menstrual periods recently begun and not yet regular (young teens)
*25. Breast feeding
26. Previous Pill use for five years or more
27. Past exposure to diethylstilbestrol during pregnancy (DES daughter or DES mother)
28. Compromised ability to use Minipills safely (no access to emergency care for Minipill problems, emotional or intellectual impairment that would make it difficult to follow Minipill schedule or recognize danger signs)

Some clinicians do not agree that all these conditions should be treated as relative contraindications, and some would add factors to the list, such as high cholesterol levels and recurrent urinary tract infections.

Minipill Interactions with Other Drugs

Numerous drugs are known to interact with regular combined Pills to result in altered activity of the drugs or in reduced effectiveness of the birth control Pills themselves (see Chapter 11). No specific interactions have yet been documented for Minipills, but you need to be aware of the potential problems. Drugs that reduce the effectiveness of regular Pills include ampicillin; antihistamines (including nonprescription cold products that contain antihistamines); Librium (chlordiazepoxide), meprobamate, and certain other tranquilizers; phenobarbital and other sedatives; Dilantin (diphenylhydantoin) (for epilepsy); rifampin and other tuberculosis drugs; and phenylbutazone (for arthritis). Drugs whose activity may be altered by regular Pills include: insulin; anticoagulants (blood-thinning medication); promazine and certain other

---

*Factors of special importance for Minipill use.

Please

read sections

on:

Menstruation (p. 18 in book)

anatomy

condoms &

foam

+ gyn

Ken

Know info
on Handouts
at tip of tongue

+ p. 74-76
in book

Diaphrams   method   Cervical Cap
Sponge

Date _____   Time in: _____

Counselor(s) _____   Time out: _____

Client(s): # of men _____ # of women _____

                                        Walk in _____
                                        Call in _____
                                        GYN referal _____
                                        Other _____

Counseled on: Gyn exam _____ Pill _____ Diaphragm _____ I.U.D. _____ Non prescription _____

Medical problem _____ V.D. _____ Relationship _____ Pregnancy testing _____

Abortion referal _____ Gave literature _____

Other _____

Outcome: Resolved _____ Will return _____ Will call back _____

Referred to: Counseling Center _____ Infirmary GYN _____ Off campus facility _____

Other _____

PILL DANGER SIGNS

* CHEST PAIN, shortness of
  breath, coughing
* PAIN IN CALF (leg)
* severe HEADACHE,
  vomiting, dizziness,
  faintness, muscle
  weakness or numbness,
  or speech disturbance
* VISION CHANGES or loss
* breast lump
* severe abdominal pain
* severe depression
* yellowing of the skin

Illustration 1   See your clinician at once if you develop a danger sign. (Reproductive Health Resources, Inc. Used with permission.)

tranquilizers; Demerol (meperidine) pain medication; and tuberculin skin tests. *Be sure that any clinician who cares for you, no matter for what reason, is aware that you are using Minipills.*

To minimize your risks using Minipills, read and consider the advice about Pill risks in Chapter 11. Remember the Pill danger signs (see Illustration 1), and see your clinician immediately if you think you may have a problem. The danger signs alert you primarily to blood-clotting disorders.

Advantages of Minipills

Minipills offer protection about equal to that of the IUD or diaphragm: 98-99% when used carefully and correctly. Minipills do not interrupt lovemaking and require minimal paraphernalia. They are easy to take, one pill every day, and you do not have to remember a cyclic pattern. Minipills provide continuous protection, no matter how frequently you have intercourse.

Although menstrual periods may be less regular than during

natural cycles, bleeding is often lighter, premenstrual symptoms such as breast swelling, headache, and tension are often less severe, and menstrual cramps are usually mild or absent.

SAFETY

The primary advantage of Minipills compared to regular combined Pills is probably safety. The word "probably" is stressed because there is as yet no research evidence that proves this advantage. Theoretical factors that do make it seem likely that a safety advantage will someday be documented, include the following: Minipills contain no estrogen. Minipills contain a lower dose of progestin than regular combined Pills. Minipill effects on chemical processes involving sugar, fat, and blood clotting appear to be less significant than combined Pill effects. Minipills do not totally suppress the pituitary hormone cycle, as combined Pills do.

These differences do not mean that progestin-only pills will be completely safe. Rather, they are good indications that Minipills are likely to be at least somewhat safer than combined Pills.

Using Minipills

Evaluation and examination procedures for starting Minipills are the same as those necessary for regular Pills (see Chapter 11); so you will need to see your clinician.

Choosing which Minipill to use is fairly easy because only three brands are now available in the United States and two of them are identical in hormone content. They are:

Brand	Progestin Dose	Type of Progestin
Micronor	0.35 mg	Norethindrone
Nor-Q-D	0.35 mg	Norethindrone
Ovrette	0.075 mg	Norgestrel

The norgestrel in Ovrette is a more potent progestin than the norethindrone in Micronor or Nor-Q-D; therefore, the progestin effect of Ovrette is probably higher than that of Micronor or Nor-Q-D even though the dose is lower. Norgestrel is a synthetic progestin that has almost no estrogen effects, whereas the other synthetic progestin, norethindrone, does have some estrogen effect in addition to the primary progestin effect.

There is no clear-cut way to choose a Minipill brand. You may find, however, that you are able to tolerate one better than another. If you do have problems such as irregular menstrual patterns, it may be worth while to try a Minipill with a different progestin.

TAKING MINIPILLS

Most clinicians and the FDA-approved Minipill leaflet information recommend that you begin Minipills on day 1 of a natural cycle; that is, on the first day of a normal menstrual period. If you begin Minipills on the first day of bleeding, the pills will probably protect you from pregnancy in your very first cycle, but you should use foam, condoms, or a diaphragm for the first two weeks to be sure. *You must not start taking Minipills if there is any chance you might be pregnant already.* It would not be safe to start your first pack, for example, during the last half of a natural cycle, for this could expose a newly conceived embryo to the potentially harmful effects of progestin during its very first few days of development. Similarly, starting Minipills on day 10, after your period, might not prevent ovulation due to occur only a few days later: you might conceive and expose the embryo to progestin.

Once you have started taking Minipills, you simply swallow one tablet each day for as long as you wish to avoid pregnancy. Do not stop taking Minipills during your period. There are no breaks and no sugar pills at all for Minipill users. Take your Minipill at about the same time each day, with no interruptions whatsoever.

Have a backup method of birth control on hand. You will need to use foam, condoms, or a diaphragm if you forget more than one Minipill or if you stop taking them for any reason.

If you miss one Minipill, take it as soon as you remember, and take your next Minipill at the regular time. For extra protection, you can use a backup method until your next period starts.

If you miss two Minipills, take one of the missed Minipills as soon as you remember, and take you regular Minipill for that day on schedule. Take the second forgotten Minipill plus the regular Minipill the next day. Use a backup method until your next period starts.

If you miss more than two Minipills, stop taking Minipills and use your backup method until your next menstrual period starts. You can safely begin taking Minipills again on the first day of your period. Use your backup method for the first two weeks of your new pack.

If you do not start a menstrual period within 45 days of starting your last one, stop taking Minipills and see your clinician promptly to determine whether you are pregnant.

If you have repeated spotting or frequent, irregular menstrual periods, discuss this problem with your clinician. She/he may decide that you need further evaluation to be certain that Minipills are truly the cause of your problem. If you have cramps or fever associated with bleeding, see your clinician at once, because you could have a pelvic infection.

Anticipate some change in your menstrual cycle length. Changes may be more likely during the first few months that you use Minipills. You may want to keep a tampon in your purse in case you have unexpected spotting or begin a period.

If you have nausea, try taking your Minipill with dinner or in the evening. If you vomit for any reason within an hour after you have taken a Minipill, take an extra Minipill immediately to replace the one vomited up.

If you accidentally damage, lose, or run out of Minipills, call your clinician. An immediate telephone refill can almost always be arranged so that you don't have to miss any Minipills. If you are traveling, you may be able to get an emergency refill from a local Planned Parenthood clinic.

Some Minipill users are able to identify their own cycles well enough to recognize signs of ovulation (see Chapter 8 for details). If you can tell when you ovulate, consider improving your protection by adding a backup method for three days before and three days after ovulation. If you add a backup method on fertile days, your effectiveness should be well over 99%, matching or outdoing the effectiveness of regular combined Pills.

STOPPING MINIPILLS

Knowing when to stop taking Minipills and when to see your clinician could be important for your safety. Read the section on stopping pills in Chapter 11; all these rules also apply to Minipill users. Remember that you also need to see your clinician if you go more than 45 days without a menstrual period. The overall chance of pregnancy and the chance of tubal (ectopic) pregnancy are higher with Minipills than with regular combined Pills; you must be alert to the early signs of pregnancy and ectopic pregnancy (see Chapter 4) (3).

If you want to stop Minipills because you have decided to use another birth control method, you can stop any time during your cycle.

If you are not bleeding when you stop Minipills, you can expect a menstrual period to begin within a few days after your last Minipill. After that you can expect your own natural cycle to resume.

PLANNING PREGNANCY

As with regular combined Pills, most clinicians recommend that you plan ahead for pregnancy. Ideally, this means stopping Minipills at least three months before you would like to become pregnant, and using another birth control method—foam, condoms, or a diaphragm —during the three-month interval. Reasons for this recommendation are explained in Chapter 11.

REFERENCES

1. Rinehart W: Minipill: A limited alternative for certain women. *Population Reports*, Ser A, No 3, September 1975. Washington, DC, The George Washington University Medical Center.
2. FDA-approved product labeling for oral contraceptives, May 1980. Manufacturers of oral contraceptives are required to provide a leaflet explaining the benefits, risks and possible complications of Pills for each patient who fills a Pill prescription. You should be able to obtain a copy of the leaflet, entitled "What You Should Know About Oral Contraceptives," from your physician or pharmacist. Manufacturer's information for physicians as well as the text of the patient leaflet appear in Physician's Desk Reference (ed. 34), Medical Economics Co., Oradell, NJ, 1980.
3. Liukko P, Erkkola R, Laakso L: Ectopic pregnancy during use of low-dose progestins for oral contraception. *Contraception* 16:575–580, 1977.

13 | Morning-After Birth Control

"Morning-after" emergencies happen to almost everyone, and it is natural to have a heart-sinking, panicky feeling the next morning when you think about the possibility of unwanted pregnancy. You may have had intercourse when you didn't expect to, or your diaphragm moved out of position, or a condom broke. It's amazing how many things can go wrong.

If you know within a couple of minutes after intercourse that you are unprotected, **try to repair the damage.** Use a full applicator of birth control foam, cream, or jelly immediately if a condom breaks or if your diaphragm seems out of position. If you don't have any foam or spermicidal cream or jelly around, douche at once with warm water and vinegar, 2 tablespoons of vinegar per quart of water.

Next, try to relax a little. The chance of pregnancy after one act of intercourse without birth control is not as great as you might think. The likelihood of pregnancy depends on your age, your and your partner's fertility, and where you are in your cycle. The chance of pregnancy may be as little as 2% if you have intercourse without birth control only once during a cycle, and is probably no more than 30% even if you have intercourse without birth control during your most fertile 24 hours (1).

You can choose from three basic approaches to emergency birth control:

1. Wait and see whether you have conceived. Have a pregnancy test and decide between abortion and continuing the pregnancy if you are pregnant.

220

2. Have an IUD inserted.
3. Take morning-after estrogen hormone treatment.

If you are considering morning-after treatment with an IUD or estrogen, you need to see your clinician within 48 hours if at all possible. Morning-after estrogen should be started as soon as possible to be most effective, within 24–72 hours at most, and an IUD must be inserted within five days.

Your clinician probably will not recommend any kind of morning-after treatment unless you had unprotected intercourse within a few days on either side of your estimated ovulation time. The likelihood of conception is quite small during the rest of your cycle. Use your menstrual period calendar to calculate your fertile days yourself by following the directions in Chapter 8.

Your clinician probably will not recommend morning-after estrogen treatment or IUD insertion if you had unprotected intercourse more than once; because if you had already conceived before treatment, a morning-after IUD or hormones could be dangerous for the developing fetus.

Wait and See

If you are really anxious, you can arrange for a highly sensitive blood pregnancy test in about 10 days. If you are not so anxious, you can wait to see whether your next period arrives on time and is normal, and then arrange for a regular two-minute urine pregnancy test if your period is two weeks overdue. (Pregnancy tests are discussed in detail in Chapter 4.) In the meantime, try to decide whether you would continue pregnancy or whether you would have an abortion.* If abortion is your choice, make your arrangements promptly. Abortions are safest when

---

*If you definitely do not want to be pregnant but are unable to face the issue of abortion, you can probably find a clinic or physician willing to perform "menstrual extraction," a vacuum procedure, at about the time your period should start. It is safer to have a blood pregnancy test beforehand so that your clinician will know that you are pregnant when the procedure is done and so that you can avoid having an unnecessary procedure if you are not pregnant; but it *is possible* to have the vacuum procedure without being told whether you are pregnant, if you prefer.

they are performed early in pregnancy. (Abortion is covered in Chapters 18, 19, and 20.)

IUD Insertion

Several researchers have had good morning-after results with copper IUDs (2). IUD insertion within five days after unprotected intercourse probably interferes with implantation of the embryo in the uterine lining. Read Chapter 10 to review potential risks and problems that can occur with an IUD. This approach would make the most sense if you would seriously consider the IUD for ongoing birth control protection.

Hormone Treatment

The most widely recognized morning-after hormone treatment is diethylstilbestrol (DES); its manufacturer is the only one so far to seek FDA approval specifically for morning-after use. A high dose of DES, 25 mg twice daily for five days (equivalent to the estrogen in 25 to 50 low-dose birth control Pills) interferes with conception and/or implantation. Many women who take morning-after DES have temporary nausea and vomiting, and clinicians often prescribe anti-nausea drugs along with the estrogen.

DES is a synthetic estrogen. Because of the many problems linked to DES exposure for women treated with DES during pregnancy and for their daughters and sons (see DES Risks below), many clinicians feel that it makes sense to choose one of the other synthetic estrogens available instead of DES. Research with other estrogens for morning-after treatment has shown that ethinyl estradiol (Estinyl), 5 mg daily for five days, or conjugated estrogen (Premarin, for example), 30 mg daily for five days, appears to be effective as morning-after birth control (4).

Another morning-after hormone approach uses a regular birth control pill (Ovral) containing ethinyl estradiol and norgestrel. This method is particularly appealing because it is so simple, and because the total hormone dose—two pills immediately (within 24–72 hours after intercourse) and two more pills 12 hours later—is quite low. Researchers reported on 608 women who used this treatment for morning-after emergencies. Only 1 pregnancy occurred, in a woman who did not begin treatment until 70 hours after intercourse. Without morning-after treatment, between 12 and 30 pregnancies would have been expected in this group (4).

There are several important factors to consider as you weigh the risks and benefits of morning-after estrogen treatment, both in relation to estrogen in general and to DES in particular.

DES RISKS

DES morning-after treatment could fail, and a developing fetus could be exposed to DES. DES exposure during fetal development may cause serious problems that appear years later as the exposed person reaches sexual maturity. Read Chapter 37 to review possible hazards for DES-exposed sons and daughters. If you would seriously consider continuing a pregnancy, then avoid DES morning-after treatment.

DES may also be linked to serious problems for women who took the drug for prolonged periods during pregnancy. Pregnant women who took DES between 1940 and 1970, when it was often used during pregnancy, appear to have an increased risk of breast cancer, and possibly of uterine and ovarian cancer as well. It is not known whether women who use DES for a brief time, as with morning-after treatment, will have risks comparable to those of DES mothers who took the drug throughout pregnancy.

GENERAL ESTROGEN RISKS

Problems that can be caused by estrogens generally, including DES, are discussed in detail in Chapter 11. The most serious immediate risk is abnormal blood clotting. If you have had clotting problems in the past, such as stroke, heart attack, or thrombophlebitis, you must not take hormones for morning-after treatment. Don't take estrogen if you have a breast lump or unusual vaginal bleeding whose cause is not yet known. Be sure to review the other conditions that would make hormone treatment unwise or unsafe. See the contraindications section in Chapter 11.

Evaluating Your Options

It may be hard for you to decide whether morning-after treatment is a good choice or not. If your own health and safety are your main concerns and you would have an early abortion if you did conceive, then the "wait and see" option is certainly reasonable, because the likelihood of pregnancy is not high and your health risks with early abortion are quite low.

Your own health and safety, however, may not be the only factors you are considering. If abortion is not an option for you, then morning-after IUD or hormone treatment may well be a good choice and may be your safest option. You may decide that preserving your peace of mind justifies the possible risks of morning-after treatment.

REFERENCES

1. Tietze C: Probability of pregnancy resulting from a single unprotected coitus. *Fertility and Sterility* 11:485–488, 1960.
2. Lippes J, Tatum HJ, Maulik D, et al: Post coital copper IUD's. *Advances in Planned Parenthood* 14(3):87–94, 1979.
3. Blye R: The use of estrogens as postcoital contraceptive agents. *American Journal of Obstetrics and Gynecology* 116:1044–1050, 1973.
4. Yuzpe AA, Lancee WJ: Ethinylestradiol and dl-norgestrel as a postcoital contraceptive. *Fertility and Sterility* 28:432–436, 1977.

14 | Making a Decision About Sterilization

Surgical sterilization—tubal ligation for women or vasectomy for men—is the most popular method of birth control among married couples over age 30 in the United States. Sterilization offers an extremely high level of effectiveness, and the surgical procedures are simple and quick, with few complications and side effects.

The key word with sterilization is **permanence.** If there is any chance you might want to have a child in the future, you are not ready for a tubal ligation or a vasectomy. Success with reversal surgery after vasectomy and tubal ligation has varied, but overall success rates are relatively low. The increasing number of men and women clinicians are seeing who would like surgery to reverse a previous sterilization shows that the decision about sterilization may be difficult, and needs to be made carefully.

The real news in the area of surgical sterilization is the change in public policies and legal restrictions. In the last few years, arbitrary guidelines that limited sterilization to married people with large families have been abandoned. Today a single person or a married person without children can be sterilized if she/he wishes, and that was not a realistic possibility ten years ago. Sterilization surgery is now a covered benefit in many standard health insurance programs.

A couple contemplating sterilization should consider both vasectomy and tubal ligation. If the two are equally acceptable, the medical recommendation would be vasectomy. Compared to other common kinds of surgery, both vasectomy and tubal ligation are relatively safe, but vasectomy is safer, simpler, and cheaper than tubal ligation.

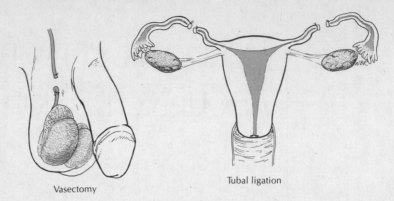

Vasectomy

Tubal ligation

Illustration 1 Tubal ligation interrupts the fallopian tubes. Vasectomy interrupts each of the two vas deferens.

Sterilization usually refers to any surgical operation that permanently prevents pregnancy; surgical sterilization is the only common method of permanent birth control. (Certain drugs and radiation techniques will result in sterilization, but they are almost never used.)

Vasectomy is the sterilization operation for men. The vasectomy procedure severs and seals shut each of the two vas deferens, the tubes that transport sperm from the testicles to the penis. The parallel operation for women is called tubal ligation. The fallopian tubes that transport a fertilized egg from the ovaries to the uterus can be severed and/or sealed shut by any one of five common surgical techniques.

None of the sterilization operations involves surgery on the sex glands themselves. The testicles or ovaries continue to produce hormones, and there is no chemical or medical reason to expect a change in sex drive. Male and female sex hormones are carried in the bloodstream, not in the tubes. Sterilization surgery simply blocks transport of egg cells or sperm cells, and when egg and sperm don't meet, pregnancy can't begin (see Illustration 1).

Other kinds of surgery can result in sterilization: hysterectomy (removal of the uterus) for women, and prostate surgery for men. When sterilization is the primary or sole purpose of surgery, however, these operations will not be recommended, because they involve a higher complication risk than vasectomy and tubal ligation.

History of Sterilization

Hippocrates described sterilization procedures in ancient Greece. Wide availability and popularity of surgical sterilization are recent, partly because of the moral and religious restrictions on all forms of birth control that dominated Western medicine until after World War II, and partly because all surgery was risky until 30 to 40 years ago. Better anesthesia, antibiotics, blood transfusions, and improved surgical techniques have greatly decreased all types of surgical risks. More than 1 million sterilization procedures have been performed in the United States every year since 1973 (see Illustration 2).

Simple tubal ligation—closing the fallopian tubes with suture

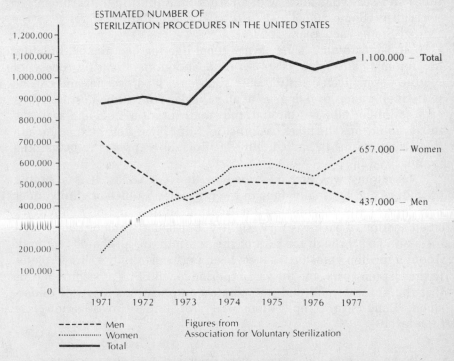

Illustration 2   By 1973, men and women were having sterilization procedures in almost equal numbers. (Annual estimates of voluntary sterilization procedures for men and women are compiled by the Association for Voluntary Sterilization; estimates do not include hysterectomies.)

thread—was the earliest sterilization procedure for women, and was described in Western medical journals in 1880 (1). This technique often failed to prevent pregnancy and has been replaced with other techniques that add destruction or removal of part of each fallopian tube to the suturing or ligation approach.

All the traditional approaches to tubal ligation have used standard surgical instruments and techniques, general anesthesia, and a standard 5-inch abdominal incision. The 70 years of experience with these operations include millions of procedures, and success rates and complications are well understood.

"Band-aid" surgery, or laparoscopic tubal ligation, was introduced on a large scale in the late 1960s. The laparoscope is a tube equipped with light and magnification lenses. It is inserted into your abdomen through a 1-inch incision so that your surgeon can see your uterus and tubes and seal your tubes with a cauterizing (burning) instrument, or with clips. Some 200,000 such tubal ligations are performed in the United States each year.

Mini-laparotomy is the newest tubal ligation technique. Miniature laparotomy calls for a 1- to 1½-inch abdominal incision, does not require sophisticated instruments such as a laparoscope, and can be performed under local or general anesthesia. Your surgeon simply lifts each fallopian tube out through the small incision, cuts and seals the tubes, and drops the tubes back inside. Mini-laparotomy experience in the United States is limited, but the procedure appears to be gaining popularity (2).

Vasectomy was first described in the late 1890s. It is a simple procedure and is usually done in the physician's office or clinic under local anesthesia. Techniques for ligating (tying) and/or removing a small section of each vas vary slightly, but usually one or two ½-inch incisions just through the skin of the scrotum are all that is required. About 5 million vasectomies have been performed in the United States in the last ten years, and the vast experience with this procedure means that the success rates and immediate complications are well understood. Long-term complications are still under investigation (see Chapter 16).

> When I first discussed vasectomy with my urologist and asked him about sperm banks, he said if that was *important* to me then I wasn't ready for vasectomy.
>
> —Man, 32

Most clinicians will discourage you from relying on a sperm bank. The idea makes sense, but it is extremely difficult to store human semen safely. Many researchers believe that sperm swimming ability is diminished by freezing. There have been very few pregnancy attempts using frozen semen; so it is impossible to evaluate what risks, if any, are associated with sperm banking. Besides, your sperm bank may go out of business; many have.

There are new surgical sterilization techniques under investigation that use metal clips or silicone bands to seal the fallopian tubes. Techniques for closing the tubal openings inside the uterus and for covering the open ends of the tubes are in early stages of investigation. Experimental vasectomy techniques are under study to close the vas with plugs or valves. The hope is that one or several of these new techniques will prove to be more reversible and/or safer than present techniques. Research experience to date is limited, and we cannot expect a real breakthrough in reversible sterilization surgery for some time—probably years.

Effectiveness

Vasectomy and tubal ligation procedures have fewer failures than any of the temporary birth control methods. Most tubal ligation "failures" actually represent pregnancies that began just before surgery. True postoperative failures do occasionally occur with both vasectomy and tubal ligation and may be caused by incomplete tubal closure, accidental ligation of a ligament instead of a tube, the presence of an extra tube, or regrowth of a tube. Table 1 lists typical effectiveness rates for the different sterilization procedures.*

Pregnancy rates after abdominal, vaginal, and postpartum tubal ligation vary widely. It makes sense to select a surgeon who is experienced with tubal ligation procedures; if you do, your risk for complications or failure will probably be low.

---

*Remember that effectiveness for temporary birth control methods is calculated per 100 women per one year of use. Sterilization effectiveness rates are calculated per 1000 individuals as a one-time risk. An IUD effectiveness rate of 98% means that 20 pregnancies occur each year for every 1,000 IUD users (2 pregnancies for each 100 women); so over a period of five years 100 IUD pregnancies would occur. If 1,000 couples rely on vasectomy or laparoscopic tubal ligation for five years, however, the total number of pregnancies would be 1 or 2.

Table 1   PREGNANCIES AFTER STERILIZATION SURGERY

Method	Pregnancies per 1,000 Procedures
Vasectomy[a]	1.5
Laparoscopic tubal ligation[b]	2.0
Abdominal, vaginal, or postpartum tubal ligation[c]	1–20

SOURCES:

[a] Judith Wortman, PT Piotrow: Vasectomy: old and new techniques, *Population Reports*, Ser D, No 1, December 1973. Washington, DC, The George Washington University Medical Center.

[b] J Phillips, et al: Gynecologic laparoscopy in 1975, *Journal of Reproductive Medicine* 16:105–117, 1976.

[c] Judith Wortman: Sterilization: Tubal sterilization—review of methods, *Population Reports*, Ser C, No 7, May 1976. Washington, DC, The George Washington University Medical Center.

Deciding About Sterilization

Making your own decision about sterilization involves both logical and emotional factors. It is a very personal decision for the man or woman considering surgery, and a joint decision for a couple. Feelings deserve full consideration along with facts, and it is important that your decision be made without subtle or overt pressure. *It is a permanent decision:* sexual problems and feelings of regret after sterilization are more likely among people who had misgivings about the surgery beforehand.

If you are uncomfortable about abortion, the effectiveness of sterilization may be its most important advantage for you. Even if 100 couples of average fertility are able to use temporary birth control methods diligently at a 98% effectiveness level, about 20 of the couples will experience at least one unwanted pregnancy every five years.

I had thought about having a tubal ligation after Toni was born, but I wasn't really sure how I would feel if she turned out to have some kind of a problem. I didn't worry much about it until I thought I was pregnant *again*. After that scare my mind was made up. I just couldn't see having to worry for the next 20 years.

—*Woman, 30*

Some childless couples and individuals choose sterilization. Concern about serious inherited diseases may be a deciding factor for some. For others, the decision is strictly personal. Some people simply don't want children. Other couples believe that adoption is a more attractive alternative than childbearing. (The number of healthy infants available for adoption is very small compared to the number of couples trying to adopt. The adoption outlook is better for couples who are willing to accept responsibility for older children or children with known handicaps.)

Most clinicians and sterilization counselors encourage a substantial "thinking-it-over" period if you are very young or have not had children, because they fear that you may regret your decision later on. There is no doubt that life situations, feelings, and hopes change over time for most people; significant changes are a natural part of youth, especially. Clinicians are seeing more and more patients who request surgery to reconnect the fallopian tubes or vas deferens, and the success rates for reversal surgery can be low. Some clinicians even recommend that young or childless women have a tubal ligation procedure more amenable to later reversal than the popular laparoscopy/cautery method that has very little likelihood of reversal.

Consider your own feelings about the impact of major life changes or tragedies before you make a final sterilization decision.

- *Divorce and remarriage.* One-third to one-half of all marriages now end in divorce. Remarriage and a desire for a child with a new partner is one of the most common reasons people request sterilization reversal surgery.
- *Death of a spouse or child.* About 52 out of 100,000 children aged 1 to 15 die in the United States each year (3).

WHICH OF YOU SHOULD BE STERILIZED?

If you have a stable relationship with your partner and each of you feels comfortable about sterilization, vasectomy makes sense as a first choice because it is a less complex procedure than tubal ligation, has a lower risk of complications, and costs less. In many cases, however, one partner (often the woman) will feel more certain about not wanting children in the future than will the other partner, perhaps because pregnancy, childbearing, and parenting can have a different impact on men and women. Often a woman is ready for a sterilization decision several years before her partner.

Hysterectomy can be an appropriate choice if you want to be sterilized and you also have a pelvic disease that might require surgery at some future time. For example, if you have severe uterine fibroid tumors that cause pain or heavy bleeding, you might choose hysterectomy rather than tubal ligation now and hysterectomy later. Base your decision on a thorough medical assessment of the likelihood of your future problems and on your own feelings about your alternatives. Your risk of complications with hysterectomy is significantly greater than with tubal ligation, and recovery from surgery will require at least four to six weeks. Most clinicians would not recommend hysterectomy unless there were good reasons for hysterectomy apart from your desire for sterilization.

Sometimes the argument is made that hysterectomy for sterilization is justified because hysterectomy eliminates the risk of your developing cancer of the uterus or cervix later on. Detailed analysis of this argument indicates, however, that for most women in the United States the overall risk of routine hysterectomy is too high to justify the operation as a preventative measure.

Legal Aspects of Sterilization

Sterilization surgery historically has been subject to many legal restrictions. Within the last five years, court decisions and new laws have struck down many restrictions, and each person has the right to sterilization without having to meet arbitrary qualifications. No state or hospital can impose rigid standards for age, marital status, or previous childbearing. The sterilization decision is up to the person and her/his clinician.

Private hospitals may, if they choose, decline to perform sterilization surgery. Similarly, no surgeon can be compelled to perform sterilization surgery if she/he feels that sterilization is not appropriate in a particular case, or if she/he is opposed to sterilization on religious grounds. Many clinicians are reluctant to consider sterilization for very young or childless patients, but it has become easier to find surgeons willing to respect a patient's sterilization wishes. Local health departments or Planned Parenthood agencies may be able to help you with referrals in your community.

You do not have to obtain your spouse's consent if you want to be sterilized. Many hospitals and physicians, however, will ask your spouse to sign a consent form whenever possible. Obviously it is desirable for you and your partner to agree about sterilization, but legally you can make a sterilization decision on your own even if you are married.

Sterilization services for persons under 21 years old are indirectly limited by current federal funding policies, because federal funds cannot be used to pay for sterilization for minors. If you rely on federally subsidized health funds such as welfare or Medicaid, you will not be able to have sterilization surgery through the program until you are 21 unless your state pays for sterilization procedures with state funds.

Federally funded health programs also impose special requirements, including a minimum 30 day waiting period, to be sure that each person can give a truly informed consent before sterilization surgery. The regulations establish seven steps for consent, and you have a right to all this information before your surgery:

- A full explanation of the procedure
- A description of the possible risks and side effects, including all major life-threatening risks and all common minor risks
- A description of the benefits you can expect
- An explanation of alternative methods of birth control and of the impact of the sterilization procedure, including the fact that you must consider it irreversible
- An offer to answer any questions about the procedure
- A reminder that you are free to withhold or withdraw your consent at any time without prejudicing your future care, and without the loss of other health or welfare benefits to which you might otherwise be entitled
- Written documentation of informed consent, which you yourself must sign

Surgery to Reverse Sterilization

Despite recent advances in surgical techniques, sterilization reversal still remains an uncertain and costly medical procedure.

For men who have undergone vasectomy, reversal surgery (called vasovasostomy) is a 1½ to 3 hour procedure that often requires general anesthesia. The best results have been reported for surgery done with an operating microscope and very delicate stitching techniques (called "microsurgery"). The most successful surgeons, using microsurgery, report that 85 to 90% of their vasovasostomy patients regain motile sperm, but that pregnancy rates are only 55 to 70% (4,5).

Surgery to rejoin the fallopian tubes after female sterilization is also most successful when microsurgery techniques are used. If success seems unlikely, because of the type of tubal ligation procedure originally performed or because of other medical problems, then reanastomosis surgery will not be recommended. As many as 70% of women considering reversal may be advised against it (6). Fallopian tube reanastomosis involves major abdominal surgery, and always requires general anesthesia and hospitalization for 5 or 6 days.

Reported rates for successful pregnancy after microsurgery reanastomosis of the fallopian tubes average about 56% (6). Ectopic (tubal) pregnancy rates after reversal surgery are high, so early confirmation of pregnancy and early pelvic examination are especially important (see Chapter 4 for danger signs of ectopic pregnancy).

REFERENCES

1. Wortman J: Sterilization: Tubal sterilization—review of methods. *Population Reports*, Ser C, No 7, May 1976. Washington, DC, The George Washington University Medical Center.
2. Wortman J: Female sterilization by mini-laparotomy. *Population Reports*, Ser C, No 5, November 1974. Washington, DC, The George Washington University Medical Center.
3. Mortality Statistics Branch, Division of Vital Statistics, National Center for Health Statistics, Department of Health, Education and Welfare: Unpublished table, 1976 data.
4. Bradshaw LE: Vasectomy reversibility—a status report. *Population Reports*, Ser D, No 3, May 1976. Washington, DC, The George Washington University Medical Center.
5. Amelar RD, Dubin L: Vasectomy reversal. *The Journal of Urology* 121: 547–550, 1979.
6. Henry A, Rinehart W, Piotrow PT: Reversing female sterilization. *Population Reports*, Ser C, No 8, September 1980. Baltimore, Md, The Johns Hopkins University.

15 | Sterilization Operations for Women

There are *five different operations* that can be used for ligating (tying) a woman's fallopian tubes. Not all of the operations are appropriate for all women—you can discuss the pros and cons of different options with your surgeon beforehand so that together you can choose the best and safest approach for you.

Each operation is discussed in detail later in this chapter. The tubal ligation operations are briefly summarized in Table 1.

In addition to different surgery approaches to reach the tubes, there are also different techniques for closing them as well. Your surgeon may close your tubes with suture thread, she/he may suture the tubes and remove a section of each tube, or she/he may cauterize your tubes (burn and seal them with an electric cautery instrument). Alternatively, some surgeons are now using metal clips or elastic rings to close each tube.

Three common tubal closure techniques are Pomeroy, Irving and fimbriectomy (see Illustration 1). Pomeroy ligation and fimbriectomy can be carried out with any of the tubal ligation operations except laparoscopic tubal ligation. The Irving technique may be used for an abdominal tubal ligation or in conjunction with cesarean section delivery. Cautery is usually used for laparoscopic tubal ligation.

The closure techniques differ from each other somewhat in failure rates and in the likelihood that reversal surgery would be successful later on. Surgery to reconstruct the fallopian tubes is more successful after the Pomeroy method—success rates of 50 to 75% are reported

Table 1 STERILIZATION OPERATIONS FOR WOMEN

Name	When Performed	Type of Anesthesia	Incision
Laparoscopic or "Band-aid" tubal ligation	Any time	Usually general; local may be possible	1-inch incision just below the navel; perhaps an additional tiny incision near the pubic hairline
Postpartum tubal ligation	Within 48 hours after delivery	General or spinal; sometimes local	1- to 1½-inch horizontal incision just below the navel
Abdominal tubal ligation	Any time	General	5-inch horizontal or vertical abdominal incision (may be shorter or longer)
Vaginal tubal ligation	Any time	General; sometimes local	1½- to 2-inch incision inside the vagina
Mini-laparotomy tubal ligation	Any time	Local or general	1- to 1½-inch horizontal incision just above the pubic hairline

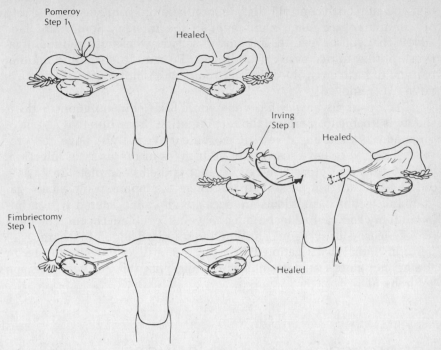

Illustration 1   Three techniques for closing the fallopian tubes.

(1)—than it is after laparoscopy cauterization. As you might suspect, the Pomeroy technique probably has a higher failure rate as well. Fimbriectomy is essentially non-reversible but, like all tubal ligation methods, can fail to protect against pregnancy in rare cases.

Preparing for Tubal Ligation

Be sure to read Chapter 39 to learn what preoperative exams and tests you will need, what your hospital stay will be like, details about anesthesia, and what to expect during your recovery.

Your surgeon will want to be sure you understand that tubal ligation must be considered permanent and that you understand all the possible complications. You (and your spouse, if appropriate) may be asked to sign a consent form. Your clinician will probably recommend that you stop birth control Pills one month before your surgery and rely on condoms, foam, or a diaphragm in the interim. Some clinicians advise that you have an IUD removed several weeks before tubal ligation in order to decrease infection risk. Be sure to change to another method of birth control—condoms, foam, or a diaphragm—if you have your IUD removed.

Decide in advance what you would like your surgeon to do if she/he is unable to complete the tubal ligation procedure that you have planned. For example, if you are extremely overweight, have had previous surgery, or have scarring of your tubes or uterus from infection, your sterilization procedure can be impossible to complete. In 7 cases out of 1,000 it is not possible to complete the laparoscopic tubal ligation, and technical problems are occasionally encountered with mini-laparotomy and vaginal techniques as well. If problems occur, you have two choices: your surgeon can switch to standard abdominal surgery to perform your tubal ligation while you are still under anesthesia, or she/he can stop. Decide which you prefer, and talk to your surgeon beforehand.

Laparoscopic Tubal Ligation ("Band-aid" Sterilization)

Laparoscopic tubal ligation is usually performed in a hospital or surgical center with general anesthesia. Sometimes it is possible to have the procedure using local anesthesia and sedatives or tranquilizers. Discuss the pros and cons of each with your surgeon.

You are positioned on the operating table with your feet in stirrups and your hips raised. Your abdomen and vagina are thoroughly scrubbed, and sterile drapes are placed over all of your body except your abdomen and vaginal area.

Once anesthesia is complete, your surgeon puts a speculum in your vagina and places a small clamp on your cervix to hold it steady, and then inserts an elevator—a blunt metal rod—into your uterus. These instruments will be used later to move your uterus and tubes into position for clear visualization. If you are having a D&C (see Chapter 40) or an abortion at the same time as your sterilization, it is done at this stage.

Next your surgeon makes a 1-inch incision just below your navel and inserts a needle through the incision into your abdomen. Carbon

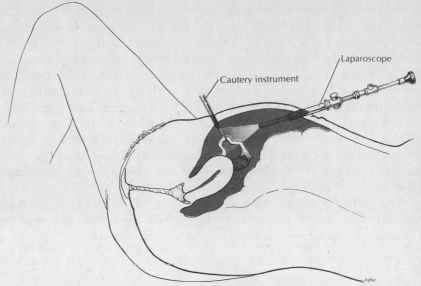

Illustration 2   The laparoscope light illuminates the abdomen. The tubal ligation instrument is usually inserted through a second small incision near the pubic hairline. (Reproductive Health Resources, Inc., used with permission.)

dioxide gas is gently pumped through the needle to lift up the abdominal wall so that your intestines will shift out of the way. Next, the laparoscope is inserted (see Illustration 2) through the incision. Your surgeon is able to see your tubes, uterus, and other abdominal organs through the laparoscope (see Illustration 3).

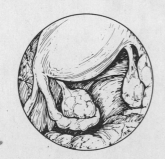

Clinician's view through laparoscope

Cautery burns and seals tube

Illustration 3   Laparoscopic tubal ligation. (Reproductive Health Resources, Inc., used with permission.)

Once the laparoscope is in place, your surgeon inserts the electric cautery instrument that will burn and seal a section of each tube. The cautery instrument is usually inserted through a second tiny incision just above your pubic hairline. (Some surgeons insert the cautery instrument directly alongside the laparoscope.) Your surgeon manipulates the elevator in your uterus to move the uterus and tubes into position so that she/he can grasp a tube with the cautery instrument. The cautery instrument is turned on, and your surgeon burns and seals 1 to 2 inches of tube (see Illustration 3). Some surgeons then use the cautery or scissors to remove a small segment of the tube; others believe that cautery alone is preferable. Clips or elastic rings may be used instead of cautery to close the tube. Next, the other tube is located and sealed in the same way.

The instruments are removed, and most of the gas escapes from your abdomen. Your incision(s) is closed with one or two stitches (see Illustration 4) and covered with one or two band-aids.

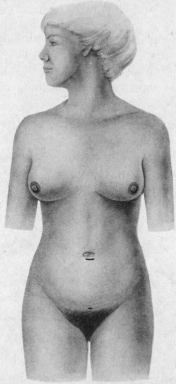

Illustration 4   Laparoscopic tubal ligation is usually performed with two small incisions.

Postpartum Tubal Ligation

In the first 48 hours after full-term delivery, surgical tubal ligation can be carried out very simply. The enlarged uterus remains high in the abdominal cavity (see Illustration 5), and the tubes can be reached through a 1- to 1½-inch incision just below the navel. If epidural block anesthesia has been used for delivery, it may be possible to perform tubal ligation without further anesthesia. Tubal ligation can also be performed at the same time as cesarean section delivery.

After general, epidural, spinal, or possibly local anesthesia is completed, your abdomen is scrubbed, shaved, and draped. Your surgeon makes an incision along the curve of your navel and is able to see the top of your uterus and your tubes clearly. The first tube is grasped with a small blunt clamp, lifted out through the incision, and then ligated. The Pomeroy method (see Illustration 6) is the most common because it can easily be performed with the small incision.

After ligation, the first tube is released and drops back into your abdominal cavity; then the second tube is grasped and ligated. Next your surgeon inspects both tubes to be sure that there is no bleeding, and closes the incision (see Illustration 7).

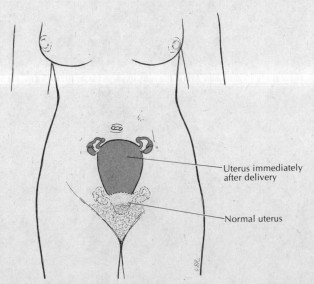

Uterus immediately after delivery

Normal uterus

Illustration 5 Tubal ligation is easy to perform immediately after delivery, when the uterus and tubes are high in the abdomen.

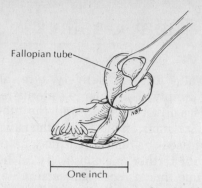

Fallopian tube

One inch

Illustration 6 A loop of fallopian tube is sutured shut with the Pomeroy technique, and then the top part of the loop is cut away.

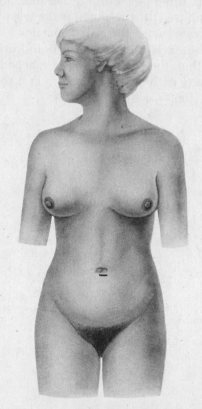

Illustration 7 Incision for postpartum tubal ligation.

242

The postpartum incision heals quickly and causes minimal discomfort. Most women find that postpartum tubal ligation does not require any additional recovery time; they are able to leave the hospital two to three days after delivery, just as they normally would.

Abdominal Tubal Ligation

When your surgeon performs an abdominal tubal ligation, an incision about 5 inches long through your lower abdomen exposes your uterus, tubes, and ovaries (see Illustration 8). Your surgeon may use a vertical "midline" incision or, more commonly, a horizontal "Pfannenstiel" incision. The Pfannenstiel incision results in a less noticeable scar; it is usually covered even by a low-cut bathing suit (see Illustration 9). If you have had previous pelvic surgery, however, your surgeon will

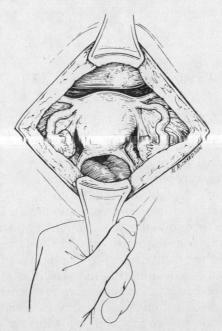

Illustration 8   Your surgeon has an excellent view of your entire pelvis during abdominal tubal ligation.

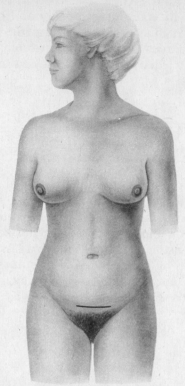

Illustration 9   Pfannenstiel incision for abdominal tubal ligation.

follow your old incision line so that old scar tissue can be removed to leave only one scar after tubal ligation.

Abdominal tubal ligation requires general anesthesia. Any of the ligation procedures can be used (see Illustration 1), including techniques that are not adaptable to smaller incisions. Once ligation is completed, your incision is closed with stitches in layers.

Recovery after abdominal tubal ligation is not as rapid as with other tubal ligation procedures because of the larger incision. Most women remain in the hospital three to five days and rest at home for several weeks. You can resume routine activities after three to four weeks, but full recovery often requires five to six weeks.

Abdominal tubal ligation has three main advantages. First, the large incision permits a more thorough evaluation of your total pelvis. If you are having surgery because of an enlarged ovary or tumor, for example, you might wish to have a tubal ligation performed at the same time. Second, it is almost always possible to carry out tubal ligation successfully with an abdominal incision, even in situations where other techniques are difficult or unsuccessful. For example, scar tissue on your fallopian tubes from previous infection or surgery may make it impossible to locate or grasp your tubes through a small abdominal or vaginal incision. The 5-inch abdominal incision is large enough to allow your surgeon to remove scar tissue and perform tubal ligation successfully. Finally, abdominal surgery is a technique with which all competent gynecologists, general surgeons, and many general practitioners are experienced. Not all gynecologists have had the training or experience necessary for laparoscopic tubal ligation; not all are comfortable with vaginal surgery; and only a few in the United States have begun to use the mini-laparotomy technique. In general, it is wise to select a surgical technique with which your particular surgeon is comfortable and experienced.

Vaginal Tubal Ligation

Some women may be able to have tubal ligation performed through an incision *inside* the vagina. It is most likely to be successful if your uterus, tubes, and ovaries are freely movable, if your pelvic muscles are relatively lax, and if your uterus is not abnormally enlarged.

Because the vagina normally contains many types of bacteria, preoperative cleansing is especially important. Some surgeons recommend that you use antibacterial vaginal suppositories or douches and perhaps antibiotic pills at home in preparation for surgery. At the time of surgery, your vagina and vulva are cleansed and pubic hair around the vaginal opening is usually shaved.

Once general (or sometimes local) anesthesia is complete, your surgeon places a speculum inside your vagina so that she/he can see your cervix and the back of the vagina. A steadying clamp is placed on your cervix, and the surgeon makes a 1½- to 2-inch incision inside your vagina just below your cervix (see Illustration 10). Only a thin layer of connective tissue separates the vagina from the abdominal lining, and when these layers are separated and opened, your surgeon can see the back side of your uterus. She/he manipulates your uterus with the cervical clamp until the first tube is located. Then the tube is grasped

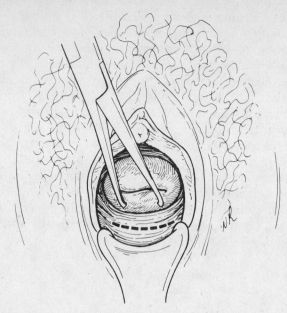

Illustration 10   Incision for vaginal tubal ligation.

and pulled down through the incision into the vagina. The Pomeroy or fimbriectomy ligation technique is usually used (see Illustration 1), and the tube is then released back into your abdomen. The second tube is then located and ligated. Your surgeon inspects both tubes to be sure that there is no bleeding and closes the incision.

Your surgeon may permit you to return home the same day, or may recommend hospital observation for a few days. Because the incision is small and does not involve an opening in your abdominal muscles, discomfort after surgery is usually minimal and recovery is rapid. Most women are able to resume normal activities (with the exception of intercourse) within one or two weeks. Avoid intercourse until four to six weeks after surgery so that your incision will have plenty of time to heal. The cosmetic results of vaginal surgery are a major advantage for some women because the scar inside the vagina doesn't show.

A disadvantage of vaginal surgery is that infection risk is higher than for the other tubal ligation techniques because of the large numbers of bacteria in the vagina. Some surgeons prescribe antibiotics after vaginal surgery to decrease the risk of infection.

Mini-Laparotomy

Mini-laparotomy is similar to abdominal tubal ligation except that the incision is only 1 to 1½ inches long instead of about 5 inches long, and the procedure is well suited for local anesthesia. General anesthesia may also be used.

Your abdomen, inner thighs, and vulva are thoroughly cleansed, hair over your pubic bone is shaved, and your abdomen is draped. If you are having local anesthetic, your surgeon injects the drug just under the skin in the area of the incision (see Illustration 11). Most women feel an initial stinging sensation with the local anesthetic; the stinging lasts only a few seconds because the anesthetic rapidly blocks

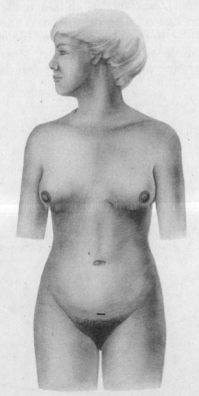

Illustration 11   Incision for mini-laparotomy tubal ligation.

the pain nerves to the skin. The anesthetic is then injected into the entire incision area and into the connective tissue and muscle layers under the skin. During this process you may be aware of a pressure sensation, but you should feel little or no pain. Once local or general anesthesia is completed, your surgeon inserts a speculum in your vagina, clamps your cervix to hold it steady, and inserts an elevator—blunt metal instrument—into your uterus. The elevator will be used later to move your uterus and tubes close to the incision opening to bring the tubes into your surgeon's view.

Next your surgeon makes the incision about an inch above your pubic bone and uses the elevator to bring your uterus up against the incision (see Illustration 12). Your surgeon moves your uterus gently from side to side and locates and grasps the first tube with a blunt clamp. The fallopian tube is brought out through the incision and ligated with the Pomeroy or fimbriectomy technique (see Illustration 1). The first tube is released back into the abdomen; then the second tube is located, grasped, and ligated. The surgeon next checks both tubes to be certain there is no bleeding and closes your incision with stitches.

Recovery after mini-laparotomy is rapid. Most women are able to return home a few hours after surgery and resume normal activities,

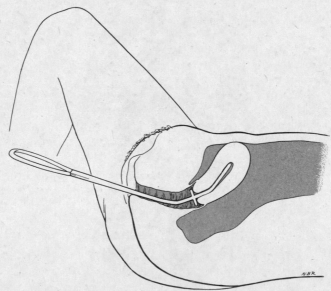

Illustration 12   A metal wand elevates the uterus so that the uterus and tubes will be closer to the skin and muscle layers.

including intercourse, within one or two days. The incision is very small, and discomfort following surgery is fairly mild.

Mini-laparotomy is suitable only for women who are slender (less than 20% above their ideal weight for height) and who have a normal, freely mobile uterus and tubes. It is a relatively new procedure in the United States, and few surgeons have had wide experience with it.

What to Expect After Surgery

Most women are ready to return home four to six hours after laparoscopic, or mini-laparotomy tubal ligation. You can go home once you are able to get up and walk without difficulty and are fully awake. Be sure to arrange for someone to accompany you home from the hospital.

> I had a little discomfort after the operation. My muscles were sore that evening, but I didn't even need to use the pain medication my doctor gave me.
>
> —Woman, 30

Don't try to drive for at least 24 hours: anesthesia medications slow down your reflexes for some time.

Some women are ready to go home the same day they have vaginal tubal ligation, but surgeons sometimes recommend a one- or two-day period of hospital observation. Plan on a two- or three-day hospital stay with postpartum sterilization, and a three- to five-day stay with abdominal tubal ligation.

For most women, recovery from tubal ligation surgery is rapid, and most discomfort is caused by the anesthesia. (Women who have abdominal tubal ligation may not feel at all well for the first three days.) It is common to feel weak, tired, and nauseated during the first 24 hours. If you had general anesthesia, you may notice general muscle soreness from the muscle relaxant drug, and a mild sore throat from the windpipe tube. Some women experience shoulder pain after laparoscopic tubal ligation. This pain is caused by irritation of your diaphragm from the carbon dioxide gas used to inflate your abdomen. As the gas is absorbed over the first 24 to 36 hours your pain will subside, as will the "bloated" feeling in your abdomen.

It is very unusual to have any major problems or delays in recovery. The common aches and pains are mild and are usually relieved by aspirin, rest, and good fluid intake.

> I was much drowsier and weaker than I anticipated. By evening I had some abdominal pain, but after I got up and went to the bathroom the pain went away. I was able to sleep easily. The next day I was able to go out for dinner. I've been fine ever since.
>
> —*Woman, 37*

A full bladder can add to your discomfort; so be sure to urinate if pain is bothersome.

It is not uncommon to have some vaginal bleeding or spotting for a few days after surgery. If you had an abortion along with your tubal ligation, bleeding may last several days, and you may have spotting or light bleeding for as long as two or three weeks.

As your incision heals you may notice thickening or a lump just under the skin. This lump is caused by the regrowth of connective tissue and will gradually diminish in a few months. The scars from the laparoscopic tubal ligation, postpartum tubal ligation, and mini-laparotomy are usually almost invisible after they are healed.

Danger Signs

Complications after tubal ligation are uncommon, but it is very important to watch for danger signs of infection, bleeding, or abnormal blood clotting (thrombophlebitis). Get in touch with your surgeon immediately if you develop any of these danger signs:

- Fever: oral temperature more than 100.4 degrees (Fahrenheit)
- Pain that is not relieved by aspirin, or that lasts longer than 12 hours
- Faintness, chest pain, cough, or shortness of breath
- Moderate or heavy bleeding from your incision or from your vagina

Problems and Risks

Many investigators have studied the risks of surgical tubal ligation, and there are many published reports about the incidence of serious complications and death. There is a substantial difference in the complication rates, depending on which study you read. Complication rates for vaginal tubal ligation, for example, vary from 3.3 to 13.3 per 100 patients (2). With such a large difference between studies, it is impossible to select one "true" complication rate, and it is difficult to make meaningful comparisons between different tubal ligation operations.

Laparoscopic tubal ligation is one of the most thoroughly studied of all surgical procedures. The American Association of Gynecologic Laparoscopists has compiled extensive records on more than 300,000 procedures performed in the United States in the past five years (3).

For rough comparison, average overall complication rates for each operation are listed in Table 2. These rates include both serious and minor problems. Most complications are not serious. Although about 5% of women who have laparoscopic tubal ligation experience some problem, only about 1% will have a problem serious enough to require overnight hospitalization for treatment. A similar ratio of minor to major complications applies to the other tubal ligation operations as well.

Problems serious enough to cause death are very rare. Death risk estimates vary, depending on the particular population studied. Deaths from vaginal, abdominal, and postpartum tubal ligation are in the range of 25 per 100,000 procedures (4), and deaths from laparoscopic tubal ligation are about 2.5 per 100,000 procedures (3).

Table 2 TUBAL LIGATION COMPLICATION RATES

Operation	Total Major and Minor Complications per 100 Women
Laparoscopic tubal ligation[a]	5.0
Postpartum tubal ligation[b]	7.8
Abdominal tubal ligation[b]	7.4
Vaginal tubal ligation[b]	11.5
Mini-laparotomy tubal ligation[c]	7.0

SOURCES:
[a]J Wortman, PT Piotrow: Laparoscopic sterilization II: What are the problems? *Population Reports,* Ser C, No 2, March 1973.
[b]LE Edwards, EY Hakanson: Changing status of tubal sterilization, *American Journal of Obstetrics and Gynecology* 115:347–353, 1973.
[c]J Wortman: Female sterilization by mini-laparotomy, *Population Reports,* Ser C, No 5, November 1974.

Table 3   RISK OF DEATH FROM LAPAROSCOPIC TUBAL LIGATION

Year	Number of Laparoscopic Tubal Ligation Procedures Reported	Total Number of Deaths	Death Rate per 100,000 Procedures
1971–1972	7,000	1	14.3
1973	—	—	13.0
1974	66,474	5	7.5
1975	201,565	5	2.5

SOURCES: Jordan Phillips, Jaroslav Hulka, Donald Keith, et al: Laparoscopic procedures: a national survey for 1975, *Journal of Reproductive Medicine* 18:219–225, 1977; and Jordan Phillips, Donald Keith, Jaroslav Hulka, et al: Gynecologic laparoscopy in 1975, *Journal of Reproductive Medicine* 16:105–117, 1976.

Many factors influence complication rates, such as the woman's general health status, specific medical problems, and anatomy. The skill of the surgeon is an important factor. Several studies have shown that the surgeon's experience with vaginal tubal ligation is directly related to the complication rate (5). Similarly, laparoscopic tubal ligation complication rates were found to be four times higher (14.7 per 1,000 versus 3.8 per 1,000) among women whose surgeons had performed fewer than 100 procedures than among women whose surgeons had had more extensive experience (6). The risk of death from laparoscopic tubal ligation has decreased as surgeons have become more experienced with the technique (see Table 3).

Remember to put the serious complications of tubal ligation in perspective with other birth control risks. Look at Illustration 1 in Chapter 5 to compare tubal ligation one-time death risks with the per year death risk with Pills, IUDs, and the other temporary methods of birth control.

ANESTHESIA COMPLICATIONS

As with any surgical procedure, anesthesia complications such as cardiac arrest or death are possible. This risk is increased if you have asthma or heart disease, are overweight, or if you smoke. Be completely honest in reporting your medical history to your surgeon. The overall risk of anesthesia problems is small (see Chapter 39). Serious anesthesia complications during laparoscopic tubal ligation occur in about 7 to 8 women for every 10,000 operations (7).

DAMAGE TO INTERNAL ORGANS

Injury to the intestines, bladder, cervix, uterus, uterine ligaments, or blood vessels can occur during any tubal ligation procedure. Injury might occur when laparoscopy instruments are first inserted into the abdomen, or during the cautery procedure, or at any time during abdominal, vaginal, or mini-laparotomy surgery. The carbon dioxide gas used to inflate the abdomen for laparoscopic tubal ligation can cause injury if gas is released directly into the skin or muscle tissue or if gas pressure in the abdomen interferes with breathing or stimulates changes in the heart rate. These problems are rare.

Further surgery may be required to correct internal bleeding. Your surgeon will make a regular 5-inch abdominal incision to stop bleeding or remove any damaged intestine. About 4 patients out of 1,000 require further surgery because of bleeding, infection, or bowel injury after laparoscopic tubal ligation (3).

INFECTION

The risk of infection in the uterus, tubes, or bladder is increased after any surgery that involves these organs. Infection usually causes pain, fever, and an unusual vaginal discharge. In most cases, infection remains localized in the incision area or in the uterus and tubes and can be effectively treated with antibiotic pills. If the infection spreads to the lining of the abdominal cavity (peritonitis) or if a large collection of pus develops (an abscess), then hospitalization may be necessary so that you can be treated with intravenous antibiotics. In some cases, further surgery may be required to drain an abscess or even to remove the uterus, tubes, and ovaries.

The higher infection risk following vaginal tubal ligation is the primary reason overall complication rates for this procedure are higher than overall rates for the other tubal ligation methods. Reported rates vary, but typically show that between 1 and 6 patients out of 100 develop infection after vaginal tubal ligation (2).

About 1 patient in 1,000 develops an infection that requires further treatment after laparoscopic tubal ligation (6).

GENERAL SURGICAL COMPLICATIONS

With any type of surgery, you may have an increased risk of thrombophlebitis (blood clot formation), embolism (clot lodging in the lungs, heart, or brain), and pneumonia during the immediate post-operative period. These problems are rare in young, healthy women.

LATER PROBLEMS INVOLVING TUBES AND OVARIES

Some researchers suggest that tubal ligation may cause later fluid swelling in the tube (hydrosalpinx). Unsuspected damage to the blood vessels that supply the ovary could occur during surgery, and might result in loss of ovarian hormone production, premature menopause, or menstrual irregularity. Ovary damage might also cause pelvic pain or pain during intercourse. Whether such problems could be a result of tubal ligation surgery or whether the relationship is coincidental is not known. These problems do occur in some women who have not had surgery. The largest study of long-term problems after laparoscopic tubal ligation did not show any increase in the frequency of these problems later on among women who had had laparoscopy tubal ligation as compared with women who had not had laparoscopy (8).

Contraindications

Women should not undergo tubal ligation in certain cases. Your clinician will want to be sure that you don't have any of the following conditions that may increase your risk of complications. These conditions are contraindications, problems that render a treatment or procedure inadvisable that might otherwise be recommended.

PREGNANCY

A woman who is pregnant or suspects that she may be pregnant and would plan to continue the pregnancy should not undergo any elective surgery. Many surgeons prefer to schedule tubal ligation during the first week or two after a normal menstrual period to be certain that you are not pregnant at the time of surgery.

ACTIVE PELVIC INFECTION

The presence of infection in your tubes, uterus, or cervix at the time of surgery will increase your risk of infection complications. Infection must be treated and cured before surgery.

ABNORMAL UTERINE OR TUBAL STRUCTURE

If your tubes and uterus are scarred from previous surgery or infection, or if they are abnormal in location or shape, it may not be possible for your surgeon to perform the laparoscopic, vaginal, postpartum, or mini-laparotomy procedure. A full 5-inch abdominal incision may be required.

SERIOUS MEDICAL PROBLEMS

Asthma, heart disease, and other serious medical problems may increase your surgery risks. Be sure that you have careful evaluation and treatment of these problems before surgery.

OBESITY

Tubal ligation may be more difficult, or impossible, if you are seriously overweight.

HERNIA

An unrepaired diaphragm (hiatal) hernia may be aggravated by gas inflation of the abdomen; before laparoscopic tubal ligation your surgeon may recommend further evaluation or an alternative tubal ligation operation.

Advantages of Tubal Ligation

No contraceptive method, including tubal ligation, is 100% effective. The effectiveness rate of tubal ligation is higher than that of any of the temporary methods of birth control, and tubal ligation is permanent. The overall risk of minor and major complications and death with tubal ligation is low compared to the risks with long-term use of birth control Pills or an IUD.

Tubal ligation surgery takes only 15 to 20 minutes. Most women are able to resume normal activity within 24 to 48 hours after laparoscopic tubal ligation, mini-laparotomy, or postpartum tubal ligation. Full recovery from vaginal or abdominal tubal ligation takes longer.

Tubal ligation does not change hormone levels except in rare cases when the ovary's blood supply is damaged; thus, there is no chemical reason to expect your sex drive to change. Menstrual periods should be unchanged.

REFERENCES

1. Leluyer A: Reversing sterilization with microsurgery—a report from London. *Contemporary OB/GYN* 9:109–114, 1977.
2. Wortman J, Piotrow P: Colpotomy: The vaginal approach. *Population Reports*, Ser C, No 3, June 1973. Washington, DC, The George Washington University Medical Center.
3. Phillips J, Hulka J, Keith D, et al: Laparoscopic procedures: A national survey for 1975. *Journal of Reproductive Medicine* 18:219–225, 1977.
4. Roe R, Laros R, Work A: Female sterilization: 1. Vaginal approach. *American Journal of Obstetrics and Gynecology* 112:1031–1036, 1972.
5. Akhter M: Vaginal versus abdominal tubal ligation. *American Journal of Obstetrics and Gynecology* 115:491–496, 1973.
6. Phillips J, Keith D, Hulka J, et al: Gynecologic laparoscopy in 1975. *Journal of Reproductive Medicine* 16:105–117, 1976.
7. Hulka J, Soderstrom R, Corson S, et al: Complications Committee of the American Association of Gynecologic Laparoscopists, First Annual Report. *Journal of Reproductive Medicine* 10:301–305, 1973.
8. McCann M, Kessel E: Late effects of female sterilization. *Advances in Planned Parenthood* 12(4):199–211, 1978.

16 | Vasectomy: The Sterilization Procedure for Men

Vasectomy is a simple 30-minute office procedure. Your clinician will want to be sure, however, that you don't have any medical problems that would increase your risk with surgery, and in rare cases you may not be able to have a vasectomy at all.

Certain conditions are considered contraindications to vasectomy. A contraindication is a medical condition that renders a course of treatment inadvisable or unsafe that might otherwise be recommended. In almost all cases the medical conditions can be cleared up, and you will be able to have a vasectomy safely.

Your clinician will take special precautions for your surgery if your **blood clotting is not normal** because of anticoagulant (blood-thinning) medication or a bleeding disease such as hemophilia. Similarly, if you have **high blood pressure** or **diabetes,** your clinician may prefer to perform your vasectomy in a hospital rather than an office or clinic.

Infection of the skin or reproductive tract should be treated and cured before your surgery. Infection can interfere with the healing process and increases your risk of postoperative complications.

Vasectomy may be more difficult to perform if you have a **hernia,** previous hernia repair, an **undescended testicle,** or other abnormalities. Your clinician will evaluate these problems before your surgery, and in some cases will recommend general anesthesia and surgery in a hospital setting.

257

Preparing for Surgery

Your clinician will review your medical history and perform a general physical exam, and may order a blood test for anemia or abnormal bleeding tendencies. She/he will want to be sure that you understand that the surgery is permanent and that you understand the possible complications of the procedure. You (and your spouse, if appropriate) may be asked to sign a consent form.

Your surgeon will probably recommend a thorough shower or bath just before your surgery appointment, and may ask you to trim or shave the hairs from your scrotum yourself. In other cases, your surgeon or an assistant will shave you. (You will not have to shave the pubic hair around your penis.)

Arrange for someone to accompany you and drive you home after your surgery. Bring snug jockey shorts or an athletic supporter with you. Make plans so that you can stay at home and be quiet for the first 48 hours after surgery. Some surgeons also recommend that you have an ice pack ready for use after your procedure.

The Vasectomy Procedure

First, your clinician will clean and shave your scrotum and drape the area with a sterile cloth. Some surgeons will give you a mild sedative or tranquilizer such as Valium.

Your surgeon first locates each vas deferens where it passes just under the skin along the middle of your scrotum above your testicles (see Illustration 1). Next, she/he injects a local anesthetic similar to Novocain to make a small area of your skin numb. The anesthetic takes effect within a few moments—much more quickly than dental anesthetic—and most men find that the anesthetic procedure is not particularly painful.

After the anesthetic has taken effect, your surgeon makes one or two ½-inch incisions through the skin and thin muscle layer of the scrotum. Each vas is identified and lifted through the incision with scissors or a small clamp. A ½- to 1-inch section of each vas is removed, and then the two cut ends are tied and/or cauterized to seal them shut. Some surgeons then fold each cut end back on itself or cover each end

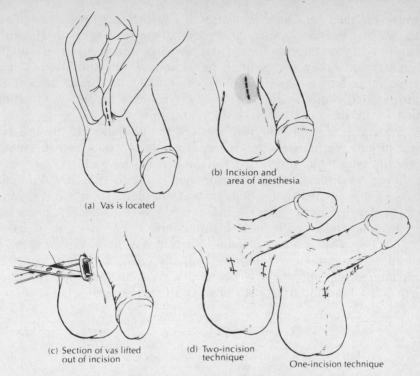

(a) Vas is located

(b) Incision and area of anesthesia

(c) Section of vas lifted out of incision

(d) Two-incision technique

One-incision technique

Illustration 1 Vasectomy is usually performed using local anesthesia in an office or clinic setting.

with connective tissue to insure that they will remain separated. Once both tubes are tied, your surgeon closes your incision(s) with one or two stitches. (Some surgeons use absorbable thread that does not need to be removed, and others use standard silk thread, in which case your stitches will need to be removed in about four days.)

Your surgeon places a small gauze bandage over the incision, which is held in place by an athletic supporter or scrotal suspensory. The entire vasectomy procedure takes 20 to 30 minutes.

What to Expect After Surgery

You will be advised to rest for the first 24 to 48 hours after surgery, because rest decreases the likelihood of bleeding (hematoma) and swelling in the scrotal area. An ice pack may also help prevent swelling and will relieve discomfort. You may have a dull ache or dragging sensation in your scrotum for the first few days, and wearing an athletic supporter or jockey shorts often helps relieve this sensation. Use a supporter as long as you are more comfortable with it than without it. Pain is usually mild and will probably be relieved by pain medication such as aspirin.

Most men feel able to return to work and normal activities the day after surgery, but most surgeons recommend that you avoid strenuous activities, straining, and lifting for the first week or so.

Keep your incision area dry for the first 24 to 48 hours. You can bathe or shower after that time. Tub soaks in plain warm water several times a day (beginning after 48 hours) may speed the healing process.

Recommendations regarding intercourse vary, but in most cases surgeons say that you can resume intercourse as soon as you think it would be comfortable. *Remember that the vasectomy does not provide immediate contraceptive protection.* You must rely upon another birth control method until your postoperative sperm counts show zero sperm.

Postoperative Sperm Counts

Live sperm are present in your semen for some time after vasectomy because mature sperm are stored in the part of your vas deferens near your prostate gland and seminal vesicles above the vasectomy site. Most men have to ejaculate 10 to 20 times to clear sperm completely from the reproductive tract. *The only way to be certain that your semen is free of sperm is to have a sperm count,* a microscopic examination of a semen sample. Arrange for your sperm counts when you see your surgeon for a postoperative checkup. You will simply take a fresh semen sample to your surgeon's office or to a lab, and it will be examined for sperm. Use another form of birth control until you have had two consecutive sperm counts that show no sperm at all.

Some clinicians recommend that you see your regular clinician for a sperm count once a year to detect possible regrowth of the vas. The likelihood of regrowth is very small, but a sperm count is a simple, cheap, and harmless test that could help you prevent unwanted pregnancy.

Problems and Risks

About 5 men out of 100 will experience some problem after vasectomy (1). Problems are almost always minor, and require simple treatment only. The five vasectomy-related deaths that have been reported all occurred in India and were due to tetanus infection.

One or 2 men out of 100 will develop a blood clot (hematoma) under the skin in the incision area. In most cases, the clot dissolves spontaneously without treatment. In some cases, the surgeon must reopen the incision to remove the clot and prevent further bleeding.

Infection can develop in the incision itself or in the vas, testes, or other parts of your scrotum, and 1 or 2 out of 100 men develop infection following vasectomy. In some cases, infection is severe enough to cause fever, pain, and swelling of the scrotum. Treatment with antibiotics usually results in prompt healing, but should a pus pocket (abscess) develop, surgery to drain the infection may be necessary.

Painful swelling of the sperm-carrying tubules on top of each testicle (epididymitis) or the testicles themselves as a consequence of sperm engorgement occurs in less than 1% of men. Swelling usually subsides within a week and is treated by rest, cold packs, and wearing a support.

Formation of a granuloma—a lump of inflammatory tissue—occurs in a small percentage of men. A granuloma can be caused by leakage of sperm from the cut end of the vas, but usually does not cause symptoms or require treatment. A granuloma can become infected and may increase your risk of tube regrowth and lead to vasectomy failure.

Danger Signs

Watch for signs of serious problems and call your clinician immediately if they occur. Possible danger signs are:

- Fever: oral temperature over 100.4 degrees (Fahrenheit)
- Bleeding: a small amount of bleeding and black and blue skin near the incision are normal. If bleeding is prolonged or heavy, or forms clots, call your clinician.

• Excessive pain or swelling: Pain and/or swelling that is not relieved by aspirin and an ice pack should be reported promptly. An enlarging, tender mass could be a symptom of infection or internal bleeding.

Long-range Effects of Vasectomy

There are as yet no known harmful long-range effects associated with vasectomy. Several reports appeared between 1968 and 1971 concerning men who developed antibodies to sperm following vasectomy, and there was active debate about the possibility that such antibodies could cause arthritis and other problems (2). (Sperm antibodies are special proteins that would attach to any sperm they encounter, just as polio antibodies coat polio viruses once you've been immunized.) Considerable research in recent years has confirmed the antibody finding. About one-half to two-thirds of men develop antibodies to sperm after vasectomy (1). (Similar antibodies are also found in some men who have not had vasectomy.) There is no evidence so far that sperm antibodies cause any medical problems (3).

In mid-1978 the media reported a study that seemed to show an increased risk of heart attack and stroke among vasectomized monkeys. Only five vasectomized monkeys and five nonvasectomized monkeys were studied, and all ten monkeys were fed high cholesterol diets. (High cholesterol diets are known to increase circulatory disease risks for animals.) It is impossible to tell from such limited studies whether there is an increased heart attack and stroke risk for vasectomized men (4).

Advantages of Vasectomy

Vasectomy is about 99.85% effective—1.5 failures for every 1,000 procedures. Vasectomy is more effective than any temporary method of birth control. The overall risk of problems or complications is lower for vasectomy than for tubal ligation surgery. The risk is very low compared to the risks associated with temporary birth control for women. Vasectomy is permanent. Surgery requires only 20 to 30 minutes, and recovery is rapid. Most men feel able to resume normal activities within 24 to 48 hours. Vasectomy does not cause any change in hormone levels or in the appearance or volume of semen. There is no medical reason to expect vasectomy to cause a change in sex drive.

REFERENCES

1. Wortman J: Vasectomy: What are the problems? *Population Reports*, Ser D, No 2, January 1976. Washington, DC, The George Washington University Medical Center.
2. Jones F: Vasectomy sequelae: Empirical studies. *Journal of Reproductive Medicine* 19:254–258, 1977.
3. Roberts H: Delayed thrombophlebitis and systemic complications after vasectomy; possible role of diabetogenic hyperinsulinism. *Journal of the American Geriatrics Society* 16(3):267–280, March 1968.
4. Alexander NJ, Clarkson TB: Vasectomy increases the severity of diet-induced atherosclerosis in Macaca fasacularis. *Science* 201:538–541, 1978.

17 | Abandoned Methods of Birth Control and Prospects for the Future

You probably won't believe this, but the first birth control I ever tried was the Dalkon Shield; I had it put in in 1973 when I was 18. When I read about the problems with it and that it wasn't being used any more, I decided to switch to Pills. My doctor took out the Dalkon Shield and gave me a prescription for Pills in 1974, but it *wasn't even a year later* when they took my brand of Pills off the market! I never did have any problems, but it makes you wonder.

—*Woman, 23*

Abandoned Methods of Birth Control

Other women did have problems. Since 1970 seven birth control products have been abandoned because of medical hazards: Dalkon Shield and Majzlin Spring IUDs; Provest, C-Quens, Norquen, Oracon, and Ortho-Novum SQ Pills.*

---

*A number of other IUD types were evaluated in clinical trials and announced in the press but never were marketed and are no longer available. Several early IUD types are no longer marketed, including the Birnberg Bow, the Margulies Spiral, and the Lem.

Dalkon Shield sales were stopped in 1975 because of serious and fatal infections, and Majzlin Spring sales were stopped because of extremely difficult and traumatic removal problems. Provest and C-Quens were withdrawn in 1970 because the specific progestin hormone they contained was shown to cause breast cancer in dogs. Three sequential oral contraceptives, Norquen, Oracon, and Ortho-Novum SQ, were withdrawn in 1976 because of evidence linking them to uterine cancer.

An eighth birth control product, Depo-Provera, should probably be included in this list as well, but it never was approved by the FDA in the first place. In 1978 the FDA announced that the manufacturer's application for approval (filed in 1967) of Depo-Provera as a contraceptive would be denied. The announcement came after more than ten years of deliberation, and after at least 20,000 women in this country had used Depo-Provera for birth control. (The FDA did approve experimental use of Depo-Provera for birth control in several large family planning clinics.)

THE DALKON SHIELD

The Dalkon Shield became very popular soon after it was introduced in 1970 because it was the first IUD small enough to be tolerated well by women who had never been pregnant (see Illustration 1). By 1974 about 2 million Dalkon Shields had been inserted, and a national controversy was raging because of 11 deaths among Dalkon Shield users who developed infections during pregnancy. Similar infections were known to occur with other IUDs as well, but the threat appeared to

Dalkon Shield
1 thick string:
Black with a knot

Illustration 1　The Dalkon Shield IUD was withdrawn from the market in 1975.

be greater with the Dalkon Shield. The Food and Drug Administration temporarily halted Dalkon Shield distribution to study the infection problem, and in 1975 the manufacturer announced that the company would no longer distribute the device.

The Dalkon Shield's string was unique, composed of many fine strands of plastic thread surrounded by a plastic sheath. All other types of IUDs have had a single, thicker (solid) strand of plastic for their strings. Some researchers believe that the Dalkon Shield string acted as a wick to transport bacteria into the uterus. As of mid-1980, there is still no definite agreement about whether the Dalkon Shield's string really did make it more dangerous than other IUDs. It is possible that the problems occurred because the Shield had a higher pregnancy rate than other IUDs, or that the same complications would have occurred with other IUDs if they had been as widely used among young women. In any case, the Dalkon Shield is gone, and the controversy had one major beneficial effect: Clinicians and women are now aware of the potential seriousness of IUD-related pregnancy and infection; early treatment has undoubtedly saved lives of IUD users who have become pregnant and developed infection since 1974.

As of September 1980 the Dalkon Shield manufacturer has recommended that any woman still wearing a shield should have it removed. In a letter to physicians, the A.H. Robbins Company cited recent studies linking long-term IUD use to uterine and pelvic infection caused by *Actinomyces* (1). Women who are still wearing Dalkon Shields have had them for at least 6 years and may therefore face the higher risk of *Actinomyces* that researchers fear faces any plain plastic IUD user after prolonged use.

DEPO-PROVERA

Depo-Provera is a long-acting progestin hormone given by injection that provides continuous birth control protection for at least three months. The progestin in Depo-Provera is called medroxyprogesterone acetate. (The identical progestin was in Provest, one of the withdrawn Pill brands.) This progestin and one other, chlormadinone acetate (C-Quens Pills used this progestin), caused breast cancer in beagle dogs. Other commonly used progestins, such as norethindrone, have not been shown to cause breast tumors. Provest and C-Quens Pills were withdrawn in 1970, and they are not mourned, because plenty of effective Pill brands are still available.

Depo-Provera is unique, however, and the FDA decision concerns some family planning specialists. Many family planning experts believe that Depo-Provera is an important birth control method, despite the safety questions raised by the breast cancer findings in dogs (2). Depo-Provera is widely used for birth control in other countries and by as many as 20,000 women annually in the United States; it is also used for treatment of certain other medical problems. Beagle dogs are known to be peculiarly susceptible to breast cancer, and the chemical effects of progestin in beagle dogs seem to be quite different than the chemical effects in other animals, including humans. Researchers do not yet know whether Depo-Provera causes breast cancer in women.

Obviously, the Depo controversy presents a dilemma if you have been using and would like to continue to use Depo-Provera. Many clinicians believe that Depo-Provera is probably safer than birth control Pills that contain estrogen as well as progestin. Using a diaphragm, foam, or condoms backed up by early abortion is probably safer still. If you do choose to use Depo-Provera, be alert for breast lumps, and be aware that if you become pregnant because the drug fails and your developing fetus is exposed to progestin in early pregnancy, birth defects may result. Fetal exposure is an important consideration if you would continue your pregnancy.

SEQUENTIAL PILLS

Sequential birth control Pills were developed in an attempt to mimic the hormone patterns of a natural cycle. Pills for the first two weeks of each pack of sequential Pills contained estrogen alone, the third week they contained progestin and estrogen together, and the fourth week was a no-Pill interval between packs. Manufacturers withdrew sequential Pills (Norquen, Oracon, and Ortho-Novum SQ) after reports of uterine cancer in relatively young users of sequential Pills.

What caused these sequential Pill users to develop uterine cancer is not known. Some researchers believe that estrogen was responsible. Sequential Pills contained twice the amount of estrogen in other oral contraceptives and exposed the uterus to estrogen *alone*, without the protective effect progestin may offer, for two weeks out of three. Estrogen used for menopause symptoms has also been linked to uterine cancer. It is also possible, however, that the pattern of hormone exposure may have played a role. Clearly it is not always safe to second-guess nature, and risks can only be reliably assessed with careful, long-term research.

Contraceptives for the Future

Family planning experts say that it is unlikely that hormone methods for men, new sophisticated hormones for women, or reversible sterilization valves and other devices will gain FDA approval in the near future. Glowing descriptions of research breakthroughs often appear in the news, but remember as you read that initial research reports are often the most promising; realistic effectiveness rates and complication rates are usually discovered somewhat later. We looked hard to find new methods of birth control for men that look promising for the near future, but could find only one, a condom/spermicide combination (see below).

Several birth control methods are used in other countries but are not available in the United States. Some of these methods may appear on our list of birth control options in the future.

THE CERVICAL CAP

The cervical cap is popular in England and mainland Europe but has not been widely used in the United States. The one manufacturer that did make plastic cervical caps in this country stopped, presumably because sales were low. The cervical cap, which looks like a small, deep diaphragm (see Illustration 2), fits snugly over the cervix and stays in place by suction. It is used with spermicidal cream or jelly and works very much like a diaphragm. Caps were developed at the same time as the diaphragm and were originally custom made of silver or gold. Plastic cervical caps were available in England and the United States 30 years ago but have now been replaced by latex models. The metal and plastic caps had the advantage that a woman could insert her cap and leave it in place for weeks at a time, and the one United States study of cervical caps found an effectiveness rate of 92% when caps were used in this manner (3).

Caps currently available are not intended for prolonged continuous use. They are made of latex, and as any diaphragm user can testify, vaginal odor can be a problem when a latex object remains in the

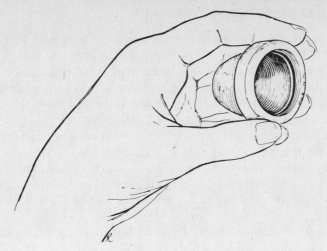

Illustration 2 The cervical cap.

vagina for longer than 24–36 hours. Instructions that accompany latex caps recommend use of spermicide and cite insertion and removal rules similar to those for a diaphragm.

There are as yet no published studies of latex cap effectiveness; clinicians experienced with the cap, however, feel that latex cap effectiveness is probably lower than diaphragm effectiveness (4).

No serious cap side effects have been reported, but safety concerns have been raised. If a cap adheres so snugly to the cervix that the normal downward flow of mucus is impeded, it is conceivable that the normal cervical defense against infection might be impaired. Also, prolonged pressure or friction on the cervix might possibly cause unforeseen problems.

Overall, the latex cervical cap method is quite similar to the diaphragm method. The cap may be an important option for a woman who has discomfort or pressure or recurrent urinary tract infections with a diaphragm, or who cannot be fitted with a diaphragm satisfactorily.

As of July 1980 the cervical cap was classified as an investigational device by the Food and Drug Administration (FDA). Caps imported into the United States are marked "For Investigational Use Only," and an approved research protocol is required for any physician or clinic dispensing caps. Cervical caps can be ordered (by your clinician) directly from the English distributor, Lamberts (Dalston) Limited, 200 and 202 Queensbridge Road, Dalston, London E8, England.

BETTER BARRIERS, NEW HORMONES

Improvements in existing barrier methods, and new barrier ideas are likely to be the "news" in contraception in the next few years. One promising product is a condom lubricated with or containing spermicide. The very high effectiveness you might expect with this winning combination was actually achieved in a pilot research project—couples using the product had a 99+% effectiveness rate (5).

The Collatex Sponge is based on a similar idea of combining spermicide with a barrier, in this case a diaphragm-shaped sponge. The Collatex Sponge has been tested in other countries where success rates and acceptance by users have varied. Work is also under way to perfect a custom-fitted cervical cap that would stay in place much as a contact lens does.

Research continues in the field of hormone contraception. It is possible that minor changes in hormone composition or scheduling may make new hormones safer than those presently available. In this category are Once-A-Month pills, "holiday" pills to take for a few days when you anticipate intercourse (currently used in China), pills that contain hormones in every other tablet (alternating with blank pills), and hormone implants under the skin or in a vaginal dispenser. Implants and dispensers would provide continuous hormone release but could be quickly removed if problems occurred.

Research also continues on contraceptives for men. Problems with side effects and long-term risks are similar to problems with women's hormone methods, however, and it does not seem likely that any men's methods will be approved in the near future. As one researcher said, "The more I study these sophisticated hormones and other drugs, the better I like condoms, diaphragms, and vaginal spermicides. It's back to Square One for birth control technology."

REFERENCES

1. Owen FB: Recommendation that the Dalkon Shield be removed from asymptomatic patients. Letter to physicians dated 25 September 1980, AH Robbins Company, 1407 Cummings Drive, Richmond, Virginia.
2. Maine D: Depo: the debate continues. *Family Planning Perspectives* 10:342–345, 1980.
3. Tietze C, Lehfeldt H, Liebmann H: The effectiveness of the cervical cap as a contraceptive method. *American Journal of Obstetrics and Gynecology* 66:904–908, 1953.
4. Lehfeldt, Hans: Personal communication, 1977.
5. Potts M, McDevitt J: A use effectiveness trial of spermicidally lubricated condoms. *Contraception* 2:701–710, 1975.

18 | Personal Decision Making About Unplanned Pregnancy

"Your pregnancy test was positive. You **are** pregnant."

These words can make you feel jubilant, or they can make you feel devastated; but if you are like many women you won't immediately be sure exactly how you do feel. Most women have a powerful emotional reaction to a new pregnancy, and if the pregnancy is unplanned, the emotional reaction can be extremely complex and ambivalent. Within a very short time, a pregnant woman must sort out her feelings and decide whether or not to continue the pregnancy.

Some women are able to decide in advance which option they would choose in the event of accidental pregnancy. Other women may not give the choices any serious thought before accidental pregnancy happens. Many women who choose abortion, for example, say that they never imagined themselves having an abortion before they had an unplanned pregnancy.

If you have an unplanned pregnancy, it makes sense to consider your options carefully before you make a decision. The choice is almost never easy when pregnancy is unplanned, but since you are the person who will live with the decision, be sure to make it for yourself. You may never feel absolutely great about what you decide, but you will feel better if you are sure that you made the best choice you could at the time. Hardly anyone gets through life without confronting some hard choices, and you may even learn valuable lessons about yourself and your life. The right decision about your unplanned pregnancy is the decison that you yourself believe is right.

271

Time Pressure and Your Options

If you think you may be pregnant, find out promptly whether you really are. Have a pregnancy test and a pelvic examination to determine how many weeks pregnant you are. (Pregnancy testing is discussed in Chapter 4.) *If you find that you have to wait more than a week for an appointment, look for another clinician who can see you sooner.* Be sure to tell the appointment clerk that you need a pregnancy test and exam to verify pregnancy so that she/he will recognize that it is important for you to be seen without delay.

Don't wait and worry trying to decide what to do about the pregnancy. *Find out first and then decide.* Only an examination will tell you how long a "thinking" time you have. No one is really prepared for an unplanned pregnancy, and faithful birth control users are often totally surprised and dismayed.

> We wanted two children. When Sheryl was 6 and Peter was 3, I got pregnant, even though I was a *very* careful diaphragm user. My husband and I discussed it some, but basically we decided very quickly that three children would be fine; no big problem.
>
> I got an IUD after Erica was born, and I got pregnant *again* when she was 2½. We didn't have enough room for another child; we were spending all kinds of money fixing up the house, and neither of us wanted a fourth child *at all*. I was 36 years old, and it was the first time I had ever considered abortion in my life. I thought I'd never get pregnant if I was careful about birth control, but I was wrong.
>
> —*Woman, 38*

Other women have taken chances—consciously or unconsciously —with unprotected intercourse.

> I didn't use anything. Dumb, right?
>
> —*Woman, 19*

There are only three options as you face an unplanned pregnancy:

- Continue the pregnancy and assume parenthood of the child
- Continue the pregnancy and relinquish the child for adoption
- Terminate the pregnancy

Most women find this a difficult choice and discover that they have ambivalent feelings. Even if you have thought about the issue and have already made up your mind, ambivalent feelings can be more intense and distressing than you imagined. It is common for a woman to change her mind repeatedly as she assesses the pros and cons of continuing a pregnancy; she decides that continuing her pregnancy is the best option one day, and the next day she goes over the same facts and arrives at the opposite conclusion.

Time pressure is one factor that makes this a difficult decision. Prenatal care should begin early in pregnancy, or abortion should be performed early when health risks are lowest. For most women this means no more than *one month* for decision making, since most women are already at least six weeks pregnant by the time they suspect and confirm pregnancy. Very long delays can lead to decision by default, for legal abortion is limited to the first 24 weeks of pregnancy.

Assessing Your Life Situation

Another important factor is the meaning of pregnancy to a woman's life situation. An accidental pregnancy can force a woman to reassess her basic feelings about a current relationship: If it is a good relationship, why does pregnancy seem undesirable? If this is not an optimal time or if financial considerations are unfavorable, when, if ever, will the situation be ideal for pregnancy? If the relationship is not good, what can be done to improve it? Should the relationship be continued, or should it be ended, in the hope of finding a better one?

Deciding about an unplanned pregnancy often raises questions about overall life goals: Is childbearing desirable at all? How does parenthood fit into education and career goals? What priorities should be assigned to each of these aspects of life?

The decision-making process about pregnancy is intimately related to major, life-changing issues that most people find difficult to assess, and that certainly deserve more than one month's thought. Decision making can be difficult and stressful, and women, couples, and families often find that counseling is beneficial. Many agencies (Planned Parenthood associations, local health departments, family services agencies) offer pregnancy counseling services. Counseling usually involves one or two sessions with a counselor especially trained in pregnancy decision making; often the counselor is a psychiatric social worker, psychologist, or trained medical worker. The goal of counseling is to help the individual(s) clarify feelings about pregnancy and come to a decision. *Counselors at reputable agencies do not attempt to influence your decision in any way.* Some of the guidelines that experienced counselors recommend are:

- Be sure of the facts. Don't rely on secondhand information about questions like welfare support or medical costs, and don't assume that your experience will be the same as that of a friend. Get the facts directly from an expert.
- Be sure that you are making your own decision. Even the wisest and most sympathetic physician, religious advisor, parent, or close friend may not weigh all the factors as you would. *You* are the one who will live with the decision.
- Try to consider all three options realistically and fully. It may be helpful to list each option and your own pros and cons for each, especially the practical and emotional impact for yourself, your family, and your close friends.

Teenagers and Pregnancy

Many pregnant teenagers wonder whether or not to involve their parents in the decision. They are reluctant to upset their parents, and they worry that their parents will disapprove or even reject them. Despite these natural fears, however, most young women find that their parents are supportive and helpful. Often the family has already sensed that something is wrong; an unspoken problem this significant may create tension and block communication, which both the young woman and her parents find very distressing. Parents often express relief when the truth is finally open for discussion. For many young women, the choice about an unplanned pregnancy is the very first major decision they have ever made. The support of concerned parents can mean a great deal, and may be especially important for finding good medical care and arranging the finances for care. Many teens, however, decide to handle the whole pregnancy experience on their own. Parental consent is not legally required for pregnancy care or for abortion.

It can be difficult for a teenager to find a good way to bring up "The Problem." Sometimes it is easier to approach one parent first. You might ask a parent to help you find a doctor for your nausea or fatigue to open the door just enough to begin a real discussion. Your clinician or pregnancy counselor may also be able to help you discuss the pregnancy with one or both parents if you wish.

Age and Genetic Factors

Fear of birth defects such as Down syndrome (mongolism) leads some women to consider abortion, and this is a real concern for older women. The risk of Down syndrome is low in the early reproductive years (about 1 in 1,300 births at age 22) but rises sharply after the mid-30s (about 1 in 110 births at age 40) (1).

It is possible to detect the chromosome defects that cause mongolism and certain other genetic disorders by analyzing a sample of fluid drawn from the amniotic sac surrounding the fetus in a procedure called amniocentesis. Amniocentesis is usually performed at about 15 weeks of pregnancy; 4 weeks are needed to evaluate the fluid samples.

Counseling to determine whether amniocentesis testing would be advisable in your case and to assess the statistical likelihood of genetic disorders is available through federally supported genetics centers. Your clinician can obtain a free directory of genetic centers from The National Foundation—March of Dimes, Box 2000, White Plains, New York 10602. Consider genetic counseling in any of these situations:

- You are 35 or older
- You have already had a child with a birth defect such as mongolism, Tay Sachs disease, spina bifida, or hydrocephalus. (Amniocentesis may be recommended for detecting these problems and other disorders such as hemophilia or hereditary anemia as well.)
- You or your partner has a birth defect or genetic disorder or a family history of birth defects or genetic disorders
- You have had three or more miscarriages, or your partner has fathered several pregnancies ending in miscarriage.

The ideal age for childbearing is 20 to 35, when risks of maternal and infant complications are lowest. Problems such as prematurity, birth defects, infant deaths, high blood pressure, hemorrhage after delivery, anemia, and maternal death are all related to the pregnant woman's age.

Table 1   MATERNAL DEATH RATES IN
THE UNITED STATES BY AGE
OF THE MOTHER

Age	Rate per 100,000 Live Births (U.S. 1972–1974)
15–19	11.1
20–24	10.0
25–29	12.5
30–34	24.9
35–39	44.0
40–44	71.4

SOURCE: C Tietze: New estimates of mortality associated with fertility control, *Family Planning Perspectives* 9:74–76, 1977.

Table 1 shows that pregnancy-related death risks are higher both for the very young and for older mothers. There is, however, no clear-cut upper or lower age limit. A 36-year-old pregnant woman faces a risk of death (44 per 100,000 live births) that is comparable to the risk for all pregnant women 20 years ago (see Table 2).

Table 2   MATERNAL DEATH RATES IN THE
UNITED STATES, 1940 TO 1975

Year	Rate per 100,000 Live Births
1975	12.8
1970	21.5
1960	37.0
1950	83.0
1940ᵃ	376.0

SOURCES: *Monthly Vital Statistics Report*, Provisional Statistics, Annual Summary for the United States, 1976: Births, Deaths, Marriages, and Divorces. US Department of Health, Education and Welfare, Public Health Resources Administration, National Center for Health Statistics, Rockville, MD. DHEW Publication No. (PHS) 78-1120, vol 25, No 13, December 12, 1977.
ᵃD. Nortman: Parental age as a factor in pregnancy outcome and child development, *Reports on Population-Family Planning*, No 16, August 1974.

For many women 35 or older considering motherhood, the national risk statistics may not really be a valid way to assess personal risks. Variables other than age influence these statistics heavily. Many of the women over 35 in the statistics in Table 1 were also economically disadvantaged, perhaps facing a fourth or fifth pregnancy, and did not receive adequate medical care. A woman who is considering a first pregnancy at 35, and who has some of the advantages that later parenthood can confer—enough money, access to good medical care, and good knowledge about her body and health needs—almost certainly has a lower death risk than Table 1 would suggest.

More and more couples are delaying parenthood. They, and their clinicians, can certainly face a late pregnancy without overwhelming fear. When good prenatal care is begun early, ideally even before conception (see Chapter 4 for recommendations on optimal pregnancy), medical risks can often be minimized. Similarly, when genetic counseling and amniocentesis are utilized, a woman 35 to 45 can reduce her risk of bearing a child with serious birth defects to about the same risk level she would have faced when she was 25 years old (2).

If your decision is to continue the pregnancy, begin immediately with routine prenatal care. Resources for prenatal services and other information might include your clinician, Planned Parenthood, and your health department. If your decision is to terminate the pregnancy, your immediate task is to learn about various abortion options and select an appropriate source for your own care.

REFERENCE

1. Hook EB, Lindsjo A: Down syndrome in live births by single year maternal age interval in a Swedish study: comparison with results from a New York Study. *American Journal of Genetics* 30:19–27, 1978.
2. Goldberg MF, Edmonds LD, Oakley GP: Reducing birth defect risk in advanced maternal age. *Journal of the American Medical Association* 242:2292–2294, 1979.

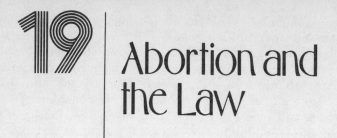

19 | Abortion and the Law

On January 22, 1973, the United States Supreme Court announced two decisions—*Roe v. Wade* and *Doe v. Bolton*—that made abortion legal throughout the country. These decisions extended the time limit for abortion through approximately 24 weeks and eliminated requirements for "justifying" abortion on medical or psychiatric grounds. The Supreme Court stated in part (1):

> For the stage prior to approximately the end of the first trimester, the abortion decision and its effectuation must be left to the medical judgment of the pregnant woman's attending physician.

During the first 12 weeks of pregnancy, state and federal law may not impose any restriction, qualification, or prerequisites on how, when, or where an abortion is performed.

> For the stage subsequent to approximately the end of the first trimester, the state, in promoting its interest in the health of the mother, may, if it chooses, regulate the abortion procedure in ways that are reasonably related to maternal health.

During the second 12 weeks of pregnancy, the states may impose requirements intended to protect a woman's health. For example, a state may, if it chooses, require that all second trimester abortions be performed in a licensed hospital.

*For the stage subsequent to viability a state, in promoting
its interest in the potentiality of human life, may, if it chooses,
regulate, and even proscribe, abortion except where it is necessary, in appropriate medical judgment, for the preservation
of the life or health of the mother.*

Once pregnancy has reached the third trimester (after 24 to 26
weeks), the possibility that the fetus could survive outside the uterus
increases with each subsequent week. During this portion of pregnancy, a state may prohibit abortion if it chooses.

New federal regulations have **prohibited the expenditure of federal
funds** for abortion except in the case of rape or incest or when pregnancy endangers a woman's life. **These regulations do not make abortion illegal.** Unless the Supreme Court reverses its 1973 position or an
amendment to the Constitution is passed, abortion will remain legal
throughout the United States.

In most cases, a woman seeking abortion will be required to sign an
informed consent document beforehand. The clinician or hospital may
request that her spouse or parent also sign the consent form and may
make this a prerequisite for care, even though court decisions have
upheld a woman's legal right to abortion without a spouse's or parent's
consent. If this request is unacceptable to the pregnant woman, her
alternative is to choose another clinician and/or hospital willing to
perform the abortion without spouse or parent consent.

The Medical Impact of Legal
and Illegal Abortion

The decision between continuing a pregnancy and electing abortion is
often portrayed as a mere matter of convenience, but it is seldom such a
simple choice. In terms of health consequences, it is not a choice of
mere convenience. For most people, the primary factors that influence a
decision about unplanned pregnancy are personal, but it is reasonable
at least to be aware of the medical impact of each option as well. Your
decision involves a choice between substantially different health risks.
Neither full-term pregnancy nor legal abortion is very dangerous. However, **full-term pregnancy incurs a risk of death that is 25 times**

higher than the death risk of abortion during the first eight weeks of pregnancy (2). Full-term pregnancy is more likely than abortion to result in major surgery; approximately 1 in 10 full-term deliveries requires cesarean section surgery. The likelihood that abortion complications will necessitate major surgery is less than 1 in 500 (3).

Abortion has always been with us. In many diverse cultures worldwide, women seek—and find—illegal abortions when no legal services exist. About 70% of the legal abortions performed in New York City replaced what would have been illegal procedures, according to one study on the first two years of legal abortion in that city (4). Investigators have documented the same pattern in other countries following legalization of abortion.

From a worldwide perspective, the current pattern of abortion in the United States is fairly typical; about 20 abortions per 1,000 women aged 15 to 44. Factors such as contraceptive availability and general fertility probably account for the differences from country to country (see Table 1). Most people in the world do have access to legal abortion at least in some circumstances (see Table 2).

Before 1973, complications of *illegal* abortions were leading causes of illness and death for pregnant women in the United States. Since legalization of abortion, there has been a significant decline in the number of hospital admissions for complications of abortion (5). Total

Table 1   ABORTION IN SELECTED COUNTRIES, 1976

Country	Number of Abortions per Year per 1,000 15- to 44-Year-Old Women
Czechoslovakia	26.7
Denmark	25.8
England and Wales (1974)[a]	11.7
Hungary	41.5
Japan	24.9
Sweden	20.1
U.S.A.	20.5

SOURCE: Center for Disease Control: *Abortion Surveillance, 1976.* U.S. Department of Health, Education and Welfare. Public Health Service. HEW Publication No (CDC) 78-8205, 1978.

[a]C Tietze, J Bongaarts: The demographic effect of induced abortion, *Obstetrical and Gynecological Survey* 31(10):699–709, 1976.

Table 2 ACCESS TO LEGAL ABORTION: ESTIMATED PERCENTAGE
OF WORLD POPULATION, 1975

Legal Status of Abortion	% of World Population
Legal on Request	36
Legal for social reasons	24
Legal for medical reasons	29
Illegal	8

SOURCE: M Potts, P Diggory, J Peel: *Abortion*. Cambridge University Press, Cambridge, England, 1977, p. 411.

Table 3 DEATHS FROM ILLEGAL AND LEGAL
ABORTION IN THE UNITED STATES

Year	Total Abortion Deaths	Annual Rate per 100,000 Women Aged 15 to 44 Years
1933–1935	2,740	9.0
1959–1961	299	0.8
1972–1974	64	0.14

SOURCE: C Tietze, J Bongaarts: The demographic effect of induced abortion, *Obstetrical and Gynecological Survey* 31(10):699–709, 1976.

maternal deaths due to abortion also decrease when abortion is legalized. *The current annual United States death rate from abortion is about one-fifth what it was when abortion was illegal* (see Table 3).

Overall data for the United States so far indicate that since legalization of abortion there has been a significant decrease in prematurity rates and *infant mortality* rates, as well as *maternal mortality* rates (3). It is not possible to prove what has caused the improvements in infant mortality. It may be that "high-risk" pregnancies are now being aborted more often than "low-risk" pregnancies are; or it may be that a completely unrelated factor such as better nutrition is entirely responsible for the decline in mortality rates.

Abortion is probably a necessary part of family planning for any population group that seeks a stable size. Population stability is achieved at a fertility rate of about 2,100 pregnancies per 1,000 women.

Even if couples with two children use extremely good methods of birth control (98% effectiveness level, such as Pills, diaphragms, or an IUD used exactly according to instructions all the time) for all the years of their remaining fertility, at least 500 couples out of 1,000 (50%) will experience one or more additional unwanted pregnancies because of birth control failure. Average couples have about 25 more years of fertility after the second child is born. Two percent annual failure risk times 25 years equals a 50% risk of method failure. *Even if a population group is able to use birth control at a 98% level of effectiveness, the fertility rate will probably exceed the 2,100 no-growth rate because of birth control failure alone.* Sterilization and/or abortion may be the only recourse for some couples.

REFERENCES

1. Supreme Court of the United States, Number 70-18. *June Roe*, et al, *Appellants versus Henry Wade.* January 22, 1973. On appeal from the United States District Court for the Northern District of Texas.
2. Cates W, Tietze C: Standardized mortality rates associated with legal abortion: United States, 1972–1975. *Family Planning Perspectives* 10:109–112, 1978.
3. Center for Disease Control: *Abortion Surveillance, 1974.* US Department of Health, Education and Welfare, Public Health Service, HEW Publication No (CDC) 76-8276, 1974.
4. Tietze C: Two years experience with a liberal abortion law: Its impact on fertility trends in New York City. *Family Planning Perspectives* 5:36–41, 1973.
5. Stewart G, Hance F: Legal abortion: Influences upon mortality, morbidity, and population growth. *Advances in Planned Parenthood* 9(2):1–7, 1976.

20 | Abortion Procedures

Be careful that you don't rush yourself into the decision to have an abortion. Take time to consider all three choices for unplanned pregnancy: abortion; continuing the pregnancy and raising the child; continuing the pregnancy and relinquishing the child for adoption. The right decision about your unplanned pregnancy is the decision that you believe is right.

Once you decide to have an abortion, however, **make your arrangements as quickly as you can.** Each week of delay significantly increases your risk of abortion-related medical complications. Perhaps the most important factor to check as you choose a doctor or clinic to perform your abortion is the arrangement for around-the-clock emergency care. All reputable physicians who perform abortions have 24-hour phone numbers for you to call, and they have immediate access to a hospital emergency room in case you develop a problem of any kind after your abortion. Infection, bleeding, and other abortion complications can almost always be treated successfully if treatment begins promptly. Don't hesitate to call your clinician if you have a problem after your abortion, even in the middle of the night.

Think carefully about why you had an unplanned pregnancy, and try to determine if you can do anything different in the future to help prevent another unplanned pregnancy. You may need a better birth control method, or you may need to pay closer attention to your fertility cycle, for example.

Hundreds of thousands of American women (including doctors)

283

have abortions each year. You are certainly not alone if you risked intercourse without birth control or if your birth control method let you down; no one goes through life without taking chances, and birth control technology is far from perfect. There is no reason to think of yourself as anything but a normal person in a less than perfect world.

If you don't already have a gynecologist or family physician who you can rely on for abortion, selecting a physician or clinic for your abortion may take a little research on your part. Remember that when you choose a specific physician or clinic you may be limiting medical choices about anesthesia and about which particular procedure will be used. Many abortion facilities offer only a limited range of services.

Local health departments and Planned Parenthood associations often offer information and referral services, and the Planned Parenthood national organization has formulated detailed guidelines for the evaluation of abortion services. In order to be included on a local Planned Parenthood referral list, each abortion facility must be reviewed by a team from Planned Parenthood to be sure that it meets acceptable standards of care. If you get the name of an abortion clinic from an agency other than Planned Parenthood, it may be wise to inquire whether the clinic has been reviewed, by whom, and whether there are any other clinics you might consider.

Watch carefully for biased counseling: Is the counselor familiar with several different alternatives? Do you feel pressured to choose one particular clinic, doctor, or procedure? Does the counselor seem to be urging you to continue the pregnancy? to terminate the pregnancy?

The choices are yours, and no one has the right to influence you against your will. If you feel pressured, find another source for counseling and information even if it means long distance phone calls or a trip out of town. You might call the nearest Planned Parenthood regional office listed below for advice on reliable services in your area. In any case, do not be discouraged, and do not delay once you have decided to have an abortion. ***The sooner your procedure is done, the safer it is.***

PLANNED PARENTHOOD REGIONAL OFFICES

785 Market Street, Room 1017
San Francisco, California 94103 (415/777-1217)

3030 Peachtree Road, NW, Room 303
Atlanta, Georgia 30305 (404/262-1128)

234 State Street, Suite 802
Detroit, Michigan 48226 (313/962-4390)

406 West 34th Street, Room 725
Kansas City, Missouri 64111 (816/531-2243)

810 Seventh Avenue
New York, New York 10019 (212/541-7800)

Medical Towers Building
255 South 17th Street, Suite 2005
Philadelphia, Pennsylvania 19103 (215/732-4744)

302 West 15th Street
Lavaca Square, Suite 201
Austin, Texas 78701 (512/472-4075)

Factors to Consider as You Choose an Abortion Clinic or Physician

- Do you prefer general anesthesia (to be asleep during the procedure), or do you prefer local anesthesia?
- Do you prefer individualized care with a physician who can perform the abortion in an office or hospital, or do you prefer a clinic setting where most of the other women are also undergoing abortion?
- Is there good provision for emergency care and followup?
- Do you feel assured about the quality of service?
- Do you have a strong preference regarding the choice between D&E, saline, prostaglandin, and urea methods for second trimester abortion? (These procedures are described later in this chapter.)
- Do the cost and convenience seem fair and satisfactory?

ANESTHESIA

General anesthesia is not used in reputable clinics or physicians' offices: it requires a hospital or surgical center setting. But an office or clinic setting may be preferable for local anesthesia, because you may be better able to relax and therefore may experience less discomfort. Your feelings about anesthesia may dictate your selection among abortion options.

General and local anesthesia each have pros and cons, and both techniques carry low risks for young, healthy women. A small number of women have died as a result of abortion anesthesia complications with both local anesthesia (1) and general anesthesia (2), however. Many more abortion procedures are performed under local anesthesia than under general anesthesia, and most clinicians believe that local anesthesia is probably safer; but research evidence has not uniformly shown that one anesthesia technique is safer than the other. The primary advantage of general anesthesia is the elimination of all discomfort.

Local anesthesia (you are awake, your cervix and uterus are partially numb) significantly reduces the overall cost of abortion because you do not use hospital facilities, have an anesthesiologist, or undergo elaborate preoperative tests; and you have a much briefer recovery period. After general anesthesia abortion, you may not feel like yourself for a full day or even longer. After local anesthesia abortion, you will require only two or three hours for recovery.

SPECIAL CLINICS

Many cities have specialized abortion clinics. In most areas, such clinics offer high-quality abortion care at a significantly lower cost than a hospital. The relatively anonymous atmosphere in a large clinic appeals to some women. Clinics are usually staffed by helpful and sympathetic counselors who assist you through the preoperative and postoperative procedures and often remain with you during the abortion procedure itself. The physician plays a relatively less prominent role; you will probably be with her/him for only about ten minutes if you have an early vacuum abortion.

Abortion clinic physicians are likely to have more than average experience with the procedure, and that can be a significant advantage. Because of the specialized nature of most abortion clinics, your care is usually limited to the abortion procedure itself and a followup examination two weeks later. You will need another source for your routine care or problems other than unwanted pregnancy.

PRIVATE PHYSICIANS

Most private gynecologists and some family physicians perform in-hospital abortion procedures. Some physicians perform early vacuum abortion in their offices. This service is commonly available in some areas and quite uncommon in other parts of the country. The cost of abortion in an office setting is about the same as or even less than abortion clinic costs. You have the advantages of individualized care and continuity for other kinds of health needs in the future.

SECOND TRIMESTER PROCEDURES

The choice among the various second trimester procedures is complex. (Descriptions of each technique follow later in this chapter.) If you are between 13 and 16 weeks pregnant, it makes sense to try to find a physician or clinic able to use the Dilation and Evacuation (D&E) method. The national Center for Disease Control has carefully studied complications of D&E and complications of saline and prostaglandin procedures and has shown that D&E performed between 13 and 16 weeks is definitely safer than saline or prostaglandin procedures (2). The overall risk of death with D&E is about half as high as the risk with saline or prostaglandins. The D&E procedure is also much shorter, can often be performed without an overnight hospital stay, does not involve labor contractions, is cheaper, and avoids the two- or three-week delay that you would face at 13 weeks waiting for a saline or prostaglandin procedure (3). If you are between 16 and 24 weeks pregnant, the D&E procedure may still be your safest alternative, but the choice is somewhat less clear-cut.

Your physician's skill and experience with a particular procedure or drug are important factors in overall safety. A wise approach might be to find a physician experienced with second trimester abortion with whom you feel comfortable, and then rely upon her or his recommendation for which procedure would be best for you.

D&E is a procedure that is not available in all areas, and it may not be easy for you to arrange. You may even have to travel to another area. If you do go to another city for your abortion procedure, be sure to make good arrangements for emergency and followup care in your home town.

FOLLOWUP CARE FOR PROBLEMS

It is crucial that the clinic or physician you choose be able to provide immediate access to a hospital, because true medical emergencies do occur with abortion in rare cases. Geographical proximity to a hospital is important, but it is even more important that the physician performing your abortion have staff privileges at the hospital.

Most important of all is the ability of your clinic or doctor to handle any emergency problems after your abortion. The most common serious complications are likely to develop in the first three or four days after your abortion. Competent care 24 hours a day for complications is absolutely essential. *Make sure you know a 24-hour emergency phone number for problems.*

ASSESSING QUALITY OF CARE

Assessing the quality of care you can expect from a physician or clinic is difficult. It is perfectly all right to ask what kind of training and specialty certification the physician has and how much experience she/he has had with your particular procedure. It may be helpful to call a physician you trust or perhaps another health agency to inquire about the reputation of the clinic or physician you are considering. You can call your local hospital to verify that the physician is a member in good standing of the hospital staff.

It is also important to use your own judgment. Your assessment, based on what you see and hear, is likely to be sound. Does the staff seem sympathetic and competent? Does the facility appear clean and well equipped? If not, you have the absolute right, in fact a responsibility, to decline treatment. If you don't want to explain your decision, you can simply leave.

The range of costs for abortion is wide. An early vacuum abortion in a physician's office or clinic may cost as little as $120 to $125 (a mid-1978 national average is approximately $160 to $180). D&E procedures are usually somewhat more expensive. An early vacuum procedure or D&E performed in a hospital with general anesthesia might be $400 to $600. Saline or prostaglandin procedures require at least 24 to 36 hours of hospitalization and often cost $600 to $900 or more.

Preparing for Abortion

Your clinician will review your general medical history before your abortion. Serious medical problems such as heart disease, bleeding or clotting disorders, or epilepsy may influence the choice of setting for your abortion, and you may need special care during and after surgery. For example, a woman who has had rheumatic heart disease may be treated with penicillin before her abortion to reduce the risk of infection that could spread to her damaged heart valves.

Your clinician will want to know about any adverse drug reactions you may have had, especially if they involved general anesthesia, local anesthetic drugs such as dental Novocain, or disinfectants such as iodine.

Your clinician will carefully review your menstrual history. It is important for you to know precisely when your last normal period started, because *pregnancy length is calculated in weeks, starting from the first day of your last normal period.* Your clinician relies on your menstrual period dates and on the size of your uterus to determine how long you have been pregnant. Since pregnancy length is the key factor in choosing the best and safest abortion method, it is essential for you to be as accurate and honest as possible about your menstrual dates.

You will need a urine pregnancy test, a blood count for anemia, and a determination of Rh type. Additional tests, such as urinalysis or chest x-ray, may be recommended if you are having general anesthesia.

Your clinician will want to be sure that you understand the abortion procedure and its possible complications and that you feel certain about your decision to have an abortion. You will probably be asked to sign an informed consent document.

You will be given specific instructions about how to prepare for your abortion. Be sure that you understand them, and be sure to arrive on time. Many clinics and hospitals have strict rules requiring that your appointment be canceled if you do not check in on time. Plan to have someone accompany you home after your abortion.

If you will be having general anesthesia, an empty stomach is essential to decrease the likelihood of vomiting and inhaling fluid into your lungs. Don't eat or drink *anything* for at least eight hours before your abortion. If you are having local anesthesia, your clinic or physician will recommend either a light breakfast or no breakfast at all.

Early Vacuum Abortion: 4 to 12 Weeks of Pregnancy

I ran out of Pills. Planned Parenthood closed at four, and I didn't get off work till five. I couldn't get a ride, and I would have been too late on the bus. Anyway, they said I had to have an exam before I could get more Pills.

So here I am. My sister came here, and she told me about it. I only got scared when I heard them turn on the machine in the next room. It wasn't as bad as I thought, though.

—Abortion clinic patient, 18

Early vacuum abortions account for 80% of all the abortion procedures now done in the United States. The vacuum procedure is *the* accepted technique for terminating pregnancy from 4 to 12 weeks in length. Vacuum abortions are usually done using local paracervical block anesthesia, but general anesthesia can also be used. (In the case of general anesthesia, the procedure is identical except that anesthetic drugs are given intravenously to induce sleep, followed by gases during the procedure to maintain anesthesia. Recovery time is somewhat longer, because you must rest until the anesthetic effect wears off.)

The first step is pelvic examination to confirm the size and position of your uterus (see Chapter 21 for a complete description of the pelvic exam). Next, your physician inserts a speculum in your vagina so that she/he can see your cervix, and then cleans your cervix and vagina with iodine solution or another disinfectant. Then she/he steadies your cervix with a clamp (tenaculum) and injects local anesthetic into your cervix and into the uterine ligaments (see Illustration 1); the anesthetic begins to take effect within seconds. Since the cervix has few nerve receptors sensitive to pinprick, you may not even be aware of getting a shot; but you may have some cramping during the injection. Local anesthesia can cause a sensation of numbness in your mouth or fingertips, or dizziness and ringing in your ears. The anesthetic is rapidly absorbed by the many blood vessels near the cervix and small amounts quickly travel through your circulation throughout your body. These effects subside within two or three minutes.

After the anesthesia takes effect, your physician gently pulls on the tenaculum to straighten out your cervical canal and widens (dilates) your canal with a series of metal dilating rods (see Illustration 2) until the opening is big enough for the appropriate vacuum tube (see Illustration 3); the vacuum tube size depends upon the length of your pregnancy.

Once the vacuum tube is in place in your uterus, the tube is connected to an electric vacuum pump machine (see Illustration 4). The vacuum pump motor often has a loud rumble; so don't be startled when it is turned on. (Some physicians use a large plastic syringe to create the vacuum, rather than an electric pump, for procedures before about nine weeks.)

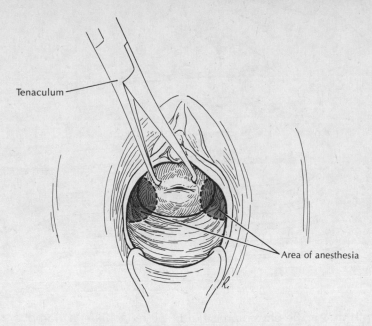

Tenaculum

Area of anesthesia

Illustration 1   The tenaculum steadies the cervix during the abortion procedure. Local anesthesia numbs the cervix.

The vacuum procedure usually takes three to five minutes. The vacuum tube is rotated inside your uterus and moved back and forth to remove the pregnancy sac and part of the thick uterine lining that is formed during pregnancy (see Illustration 5). The total amount of tissue and blood removed depends on the length of pregnancy. If you are five to six weeks pregnant, there may be only 1 or 2 ounces (15–20 grams); at 11 to 12 weeks, there may be as much as 12 to 16 ounces (100–150 grams).

Many physicians use a sharp, spoon-shaped instrument (curet, see Illustration 6) to explore your uterine cavity and make certain that all the tissue has been removed.

When your physician is sure that your uterus is empty, she/he removes the tenaculum and speculum.

The vacuum part itself wasn't really painful, but it felt very peculiar: a sensation deep inside my abdomen. I did have strong cramps during the last part, maybe 30 seconds or a minute before the machine was turned off. After that the cramps just gradually went away, and I was okay.

—Abortion clinic patient, 20

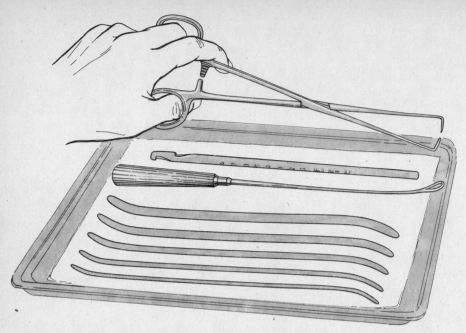

Illustration 2 The physician is holding a tenaculum, a clamp to steady the cervix. The tray holds (from the bottom) five graduated dilating rods, a curet, and a vacuum tube.

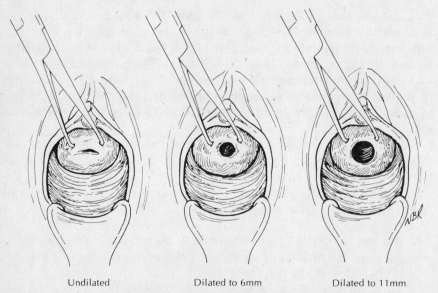

Undilated   Dilated to 6mm   Dilated to 11mm

Illustration 3 The physician uses metal dilating rods to widen the cervical canal.

Illustration 4   A commonly used vacuum machine for abortion. (Photograph by Rita R. Harris, Medical Photographer.)

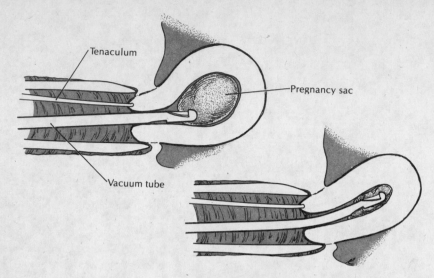

Illustration 5 The vacuum tube draws the pregnancy sac out of the uterus. Near the end of the abortion procedure, the uterus begins to contract.

Illustration 6 The physician may explore the uterus with a curet once the vacuuming procedure is completed.

It is natural to be concerned about how much pain you should expect during a vacuum abortion, especially if you will be having local anesthesia. You may have a reassuring friend who tells you that she had no real pain at all. Some women do have only the most minimal discomfort. *Most women say that vacuum abortion hurts, but that the pain is tolerable.*

> During the dilating and also during the vacuum part, I had cramps that were really bad, like my absolutely worst menstrual cramps, but they didn't last very long.
>
> —*Abortion clinic patient, 23*

As the vacuuming begins, most women notice a tugging sensation in the lower abdomen. Toward the end of the procedure when most of the tissue has been removed, the uterus itself contracts. You will probably find that this causes a strong cramping sensation that lasts for 2 to 20 minutes or so after your procedure is completed.

Most women are able to get up soon after abortion, and in many clinics patients routinely walk from the procedure room to a recovery lounge. Your physician will probably ask you to remain at the office or clinic for about an hour after the procedure. During the first 20 or 30 minutes it is common to experience cramps and sometimes nausea, but you will probably feel ready to leave after your hour of observation.

Menstrual Extraction

Terms such as "menstrual induction," "menstrual extraction," and "aspiration without dilation" have been used in the past to refer to vacuum procedures performed very early in pregnancy before a routine urine pregnancy test could confirm pregnancy. Since it is now possible to confirm pregnancy as early as one week after conception, these terms are no longer meaningful. (Read more about early pregnancy tests in Chapter 4). In other words, a woman who requests "menstrual induction" because her period is a few days late can now find out for certain whether or not she is pregnant. If the pregnancy test is positive, her vacuum procedure should properly be called an abortion. *If her pregnancy test is negative, she is not pregnant, and there is no justification for performing a procedure at all.*

If a vacuum procedure is performed before the sixth week of pregnancy, there is a higher risk of retained fetal and placental tissue and failure to terminate the pregnancy compared to abortions performed after six weeks (4). This is especially a problem if your physician does not know for certain whether you are pregnant. Be certain you have a positive pregnancy test before you have any abortion procedure.

The technique for menstrual induction or extraction is identical to that for early vacuum abortion.

Dilation and Evacuation Abortion (D&E): 13 to 24 Weeks of Pregnancy

The dilation and evacuation (D&E) procedure is similar to the vacuum procedure except that general anesthesia is usually recommended and cervical dilation is significantly greater (12 to 14 mm or more). About 4% of all abortions are done with the D&E procedure. It is most often used for abortion between 13 and 16 weeks of pregnancy. Some clinicians also use D&E for more advanced pregnancies. Surgical instruments are necessary, in addition to the vacuum tube, in order to remove the large volume of fetal and placental tissue. The procedure takes about 20 to 30 minutes. Laminaria rods (see following section) are often used 6 to 12 hours before a D&E procedure to dilate the cervical canal, and drugs to promote uterine contraction at the conclusion of surgery are usually required.

From the patient's point of view a D&E procedure is very similar to vacuum abortion. Sensations during the procedure and discomfort are similar when local anesthesia is used, although the D&E procedure takes somewhat longer (20 to 30 minutes). When general anesthesia is used, of course, there is no discomfort during the procedure. Recovery after a D&E procedure is also similar to that after a vacuum abortion.

Amniocentesis Abortion (Saline, Prostaglandins, or Urea): 15 to 24 Weeks of Pregnancy

"Amniocentesis" means inserting a hollow needle into the fluid-filled amniotic sac surrounding the fetus in order to remove amniotic fluid or introduce medicine. About 6% of all abortions in the United States use the amniocentesis procedure. It is very difficult to perform amniocentesis before about 15 weeks of pregnancy. Some clinicians advise a woman who is 13 weeks pregnant to wait two or three weeks before an amniocentesis abortion is scheduled. Statistics on abortion complications compiled by the national Center for Disease Control, however, indicate that D&E abortion (see above) *without waiting* is probably a safer option in this situation. Amniocentesis abortion is almost always performed in a hospital so that emergency problems that might occur during the drug injection or later during labor or expulsion can be safely managed.

The physician uses the amniocentesis procedure to insert saline, prostaglandins, or urea into the amniotic sac surrounding the fetus. Saline is a concentrated salt solution. Prostaglandins are a family of hormone drugs. Urea is a concentrated solution of a nitrogen waste product excreted by the kidneys. Each of these drugs will induce premature labor. *You will be fully awake and alert during amniocentesis,* because your physician relies on you to report *immediately* any unusual sensations that might mean you are having a drug reaction.

The first step in the amniocentesis procedure is examination of your abdomen. Your clinician locates the top of your uterus, and a small area on your lower abdomen may be shaved. Next your clinician injects a small amount of local anesthetic to deaden a 1-inch circle of skin, muscle, and connective tissue (see Illustration 7). Most women experience a brief stinging sensation as the anesthetic is injected.

Next your physician inserts a slender hollow needle or plastic tube through the anesthetized area into the amniotic sac (see Illustration 8). Most women feel pressure and a short twinge of discomfort as the tube is inserted, but once the tube is in place, most women feel no discomfort. Either saline, urea, or prostaglandins is inserted through the tube into the amniotic sac. You may notice a slight sense of fullness or pressure in your uterus; if you have any pain or a sensation of warmth, tell your physician at once. After the saline, urea, or prostaglandins is in place, your physician withdraws the tube and the injection site is covered with a band-aid.

Many physicians insert one or two laminaria rods into the cervical canal immediately after amniocentesis in order to widen (dilate) the canal gently before strong labor contractions begin. (Laminaria are described later in this chapter.)

Most women have a quiet period of several hours after amniocentesis before labor contractions begin. You may be given a drug called oxytocin through an intravenous tube (IV) in your arm to encourage or strengthen contractions. Oxytocin sometimes causes increased fluid retention; so you and the hospital staff must keep careful records of

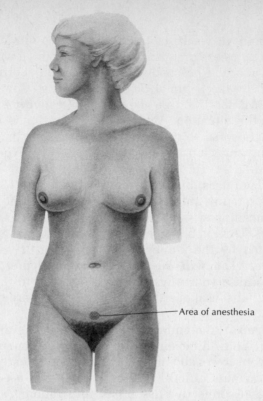

Illustration 7 A small area of skin will be anesthetized for amniocentesis abortion.

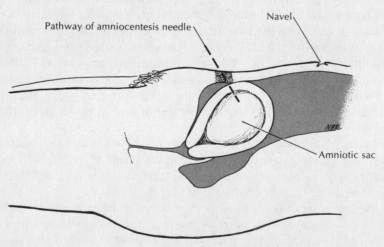

Illustration 8 The slender amniocentesis needle enters the amniotic sac.

your urine output and all fluids you are given by mouth and by IV. Keep your records carefully so that excessive fluid retention can be recognized and corrected promptly; untreated fluid retention can cause serious complications, including coma and convulsions.

Uterine contractions cause expulsion of the pregnancy in amniocentesis abortion. There is wide variation in the length of time that abortion labor lasts and in the amount of discomfort women have. You can have pain medications if you need them.

As the time for abortion approaches, most women feel a sense of fullness and pressure in the vagina, similar to the pressure and urge for a bowel movement. In most cases, the fetus is expelled first, followed a short time later by the placenta. Because the fetus is relatively small, expulsion is usually not painful, usually does not cause tearing, and does not require an incision in the vaginal opening (episiotomy) that is often used with full-term pregnancy.

The hospital nursing staff usually assists you during expulsion. In case expulsion occurs before a nurse arrives, it is important to be prepared for the fact that the fetus is recognizable at this stage of pregnancy.

In about one out of four cases, expulsion of the placenta is delayed, and it may be necessary for the physician to remove the placenta. She/he will first try to pull the placenta free with a blunt grasping instrument; if this technique fails, you may need general anesthesia and a D&C procedure (see Chapter 40).

Most women are encouraged to remain in the hospital for observation for at least three to four hours after amniocentesis abortion. Most women feel well during this time and are able to shower and prepare to go home.

The total time in the hospital for amniocentesis abortion varies widely and is not predictable. On the average, saline and prostaglandin abortions require about a 24-hour stay. But abortion may occur quite a bit earlier (six to eight hours) or later (36 to 48 hours). You must be prepared to remain in the hospital for 48 hours or even longer.

Drugs for Abortion

The newest abortion method, approved in 1977 by the Food and Drug Administration, is a prostaglandin vaginal tablet. The tablet is simply inserted in your vagina, and the drug is absorbed through the vaginal walls. The tablet causes labor contractions similar to those caused by saline or prostaglandin injected into the amniotic sac itself (5). Compared to saline and prostaglandin techniques, vaginal prostaglandin tablets have advantages: the amniocentesis injection is eliminated, and the hormone tablet can be quickly removed if you develop an adverse reaction to the drug. Experience with the tablet is very limited, and there are no extensive data on which to base an estimate of the safety of this method. The risk of serious or fatal reactions to the vaginal tablets is not known.

The idea of a simple vaginal tablet for abortion is very appealing. It is not considered a likely replacement for current abortion procedures, however, because early vacuum abortion has such a good safety record. Even commonly accepted and widely used drugs usually carry higher risks: the death rate associated with penicillin shots, for example, is 1.5 to 2.0 per 100,000 people (see Chapter 22, gonorrhea treatment section). The comparable risk for abortion during the first eight weeks of pregnancy is 0.6 per 100,000 procedures (2). It is unlikely that a complex and potent drug like the prostaglandin vaginal tablet will prove to have comparable safety.

Experts in the abortion field believe that it is unlikely that *any* elective abortion drug will be found to match the early vacuum procedure for safety. A general rule in pharmacology is that any substance with powerful therapeutic effects is likely to have powerful side effects as well. There are drugs that could be used to induce abortion; anticancer drugs (chemotherapeutic agents) are one example. The seriousness and likelihood of severe side effects, however, is so high that such drugs are not even considered when abortion is the goal. The alternative means for inducing abortion (vacuum, D&E, and amniocentesis procedures) are much safer.

SPECIAL WARNING. Three cases of poisoning caused by *pennyroyal* oil (*Mentha pulegium*, also called squawmint or mosquito plant) have recently been reported to the Center for Disease Control (6). In one case, a young woman who drank 1 ounce of pennyroyal oil died six days later despite intensive treatment for massive liver destruction apparently caused by the poison. Pennyroyal is clearly *not* a safe abortion option.

Herbal remedies, like conventional drugs, can have serious side effects. Any preparation that has active ingredients potent enough to have beneficial effects is likely to have detrimental effects for at least some individuals. A major problem in using herbal remedies is that the identity of the active ingredient is, in many cases, unknown and there is no good way to determine an effective, but safe, dose.

Hysterotomy and Hysterectomy

Abortion methods that are very rarely used today are hysterotomy and hysterectomy. Hysterotomy, a miniature cesarean section, was more common in the first few years after abortion was legalized in the United States. These procedures are now reserved for women with specific, serious medical problems that make it dangerous to use saline, prostaglandin, or urea, or for cases in which other abortion methods have failed.

Laminaria

Laminaria is a type of seaweed. One or sometimes two slender dry laminaria rods are inserted into your cervical canal, and after several hours they absorb moisture, swell, and gently widen (dilate) the canal (see Illustration 9). Laminaria rods are often used the day before a vacuum or D&E abortion, and they can also be used in conjunction with saline and prostaglandin amniocentesis procedures. The laminaria rod is inserted while you are in the standard pelvic examination position. You may feel some cramping during laminaria insertion, but once the

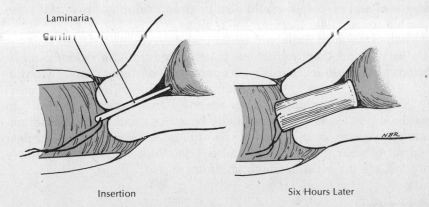

Laminaria

Cervix

Insertion   Six Hours Later

Illustration 9   The physician may insert a laminaria rod in the cervical canal. The laminaria will absorb moisture, swell, and gradually widen the canal in about six hours.

insertion is complete, you probably won't have any discomfort. A folded gauze square is placed against your cervix to hold the laminaria rod in place.

The rod may come out on its own before or during your abortion. Watch for it—laminaria rods look like small brown tampons—when you go to the bathroom, because if it is flushed away unnoticed, you will need an abdominal x-ray to be certain that it is not still inside.

Complications and Risks

Serious complications and deaths from legal abortion are rare. For 1976 the national Center for Disease Control recorded 10 deaths among a total of 988,267 legal abortions reported. This gives an overall legal abortion mortality of 1 death per 100,000 procedures.

The small number of deaths in 1976 (10 total) makes safety comparisons between different pregnancy lengths and types of procedures impossible on a one-year basis. For this reason, the comparisons below are based on cumulative statistics. During the four-year period 1972 through 1976 a total of 116 deaths were reported, equivalent to a rate of 3 deaths for every 100,000 legal abortion procedures. Note that this cumulative rate is somewhat higher than the rate for 1976 alone. Death rates for legal abortion have declined each year since 1973. Presumably, the complication rates and death rates for each of the abortion categories shown below would also be proportionally lower if it were possible to calculate them for 1976 alone.

By far the most important factor that determines abortion safety is how early in pregnancy you have your procedure. *The risk of complications and death increases with each week of delay* (see Illustration 10). Risks are lowest for early vacuum procedures (see Table 1).

Most abortion complications are mild and respond promptly to treatment. Problems can occasionally be serious and can cause permanent damage to your reproductive organs or even require surgical removal of your uterus, tubes, and ovaries. Infection and incomplete abortion are the most common complications.

INFECTION

Infection in the uterus and/or fallopian tubes usually causes persistent cramps and abdominal pain that become worse over time. In-

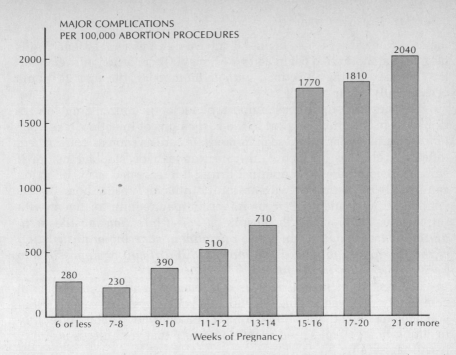

MAJOR COMPLICATIONS
PER 100,000 ABORTION PROCEDURES

Weeks of Pregnancy

Illustration 10 The risk of serious complications increases each week that an abortion procedure is delayed. Complication rates shown here for abortion after 14 weeks are rates for amniocentesis procedures. When the D&E technique is used, complication rates are lower (approximately 700 per 100,000 procedures). SOURCE: Center for Disease Control: Abortion Surveillance 1974. US Department of Health, Education and Welfare. Public Health Service. HEW Publication No (CDC) 76-8276.

Table 1 DEATHS FROM ABORTION BY TYPE OF PROCEDURE (1972–1976)

Abortion Procedure	Deaths per 100,000 Procedures
Vacuum	1.3
D&E	9.9
Saline amniocentesis	18.3
Prostaglandins amniocentesis	13.1
Hysterotomy/hysterectomy	44.7

SOURCE: Center for Disease Control: Abortion Surveillance 1976. US Department of Health, Education and Welfare. Public Health Service. HEW Publication No (CDC) 78-8205, 1978.

303

fection often causes fever, vaginal discharge, and general fatigue. Signs of infection most often begin 24 to 36 hours after abortion or even later. Rapidly developing infections with symptoms in the first 24 hours occasionally occur as well.

You are the single most important factor in minimizing the seriousness of infection. Be alert to the early signs of infection, take your temperature regularly, and seek immediate care as soon as you suspect infection; chances are good the infection can be stopped before it spreads to your tubes or abdominal lining if it is treated early. Infection can usually be controlled with antibiotic pills and rest at home if it is confined to your uterus. Serious infection may require treatment with intravenous antibiotics in the hospital. *Even if infection subsides with antibiotic treatment, it can cause permanent scarring or obstruction of the fallopian tubes, and you may find it difficult or impossible to become pregnant in the future.*

The risk of infection is increased if fetal and placental tissue is not completely removed during abortion. If your physician suspects that you have retained tissue or if your infection does not respond promptly to antibiotics, you may need a D&C to be sure that your uterus is empty (see Chapter 40).

Infection risk is also increased if you have gonorrhea or a cervical infection caused by other bacteria. *If you suspect that you may have been exposed to gonorrhea, have a gonorrhea culture test and treatment before your abortion.* Be careful to avoid exposure to gonorrhea after your·abortion, especially for the first four weeks.

INCOMPLETE ABORTION

Incomplete abortion means that you have retained fetal or placental tissue in your uterus.

Bleeding and strong cramping can alert you to incomplete abortion. The absence of fever and malaise distinguish this problem from infection; however, your risk of infection is increased if you have retained pregnancy tissue.

Incomplete abortion can mean that your pregnancy is not terminated. You may continue to have symptoms of pregnancy, such as fatigue, nausea, and breast soreness. You may have less postabortion bleeding than would be expected. Other women with continuing pregnancy have no symptoms at all.

Your most important assurance that your abortion was complete is a normal uterus at the time of your followup examination; so be sure to keep your followup appointment. If your abortion is incomplete, your clinician probably failed to empty your uterus completely. Occasionally, incomplete abortion means that you have a tubal (ectopic) pregnancy, twin pregnancy, or an abnormal uterine shape.

Your clinician will repeat your vacuum procedure or perform a D&C under general anesthesia (see Chapter 40).

About 1 in 1,000 women who have early vacuum procedures experience another more immediate form of incomplete abortion: accumulation of blood clots in the uterus during the first few hours after abortion. This complication, called "re-do" syndrome, causes severe, progressive cramps that begin within the first few hours after an abortion procedure and subside as soon as the clots are removed by a repeat vacuum procedure.

HEMORRHAGE

Excessive bleeding during or after abortion can occur with any of the abortion procedures, but hemorrhage is minimized when your physician uses local anesthesia for early abortion; general anesthesia can decrease the strength of normal uterine contractions that help stop bleeding. Hemorrhage is a more frequent complication of late abortion procedures with prostaglandin or saline. Saline can temporarily alter blood coagulation factors. Hemorrhage is most likely to occur during the actual abortion process while you are in the hospital, and immediate removal of remaining pregnancy tissue, uterine scraping, and uterine massage can usually stop the bleeding effectively. Blood transfusions are sometimes necessary to replace the blood that you have lost.

Hemorrhage risk is increased if you have a bleeding disorder or take medications that alter blood coagulation. Large doses of aspirin for a long period of time can be a cause of excessive bleeding. Blood-thinning medications (anticoagulants) have a similar effect.

Excessive bleeding after an abortion is rare. Heavy or prolonged bleeding may indicate incomplete abortion, a tear in the cervix or uterus, or inadequate uterine contraction and must be investigated and treated.

INJURY TO THE CERVIX, UTERUS, OR OTHER ABDOMINAL ORGANS

Perforation is very rare, but damage to the cervix, uterus, and lower abdominal organs can occur any time instruments are inserted into the uterine cavity. A puncture wound in your uterus caused by an abortion instrument will usually close spontaneously and heal without treatment. If nearby organs such as the bladder, rectum, intestines, or major arteries or veins are injured by the puncture, however, emergency surgery to repair the damage will be necessary. Even if you have no evidence of internal damage, your physician may want you to stay in the hospital for observation if she/he suspects that you have a perforation.

Injury to the cervix is a more common problem than perforation and can occur with both early vacuum and later procedures. The cervical clamp used in vacuum abortion and D&E can tear your cervix, and you may need stitches to control bleeding. Tearing of the cervix can also occur as a result of forceful labor contractions with saline or prostaglandin abortion. Cervical injury may be a cause of miscarriage (spontaneous abortion) and premature delivery in future pregnancies.

ADVERSE REACTIONS TO DRUGS

Rash, hives, difficulty in breathing, heart arrest, or even death can be caused by drug reactions, but allergy to the drugs used in abortion procedures is rare.

Local Anesthetics. Be sure to inform your physician if you have ever had a reaction to other local anesthetics such as dental Novocain. You may be able to have a different type of local anesthetic or general anesthesia may be recommended. Heart rhythm changes and seizures can occur when drug reactions are severe.

Tetracycline. For some people, taking tetracycline can trigger severe skin rashes on areas of the body exposed to sunlight. Avoid sunbathing or sunburn when you are taking this drug. Severe allergy reactions are rare.

Methergine. This drug is sometimes prescribed after abortion to stimulate contraction of the uterus. Some women find that it causes excessive cramping. Consult your physician if cramps are severe. Methergine can also cause a rise in blood pressure that would be especially dangerous for a person who already had high blood pressure.

Saline. Saline does not cause allergic reactions, but adverse reactions do occur if it is absorbed too rapidly or is injected accidentally into the bloodstream or uterine muscle. Excessive levels of saline in the bloodstream can cause rapid absorption of fluid; in severe cases this can cause coma or death. Retention of extra fluid in the lungs or circulation can also cause heart strain that would be hazardous for a woman with preexisting heart disease. Concentrated saline can destroy muscle tissue if it is accidentally injected directly into the muscle itself.

Prostaglandin. If prostaglandin is absorbed too rapidly into the bloodstream, it can cause difficulty in breathing (much like an asthma attack), rapid heart rate, change in blood pressure, and immediate strong contractions of the uterus, intestine, and stomach. These symptoms usually subside within a few minutes and usually do not require treatment. Prostaglandin commonly causes nausea, vomiting, and diarrhea. Many physicians routinely prescribe additional medications to counteract these effects.

Oxytocin. In addition to causing strong uterine contractions, this hormone causes the kidneys to retain fluid. Large amounts of oxytocin over a period of many hours can cause serious brain swelling, coma, and convulsions.

EFFECTS OF ABORTION ON FUTURE FERTILITY

Abortion *complications* can clearly jeopardize your future fertility. Infection can scar and obstruct your fallopian tubes, or an injured cervix can be the cause of miscarriage (spontaneous abortion) and premature delivery in future pregnancies. This problem, called incompetent cervix, can be treated by placing a temporary tie (cerclage) on the cervix to hold it closed during pregnancy. The tie is removed when pregnancy reaches full term or labor begins.

Complications like these are rare, however, and it may be that the statistics on overall long-term effects will never be able to measure the impact of such problems on future fertility, even though the impact is certainly real for an individual woman.

Although some studies in other countries have linked abortion to later problems with fertility, prematurity, low birth weight infants, and abnormal placenta, reports so far from the United States have been fairly reassuring. One study of 5,003 pregnancy records showed that women who reported one previous induced abortion had no higher rates for prematurity, low birth weight, placenta problems, or newborn abnormalities (8). Researchers studying spontaneous abortion (miscarriage) rates for 31,900 women in California, however, found that women with one or more previous induced abortions had higher rates of miscarriage late in pregnancy than did other women. They also showed that the excess risk had decreased over time and concluded that improvements in abortion techniques, with more gentle dilation using laminaria, might explain the drop in risk (9). It may be that significant differences in techniques used for abortion explain why research results from other countries are contradictory.

When you are careful to watch for danger signs of infection after an abortion, you minimize the risk of impairing your fertility.

Contraindications

A contraindication is a medical condition that renders a procedure inadvisable or unsafe that might otherwise be recommended. ***There are no true contraindications to abortion.*** Any medical problem that might make abortion risky would make continuing pregnancy even riskier.

Your physician will consider certain medical issues as she/he advises you about the safest abortion procedure for you, and decides whether you need to be hospitalized for your procedure.

- If you are allergic to local anesthesia, then general anesthesia in a hospital setting may be recommended.
- If you have severe anemia, a bleeding disorder, asthma, heart disease, diabetes, epilepsy, or an orthopedic problem, a hospital setting may be safer.
- If you have an emotional disorder that might interfere with your ability to be calm and cooperative during a local anesthesia procedure, you and your physician may prefer general anesthesia in a hospital setting.
- If your physician is unable to determine exactly how far along in pregnancy you are, because of obesity or tense muscles during your exam, she/he may want you to have a sonogram (a test to measure your pregnancy size, see Chapter 21) or may suggest general anesthesia for your procedure. General anesthesia permits her/him to examine you when your muscles are completely relaxed and may make it easier to perform a vacuum or D&E abortion.
- If you have serious heart or kidney disease, your physician will probably avoid saline, because you might have serious complications if saline caused abnormal fluid retention.

- If you have an active pelvic infection, your physician will probably recommend that abortion be temporarily delayed while your infection is treated.
- Your physician will avoid prostaglandins if you have a known allergy to the drug or if you have medical problems that may be aggravated by prostaglandins, including high blood pressure, asthma, heart disease, lung disease, epilepsy, or glaucoma.

The Rh-Negative Woman and Abortion

Rh disease of the newborn infant was a common cause of severe newborn jaundice and fetal or infant death until ten years ago. This problem arises when a **woman who is Rh-negative** herself becomes pregnant with an **Rh-positive fetus.** At the time of delivery, miscarriage, or abortion, Rh-positive cells from the infant or fetus can enter the woman's bloodstream and cause her body to build antibodies, special proteins that attach to the "foreign" Rh-positive cells. This antibody buildup is a normal defense against invasion by foreign chemical structures.

Usually, antibodies are not a problem during a first Rh-positive pregnancy. If the same woman becomes pregnant again with another Rh-positive fetus, the antibody response that was established during her first pregnancy is stimulated and antibody levels in her blood rise. These antibodies are able to cross the placenta into the blood circulation of the fetus, where they can attack *fetal* Rh-positive cells. Breakdown of fetal blood cells can cause severe anemia and jaundice in the fetus, called Rh hemolytic disease. It tends to be worse with each succeeding Rh-positive pregnancy.

Today, Rh hemolytic disease can almost always be prevented. In 1968, the Food and Drug Administration approved a drug containing Rh immune globulin which, if given to the Rh-negative woman at the time of delivery, miscarriage, or abortion, prevents her buildup of antibody response. The globulin in the drug acts by coating any Rh-positive cells that do enter the woman's circulation; consequently, her own body does not perceive that a foreign chemical has entered her bloodstream, and she does not build antibodies. This drug must be administered by injection, if possible within 36 to 72 hours after delivery, miscarriage, or abortion. *That is why every woman who has an abortion must have a blood test to determine whether she is Rh-positive or Rh-negative.*

Without treatment, about 4% of Rh-negative women develop antibodies after an early vacuum abortion. The percentage is somewhat higher for women undergoing second trimester abortion (10). Fewer than 1% of the Rh-negative women treated with Rh immune globulin shots develop antibodies (10).

It is wise to have Rh treatment even if you don't plan any future pregnancies. You could change your mind, for one thing; and also, you may protect yourself against future problems with blood transfusions.

The standard Rh immune globulin drug costs between $35 and $55. In 1977, the FDA approved a small dose of Rh immune globulin medication specifically for Rh-negative women undergoing abortion in the first 12 weeks of pregnancy, when a smaller dose can provide effective protection (11) at a cost of only about $16.

Caring for Yourself After Abortion

You may eat or drink anything you like and return to most of your normal activities as soon as you feel like it. Most women find it best to avoid especially strenuous exercise for a few days. Be guided by how you feel.

Most women have some cramps and vaginal bleeding during the first couple of weeks. If your bleeding is heavier for three days than on the heaviest day of a normal menstrual period, call your clinician. It is not unusual to have spotting as long as four weeks after abortion. Spotting may stop completely and then start up again several days later. *Severe cramps are not normal.* Arrange to see your clinician if your cramps are persistent or if you have pain more severe than menstrual cramps.

Your first normal period should begin in four to six weeks. If you are taking birth control Pills, your first period will come after you finish your first pack. *It is possible to become pregnant again even before your first period begins.* If you want to avoid another pregnancy, begin using a method of birth control as soon as you begin having intercourse again.

No one will be able to tell for sure that you have had an abortion. In the rare event that your cervix is damaged during the procedure, it may have scar tissue after it heals. A clinician who examines you in the future might see the scar and surmise that you have had an abortion.

DO'S AND DON'TS

- Be sure that you have a 24-hour emergency telephone number to call in case you have problems.
- Take your temperature carefully each morning and late afternoon, and anytime you feel warm or have chills, for one week. If you are taking aspirin or an aspirin substitute, record your temperature before you take each dose. Call your physician if your temperature is 100.4 degrees (Fahrenheit) by mouth, or higher.
- Do not have intercourse for the first two weeks.
- Do not douche for two weeks.
- Use sanitary pads only. No tampons for the first two weeks.
- Baths, showers, and shampoos are fine.
- If you develop breast milk after abortion, wear a snug bra day and night for two or three days and avoid any stimulation of your nipples. Squeezing milk from your breast will result in increased milk flow.
- Keep your appointment for your followup exam in two weeks.

DRUGS

Make sure you have written instructions for any medications you will take at home, and be sure to take your medication on schedule.

Methergine. This drug, a preparation of methylergonovine, is sometimes prescribed for the first 24 to 48 hours after surgery to help your uterus contract to normal size. If you have severe cramps or pain radiating down to your thighs, call your clinician. She/he may want you to stop Methergine to reduce your cramping.

Tetracycline. Some clinicians prescribe tetracycline to protect against infection during the first three to four days after surgery. Avoid milk and milk products for two hours before and after each dose, and do not sunbathe while you are taking tetracycline.

Pain Medications. If your cramps are so severe that aspirin or an aspirin substitute does not relieve your pain, call your clinician. Two or three aspirin tablets every three to four hours usually provide good pain relief. Remember that stronger medications such as codeine, Darvon (propoxyphene), Fiorinal (butalbital), and others can slow reflexes and make you less alert; so don't try to drive.

DANGER SIGNS

Be alert to the danger signs of serious trouble. Prompt medical attention can mean that a minor problem never becomes a major problem. Call your clinician at once if you develop any of these danger signs:

- Fever: temperature of 100.4 degrees (Fahrenheit) by mouth, or higher, chills or malaise (fatigue, aching)
- Significant cramping or abdominal pain—especially if it becomes more severe over a few hours
- Abdominal tenderness, sensitivity to pressure or activity such as walking, coughing, or jumping
- Prolonged or heavy bleeding that lasts more than three weeks after your abortion, or is heavier than a heavy menstrual flow for three days or more
- Unusual or foul-smelling vaginal discharge
- Allergy symptoms such as rash, hives, asthma, or difficulty in breathing that may indicate a drug reaction
- Your first menstrual period does not begin within six weeks

BIRTH CONTROL

I don't like taking the Pill. But I don't want to do this again either *(patting her stomach).*

—Abortion clinic patient, 27

Most physicians discuss contraception with abortion patients and can prescribe a method of birth control at the time of abortion. If you choose a diaphragm, condoms, or foam, be sure to use them as soon as you begin having intercourse. If you choose birth control Pills, take your first Pill the first Sunday after your abortion. If you choose an IUD, plan to have it inserted at the time of your two-week followup examination. (Some clinicians are willing to insert an IUD immediately after an early vacuum abortion.)

Plan for and be prepared to use birth control immediately after an abortion. Ovulation usually returns two or three weeks after abortion, but some women may ovulate within a week or ten days and another pregnancy is entirely possible.

YOUR EMOTIONS

It is normal to have strong emotional feelings after abortion.

I still think it's—unnatural—to just erase it like that. I feel all washed out. I had intercourse just *one time* without protection.

—Woman, 22

You may be sad; angry at your partner; angry at yourself; uncertain that you did the right thing. It will probably comfort you to remember that you made the best decision you could at the time.

Many women express a sense of relief after an abortion, and the overall emotional impact of abortion can be positive.

It was such a relief to have the whole thing over with, the worrying and tension, and dreading the surgery. The abortion did hurt, but it wasn't as bad as I had expected. I did feel sad as well, but mostly just relieved.

—Woman, 28

From in-depth psychological interviews with vacuum abortion patients, researchers found that six months later about half felt that the experience had had positive effects, such as personal growth or improvement in family relations; about 10% had negative reactions, such as guilt or fear of men; and about 25% had no change in their feelings at all (12). Another study compared women who had vacuum abortion with women who completed pregnancy and found no significant psychological differences between the groups one year later (13).

Repeat Abortion

The need for a second abortion is sometimes viewed with dismay by health care providers, and a pregnant woman herself may feel a sense of failure. Dismay is understandable in view of the physical and emotional stress, inconvenience, and expense of abortion, especially after the intensive education most abortion providers offer women to help them prevent accidental pregnancy in the future.

What must be understood is that *there is a quite significant likelihood of another unwanted pregnancy, even when a woman faithfully uses very effective birth control.* One study demonstrated that if 100 women rely on a method that provides 98 to 99% effectiveness after a first abortion, about 21 to 51 women will probably have at least one more unplanned pregnancy within ten years. Some 69 to 97 out of 100 women who rely upon foam or condoms (90 to 95% effectiveness) will face unplanned pregnancy at least once more within ten years. Even within the first year, a significant number of repeat unwanted pregnancies can be expected (14).

In light of these statistics, it seems inappropriate to view repeat abortion as proof of a deep-seated psychological problem or an educational failure. In some cases, of course, repeat unwanted pregnancy may be a symptom of emotional disorder. In most cases, however, it is not; repeat abortion rates may reflect nothing more than statistical odds. Our methods of birth control are far from perfect.

REFERENCES

1. Grimes DA, Cates W: Deaths from paracervical anesthesia used for first-trimester abortion, 1972–1975. *New England Journal of Medicine* 295(25):1397–1399, December 16, 1976.
2. Center for Disease Control: *Abortion Surveillance* 1976. US Department of Health, Education and Welfare. Public Health Service. HEW Publication No (CDC) 78-8205, 1978.
3. Cates W, Schulz KF, Grimes DA, et al: The effect of delay and method choice on the risk of abortion morbidity. *Family Planning Perspectives* 9:266–273, 1977.
4. Miller ER, Fortney JA, Kessel E: Early vacuum aspiration: minimizing procedures to nonpregnant women. *Family Planning Perspectives* 8:33–38, 1976.
5. "A vaginal suppository for abortion." *The Medical Letter on Drugs and Therapeutics* 19(22):89–90, November 4, 1977.
6. Center for Disease Control: Fatality and Illness Associated with Consumption of pennyroyal oil—Colorado. *Morbidity and Mortality Weekly Report* 27(51):511–512, 1978.

7. Tietze C: Induced abortion: 1977 supplement. *Reports on Population-Family Planning*, No. 14 (ed 2), Suppl, December 1977. New York, The Population Council.

8. Schuenbaum SC, Monson RR, Stubblefield PD, et al: Outcome of the delivery following an induced or spontaneous abortion. *American Journal of Obstetrics and Gynecology* 136:19–24, 1980.

9. Harlap S, Shiono PH, Ramcharan S, et al: A prospective study of spontaneous fetal losses after induced abortions. *New England Journal of Medicine* 301:677–681, 1979.

10. Prevention of Rh Sensitizations, Report of a World Health Organization Group. WHO Technical Report Ser No 468, 1971.

11. Stewart F, Burnhill MS, Bozorgi N: Reduced dose of Rh immunoglobulin following first trimester pregnancy termination. *Obstetrics and Gynecology* 51:318–322, 1978.

12. Margolis AJ, Davison LA, Hason KH, et al: Therapeutic abortion followup study. *American Journal of Obstetrics and Gynecology* 110:243–249, 1971.

13. Athanasiou R, Oppel W, Michelson L, et al: Psychiatric sequelae to term birth and induced early and late abortion; A longitudinal study. *Family Planning Perspectives* 5:227–231, 1973.

14. Tietze C: The "problem" of repeat abortion. *Family Planning Perspectives* 6:148–150, 1974.

21 | The Pelvic Examination and Common Office Tests and Procedures

A pelvic examination provides your clinician—and you—with essential basic information about the health of your reproductive system; yet thousands of women avoid or delay pelvic exams. Some women fear that the exam will be painful, especially if they have had uncomfortable exams in the past. You probably won't ever like having a pelvic exam, but it does help to know what happens during your exam and why. It also helps to know how to prepare for an exam and what you can expect your exam to accomplish.

Most reproductive system problems can be treated successfully if they are detected early, so it is very important to be realistic about your health needs and put fear and embarrassment in perspective. "I guess I'd rather be mortified for a few minutes than put up with this itching another month," one woman said.

Preparing for a Pelvic Exam

My memory deserts me when I take off my clothes. The minute I get on an exam table—just me and that sheet—I forget *everything* I wanted to ask about. And I'm too embarrassed to call back and ask questions later!

—*Woman, 35*

Make a list of your questions at home and take them with you, right into the exam room if necessary. Start with your most important concerns, and be sure that your clinician is aware of them before beginning your examination. Write down the dates of your last few periods, the dates you first noticed any symptoms that concern you, and the names of any drugs you have taken recently. (See Chapter 4 for a list of drugs that may interfere with pregnancy tests.) Be sure to tell your clinician if you took DES during pregnancy or if your mother took DES while she was pregnant with you. (See Chapter 37 for more on DES and its implications for your health.)

Avoid douching for at least 24 hours before your exam, especially if you think you have an infection. Your clinician can't diagnose infection if all the evidence has been washed away. Some clinicians also recommend that you avoid intercourse for 48 hours, and tampons for 24 hours, before your exam. Your Pap smear and other lab tests will be more accurate if your normal vaginal ecosystem hasn't been tampered with. Find out whether your clinician wants you to come in on schedule if you start your period. Heavy menstrual flow may interfere with a Pap test but should not be a problem for pelvic examination otherwise. If you are a diaphragm user, take your diaphragm with you. Your clinician may want to check for proper insertion and fit. Let your clinician know if this will be your first pelvic exam and ask her/him to explain the exam along the way. Your clinician can also show you the instruments she/he will use, and provide a mirror so you can see your cervix, vagina, or other areas of interest or concern.

How a Pelvic Exam Is Done and Why

A gynecologic exam begins with a careful medical history and a general physical examination. Your clinician will probably record your weight and blood pressure, listen to your heart and lungs, examine your thyroid gland, breasts, and abdomen, and may take specimens for routine blood and urine lab tests (see following section).

Before your breast exam, ask about breast changes you have noticed that puzzle or concern you. *Don't assume that your clinician will find a lump you found first yourself;* you know your breasts much better than your clinician does. Your clinician will check your breasts for lumps,

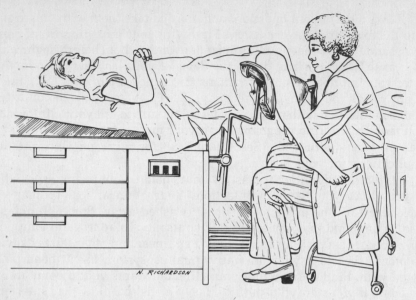

N. RICHARDSON

Illustration 1　Speculum part of pelvic exam. Your clinician usually sits on a stool.

tenderness, enlarged nodes, nipple discharge, and skin changes that might indicate the presence of a tumor. (See Chapter 32 for a full discussion of breast lumps.) Pay careful attention to your clinician's technique and compare it with your own technique for your monthly breast self-examination. If you are not sure how to examine your own breasts, ask your clinician to teach you (see Chapter 2).

For your pelvic exam you will be placed in what is clinically called the dorsal lithotomy position (commonly known as the Awkward Embarrassing Position). You lie on your back with your bottom at the very end of the table and your legs supported in knee or foot stirrups. Your clinician will sit on a stool at the end of the table, between your legs (see Illustration 1).

EXTERNAL EXAMINATION

The first step in the pelvic examination is inspection of your vulva, the area around the entrance to your vagina (see Illustration 2). Your clinician will check for redness, swelling, or lesions that might indicate infection or injury. ("Lesion" simply means any tissue abnormality or loss of function: a sore or a wound or an area of irritation, for example.)

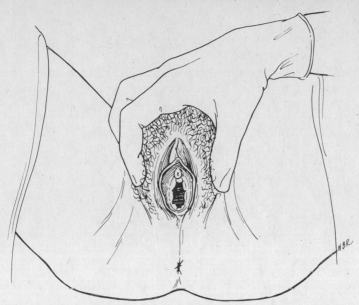

Illustration 2 Your clinician examines your vulva as the first step in a pelvic exam.

Some clinicians examine the clitoris by pushing back the fold of skin (prepuce, or clitoral hood) that covers it.

SPECULUM EXAMINATION

Examination of the lining of the vagina and the cervix is the next step in a pelvic examination. The speculum holds the vaginal walls apart so that your clinician can see your cervix and inspect the vaginal lining (see Illustration 3). Specula come in several sizes, and your clinician will choose a speculum compatible with the size of the entrance to your vagina. If speculum insertion is painful, ask your clinician to stop. She/he may be able to readjust its position or switch to a smaller size.

Many clinicians begin by inserting a gloved finger into your vagina to locate your cervix. The speculum is inserted with the blades closed. Your clinician will press downward on the bottom wall of your vagina to guide the speculum in. Once inside the vagina, the speculum is rotated to the handle-downward position and the blades are opened and locked into place at the correct width. (Plastic specula make a loud crack as they snap into the locked position, so don't be surprised. Metal

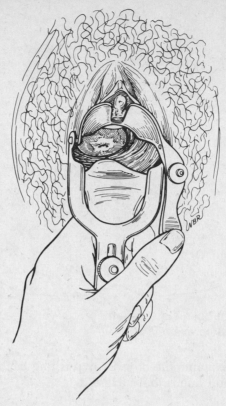

Illustration 3   A speculum holds your vaginal walls apart so that the clinician can see your cervix.

specula are mercifully silent, but they are cold unless they are warmed prior to insertion.) Your clinician inspects the vaginal walls and cervix for any redness, irritation, unusual discharge, or lesions. Specimens for lab tests are collected while the speculum is in place. A Pap smear specimen, gonorrhea culture sample, and a wet smear preparation for diagnosing infection are often included. (See the next section for details.)

Because gonorrhea is so common and because both men and women can have gonorrhea without any symptoms, many clinicians believe that the safest course is to perform a routine gonorrhea culture on every patient. Other clinicians perform a gonorrhea culture only when there is reason to suspect that the disease may be present. A gonorrhea culture is essential if you have pain or an unusual discharge, if either you or your partner has been exposed or even has reason to suspect exposure, or if you are worried. It may be wise to have frequent gonorrhea cultures if you have more than one sexual partner. Be sure to ask specifically for a gonorrhea culture; not all culture tests are reliable for gonorrhea detection, and wet smears cannot diagnose gonorrhea at all. (See Chapter 22 for a discussion of gonorrhea.)

It doesn't take as long to perform a speculum exam as it does to read about it here, you'll be happy to know.

BIMANUAL EXAMINATION

After laboratory specimens are collected, the speculum is removed. The next step in a pelvic exam is a bimanual (both hands) exam. Most clinicians stand up to perform a bimanual exam (see Illustration 4).

Your clinician inserts two gloved fingers of one hand into your

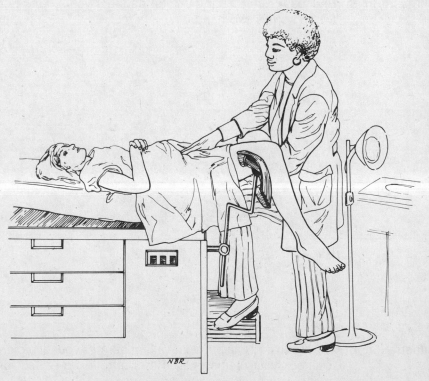

Illustration 4   Bimanual part of a pelvic exam. Your clinician usually stands, and supports a forearm with her/his knee.

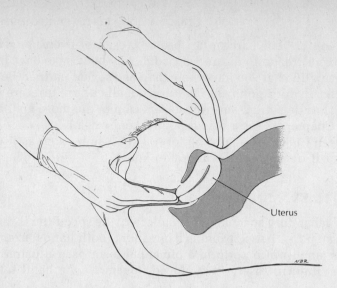

Uterus

Illustration 5   Bimanual exam. Your clinician can feel your uterus between her/his two hands.

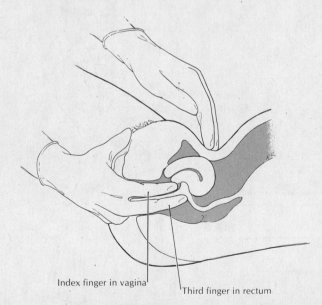

Index finger in vagina

Third finger in rectum

Illustration 6   The rectal part of a bimanual exam permits your clinician to check your uterus even if it is retroflexed—tilted towards your back—as this uterus is.

322

vagina and places the other hand on your abdomen. By pressing upward on your cervix and downward on your abdomen, she/he can feel the size, consistency, shape, and location of your uterus and will check for pain or tenderness (see Illustration 5). She/he checks both sides of your abdomen to locate your ovaries and fallopian tubes and checks your entire abdomen for masses or tender areas. At the conclusion of the bimanual exam, your clinician may insert one gloved finger into your rectum while the other remains in your vagina in order to evaluate the muscular wall that separates the rectum and vagina and to detect masses or tenderness deep in your pelvis (see Illustration 6).

Surviving a Pelvic Exam

I must have had about 30 pelvics by now, and I'm beginning to feel as blasé about them as my doctor does. After one child, two diaphragms, and a yeast infection I think I'll go to my grave with, it just doesn't bother me anymore. Last time, right in the middle of the exam, I caught myself wondering if Dr. Jackson dyed his hair! It proves you can get used to anything, I suppose.

—Woman, 33

A pelvic exam—performed on a healthy pelvis—should not be painful, but it may be uncomfortable. The speculum insertion is a strange sensation, especially if you have never had intercourse. Remember that relaxed vaginal muscles are highly flexible and elastic and that they are capable of accommodating a speculum. You can help by relaxing all your pelvic muscles completely and keeping them relaxed until the speculum is removed. When you are tense, your muscles clamp down on the speculum and increase your discomfort. If the speculum feels really awful, by all means ask your clinician to adjust it. It is almost always possible to do an adequate speculum exam without causing you significant discomfort.

A successful, informative bimanual examination is also much easier for your clinician if you are able to relax your abdominal muscles. A thick sheath of muscle completely covers your abdomen, and when muscles are tense, your clinician may find it difficult or impossible to feel your uterus underneath. Deep breathing with your mouth open helps relax these muscles. You may not even recognize tense muscles, especially if you are anxious or busy talking over your questions with your clinician. You might try tensing all your muscles on purpose and then relaxing them completely.

If you are having pain or tenderness, tell your clinician where it is before the exam begins; she/he will want to be especially gentle and especially thorough in examining that area.

Make sure to urinate just before your exam. Your bladder rests just above your uterus, and a full bladder can make the examination uncomfortable for you and more difficult for your clinician.

It is unlikely that your clinician will be able to tell if you have ever had intercourse. If she/he can't even insert so much as a fingertip in your vagina, she/he could reasonably conclude you haven't, but most women are quite easy to examine, including those who have never had intercourse even once.

Many clinics and private physicians now employ specially trained nurse practitioners who function in roles that formerly were reserved for doctors only, including routine pelvic examinations. Nurse practitioners counsel and examine women for annual exams, family planning, prenatal care, and many other health needs. They work under a physician's supervision, and the physician assists in difficult or unusual situations.

Most patients are very pleased with their nurse practitioner experience.

> She spent *much* more time with me than my doctor ever did, and she was a very good explainer. For the *first time* I understood why I get spotting when I miss a couple of Pills!
>
> —*Woman, 22*

When You Will Need a Pelvic Exam

Think of a pelvic exam as the starting place for all your reproductive health care needs. No one else can take the responsibility for the routine exams you need or for additional exams when problems occur. Plan to see your clinician for a pelvic exam:

- When you think intercourse is imminent for the first time. You'll be reassured when you know your anatomy is normal and when you are prepared with good birth control.

- If you haven't begun menstruating by age 16
- At about age 16 or 17, or earlier if you begin having menstrual periods or intercourse at an earlier age
- About every six months for a Pap smear if you have had herpes, or if your mother took DES when she was pregnant with you (see Chapters 22 and 37)
- At whatever intervals your clinician recommends if you have had an abnormal Pap smear (see the section entitled When to Have a Pap Smear at the end of this chapter)
- Any time you are bothered by itching, redness, sores, swelling, unusual odor, or unusual discharge
- Any time you have abdominal pain or painful intercourse, especially if you also have chills or fever
- Any time you have unusual vaginal bleeding
- Any time you miss a period if there is even a remote chance that you could be pregnant
- Any time you have burning when you urinate, and you urinate frequently
- Any time you have been raped or suspect that you may have been injured
- Any time you have had intercourse with a partner who might have an infection
- Any time you plan to become pregnant, for a thorough health assessment and prenatal advice before you conceive
- Any time you would like to use Pills, an IUD, or a diaphragm

Common Office Tests and Procedures

This section describes some of the common procedures that your clinician may use to help determine the cause of a specific problem. If your test can be analyzed in the office, you may know the results within a few minutes. In many cases, a test specimen is collected during your visit and is sent to an outside laboratory for analysis; or you may be asked to go to the laboratory yourself to have the test. Often it takes several days or more for your clinician to receive test results.

If your test result is not normal, your clinician will notify you by telephone or mail and will make arrangements for any further studies or treatment you might need. Many clinicians do not routinely notify patients when test results are normal (the "no news is good news" technique). If you do not hear from your clinician within a week or so, you can telephone the office or clinic and ask the receptionist to verify that your test report has been received and that it is normal.

PAP SMEAR

A Pap smear specimen is collected during your speculum examination. Your clinician gently rotates a wooden or plastic spatula over the surface of your cervix to scrape away a thin layer of cervical cells; she/he then spreads the cells across a glass slide (see Illustration 7). An additional sample of cells may be collected from your vagina as well. The slide is sprayed or immersed in a chemical that fixes the cells to the slide and preserves them; the slide is then sent from your clinician's

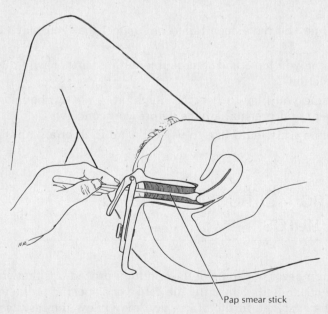

Pap smear stick

Illustration 7   Your clinician scrapes surface cells from your cervix for a Pap smear.

office to a laboratory to be stained and examined under the microscope by a specially trained technician (cytotechnologist) or a physician specialist (pathologist). You probably will not feel anything except the speculum during your Pap smear. You may have light bleeding or a few spots of blood after a Pap smear.

The Pap smear is intended primarily to detect cervical cancer. Vaginal infection or a low estrogen level is sometimes evident from a Pap smear as well. *The Pap smear is not reliable for detecting cancer of the uterus, ovary, or vagina.* Detailed information about abnormal Pap smears is in Chapter 27. Look at the last section of this chapter for recommendations on when and how often Pap tests are needed.

WET SMEAR

If you have been bothered by itching, burning, an unusual odor, or excessive discharge, your clinician will probably recommend a wet smear (wet mount, wet prep). She/he places a small sample of your vaginal discharge on a glass slide and adds 1 or 2 drops of salt solution so that vaginal cells float in suspension, or 1 or 2 drops of mild alkaline solution to dissolve vaginal cells and make yeast infection cells appear more prominent. Your clinician examines the slide immediately under a microscope to look for fast-moving, one-celled organisms that cause trichomonas vaginitis, the branched colonies of fungus that cause yeast infections, and the stippled cells that indicate a bacterial vaginitis. All competent clinicians who treat gynecologic problems have microscopes and perform wet smears frequently. *The wet smear does not provide a conclusive diagnosis for gonorrhea.* A culture specifically for gonorrhea must be performed to detect these small, fragile bacteria (see "Culture and Sensitivity Tests" later in this chapter).

URINE TESTS

Many different kinds of tests can be performed on a urine sample. Don't be misled by thinking that the normal urine test you had two months ago proves that your entire urinary system is perfect.

Two-minute urine pregnancy tests are often performed in your clinician's office. Two-hour urine pregnancy tests may be performed by an outside laboratory with your results available the next day. (See Chapter 4 for a description of pregnancy tests.)

Dipstick urine tests are routinely performed in many clinicians' offices. A small strip of chemically treated paper is dipped into a urine specimen, and the results immediately appear as a color change in the paper. The dipstick test reveals the presence of blood, abnormal protein, sugar, and diabetes acids in your urine. An abnormal dipstick result may indicate kidney disease, diabetes, or infection in your bladder or kidneys; or it may simply mean that your urine specimen was contaminated by menstrual blood or vaginal discharge washed from your vulva into your specimen cup.

Urinalysis is a more complete urine evaluation that can be performed either in your clinician's office or by an outside lab. The concentration and acidity of your urine are tested, and a dipstick test is performed. A tube of urine is spun in a centrifuge for several minutes to collect the cells and particles in a sediment at the bottom of the tube. The sediment is spread on a glass slide and examined under a microscope; if infection is present, the sediment will contain white blood cells and bacteria. Abnormal microscopic crystals or clumps of cells in your urine may indicate kidney disease. Many other less common tests can be performed on a urine sample; determination of hormone levels, for example, often requires analysis of your entire urine output over a 24-hour period. *Urine cultures* are described in a later section.

BLOOD TESTS

Hundreds of tests can be performed on a blood specimen. If you want to find out whether you have syphilis, for example, you must ask specifically for a syphilis test. It is entirely possible to submit 15 different tubes of blood and learn whether you have ever had German measles, whether your liver is damaged, whether your thyroid is low, and so forth, and still not find the answer to your question about syphilis.

One very common blood test, the *blood count,* can be done with a specimen drawn either from a vein in your arm or from a finger or earlobe prick. A blood count detects anemia. Two slightly different techniques are widely used. Your clinician may perform a blood count right in the office or clinic, or send you to an outside lab. The *hematocrit* method determines what percentage of your blood volume is made up of red cells. A result of 35 to 40% is normal, and a lower percentage means that you are anemic. The *hemoglobin* method measures the concentration of red pigment (hemoglobin) in your blood. Normal hemoglobin values are 12 to 14 gm per 100 cc of blood, and lower values indicate anemia. If you have a finger or earlobe prick test, most likely you are being checked for anemia. Most other blood tests require a tube of blood from an arm vein.

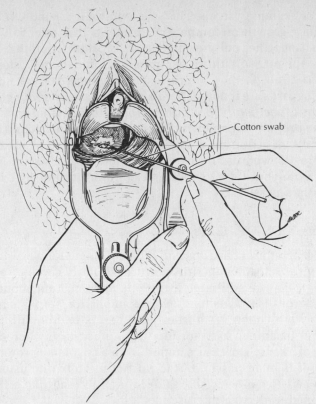

Cotton swab

Illustration 8 Your clinician collects a specimen of fluid from inside your cervical canal for a gonorrhea culture.

CULTURE AND SENSITIVITY TESTS

A culture identifies the specific bacterial agent or other organism that is causing infection. Your clinician collects a blood, urine, pus, or discharge sample from your infection site with a sterile cotton swab (see Illustration 8), transfers the sample to a jelly-like nutrient where organisms are likely to thrive, and sends the specimen to a lab, where it is incubated at roughly 98 degrees. Bacteria begin to multiply rapidly in this ideal environment. Lab specialists identify the specific bacteria and determine its sensitivity and susceptibility to various antibiotics. Incubation, identification, and sensitivity tests take several days.

Some bacteria are more difficult to culture than others and will require special handling. In order to culture the fragile gonorrhea bacteria, for example, laboratories use a nutrient treated with antibiotics to reduce growth of competitive bacteria that might overshadow gonorrhea. Gonorrhea cultures must also be protected from exposure to oxygen in the air, so culture samples are immediately stored in an oxygen-free atmosphere. Culture tests for gonorrhea are not reliable if these safeguards are ignored. *If you are concerned about gonorrhea, be sure to ask specifically for a gonorrhea culture so that your clinician can use the proper collection and storage techniques.* Many clinicians recommend that gonorrhea test samples be collected from the rectum and urethra, as well as the cervix, for maximum test reliability. A specimen from your throat should be cultured if oral sex exposure to gonorrhea is a possibility.

IDENTIFICATION OF HERPES

Many laboratories have specialized equipment for culturing herpes and other viruses. Although virus culture is a fairly complex and costly procedure, it may be advisable if there is any question about whether you have herpes (see Chapter 22). Specimens for herpes cultures are collected with a cotton swab from your cervix or from a blister.

Another technique used for identifying herpes is microscopic examination of a sample of cells scraped from a suspicious sore; if herpes is present, it is often possible to identify tiny dots (inclusion bodies) inside the cells when your cell sample is processed like a Pap smear and examined under the microscope.

SCHILLER'S STAIN

In a simple procedure often done during the speculum examination, Schiller's solution or a similar iodine mixture called Lugol's solution is painted over the surface of your cervix. A normal cervical surface absorbs iodine from the solution and is stained mahogany brown; abnormal areas remain light pink. Iodine staining was often used to pinpoint an area for biopsy before colposcopy was available. Colposcopy, described below, is probably more accurate, however.

WOOD'S LIGHT

Wood's light is an ultraviolet light bulb used to identify fungus infections of the scalp and skin. Some common fungus infections appear fluorescent under ultraviolet light.

BIOPSY

If you have a lump, a wart, or a sore, ulcerated area, your clinician may recommend biopsy: removal of a small piece of tissue for microscopic examination by a pathologist. Biopsy is a procedure that usually allows your clinician to arrive at a precise, definite diagnosis. Almost any tissue can be subjected to biopsy, including skin, vaginal lining, cervix, or uterine lining.

Taking the biopsy sample is usually a minor office procedure. Local anesthetic is often used, and discomfort is likely to be minimal. The pathologist needs only enough tissue to include several cell layers so that she/he can assess the pattern of cell changes beneath the surface layer. Laboratory evaluation of a biopsy specimen requires several days.

Vulvar Biopsy. Vulvar biopsy is particularly helpful when skin cancer is a possibility. Your clinician removes a ¼-inch patch of anesthetized skin from the junction of normal and abnormal-looking areas. In some cases, she/he will close your biopsy site with a stitch, and in other cases, it can be left to heal over by itself. Keep the biopsy area clean and dry to prevent infection. If tenderness, swelling, or redness occurs in the biopsy area, see your clinician promptly.

Cervical Biopsy. Your clinician may recommend biopsy of the cervix if you have an abnormal Pap smear. Colposcopy (see following section), careful examination of your cervix under bright light through magnifying lenses, may help your clinician pinpoint abnormal areas for biopsy. Local anesthetic usually is not necessary; pain nerves to your cervix are sparsely distributed, and you are likely to feel only mild cramping when a biopsy specimen is taken (see Illustration 9). Avoid intercourse, douching, and tampons for a week or so after biopsy so that your cervix can heal properly. It is normal to have some spotting after a biopsy, but if heavy bleeding occurs, see your clinician promptly. Symptoms of infection, such as pain, unusual vaginal discharge, or fever, require evaluation as well.

Endocervical Curettage (endocervix means the cervical canal; curettage means scraping). If an abnormal area on your cervix extends up into your cervical canal, your clinician may recommend endocervical curettage to obtain shreds of tissue for microscopic evaluation. The scraping instrument (curet) has a tiny spoon-shaped tip that removes a

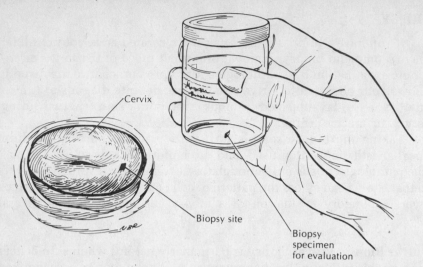

Cervix

Biopsy site

Biopsy
specimen
for evaluation

Illustration 9 A cervical biopsy requires only a tiny fragment of tissue.

shallow strand of cervical lining as it is scraped downward inside the canal. The strand is evaluated in the same way as any other biopsy sample. Endocervical scraping is unlikely to be very painful, but you may have some mild cramping. Watch for infection symptoms, such as fever, pain, and unusual discharge, and call your clinician promptly if you think you have an infection.

Endometrial Biopsy. A small scraping instrument (curet) is inserted through your cervical canal into your uterine cavity and then scraped downward along the uterine lining (see Illustration 10) to remove shallow strands of lining (endometrium). Most women experience moderate to strong cramping with endometrial biopsy. Your clinician may use a local anesthetic to decrease pain.

Endometrial biopsy may be recommended for evaluation of abnormal bleeding, especially if you are over 35 or have a family history of uterine cancer.

Endometrial biopsy is often used to evaluate fertility problems. The pathologist can determine whether your uterine lining shows evidence of normal ovulation and normal progesterone-influenced changes.

Uterine Vacuum Scraping. There are several techniques and special instruments that your clinician can use to evaluate your uterine lining

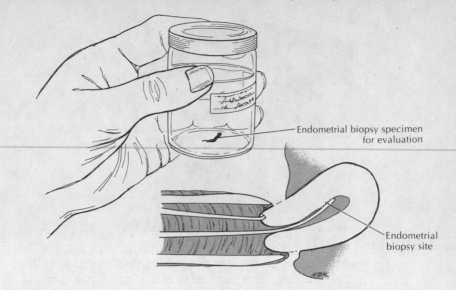

Endometrial biopsy specimen for evaluation

Endometrial biopsy site

Illustration 10   Your clinician scrapes away a narrow strand of uterine lining for an endometrial biopsy.

in the office. She/he inserts a narrow plastic tube through your cervix into the uterine cavity to obtain small shreds of uterine lining tissue that can be examined microscopically by a pathologist. The vacuum scraping procedure is similar to early vacuum abortion (see Chapter 20).

The purpose of vacuum scraping is to be sure that you do not have abnormal thickening of the uterine lining (endometrial hyperplasia) or uterine cancer. In some cases, uterine vacuum scraping can be a substitute for full dilation and curettage (D&C, see Chapter 40). Some clinicians recommend vacuum scraping as a routine test for women who choose to take estrogen replacement therapy after menopause.

Your clinician will probably use local anesthetic to block nerves in your cervix and decrease your discomfort during the procedure. You are likely, however, to have some cramping during and a few minutes after vacuum scraping. Most clinicians believe that more accurate diagnostic information is obtained with vacuum scraping than with older techniques that used a salt solution to wash cells from the uterine cavity (such as Gravlee jet wash).

If you have fever, pain, or unusual discharge after uterine scraping, be sure to call your clinician promptly.

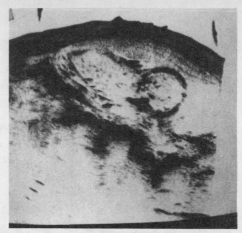

Illustration 11   The head and back of this five-month fetus are visible on the sonogram. The pregnant woman's navel is the bulge on top, and her ribs are to the left, pelvis to the right.

SONOGRAM (ULTRASOUND, SONOGRAPHY)

Sonography is an adaptation of marine sonar technology. Sound echos provide a picture of soft tissue structures inside your body. (X-ray provides some information about soft tissue but is best for evaluating bones.) A sonogram may be recommended to determine the size of the uterus, length of pregnancy, the position of a fetus, or to confirm the presence of twins (see Illustration 11). It can also be used to evaluate ovarian enlargement or a pelvic mass or to detect an ectopic pregnancy.

You will most likely be sent to an x-ray laboratory for the sonogram. Sonography does not use x-ray, but it does require special equipment and specially trained technicians. You will be asked to drink several glasses of water before your test, and your bladder will be uncomfortably full. The technician uses your full bladder to establish landmarks for the sonar echos. (You will be able to urinate immediately after your test.) During the test, you will be positioned on a hard table and the technician will move a small transmitter-receiver that looks like a microphone back and forth across your abdomen to trace the sonar echos. The procedure is painless but may require 30 minutes or more. You will probably be able to watch some of the echo patterns yourself on the ultrasound screen. Many women find it an interesting experience.

Most radiologists (physicians specializing in x-ray techniques and ultrasound) believe that risks associated with sonography are minimal. Sound waves do not have the same potential for altering molecular structure that x-rays do and are almost certainly safer. Since this is a relatively new technique, however, long-term studies of ultrasound effects are not yet available, and long-term risks, if any, are not known.

COLPOSCOPY

A colposcope is a diagnostic instrument that looks like binoculars mounted on a tripod. During a pelvic examination your clinician can look through the colposcope to see the surface of your cervix magnified 10 to 20 times normal size. With magnification and high-intensity colored lights, it is possible to see details of cervical structure that are not visible to the naked eye.

Colposcopy is a relatively new procedure and requires special training. Many clinicians did not have a chance to learn colposcopy as part of their specialty education in gynecology, and unless your clinician has been trained to interpret colposcopic findings, the procedure is not worth while.

Colposcopy is painless; the instrument does not even touch you, and the light source provides cool light. Colposcopy is time-consuming and expensive, and thorough colposcopic examination requires that you lie still for 10 to 20 minutes with a speculum in place.

Colposcopy is often used to evaluate abnormal Pap smear results (see Chapter 27) or to identify an abnormal area for biopsy. Your clinician may perform a colposcopic exam if you have pain or bleeding with intercourse that may be caused by a cervical abnormality. Colposcopic examination of both the cervix and the vaginal walls is recommended for DES daughters (see Chapter 37). The colposcope can be used to examine ulcers, sores, or other abnormal skin areas on the vulva.

Colposcopy can help your clinician identify areas of the cervix where cell multiplication is increased. These areas appear white and dense compared to the normal cervical surface areas because dense, white nuclei of young cells are closely packed together. Such areas are called *white lesions* and are often the source of abnormal cells found in a Pap smear.

The distribution of tiny blood vessels near the surface of your cervix can also be seen through a colposcope. The blood vessel pattern is often altered when precancerous changes occur, and the pattern is greatly altered by cancer. These clues may help your clinician identify the most abnormal areas for biopsy or treatment.

Biopsies performed after careful colposcopic examination (called colposcopically directed biopsies) are especially valuable, for you and your clinician have some assurance that your biopsy specimens are from the most abnormal areas. The same principle applies when your clinician uses the colposcope to examine an abnormal area on your vulva.

If your clinician is not able to see the entire extent of the abnormal areas, she/he will recommend further tests or treatment. For example, if the abnormal area extends up inside your cervical canal out of view, your clinician will probably recommend endocervical curettage (see previous section) or perhaps surgery to remove the entire surface of the cervix and the outer part of the cervical canal (called conization of the cervix).

CAUTERY AND CRYOSURGERY

Cautery (burning, heat cautery) and cryosurgery (freezing, cold cautery) are commonly used to destroy abnormal tissue such as warts on the vulva, cervix, or vaginal walls. They are often recommended for treatment of cervicitis (inflammation of the cervix, see Chapter 24) and benign or precancerous abnormalities of the cervix that are detected by Pap smear and confirmed by biopsy (see Chapter 27). When an abnormal area of surface tissue is destroyed, the nearby normal cells have an opportunity to grow into the area and replace destroyed abnormal tissue with new, normal cells. Cautery and cryosurgery treatments are often quite effective.

Heat cautery is the older of the two approaches. Cautery equipment is simple and inexpensive; electricity produces a controlled current at the tip of the cautery probe. The probe is touched to an abnormal area, and heat destroys abnormal cells. The heat current penetrates only a few cell layers: only surface cells are killed. Cautery causes mild to moderate pain, depending on what part of the body is treated and how extensively tissues are burned, but the cautery procedure lasts only a few seconds.

Cryosurgery is a newer technique and has several advantages over cautery. It is less likely to be painful and produces a more uniform area and depth of tissue destruction. Freezing can eradicate a more extensive surface area without as much risk of damage to underlying tissue; it causes less scarring and is less likely to cause narrowing of the cervical canal (stenosis) than cautery is.

Cryosurgery equipment is fairly sophisticated and expensive. The cold source is compressed nitrous oxide or carbon dioxide gas from a tank. The tank is connected to a pressure regulator and a hand-held instrument that looks like a gun. Compressed gas is released into the gun and expands rapidly to produce intense cold, about −60 degrees Fahrenheit. Cold is conducted from the gun's metal tip to any tissue that it touches.

When cryosurgery is used to treat cervical problems, your clinician first selects a metal tip that fits the contour of the area to be frozen. With the speculum in place, as in a routine pelvic examination, she/he touches the metal tip to your cervix and turns on the gas. Thorough freezing usually requires about two minutes. You may experience a vague sensation of coldness in your vagina and mild menstrual-like cramps, but discomfort usually subsides rapidly after the freezing is completed.

Cryosurgery or heat cautery can cause swelling in the cervix that might temporarily narrow or obstruct your cervical canal; therefore, these procedures are usually performed immediately after a normal menstrual period. Swelling should be resolved by the time your next period begins.

After heat cautery or cryosurgery, you will have a profuse, watery vaginal discharge lasting as long as a week or two. You may also have spotting or even bleeding, especially if your cervix is touched or bumped. Most clinicians advise that you avoid intercourse for two weeks after treatment to minimize the risk of infection. You may be advised to use medicated vaginal cream to provide an optimal environment for healing. Illustration 12 shows a typical cervix after heat cautery and after cryosurgery.

Complications after heat cautery or cryosurgery are rare. Infection may occur and may require antibiotic treatment. Bleeding can occur,

Cervix after Cryosurgery   Cervix after Cautery

Illustration 12 Cryosurgery and cautery are two common treatments for abnormal cervical cell changes.

especially if your cervix is injured before it heals. Excessive tissue destruction can result in permanent narrowing of the cervical canal, and is more likely after heat cautery than cryosurgery. Accidental damage to deeper cervical tissue could cause serious hemorrhage, especially with hot cautery when tissue destruction is rapid and difficult to gauge accurately. Extensive destruction of cervical mucus glands might result in a significant decrease in cervical mucus production and might even impair fertility.

When To Have A Pap Smear

According to the newspaper, doctors can't get together on when women need Pap smears. Just one more example of how life isn't as simple as it used to be! I got on the phone with my doctor and we worked out a schedule for me. Now if I only had a five-year calendar . . .

—Woman, 36

The medical community is not in complete agreement about how often women should have Pap smears. In fact, the American Cancer Society, the American College of Obstetricians and Gynecologists, and the National Institute of Child Health and Human Development have each recently issued *different* recommendations for Pap smear intervals. Perhaps an individual woman's wisest course is to review the three recommendations, talk with her clinician, and then decide on the most appropriate intervals for her own situation.

American Cancer Society (ACS): The current ACS recommendation (1) is that a woman have her first Pap smear soon after she begins having intercourse or when she reaches age 20, whichever comes first. She should have the test repeated a year later. If both tests are normal, she can then begin to have Pap smears at three-year intervals. ACS notes that women who begin intercourse at an early age (before 20), who have multiple sex partners, or who have other risk factors such as prenatal DES (diethylstilbestrol) exposure (see Chapter 37) may need Pap smears more frequently. Women who are "relatively inactive sexually" may prefer intervals even longer than three years.

Women need Pap smears annually between the ages of 40 and 65, according to ACS, and certain women need a pelvic exam, Pap smear, and endometrial tissue sampling at menopause. These women would include those at high risk for developing endometrial cancer because of a history of infertility, obesity, failure of ovulation, abnormal uterine bleeding, or current estrogen therapy.

American College of Obstetricians and Gynecologists (ACOG): ACOG continues to recommend annual Pap smears for most women (2) because, among other reasons, the test is inexpensive, Pap test results can be normal even in the presence of cervical disease as often as 15–40% of the time, and early cervical disease is much easier to treat and cure than advanced disease. Annual screening is especially recommended for high-risk women. The ACOG policy states that "extending the screening interval in the low-risk group should be an informed choice arrived at by the patient and her physician." Women at low risk for cervical cancer are those who do not begin intercourse before age 18–20, do not have multiple sexual partners, and did not have prenatal exposure to DES.

National Institute of Child Health and Human Development (NICHD): NICHD agrees with ACS in that Pap smears should begin as soon as a woman is sexually active (3), should be repeated in one year, and can then be extended to three-year intervals if both tests are normal. Their panel was not able to reach agreement on screening intervals for high-risk women, which NICHD defines as women who begin intercourse before age 18, who have multiple sexual partners, or who are of lower socioeconomic status. Women who have been prenatally exposed to DES may need Pap smears before they are sexually active, if intercourse is delayed beyond the teen years. If a woman has two normal tests after age 60, "further screening appears to be unproductive," says NICHD.

Appropriate Pap smear intervals depend a great deal on your own personal health and life-style factors. Certainly annual Pap smears make sense for high-risk women. If you do not fall into a high-risk category, talk with your clinician and decide on a screening interval you are both comfortable with. Remember that even one abnormal Pap smear result (see Chapter 27) means you and your clinician must rethink your testing intervals.

REFERENCES

1. Guidelines for the cancer-related checkup: Recommendations and rationale: Cancer of the cervix. *Ca—A Cancer Journal for Clinicians*, American Cancer Society 30(4):215–233, 1980.
2. American College of Obstetricians and Gynecologists: Periodic Cancer Screening for Women. Policy Statement, June 1980.
3. Consensus panel issues Pap smear recommendations, *NICHD Research Highlights and Topics of Interest*, Office of Research Reporting, National Institute of Child Health and Human Development, Bethesda, Maryland, September 1980.

22 | Common Reproductive Tract Infections

You may have read that there are two kinds of reproductive tract infections; vaginitis and venereal disease (VD). You'll probably find that most clinicians today don't make such a definite distinction. An important distinction they do make, however, is between infections that are just bothersome and infections that may cause you serious health problems. Yeast, trichomonas, bacterial infections, warts, and pubic lice can make life miserable, but they are not serious health threats. Herpes, syphilis, and gonorrhea are.

Gonorrhea is a major health threat for women, not only because it is epidemic (only the common cold afflicts more people in the United States than gonorrhea) but because for women its consequence can be serious pelvic infection. The symptoms of early gonorrhea infection are sometimes subtle. In fact, both women and men can be silent carriers of the disease, spreading infection to new partners though they themselves have no telltale discharge or symptoms at all.

If a woman becomes infected and does not receive early treatment, gonorrhea can spread from its original infection site in the cervix and vagina to invade the uterus and tubes, where it may cause serious internal damage. Gonorrheal pelvic infection necessitates hospitalization for 175,000 women each year in this country at a cost of $212 million. Many more women are ill enough that they must miss work or school. Gonorrhea and subsequent pelvic infection account for 918,000 lost school days a year. Each school day in the United States, about 5,750 young women are absent because of gonorrhea (1,2).

341

Women who have had pelvic infections are also likely to have continuing problems. Impaired fertility, persistent pain, and ectopic pregnancies are common after gonorrhea, because scarring from pelvic infection often obstructs the fallopian tubes and prevents free passage of an egg from the ovary to the uterus. One study found that 15 to 40% of women who had one gonorrhea pelvic infection became sterile, even after antibiotic treatment for infection (2).

Basic Facts About Infection

The diseases covered in this chapter have different symptoms and require different treatments. Certain basic facts about prevention and cure, however, apply to all of them:

1. *Women tend to have infections when they have a new partner, or when they have more than one partner.* You can prevent infection in many cases if you use condoms in the early going with a new partner, and any time you have more than one partner.

2. *Avoid intercourse if you have any symptoms of infection.* You may be able to avoid transmitting an infection to your partner. If you have itching, redness, pain, or an unusual discharge, intercourse may be uncomfortable and may make your symptoms worse.

3. *An examination and lab tests are the only way to learn what kind of infection you have.* Remember that gonorrhea may have no symptoms either for you or your partner in the early stages. You must be tested if you suspect that you have been exposed to gonorrhea.

    Leftover medicines from your seventh yeast infection may be just what you need to cure your eighth one! In general, however, you'll need an exam, lab tests, and a new prescription for any infection. Do not douche before your exam; if you do, your tests may not be accurate; your clinician cannot diagnose a discharge that isn't there.

    None of the common infections responds to exactly the same kind of treatment; yeast medicine may not help a trichomonas infection, for example. You may have more than one infection at the same time, and you will need two separate and distinct courses of treatment. If you are itching and miserable and have to wait three days for your appointment, frequent soaks in a bathtub full of plain warm water (sitz bath) may relieve your symptoms. Betadine douche used according to directions on the package is often effective treatment for vaginitis, and does not require a prescription. Three dangers with self-treatment for vaginitis are the possibility that you might have gonorrhea and remain untreated and unaware because no culture was done, that your treatment might interfere with tests your clinician performs later to diagnose the cause of infection and that you might have a more serious or extensive infection than simple vaginitis.

4. ***Your partner may need to be treated at the same time you are.*** With many infections you are likely to get reinfected immediately unless your partner(s) is treated along with you. Many clinicians are willing to give you medicine to take to your partner yourself, but in some cases your partner must be seen for evaluation and treatment. Sometimes men have clear symptoms of infection, but often they do not. Burning, pain, discharge, or skin irritation may be present with many of the common infections, but it is also possible that a man would have no outward signs of infection. You cannot assume that he is infection-free just because he has no symptoms. Avoid intercourse with anyone who has a discharge, sores, or warts on the penis, scrotum, or anus.

5. ***Use all the medicines you are given.*** Infections tend to feel better before they are completely cured (thank goodness). But be diligent about your medication schedule, and use the full course recommended so that you will be sure of a cure.

Bacteria respond to antibiotic therapy. Antibiotics like penicillin, ampicillin, and tetracycline are commonly used to cure gonorrhea, syphilis, and bacterial infections. If you have ever had any kind of allergic reaction to penicillin, you must not use penicillin or ampicillin (a semisynthetic form of penicillin). Be sure to tell your clinician about your history of allergy. She/he is likely to prescribe tetracycline or another substitute antibiotic.

Do not take tetracycline if you are pregnant or suspect that you could be pregnant and intend to continue the pregnancy. Tetracycline may cause dark stains on the permanent teeth of a fetus that is exposed to the mother's tetracycline. Avoid milk, all milk products, and antacids two hours before and two hours after each tetracycline pill. The calcium in these products decreases your body's ability to absorb and use tetracycline, with the result that the drug may not be fully effective. Avoid sunbathing and prolonged sun exposure of any kind while you are taking tetracycline, because you may develop a skin rash. Never use tetracycline after the expiration date on the package, because you may have an increased risk of kidney damage.

Make sure you know the exact name and danger signs for the particular drug your clinician prescribes. Diarrhea, for example, is a common and fairly harmless side effect with ampicillin; diarrhea with some other less common antibiotics may be a sign of serious trouble.

6. ***Find out from your clinician whether you will need a followup exam.*** A repeat test for you and your partner is crucial if you have gonorrhea, but you may be able to tell for yourself whether your yeast, trichomonas, or bacterial infection is under control. Even these infections can be stubborn, so see your clinician for repeat tests if you suspect that you still have a problem. It may be especially important to have followup tests when you have been treated with antibiotics such as ampicillin or tetracycline, because these drugs may ***promote*** yeast while they cure the other infection. Some clinicians routinely provide a prescription for yeast medication along with such antibiotics so that you can have the prescription filled later if you develop symptoms of yeast infection.

7. ***Use condoms until you are certain both you and your partner have been cured.***

8. ***Infections can cause abnormal Pap smears.*** Bacterial infection, yeast, trichomonas, herpes, and gonorrhea can cause significant inflammation of the cervix; and inflammation can cause abnormal but noncancerous cell changes. It is common to have abnormal Pap smears during an infection. Have your Pap test repeated when your infection is cleared up. When you are free from inflammation, your Pap test is more likely to give an accurate report on the presence or absence of premalignant or malignant cervical cells.

9. ***Remember how reproductive tract infections are spread.*** Except for yeast infection and bacterial vaginitis, which may sometimes arise spontaneously, most disease organisms are transmitted by intimate sexual contact, straight or gay: skin to skin, or mucous membrane to mucous membrane. It is unlikely that your children

who share your bathroom might catch your infection, for example. And forget all that misinformation about toilet seats and door-knobs. These disease organisms need warm, moist, mucous membrane environments for survival.

10. ***Some infections can be prevented. Condoms are the very best protection against sexually transmitted infection.*** Also, when you keep your vulva clean, dry, and healthy, you are less likely to get infections. Some suggestions for preventing infection:

Bathe carefully every day with water and a mild soap, and ask your partner to do the same.

Wipe front to back, to avoid bringing bowel bacteria into your vaginal area.

Wear cotton underpants. Avoid nylon underpants, pantyhose, and very tight pants, because they tend to hold moisture in the vulvar area.

Avoid bath oils, bubble baths, and hygiene sprays if you are frequently bothered by tender, irritated skin around your vulva.

Avoid douching. Douching may irritate your vaginal lining and make you more vulnerable to infection.

Lose weight if you are overweight. Extra pounds mean less exposure of the vulva to air, so the vulvar environment can become too moist.

If you use extra lubrication for intercourse, try contraceptive foam, cream, or jelly. All these products offer good lubrication and can help destroy infectious organisms to some degree. A good second choice for lubrication, without germ-killing capability, is a water-soluble lubricant such as K-Y Jelly, which is available in drugstores without a prescription. *Avoid petroleum jelly lubricants* such as Vaseline, because they tend to stay in the vagina, are hard to wash away, and may even promote infection.

11. ***Women tend to have infections when their general health status is not good.*** Infections seem to crop up most frequently when times are hard: after an illness, during exam week, during a long battle siege with your partner. That is why you might have six infections in one year, and then no infections for eight years. Try to maintain a healthy physical and emotional equilibrium, and you may prevent infections (and have a happier life).

Bacterial Vaginitis (Nonspecific Vaginitis, *Corynebacterium vaginalis, Hemophilis vaginalis,* or *H. influenzae)*

SYMPTOMS

Discharge is yellow to gray-green. It may be thick or watery, and it may have a foul odor. Pain on urination, vaginal itching, and/or pain in the vagina or vulva during intercourse may also be symptoms.

DIAGNOSIS

Bacterial vaginitis is caused by one (or more) of the ubiquitous bacteria such as the corynebacterium, hemophilus bacterium, or possibly a new culprit called *chlamydia.* It is transmitted via sexual intimacy or may arise spontaneously.

Your clinician will take a sample of your discharge and look at it immediately under a microscope. She/he looks for rod-shaped bacteria and stippled cells on your slide. These same bacteria may also be detected on your Pap smear. The diagnosis is often made by eliminating the possibility of trichomonas or yeast infections on the microscopic examination and eliminating the possibility of gonorrhea with a culture test.

TREATMENT

Sulfa-based creams and suppositories (Furacin, Sultrin Triple Sulfa, Vagitrol, AVC) relieve symptoms for many women, but recent research seems to show these products may not effectively cure infection. Vaginal treatment has the disadvantage that your partner is not treated at the same time you are. More and more clinicians are using oral antibiotics such as tetracycline, Flagyl (see discussion of Trichomonas below), or ampicillin for seven to ten days as the initial treatment. Oral antibiotics may be especially important for difficult or recurrent infections, because it is possible to treat you and your partner simultaneously. If you are given ampicillin to take to your partner, **be sure to tell him not to take it if he is allergic to penicillin.** If he is, he needs another type of antibiotic. An antibacterial douche such as Betadine (povidone-iodine) also works well and is often prescribed along with the oral antibiotics. You may find douches less messy than vaginal suppositories or cream.

PROGNOSIS

Bacterial vaginitis usually improves promptly with treatment, but reinfection is common. You are not contagious once the infection is cured. Vaginitis does not attack or harm your uterus or tubes, and will not affect your fertility once you are cured. Review "Basic Facts About Infection" in this chapter for help with treatment and prevention.

Yeast Infection (*Monilia, Candida*, Fungus Infection)

SYMPTOMS

Yeast infection causes a thick, white, cottage-cheese-like discharge, itching, or redness around the labia, and sometimes itching and redness on the upper thighs. Itching may be severe.

DIAGNOSIS

Yeast is a very common fungus (*Candida albicans*) that normally exists in harmony with other organisms in your body. When it overgrows, you are likely to have symptoms. Your clinician will examine a sample of your discharge under a microscope. Long, branching yeast colonies are easy to see and may also appear on your Pap smear.

TREATMENT

Yeast infections are usually treated with antibiotic vaginal cream or suppositories such as Monistat (miconazole, 7 days), Mycostatin or Nilstat (nystatin, 15 to 30 days), Candeptin or Vanobid (candicidin, 14 days) or Gyne-Lotrimin (clotrimazole, 7 days). For stubborn infections, it may be necessary to continue treatment throughout a menstrual cycle, and in some instances treatment for as long as six weeks to two months may be necessary. You can use tampons to reduce discharge caused by melting suppositories. Mycolog or another cream containing a yeast agent and cortisone will reduce swelling and itching around the entrance to your vagina and on your thighs to make you more comfortable. Gentian violet (Hyva) suppositories once a day for two weeks may be used, but these cause purple stains on clothing. Boric acid powder dissolved in a douche or inserted in the vagina in gelatin capsules has been used with considerable success in the treatment of yeast infection.

It is unlikely that your partner will have symptoms of yeast, although it can occasionally cause infection and irritation on the penis, scrotum, or inguinal area. To minimize the likelihood of reinfection from yeast that he may be harboring, your partner should wash his penis carefully with soap and water daily and use condoms for intercourse until your infection is cured.

Yogurt is very popular as a yeast remedy. Some women who have tried it recommend eating yogurt, and others insert yogurt in the vagina. There is no research to indicate what, if any, therapeutic effect yogurt has.

PROGNOSIS

Medication will almost always cure yeast infections, but reinfection is extremely common. If you have yeast over and over, your clinician may recommend further evaluation to be sure that you don't have diabetes, which would make you more susceptible to yeast infections. Yeast infections also may be more common among pregnant women and women who use birth control Pills.

Yeast does not attack or harm your uterus or tubes and will not affect your fertility once you are cured. Read "Basic Facts About Infection" in this chapter for tips on curing infection and preventing infections in the future.

I used to get yeast as regular as clockwork right after each period. I would see my doctor, get suppositories, and use them faithfully for two weeks; then *maybe* the next cycle I wouldn't have problems. But in the cycle after that yeast always came back. Now my doctor gives me suppositories to have on hand all the time. I store them in the refrigerator. Every month I use them for three days after my period stops. I haven't had any itching or discharge in a year.

—*Woman, 36*

Some women notice that yeast symptoms appear almost every cycle just after a period. One or two vinegar douches (1 tablespoon of white vinegar to a quart of warm water) or several days of antibiotic cream or suppositories just before you usually get symptoms may head off trouble.

Trichomonas Vaginitis ("Trich," Trichomoniasis. Pronounced "Trick")

SYMPTOMS

Trichomonas is apt to produce a frothy, thin, greenish white or grayish vaginal discharge, intense itching, redness, a foul odor, pain, and/or frequency of urination.

> I've had vaginitis before, but trich was something else! I had *gallons* of discharge, and it *really* burned. One day I was fine, and the next day I couldn't even go to work. It was the first time in my life I *demanded* an immediate appointment with my doctor.
>
> —Woman, 31

DIAGNOSIS

Trichomonas is caused by a one-celled protozoan called a trichomonad. Infection is usually transmitted by sexual intimacy. The trichomonad is not quite as delicate as the gonorrhea bacterium, for example; so it may be possible for trichomonads to survive for a few hours—and be transmitted—on wet towels or bathing suits.

Your clinician will examine a sample of your discharge under a microscope. Often the organisms can be easily identified because they swim quite rapidly with their whip-like tails. Trichomonads are sometimes identified on a Pap smear or in the sediment of a urine specimen. Trichomonas can also cause small, deep red spots (petechiae) on your cervix.

TREATMENT

The most effective drug for treatment of trichomonas is Flagyl (metronidazole), but Flagyl can cause serious side effects. On the other hand, safer medications such as antibiotic vaginal suppositories are not as effective and do not kill trichomonads in your urinary system or in your partner, so reinfection is quite likely.

Flagyl is an antibiotic that is given in pill form. The FDA-approved treatment is 250 mg three times a day for seven days. Many experts in the field of sexually transmitted infection believe that it may be preferable, however, to give Flagyl in a single 2,000-mg dose or in 500-mg doses twice a day for five days, because a shorter time of exposure to Flagyl may decrease your risk of harmful side effects. Your partner(s) should be treated at the same time you are.

Do not use Flagyl if you are pregnant or if you suspect that you are pregnant and would continue the pregnancy; it is not yet known whether Flagyl causes fetal abnormalities. Do not use Flagyl if you are nursing, for the drug appears in breast milk.

Side effects of Flagyl may include an allergic reaction; nausea and/or diarrhea; dryness of the mouth; tinny, metallic taste; intolerance to alcohol—many (not all) people who drink soon after or during Flagyl therapy experience nausea, vomiting, headache, and/or flushing; and a depression in the white blood cell count (leukopenia).

The FDA-approved information leaflet for physicians that accompanies each package of Flagyl begins with the following statement:

WARNING

Metronidazole [*generic name for Flagyl*] has been shown to be carcinogenic [*cancer-producing*] in mice and possibly carcinogenic in rats. Unnecessary use of the drug should be avoided. Its use should be reserved for the conditions described in the Indications section below.

The indications section says that Flagyl (for both you and your partner) should be used only when your clinician has done lab tests to be sure trichomonads are present and when you have definite symptoms or inflammation of the cervix caused by these organisms.

The FDA-approved instructions also recommend that you have a white blood cell count performed both before and after treatment, because Flagyl may temporarily decrease your body's ability to produce white cells (leukocytes). *A white cell count is especially important before taking a second course of Flagyl.* Diminished white blood cell production could impair your body's ability to fight off infection of any kind.

If you have a severe, stubborn infection and choose to take a second course of Flagyl, observe the following precautions: 1) Have another exam and a microscopic examination of your discharge to be certain trichomonads are still present. 2) Have a white blood cell count. 3) Be certain that you are not pregnant. 4) Make sure that your partner(s) and anyone he may have had intercourse with are treated. 5) Wait at least four to six weeks after your first course of treatment.

Perhaps the safest treatment approach is to try a two-week course of antibiotic vaginal suppositories (Tricofuran) or douches (Trichotine or Betadine) first, and to use Flagyl for both you and your partner(s) if your symptoms are severe or persistent or if reinfection occurs.

PROGNOSIS

Trichomonas vaginitis can sometimes be cured with antibiotic vaginal suppositories or douches, and can almost always be cured with Flagyl. Reinfection is quite common.

Trichomonas may encourage the development of venereal warts. If you have had trichomonas, watch carefully for warts developing around the entrance to your vagina or on your partner's penis, and seek treatment promptly. (A discussion of venereal warts follows later in this chapter.)

Yeast infections often flare up after a trichomonas infection. Trichomonas does not attack or harm your uterus or tubes, and your fertility will not be affected once the infection is cured.

Condoms should be used as a routine practice if your partner isn't treated at the same time you are.

Read "Basic Facts About Infection" in this chapter for tips on curing infection and preventing infection in the future.

Gonorrhea (*Neisseria gonorrhoeae*, GC, Clap)

SYMPTOMS

It is quite common for women and men to have absolutely no symptoms with gonorrhea, especially in the early stages. A woman's first clue may very well be her partner's penile discharge or burning.

At first I was shocked that my doctor wanted to do a gonorrhea test as part of my regular checkup. Why spend an extra $5 when I didn't feel sick and neither did Charlie. Still, it was reassuring to find out I don't have gonorrhea smoldering inside.

—*Woman, 23*

Many cases of gonorrhea are first detected by a routine gonorrhea culture. When symptoms do occur, they can include unusual discharge, painful urination, painful intercourse, pelvic pain or tenderness, unusual vaginal bleeding, bleeding after intercourse, and/or fever.

DIAGNOSIS

Gonorrhea is caused by a bacterium that thrives in the United States in epidemic numbers (see Illustration 1). In 1977 the **reported** case rate was 469 per 100,000 people in the United States. Atlanta and Baltimore are the gonorrhea capitals, with rates of 3,423 per 100,000 and 2,772 per 100,000, respectively (3).

A man who has intercourse one time with an infected woman has a 20 to 25% chance of becoming infected, while a woman who has intercourse one time with an infected man is "almost certain to become infected" (4), nearly 100%. Gonorrhea may be very easily spread to your tubes and uterus if you have intercourse during your menstrual period, because bacteria thrive on blood.

The fragile gonorrhea bacterium cannot survive outside warm, moist environments and is only transmitted by sexual intimacy. It most often attacks the reproductive system but can attack the throat, eyes, and rectum as well.

Your clinician cannot diagnose gonorrhea on the basis of an examination alone. (Immediate microscopic examination of discharge or a stained slide from the discharge is helpful in making a diagnosis for men, but is not reliable for women.) Diagnosis is usually made on the basis of a culture test, which takes about 48 hours to complete. (Special precautions necessary for accurate gonorrhea cultures are described in Chapter 21.) If you do have gonorrhea, a blood sample should be taken to check for syphilis as well. It is not unusual for the two infections to coexist.

TREATMENT

Gonorrhea can be cured by antibiotics such as penicillin or ampicillin. Your partner(s) must be treated at the same time you are. The

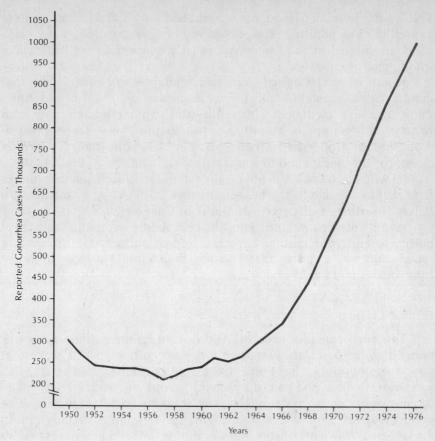

Illustration 1 The American gonorrhea epidemic. (U.S. Public Health Service, Center for Disease Control, Bureau of State Services, Venereal Disease Control Division.)

treatment most people are familiar with, penicillin shots, provide a quick, effective cure. Many clinicians choose ampicillin pills instead, because the risk of severe allergic reaction is lower than with penicillin shots. About 1.5 to 2.0 per 100,000 people who have penicillin shots have fatal allergic reactions (5).

The penicillin treatment dose is divided into two injections, one for each hip, one right after the other. Ampicillin is given by mouth; you will take about seven pills, one after the other. Both penicillin and ampicillin are often given along with a pill called probenecid that temporarily slows down the kidney excretion rate so that the antibiotic can stay in your system longer and work more effectively.

Tell your clinician if you have ever had any unusual reaction to penicillin or ampicillin in the past. If you have, you can be treated with other antibiotics, such as tetracycline (if you are not pregnant), spectinomycin, or cephalexin.

If you have abdominal pain and tenderness or other signs that gonorrhea has spread to your uterus and tubes, you will need longer, more intensive treatment with antibiotics. Your clinician may even recommend that you be admitted to the hospital for intravenous antibiotic therapy. *Gonorrhea infection in your uterus and tubes is a serious threat to your health* and to your fertility. It is estimated that 34,000 to 92,000 women in the United States become sterile each year because of irreversible damage to the fallopian tubes initiated by gonorrhea (2). Pelvic infection is discussed in detail in Chapter 25.

Avoid intercourse until you are completely symptom-free. Until both you and your partner have had repeat culture tests (including rectal cultures) to prove that you are both cured, use condoms for intercourse, and avoid oral sex.

PROGNOSIS

You must consider yourself highly contagious with early or advanced gonorrhea until you have a repeat culture test to prove that you are cured. Gonorrhea that is treated early can be cured easily with proper antibiotics, and you can probably avoid any permanent damage to your reproductive system. However, it is often difficult to recognize gonorrhea early, for it can occur with no symptoms or only subtle symptoms in the early stages. Reinfection is quite common, especially if your partner isn't treated at the same time you are.

Once gonorrhea infection has reached the fallopian tubes, you have a 15 to 40% risk of scarring, tubal obstruction, and infertility (2). The longer gonorrhea remains untreated, the greater the likelihood of permanent damage. Each time you have a repeat episode of gonorrhea, your risk of irreversible damage increases. Gonorrhea is a leading cause of fertility problems.

HOW TO PREVENT GONORRHEA

Avoid gonorrhea to protect your health, and to protect your fertility if you plan to become pregnant in the future. Some suggestions for avoiding gonorrhea:

- Have your partner use condoms. Condoms are especially important if you have more than one partner, and any time you have a new partner.

- Don't have intercourse with anyone you suspect of having gonorrhea, whether he has a discharge or not.
- Ask for a gonorrhea test each time you have a pelvic exam, and any time you think you have been exposed.
- See your clinician at once if you develop unusual discharge, pain during intercourse, abdominal pain, unusual vaginal bleeding, and/or fever. .

Read "Basic Facts About Infection" in this chapter for more suggestions on curing infection and preventing infection in the future.

Herpes Infection (Herpes Simplex Type II, Genital Herpes)

SYMPTOMS

Multiple small, extremely painful blisters (similar to cold sores on the lips or nose) appear on the vulva or buttocks (in men, sores are usually on the penis and appear somewhat drier). After about two days, the blisters open and small ulcers remain. You may also have vulvar swelling, fever, and enlarged, tender lymph nodes in your abdomen, especially the first time you are infected. An outbreak may be preceded by a tingling sensation in the area where sores later appear. Symptoms are noticeable two to seven days after you are exposed.

DIAGNOSIS

Herpes is a virus infection that is usually transmitted by sexual intimacy, but may also arise spontaneously. Techniques for identifying the herpes virus on a slide prepared from active sores or by culture or blood tests are discussed in Chapter 21.

TREATMENT

There is no known cure for herpes. Your clinician will provide you with pain-relieving pills and/or ointments, antibacterial ointments to prevent bacterial invasion in the virus ulcers, and will probably recommend sitz baths and cold, wet medicated compresses to decrease your discomfort. Sores heal spontaneously in one to four weeks.

Although the sores heal and disappear, *the virus remains inside the cells of the nerves to your vulvar area.* Sores can reappear whenever the viruses are triggered to multiply. You may have no further recurrences, or you may have many; what determines your likelihood of recurrence is not known. Recurrent attacks are usually not as severe as the initial infection. Tingling often occurs, followed by the appearance of blisters and then small ulcers just as in the initial attack, but with a faster progression and healing time. It is unusual to develop fever or swollen lymph nodes with recurrent herpes.

Several techniques for curing or ameliorating herpes have been tried in the past, including photoinactivation with neutral red dye and fluorescent light, ether, nitrous oxide, and smallpox vaccination. None of these approaches has been shown to cure herpes. It is especially important to avoid photoinactivation treatments, because it is possible they may cause viral mutations that might predispose you to develop later skin cancer; whether this actually occurs is not known.

PROGNOSIS

You are highly contagious when you have active sores during your initial attack *and* also during recurrences. *It is difficult to say how long you are contagious once sores disappear.* Lab studies have revealed infectious viruses several weeks after sores are healed.

Avoid intercourse and oral sex when you have sores and for two weeks after sores are gone. Use condoms for a full six weeks after sores have healed.

Many women who have had herpes find that they have flareups after an illness or a particularly stressful time. Flareups can occur spontaneously and do not necessarily mean that you have been reinfected by a sexual partner.

Have a Pap smear every 6 to 12 months for the rest of your life. Women who have cervical cancer are more likely than other women to have had genital herpes infections in the past, and researchers suspect that herpes may play some role in the development of cervical cancer.

HERPES AND PREGNANCY

Women who have herpes have a higher than average miscarriage rate. If you deliver a baby while you have active herpes sores, the baby is likely to become infected, and herpes can cause severe illness or death in newborns. Your clinician will deliver you by cesarean section if you have active sores at the time your baby is due.

It is extremely disheartening to have an incurable disease, even one like herpes that need not be life-threatening. Do your best to prevent flareups by maintaining a good overall health status and good nutrition. Active research to find an effective treatment for herpes is under way, so you may not have to live with it permanently.

Venereal Warts (Condylomata Acuminata, Genital Warts)

SYMPTOMS

Dry, painless warts appear on the vulva, cervix, inside the vagina, and/or around the anus. (Men usually have warts on the penis and sometimes on the anus or scrotum.) Warts may be small or large, and resemble warts on other parts of the body. If left untreated, they may go away spontaneously, but more likely they will grow in size and number, merge, and take on a cauliflower-like appearance. Warts are usually firm and rough, and are flesh colored or greyish-white.

DIAGNOSIS

Warts are caused by a virus and may follow a trichomonas or other vaginal infection. They are transmitted by sexual intimacy, and symptoms become apparent one to three months after exposure.

Your clinician can usually diagnose venereal warts by appearance alone. Warts can sometimes be confused with condylomata lata, the moist flat sores sometimes associated with secondary syphilis. If there is any question, your clinician will draw a blood sample and test for syphilis. Skin cancer on the vulva may also be mistaken for venereal warts, and your clinician may recommend biopsy to determine which disease is present in your case.

TREATMENT

Seek treatment promptly. It is much easier to cure this disease if it is treated early.

Small Warts. Your clinician will probably ask you and your partner to come in once or twice a week for treatment with podophyllin ointment or liquid, which is applied directly on the warts to dry them up. Your clinician may first put a lubricant jelly on surrounding normal skin to prevent podophyllin burns. Treatments usually are not painful. You will be asked to wash off the podophyllin six to eight hours after each treatment. Warts may go away after three to four applications, or you may need quite a few treatments.

> I guess I got warts from the guy I dated last summer while I was working at Yellowstone. I went to the health clinic a couple of times in the Fall quarter and they put medicine on them, but it didn't help much.
> By Christmas vacation they were driving me crazy. The clinic doctor said I would *have* to come in once a week till they were entirely gone. I did, and they were gone by Spring break.
>
> —*Woman, 19*

Warts are often associated with bacterial or trichomonas vaginal infections. Wart treatment is more likely to be effective if you use antibacterial vaginal cream faithfully until your warts have responded to podophyllin treatment.

Large Masses of Warts. Surgery under local or general anesthesia may be necessary to remove large masses of warts. Your clinician may also treat large warts with cautery (burning), cryosurgery (freezing), or trichloracetic acid.

Warts inside the vagina or on the cervix cannot be treated with podophyllin. Your clinician will use cautery or freezing instead. You should not be treated with podophyllin if you are pregnant, because it is not yet known whether podophyllin causes fetal abnormalities.

PROGNOSIS

Warts can be cured, and your risk of permanent scarring is greatly decreased if you seek treatment promptly. Reinfection can occur, particularly if your partner isn't treated at the same time you are.

Warts do not attack or harm your uterus or tubes, and your fertility will not be affected once you are cured.

Read "Basic Facts About Infection" in this chapter for tips on curing infection and preventing infection in the future.

Pubic Lice (Crabs, *Phthirus pubis*)

SYMPTOMS

Lice cause mild to intense itching in pubic hair areas. You may be able to see tiny lice (see Illustration 2) moving about, or feel egg cases as small bumps along the length of a pubic hair. Scratching can cause irritation of the external urinary opening (urethritis) or even lead to bladder infection (cystitis) (see Chapter 23).

DIAGNOSIS

Pubic lice are parasites much like head lice, except that they tend to inhabit the pubic area rather than the scalp. (Very hairy people may find that pubic lice spread to chest hair, underarms, and the scalp on occasion.) They are usually transmitted by sexual intimacy, but you may also be infested by sharing clothing or a bed with an infested person.

Your clinician will inspect your pubic hair carefully for lice and/or egg cases. If you have found and removed lice yourself, you might put them in an envelope and show them to your clinician to confirm the diagnosis.

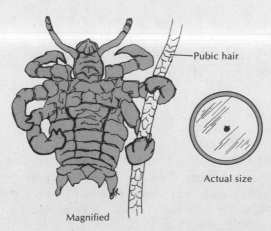

Pubic hair

Actual size

Magnified

Illustration 2   The crab louse, or "papillon d'amour" (butterfly of love) as the French say.

TREATMENT

A prescription cream, lotion, or shampoo called Kwell (gamma benzene hexachloride) kills pubic lice. Kwell is the potent pesticide Lindane, and it should not be used by pregnant women and young children. Several nonprescription products are marketed that are often effective treatments for pubic lice.

Cream or Lotion. Bathe or shower thoroughly, dry yourself completely, and apply cream or lotion to all affected areas. Wash the cream or lotion off thoroughly after 12 hours and put on freshly laundered clothes. Repeat in seven days if necessary.

Shampoo. Shampoo all affected areas thoroughly for at least four minutes, then rinse completely. Comb your pubic hair with a fine-toothed comb to remove egg cases. Repeat in seven days if necessary, but no more than twice in one week.

Change clothes and bedding at the time you treat yourself and wash combs and brushes in Kwell shampoo. Pubic lice can live about 24 hours once they leave the body, and egg cases can survive six days. All articles are safe to use after that time.

PROGNOSIS

Pubic lice are easy to cure. Reinfestation is unlikely if all infested people are treated at the same time. Lice are not a serious health risk.

Syphilis (Lues, *Treponema pallidum* Infection)

SYMPTOMS

Primary Syphilis. Primary syphilis is the first stage and occurs about three weeks after exposure. The range of time from exposure to the onset of symptoms may be anywhere from 9 to 90 days. Usually the first symptom is at the site of sexual contact: a sore called a chancre (pronounced "shanker"). The chancre is usually painless; there may be a hardened red-rimmed sore or pimple-like area on the edge of your vagina, cervix, vulva, or mouth, or on your partner's penis. These are the most common locations, but the chancre may also appear on the fingertips, lips, breast, anus, or almost anywhere there is intimate contact between you and the infected person. During this primary stage, syphilis is extremely infectious. *Only a small percentage of women who develop a chancre will notice it,* because it is painless and may be deep inside the vagina. In two to six weeks the chancre will disappear, even without treatment.

Secondary Syphilis. The second stage occurs as soon as one week or as long as six months after the chancre heals. Symptoms tend to last three to six months but may come and go for several years. They include rash, especially on the palms of the hands and soles of the feet, fever, a sore throat, headaches, a sore mouth, loss of appetite, nausea, and inflamed eyes. Scalp hair may fall out in patches. (Syphilis is sometimes called "Haircut.") Sores called condylomata lata may appear around the genitals and anus; these sores are moist, broad-based, and about ¼ inch across. *You are highly infectious* in the secondary phase of syphilis, and the infection can be spread from any affected site.

Tertiary Syphilis. After 10 to 20 years, you may develop signs of tertiary syphilis. These include heart disease, brain damage, spinal cord damage, and blindness. Approximately one in four people not treated for secondary syphilis will eventually suffer incapacity or death from the disease.

DIAGNOSIS

Syphilis is caused by a spiral-shaped bacterium and is transmitted by sexual intimacy. In 1977 the *reported* case rate in the United States was 10 per 100,000 people for infectious (primary or secondary) syphilis (3).

Your clinician will look first for a chancre, rash, or flat, moist genital sore, the outward signs of primary and secondary syphilis. Syphilis is usually confirmed by testing your blood to determine whether you have syphilis antibodies, which appear about six to seven weeks after the disease begins. If exposure to syphilis is suspected and your first blood test is normal, have the test repeated about six weeks later.

A man I had dated a few times called me and said he had syphilis, and I nearly died! I went to the health department, and their tests showed I had gonorrhea, not syphilis. I never thought I'd be *relieved* to find out I had gonorrhea!

—Woman, 22

TREATMENT

The high-dose penicillin or ampicillin treatment given for gonorrhea will destroy early incubating syphilis within ten days of exposure but will not destroy syphilis that has progressed to the chancre stage or beyond. Longer-acting penicillin or tetracycline preparations are used for the treatment of primary, secondary, or tertiary syphilis.

You and your partner(s) must be treated at the same time. Avoid intercourse and all intimacy for at least a month and until repeat tests prove that you and your partner are cured. (Some syphilis blood tests may still have positive results even when you have been completely cured. Usually, however, repeat tests will be negative if you have been cured.)

PROGNOSIS

Syphilis can be cured with antibiotics. Reinfection is likely if your partner is not treated at the same time you are. If you are cured in the primary or secondary stage, permanent damage will be prevented.

A blood test for syphilis is essential during the first four months of pregnancy whether you think you have been exposed or not. Syphilis can seriously harm or even kill a developing fetus. Syphilis can be treated and cured during pregnancy. Read "Basic Facts About Infection" in this chapter for tips on preventing infection in the future.

Bartholin's Gland Infection

SYMPTOMS

Bartholin's glands are normally inconspicuous (see Chapter 1). If a gland is invaded by infection, however, it becomes very conspicuous: an exquisitely tender, hot lump that can become as large as a lime (see Illustration 3). Infection is often caused by gonorrhea, but can also be caused by other kinds of bacteria.

An initial episode of infection can cause scarring of the gland duct and impair or block drainage of normal gland secretions. If this occurs, then subsequent, repeated attacks of infection are likely. Also, scarring can lead to gradual accumulation of gland secretions trapped within the gland, forming a large cyst.

DIAGNOSIS

Examination of your vulva should permit your clinician to decide whether or not you have a Bartholin's gland infection or cyst. *A gonorrhea culture is essential if you have an infection.*

TREATMENT

When active infection is present, your clinician will probably recommend oral antibiotics (such as ampicillin) and frequent hot soaks. In most cases, infection will resolve more quickly if the gland is also drained. Your clinician may use local anesthetic and perform an incision and drainage (I&D) in the office, or she/he may recommend that the procedure be performed with general anesthesia in a hospital or surgical clinic. Incision and drainage simply means making an incision through the skin (see Illustration 3) into the pus collection in the gland, thus allowing the pus to escape. A gauze wick is usually placed in the incision so that it will remain open for several days to allow complete drainage.

Many clinicians recommend marsupialization rather than simple I&D for treatment of an infected gland. The goal of marsupialization is to create a permanent drainage route for the gland. An incision is made

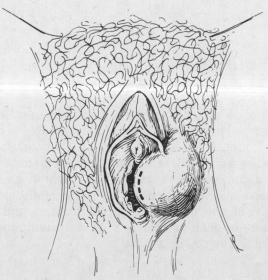

Illustration 3   An infected Bartholin's Gland. The dotted line indicates where an incision would be made to drain the gland.

through the skin into the gland, and the edges of the incision are stitched so that it will heal with a fairly large opening. In effect, the gland is converted into a pouch (hence, marsupial). Marsupialization often is successful in preventing later, repeated episodes of infection or formation of a cyst. General anesthesia is usually recommended for marsupialization.

Removal of the entire Bartholin's gland may be recommended if a cyst forms, but there is no active infection. The enlarged gland is located, cut free from its attachments to the vulva, and removed through an incision similar to the one shown in Illustration 3. General anesthesia is usually recommended for cyst removal (cystectomy).

Recovery after Bartholin's gland surgery is rapid except for localized pain, tenderness and swelling, which may last for two or three weeks. Complications of surgery are unlikely, but bleeding at the incision site or into the tissue around the gland, or damage to the rectum (which lies adjacent to the Bartholin's glands) are possible.

PROGNOSIS

Bartholin's gland infection is likely to recur and may even recur after marsupialization in some cases. Removal of the gland, however, should end problems with it.

Other Infections

This chapter covers only the reproductive tract infections that commonly occur in the United States. There are a number of other sexually transmitted infections that are rarely seen here but are fairly common in other parts of the world. These include lymphogranuloma venereum, chancroid, and granuloma inguinale. You might suspect these infections if you have a sexual partner who has recently returned from a tropical area, or if you have been in the tropics—and romancing—yourself. Be sure to mention this to your clinician; otherwise she/he may have trouble diagnosing your illness.

REFERENCES

1. Rendtorff RC, Curran JW, Chandler RW, et al: Economic consequences of gonorrhea in women: Experience from an urban hospital. *Journal of the American Venereal Disease Association* 1(1):40–47, September 1974.
2. *V.D. Fact Sheet 1976*, Joseph H Blount (ed). US Department of Health, Education and Welfare, Public Health Service, Center for Disease Control, Bureau of State Services, Venereal Disease Control Division, 1977.
3. *V.D. Fact Sheet 1977*, Joseph H Blount (ed). US Department of Health, Education and Welfare, Public Health Service, Center for Disease Control, Bureau of State Services, Venereal Disease Control Division, 1978.
4. Willcox RR: What are the chances of catching VD? *Resident and Staff Physician*, September 1976.
5. Idsoe O, Guthe T, Willcox RR, et al: Nature and extent of penicillin side-reactions with particular reference to fatalistic form: anaphylactic shock. *World Health Organization Bulletin* 38:159, 1968.

23 | Bladder and Kidney Infections

Infections frequently attack the urinary system and can cause problems ranging from mild burning sensations during urination to serious illness or even death. Most urinary infections are caused by bacteria from the vagina or from the anus that gain access to the bladder. Infection can sometimes arise spontaneously but usually occurs after injury or irritation to the external urethral opening caused by vigorous intercourse or by a urine catheter (a rubber tube inserted through the urethra into the bladder during pelvic surgery). Urinary tract infections can also be caused by poor hygiene, by diseases such as diabetes that diminish a person's resistance to infection, by kidney stones or structural abnormalities that obstruct urine flow from the kidneys, or by failure to urinate frequently enough. Infection can attack the urethra, bladder, or kidneys, or all three sites together (see Illustration 1).

Urethritis (Infection of the Urethra)

Infection of the urethra, the tube that carries urine from the bladder to the outside of the body, causes burning during urination and/or a urethral discharge. In women the urethra is about 1 inch long. Urethritis often accompanies a bladder infection (cystitis) and is usually treated with the same medication.

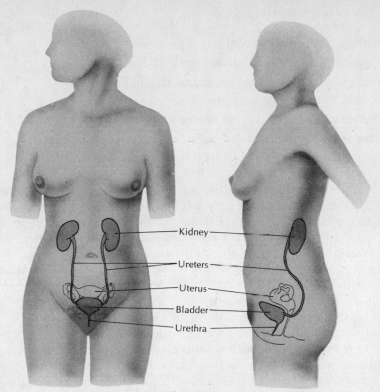

Illustration 1   The woman's urinary system.

Urethritis can occur without an accompanying bladder infection when it is associated with gonorrhea, trichomonas, or other vaginal infections. You will need a gonorrhea test if you have urethritis.

Cystitis (Infection of the Bladder)

The bladder is a storage bag for urine, the fluid waste products that the kidneys have filtered from the blood. Urine can remain in your bladder for many hours if you don't urinate frequently; and like a stagnant pool anywhere, it can be a prime target for bacterial overgrowth.

Your symptoms might include:

- Feeling of pressure, urgency to urinate
- Burning during urination or urethral discharge
- Frequency of urination; urinating in small amounts
- Having to get up at night to urinate
- Cramping and pain in the center of your lower abdomen
- Urine that has an unusual odor
- Urine that is cloudy or bloody (red or pink)

Bladder infections (cystitis) are much more common in women than in men, since bacteria only have to travel about 1 inch to reach a woman's bladder from the outside of her body, compared to the 6 inches or more bacteria must travel to reach a man's bladder.

Your clinician may be able to diagnose cystitis almost entirely on the basis of your symptoms. She/he will find that your bladder is tender to pressure during your pelvic exam (see Illustration 1), and microscopic examination of your urine will show bacteria and white blood cells, neither of which are present in normal urine.

Your clinician may also order a urine culture and sensitivity test to determine what specific bacterium is causing your infection and which antibiotics will be most effective. Culture and sensitivity results will not be available for about 48 hours. Your clinician will begin your treatment immediately with an antibiotic that is usually effective and change it after the test results come back if necessary.

Sulfa medications such as Gantrisin (sulfisoxazole) and broad-spectrum antibiotics such as tetracycline or ampicillin are commonly used to treat cystitis. (If you have certain kinds of hereditary anemia, you should not use sulfa drugs. Be sure to discuss this with your clinician.) Your clinician is likely to recommend a ten-day course of pills or tablets. *Take all the medicine prescribed for you even if your symptoms disappear* after two or three days. You need a full course of medication to kill all the bacteria and prevent another flareup of infection. Don't try to treat yourself with old antibiotics you may have at home; your urine tests will be inaccurate if you have already taken antibiotics, and you need specific doses and a full prescription to treat your infection properly. If gonorrhea or trichomonas is causing your infection, your partner will be treated at the same time you are.

If you are having severe bladder spasm and frequency of urination, your clinician may prescribe Pyridium (phenazopyridine hydrochloride) to soothe your bladder and urethra temporarily until infection begins to subside. Pyridium may turn your urine dark orange. This is a harmless, temporary effect.

Pyelonephritis (Infection of the Kidneys)

Infection of the kidney, called pyelonephritis, is much more serious than cystitis. Symptoms include fever, chills, and pain in the back at or just above waist level on one side or the other. Back pain is likely to be more persistent than simple muscular backache, and you may feel really sick. Pyelonephritis can be a very serious infection and requires prompt, aggressive antibiotic treatment and a thorough evaluation of the source of infection. Kidney infections are most common during pregnancy and can cause premature delivery.

Followup Care

Your clinician is likely to recommend a urine culture about two weeks after you have finished taking your medication to confirm that the bacteria that caused your infection have been eradicated.

Be sure to drink plenty of water while you are recovering from infection to decrease the concentration of bacteria in your urine and help flush out your bladder. Cranberry juice or ascorbic acid may help because they make your urine acidic. Avoid or at least decrease the frequency of intercourse and have your partner use condoms. If urinating burns badly, urinate in a bathtub full of warm water. Avoid tea, coffee, and alcohol.

When You May Need Further Evaluation

If you have had a serious kidney infection or repeated episodes of cystitis, your clinician will probably recommend a series of tests to evaluate your entire urinary system. She/he will test you for diabetes and may recommend an intravenous pyelogram (IVP), an x-ray evaluation of the urinary system. The radiologist injects dye into your arm vein and then takes a series of x-rays that would reveal any obstruction in the flow of urine from your kidneys to your bladder. You may be referred to a urologist for further evaluation, and you may need cystoscopy, an office procedure that permits your clinician to see the inside of your urethra and bladder through a thin lighted tube called a cystoscope. Your clinician may also recommend long-term medication to suppress infection.

If you use a diaphragm and have recurring bouts of cystitis, consider seeing your clinician for a change in diaphragm size or rim type. You may even need to change to a different method of birth control. (See Chapter 9.)

Preventing Urinary Infection—Suggestions

Many women find that infection crops up when they have very frequent and vigorous intercourse, especially after a long period of little or no intercourse. Bladder infections are sometimes called "honeymoon cystitis." You may be able to stave off infection if you follow these suggestions:

- Use plenty of lubrication during intercourse; try a water-soluble lubricant such as K-Y Jelly or birth control foam.
- Change intercourse positions frequently; rear entry and side-by-side positions may decrease friction on your urethral opening. Avoid anal intercourse to decrease the likelihood of contaminating the urethral opening with bacteria from the rectum.
- Stop having intercourse if you begin to feel sore or tender.
- Urinate before and after intercourse.
- Shower carefully every day, and ask your partner to to do the same.
- Wipe from front to back after using the toilet; the goal is to avoid transfer of bacteria from the rectum to the vulva or urethra.
- Take vitamin C or drink cranberry juice to keep your urine acidic. (Bacteria don't thrive in an acid environment.)
- Have your partner use condoms to prevent transmission of gonorrhea, trichomonas, and other infections that can cause urinary tract infections.

24 | Inflammation of the Cervix

Cervicitis is inflammation of the cervix (the ending "itis" means inflammation). Inflammation is often caused by infection, invasion of cervical tissue by bacteria or other microorganisms, and can also be caused by chemicals or foreign bodies. Inflammation is the result of normal body defenses; infection-fighting white blood cells are mobilized to enter the infected area, blood circulation in the infected area is increased, and the area becomes warm and red. (Read more about the pelvic infection process in Chapter 25.)

Symptoms

If you have mild cervicitis, you may not notice any symptoms at all. Cervicitis can cause profuse, pus-like discharge with a foul odor that persists throughout your cycle. Discharge is often thin or a mucous consistency, and grey-white or yellow in color. Cervicitis may cause pain during intercourse or when you touch your cervix, spotting or bleeding after intercourse, or even abdominal pain and back pain.

Causes of Cervicitis

Gonorrhea, trichomonas, herpes, chlamydia, and yeast organisms can cause cervicitis. Common bacteria that are normally present in the va-

371

gina can also cause cervicitis if they invade the mucus glands in the cervical canal and begin to multiply. Chemicals in vaginal hygiene products (see Chapter 3) or an IUD string can also cause inflammation.

Diagnosis

Your clinician may suspect cervicitis on the basis of your symptoms, the appearance of your cervix, or an abnormal Pap smear that shows inflammatory cells (see Chapter 27). If cervicitis is severe, your clinician will find that your cervix is swollen, reddened, and possibly tender to the touch. You may have a pus discharge from your cervix, and the surface of your cervix may look abnormal. Your clinician may use terms like erosion or eversion to describe the appearance of your cervix.

The outer surface of the cervix is normally pale pink and smooth. The surface is made up of several layers of flat, shiny cells called *squamous* epithelium. The normal lining of the cervical canal is made up of tall, red, velvety cells and a rich supply of mucous glands and is called *columnar* epithelium. The junction between the squamous cells and the columnar cells is normally located very near the opening of the cervical canal.

EVERSION

Eversion means that columnar cells spread from the normal junction close to the cervical opening out over the surface of the cervix (see Illustration 1). In some cases, columnar cells can spread to cover a large part of the cervix. Eversion may be more extensive in DES daughters, women who take birth control Pills, and young, never-pregnant women. Increasing age, pregnancy, and shifts in your vaginal acid-alkaline balance can improve eversion. With eversion, you may have a heavy mucous discharge, for you have a larger than average number of mucus-secreting glands. Eversion increases your risk of infection, because bacteria are more likely to thrive in mucus-secreting tissues.

EROSION

Erosion or ulceration of the cervix can be caused by infection, trauma, or chemicals. Erosion means that the cervical surface layer is partially or completely absent in one area. An eroded area looks raw

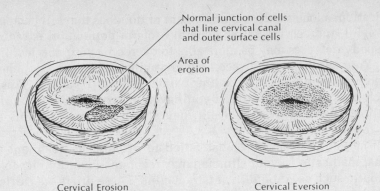

Normal junction of cells
that line cervical canal
and outer surface cells

Area of
erosion

Cervical Erosion   Cervical Eversion

Illustration 1 Cervical infection can cause raw, eroded areas. Infection is more likely if you have eversion: mucus-secreting glands and columnar cells normally present in the cervical canal that extend *outward* onto the surface of your cervix.

and red and may cause spotting (see Illustration 1). Erosion is more common in columnar cells because they are less hardy than squamous cells. Cervical injury from intercourse, tampon insertion, or speculum insertion can lead to erosion.

A gonorrhea culture is essential if you have cervicitis. Gonorrhea is a frequent cause of cervical infection, and gonorrhea cannot be detected without a special culture (see Chapter 21). Your clinician may prepare a wet smear (see Chapter 21) to look for trichomonas or yeast organisms, or excessive vaginal bacteria.

If your cervix surface appears abnormal or if you have an area of erosion, your clinician may use a colposcope (see Chapter 21) to distinguish between simple inflammatory erosion and cancerous ulceration. Biopsy (see Chapter 21) of abnormal areas is sometimes helpful in making a precise diagnosis.

Treatment

If your clinician finds that you have gonorrhea, yeast, or trichomonas infection, she/he will treat it (see Chapter 22). If a chemical irritant is causing cervicitis, your clinician will advise you to avoid it.

If your cervicitis is caused by bacteria from your vagina, it may not be possible to determine what specific type(s) of bacteria is responsible. Your clinician may treat this kind of cervicitis with "nonspecific" medication, such as sulfa vaginal cream or douches that kill bacteria in the vagina and cervix. As the general bacteria population is reduced, your body defenses may be more able to overcome your cervical infection. Your clinician may recommend vaginal creams or douches to promote an optimal acid-alkaline balance in your vagina. This approach is especially effective if you have a marked eversion but little infection. Diet and overall health may also be factors that influence your resistance to infection.

If cervicitis is severe or has failed to respond to treatment with vaginal medications, your clinician may recommend antibiotics to take by mouth, such as ampicillin or tetracycline. These drugs are carried to the cervical tissue by your bloodstream and are usually effective in destroying bacteria.

Prolonged or repeated problems with cervicitis may lead you to consider cautery or cryosurgery, which are described in Chapter 21. Prolonged cervicitis may make it difficult or impossible for you to become pregnant, for abnormal mucus production interferes with sperm's ability to penetrate your cervical canal. Treatment for your partner is crucial if your cervicitis is caused by gonorrhea or trichomonas infection. Treating your partner may also be important if you have bacterial or yeast infection. You will probably be advised to limit intercourse until your cervicitis is cured. If you do have intercourse, ask your partner to use condoms until your infection is gone and your treatment is completed.

Cervicitis that occurs with an IUD in place can often be successfully treated with vaginal creams or antibiotics without removing your IUD. If cervicitis is severe or if it recurs, you may need to have your IUD removed and change to another method of birth control. Remember that abnormal discharge can also be a sign of serious pelvic infection. Prompt, thorough evaluation is essential for any woman who is using an IUD and develops abnormal discharge.

Prevention

You may decrease your likelihood of developing cervicitis if you minimize your exposure to sexually transmitted infection. See Chapter 22 for suggestions that can reduce infection risk. Avoid chemical irritants in douching products and deodorized tampons, and seek treatment promptly for vaginal infections so that organisms don't have a chance to invade your cervix.

25 | Pelvic Infection

Pelvic infection and pelvic inflammatory disease (PID) are general terms for infection anywhere in a woman's pelvic organs. Your clinician may also use more precise terms to indicate which specific areas are infected: endometritis (uterine lining is infected); endoparametritis (uterine lining and uterine muscle wall are infected); salpingitis (fallopian tubes are infected); oophoritis (ovary is infected); and pelvic peritonitis (membrane lining of the abdomen is infected).

Pelvic infection often begins when bacteria from a cervix infection spread to the pelvic organs. Infection usually spreads upward, beginning in the uterine lining and then extending to the uterine muscle layer, the tubes, the ovaries, and finally out into the abdominal cavity itself. Early treatment will halt the spread of infection in most cases.

Symptoms

Symptoms of pelvic infection can be very dramatic, with sudden, severe pelvic pain, a temperature of 102 to 104 degrees (Fahrenheit), shaking chills, foul vaginal discharge, and vaginal bleeding. But infection symptoms can also be very subtle: annoying, persistent mild abdominal pain or backache, or pain that you only notice during intercourse, or slightly increased vaginal discharge. Your symptoms depend on the location of your infection, the type of bacteria causing it, and how quickly the bacteria multiply and spread.

If your symptoms are severe, your need for treatment will be obvious. Subtle symptoms are a real problem, however, because it is easy to ignore them and put off calling your clinician. *Subtle, smoldering infection is a leading cause of infertility, because it can permanently scar and obstruct your fallopian tubes* just as a dramatic infection can. Infection danger signs are:

- *Abdominal pain* or back pain
- Persistent *cramps*
- Unusual *vaginal bleeding* or spotting
- General *tired, achy feelings*
- *Pain during or after intercourse*
- *Tenderness* in your lower abdomen with pressure or jarring, such as when you cough or run
- Abdominal pain with bowel movements or urination
- Foul-smelling or pus-like *vaginal discharge*
- *Fever:* temperature of 100.4 degrees (Fahrenheit) or higher
- *Chills*

Suspect infection especially if you have an IUD, if you think you may have been exposed to gonorrhea, or if you have recently had a baby, a miscarriage, an abortion, or pelvic surgery.

You are unlikely to have all these danger signs. Fever, for example, does not always accompany pelvic infection. If you suspect infection, have an examination immediately to be certain.

The Pelvic Infection Process

Many kinds of bacteria normally live in the intestines and on the outer surface of the body, including the vaginal cavity. The uterus and other internal pelvic organs, however, are normally free of bacteria. The uterine cavity is protected by mucus that has a mild germ-killing (antibacterial) effect and constantly coats and cleanses the lining of the uterus and cervix. The occasional bacterium that enters the uterus usually is destroyed by white cells from the bloodstream.

Your body's normal infection defenses can be overwhelmed if a large number of bacteria or an unusually aggressive kind of bacteria, such as gonorrhea, invades your body. A large number of bacteria can enter your uterus on medical instruments during a D&C (see Chapter 40), an endometrial biopsy (see Chapter 21), or insertion of an IUD; contamination is more likely if your cervix is infected or you have vaginitis at the time.

Your normal infection defenses may prove inadequate if your uterus contains blood or unexpelled fetal or placental tissue after a miscarriage or abortion. These substances are ideal sites for bacterial growth, and your infection-fighting white blood cells have difficulty reaching them inside the uterus. The presence of an IUD may also interfere with your infection defenses. Diabetes and some medications, such as cortisone, can reduce your body defenses against all kinds of infection.

Pelvic infection is rare during a normal pregnancy, but after delivery your cervical opening does not shrink to normal size for several weeks, and the lining of your uterus does not have its normal mucus protection. Infection risk is high during the first few weeks after delivery, miscarriage, or abortion.

Infection risk is higher during your menstrual period than at other times in your cycle. Bleeding seems to make it easy for bacteria to spread upward into your uterus, and blood enhances bacterial growth. Women with pelvic infection often say that they first noticed symptoms two or three days after the beginning of a menstrual period.

Your defense against infection is impaired if you have scarring or damage from infection in the past; and you may have repeated attacks of pelvic infection months or years after your initial infection.

No matter what kind of bacteria is present or where in your body infection occurs, the infection process is fairly predictable. Bacteria are nourished by the fluid or tissue that they attack, and they produce waste products that they release into the invaded tissues. Body defenses sense the presence of bacteria and send white blood cells into the area to attack them. The infected area becomes warm, red, and swollen because of increased blood flow and the accumulation of pus, which is composed of dead bacteria, dead white cells, and fluid. Bacterial waste products can be poisonous and can cause fever, chills, and malaise (feeling tired and achy) when they enter your circulation and travel to the rest of your body.

Your normal cells can be destroyed by bacteria directly, or indirectly by the excessive swelling and poisonous bacterial wastes. Even when all bacteria are eradicated, tissue may heal slowly and may never completely return to normal.

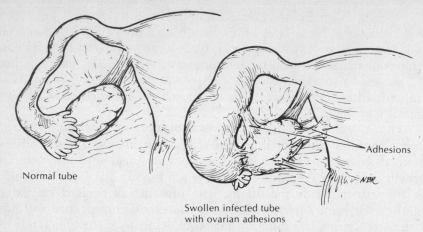

Normal tube

Adhesions

Swollen infected tube
with ovarian adhesions

Illustration 1   Pelvic Infection can cause the fallopian tubes to become grossly swollen and distended.

INFECTION OF THE FALLOPIAN TUBES

Permanent damage is especially likely if infection involves your fallopian tubes. The inner lining of the tubes is delicate and easily damaged by infection. Tube walls are thin and pliable, so fluid or pus accumulation can cause massive swelling. A fluid-filled tube that looks like a fat sausage or balloon is called a pus tube (pyosalpinx) or a fluid tube (hydrosalpinx) and is fairly common with pelvic infection. Infection can cause such severe scarring that the open end (near the ovary) of one or both tubes is literally sealed shut. Bands of scar tissue (adhesions) can distort the shape of the tubes. Infected fallopian tubes are shown in Illustration 1.

PELVIC ABSCESS

Pelvic abscess is another serious complication that can occur with infection. Pus and live bacteria leaking from the open end of a fallopian tube can enter the abdominal cavity itself and cause peritonitis, widespread infection throughout the lining of the abdomen (peritoneum). In many cases, pus collects in a puddle, and your body's normal defenses attempt to prevent its spread by producing a scar tissue wall to separate it from the rest of your abdomen. A walled-off collection of pus and active bacteria is called an abscess.

Antibiotic medications are often ineffective in treating an abscess, for antibiotics and infection-fighting white blood cells carried in your bloodstream cannot penetrate an abscess very effectively. When you have an abscess, symptoms are likely to persist despite antibiotic treatment. Surgery may be necessary to drain out the pus and bacteria so that healing can begin.

Causes of Pelvic Infection

Gonorrhea (see Chapter 22) may be responsible for as many as 45% of new pelvic infections (1). Studies of groups of women with high gonorrhea rates in general show that a large percentage of pelvic infections are due to gonorrhea. The initial stage of gonorrhea is a cervix infection, and it progresses to true pelvic infection in about 30% of women within one month if it is not treated (2). Other bacteria can also cause pelvic infection and are especially likely to be present if infection begins after pregnancy, abortion, IUD insertion, or surgery.

If you have had a gonorrheal pelvic infection, it is absolutely essential to protect yourself from any further exposure to gonorrhea. Your health and your fertility are at stake. *Your partner(s) must be treated,* and so must any other woman or man with whom either of you has had intercourse, *whether or not they have symptoms and whether or not they have been tested for gonorrhea.* Both men and women can carry early gonorrhea infection with no symptoms at all, and culture tests are not entirely reliable. As many as 10% of cultures may fail to show gonorrhea even though it is present (3). *Your body does not build immunity to gonorrhea.* If you are exposed to gonorrhea a second time, your risk of developing a second serious pelvic infection may be even higher than it was the first time.

Two or more types of bacteria can cause pelvic infection at the same time, and repeated attacks of pelvic infection are often caused by different combinations of bacteria. In some cases, bacteria may persist despite antibiotic treatment; your symptoms may subside as bacterial growth is suppressed during antibiotic treatment and then reappear once you stop antibiotics and the organisms begin to multiply once again.

Diagnosis

Your clinician will need to examine you to decide whether or not you have a pelvic infection. One of the most important clues is *tenderness* in your uterus, tubes, or ovaries during pelvic examination. If your uterus is tender or if moving your cervix back and forth (which jars the uterus, tubes, and ovaries) causes pain, your clinician will suspect infection. Sometimes infection is obvious, but sometimes it is difficult for your clinician to be certain. Even if there is some doubt, it is probably better to go ahead with treatment anyway. There is nothing to be gained by waiting until the infection becomes severe.

A gonorrhea culture (see Chapter 21) is essential, and your clinician may recommend other tests to help determine the cause, extent, and severity of your infection.

A bacterial culture from your cervix may help to identify the specific bacteria causing your infection and determine which antibiotic would be most effective. Culture results are not always clear-cut, however. Since bacteria are normally present in the vagina, your culture is likely to show growth of several of these bacteria. It may be difficult to determine which type(s) of bacteria is responsible for your pelvic infection and which types just happen to live harmlessly in your vagina.

A blood count can determine whether your body defense cells are stimulated. When you have an active infection, the number of white cells in your bloodstream is elevated and your blood proteins are altered so that your blood cell sedimentation rate is speeded up.

If your clinician suspects that you have an abscess, she/he may recommend a sonogram (see Chapter 21). Sonography uses sound waves to identify localized swelling or fluid collection and can provide your clinician with a fairly precise measurement of abscess size and location. This information helps your clinician decide whether surgical treatment is necessary, and your progress can be followed by sonography once antibiotic treatment has begun.

In some cases, surgery will be necessary for diagnosing pelvic infection. If your symptoms are so severe that your clinician suspects you could have appendicitis or an abscess, she/he will consider surgery. Either exploratory laparoscopy, viewing the inside of your abdomen through a lighted tube inserted through a 1-inch incision just below your navel (see Chapter 15), or laparotomy, a 5-inch surgical opening in your lower abdomen, might be recommended.

Treatment

Your treatment will depend on how severe your infection is. If you are gravely ill or if surgery may be necessary, then you will be hospitalized.

In the hospital your antibiotics can be administered directly into a vein in higher, more effective doses than you could absorb through your stomach.

Oral antibiotics, pain medication, and rest at home will cure pelvic infection in many cases. While you are being treated at home, pretend that you are in the hospital. ***The importance of complete rest cannot be overemphasized.*** Rest enables your body defenses to function at their best. Antibiotics do part of the job, but your own internal defenses are crucial in your cure. Your clinician will also recommend ***pelvic rest;*** by that she/he means no intercourse, no active sports, and no other activity that jars or bounces your pelvis.

Your clinician will want you to return for a checkup after one or two weeks. At that time, she/he will evaluate your improvement to decide whether you are ready to resume your normal activities gradually.

If your infection does not improve with antibiotic treatment, whether you are in the hospital or at home, your clinician will probably recommend a sonogram or other tests and will consider surgery to drain an abscess or remove infected tissue. An abscess may be best drained through an incision in your lower abdomen or through an incision in your vagina, depending on the location of the abscess. In either case, general anesthesia is usually recommended.

When infection is truly severe and antibiotic treatment is not working well, it may be necessary to remove the infected organs. Severe infection might mean removing one or both tubes, the uterus, and possibly even your ovaries. Hysterectomy is discussed in Chapter 41.

Infection that occurs after pregnancy, abortion, or miscarriage is a special situation. Your clinician will carefully evaluate the size of your uterus to assess whether there is evidence of any retained fetal or placental tissue. If there is, she/he will recommend uterine scraping (D&C or vacuum curettage, Chapters 40 and 20). A D&C may also be considered if you do not respond promptly to antibiotic treatment. Your clinician will probably prescribe a drug such as Methergine (methylergonovine) (Chapter 20) to stimulate uterine contraction and help prevent accumulation of blood inside your uterus.

If your infection is associated with an IUD, then your clinician will probably recommend that it be removed. In some cases, when infection is mild and limited to your uterus, infection can be treated effectively with your IUD in place. If infection is severe or if it does not respond promptly to treatment, then your IUD should definitely be removed.

Infection Aftermath

If pelvic infection is limited to the uterus itself, antibiotic treatment usually resolves the problem rapidly and completely with little likelihood of permanent damage or future complications. If infection has involved your fallopian tubes, ovaries, or abdominal cavity, however, long-term consequences are of significant concern. Permanent damage to the fallopian tube lining, scar tissue formation, and partial or complete obstruction of the fallopian tubes may lead to four serious long-term problems:

First of all, *infertility* is possible because of infection damage. Second, the incidence of *tubal (ectopic) pregnancy*—pregnancy that implants and grows in the fallopian tube or elsewhere rather than the uterus—is increased after pelvic infection, for partial obstruction of a tube can delay or obstruct passage of the fertilized egg to the uterus. Third, there is a significant risk that *repeated episodes of infection* will occur in the future. Finally, scar tissue (adhesions) formed during infection can be a source of *continuing pelvic pain,* sometimes severe enough to require later surgery.

It is important to remember that gonorrhea and other types of pelvic infection do not always cause infertility. Your clinician will stress the possibility of permanent damage and infertility when you have an infection, but *you cannot assume that you are infertile.* Many women have unwanted pregnancies because they assumed, quite naturally, that they would not need birth control after a warning from their clinician. If you do not want to be pregnant, you will need to continue using birth control. Your clinician can tell from examination that there may be tubal scarring that could impair your fertility, but she/he cannot tell for sure whether you are able to conceive or not. You can have a hysterosalpingogram (see Chapter 34) to determine whether or not your tubes are blocked. This test would not be recommended until at least three months after all evidence of infection was gone, to protect against contaminating your abdominal cavity with bacteria.

Preventing Infection

There are two very important ways that you can protect yourself against serious pelvic infection.

First, do all you can to avoid exposure to gonorrhea. Do not have intercourse if your partner appears to have any penile discharge or inflammation. He should use condoms any time either one of you has even the least question about the possibility of infection. Think about condoms or a diaphragm as the birth control method you might use all the time to give you added protection from infection.

Second, pay attention to any symptoms you do have, even if they are subtle. Pelvic infection usually is not a serious problem if you seek treatment right away. Be especially alert to early infection symptoms in the first few weeks after pregnancy, miscarriage, or abortion, or if you have an IUD, or if you have recently had any medical procedures involving your cervix or uterus.

REFERENCES

1. Eschenbach D, Buchanan T, Pollock H, et al: Polymicrobial etiology of acute pelvic inflammatory disease. *New England Journal of Medicine* 293:166–171, 1975.
2. Curran JW, Rendtorff RC, Chandler RW, et al: Female gonorrhea: Its relation to abnormal uterine bleeding, urinary tract symptoms, and cervicitis. *Obstetrics and Gynecology* 45(2):195–198, 1975.
3. Schmale JD, Martin J, Domescik G: Observations on the culture diagnosis of gonorrhea in women. *Journal of the American Medical Association* 210:312, 1969.

26 | Menstrual Problems

You are an unusual woman if you live your whole life without at least some problems with your menstrual cycle. Premenstrual symptoms and menstrual cramps are especially troublesome, and they are not well understood. It is astounding that so little is known about a problem as common as cramps. Cramps are responsible for 140 million lost working hours each year in this country (1). Abnormal menstrual cycle patterns and missed periods are also common, and it is comforting to know that their causes are better understood.

Premenstrual Symptoms and Menstrual Cramps

Breast tenderness and bloating (fluid retention) are very common premenstrual symptoms that many woman notice for one to seven days before each period. Many women also have symptoms they describe as "tension," such as headache, irritability, nervousness, increased or decreased activity levels, fatigue, exhaustion, crying spells, depression with no apparent cause, and inability to concentrate.

Research on the causes of premenstrual symptoms and menstrual cramps has been limited and has often emphasized psychological or cultural factors rather than chemical or hormone factors. There is fairly good research evidence that women are more likely to commit violent crimes, commit suicide, and have severe episodes of mental illness during the premenstrual week than at any other cycle times (2), but there is very little understanding of why this is so.

You may have heard or read that premenstrual symptoms are usually caused by psychological problems. Researchers now believe, however, that there are probably chemical and hormonal changes during the normal menstrual cycle that account for premenstrual tension. Severe depression and certain other serious mental illnesses are known to cause chemical alterations within the brain. More subtle chemical brain alterations probably occur with your cyclic hormone changes as well, and may some day be understood. Fluid retention itself may have some effect on the brain, in addition to its manifestations in breast engorgement, bloating, and ankle swelling.

One direct link between hormones and depression has been demonstrated; some women who take birth control Pills become deficient in vitamin B_6 and develop depression. Depression subsides when they take supplementary vitamin B_6 (20 mg per day) (3).

Premenstrual symptoms and cramps are also linked to ovulation and are rarely a problem for women who aren't ovulating. For this reason, researchers suspect that progesterone, the hormone that is produced *after* ovulation, may be involved in these disorders.

Menstrual cramps (dysmenorrhea) can be caused by specific medical problems, such as endometriosis, pelvic infection, fibroid tumors, or an IUD. Cramps associated with these conditions typically appear for the first time when a woman is in her 20s or 30s. Your clinician will call this condition *secondary dysmenorrhea,* for the cramps are secondary to (caused by) another medical problem.

Most women who have menstrual cramps don't have any underlying illness, however. Intermittent cramping pain during days of heavy menstrual bleeding is extremely common among all women; yet the cause of menstrual cramping is not understood. Severe, disabling cramps without underlying illness is most common among teenage women. A severe cramping problem that appears within the first year or so after periods begin in a healthy young woman is called *primary dysmenorrhea.* In addition to cramps, primary dysmenorrhea can cause backache, leg pain, nausea, vomiting, diarrhea, headache, dizziness, and loss of appetite. Young women with severe cramps may be unable to manage normal daily activities for the first 24 to 36 hours of each menstrual period. Primary dysmenorrhea symptoms rarely last more than two days with each cycle, and severe cramps often subside on their own when a woman reaches her 20s or has a pregnancy.

Your medical history and pelvic exam alone may provide enough information for your clinician to determine whether your cramps are caused by primary dysmenorrhea or by another medical problem. If there is any doubt, however, further evaluation, including laparoscopy, may be recommended. This procedure permits your clinician to look at your uterus, tubes, and ovaries through a narrow, illuminated tube inserted just below your navel. (See Chapter 15 for a description of laparoscopy.)

At least three theories have been advanced to explain menstrual cramps:

An old, popular theory blames cramps on a tight cervical canal. Doctors know that mechanical widening of the cervix, D&C (see Chapter 40), or full-term delivery often improves menstrual cramps. Careful x-ray studies of women with cramps have not shown any significant cervical narrowing, however (4).

A more recent theory attributes cramps to uterine muscle activity. The strength and frequency of normal rhythmic uterine contractions are altered by changes in hormone levels, and women with severe cramps have been shown to have excessive contraction strength when investigators have measured pressure inside the uterus (5). High pressure could interfere with normal blood flow to the uterine muscle itself and cause pain, because muscles tend to hurt when they don't have adequate oxygen supplies from the bloodstream.

The newest theory is that high levels of prostaglandin hormone may stimulate strong, painful uterine contractions. Research has shown that women with severe cramps have a higher level of uterine prostaglandin than other women (6).

It is possible that all of these factors contribute to cramps, and they may be interrelated. A tight cervical canal, for example, might be aggravated by excessive muscle contraction, and might retard the outflow of prostaglandin hormone present in mucus secretions from the uterine lining.

MINIMIZING PREMENSTRUAL SYMPTOMS AND MENSTRUAL CRAMPS

First, have a thorough examination to be sure you don't have a medical problem that is causing your cramps. Even if cramps are terrible, it helps to be confident you don't have a hidden illness. There are no real cures for premenstrual symptoms and cramps, but there are suggestions and treatments that may help.

1. **Keep track of your periods.** When tension symptoms appear before a period, you will be able to reassure yourself that it is just hormones and not permanent craziness.

2. **Experiment with changes in your diet.** You may be able to control bloating by reducing your sodium intake (table salt, soy sauce, salty foods) just before you expect fluid retention to appear. Foods rich in potassium (bananas) and plenty of plain water may also help to reduce fluid retention. Supplementary vitamin B complex may be worth while, especially if you feel depressed. Some women find that balanced calcium and magnesium supplements and extra Vitamin C are helpful. Also, the natural laxative effect of prunes, bran, and a high bulk diet (whole grain foods, raw vegetables and fruit) may help to diminish discomfort with cramps. Be sure that your diet is high in protein and vegetables and low in refined sugar, carbohydrates, sodium, and fat so that you will feel your best.

3. **Use your best home therapy for cramps.** Avoid standing or walking on hard pavement, and try back massage, hot pads, tub soaks, and rest. One stiff drink may help, because alcohol relaxes the uterine muscle. Orgasm also helps relax the uterine muscle, and will decrease congestion in your pelvis. **Warning:** Pennyroyal, an herbal "remedy," can cause serious and even fatal poisoning, see Chapter 20.

4. **Talk to your clinician about prescription medications** if your premenstrual symptoms or menstrual cramps are severe.

You may find that one or two codeine tablets each month is all you need, or a combination of aspirin with tiny doses of amphetamine for good pain relief without nausea and drowsiness.

Many women have found some new drugs that are a very successful weapon against menstrual cramps and also against the nausea and diarrhea that often accompany cramps. Researchers believe their potent effect on cramps comes from their ability to counteract abnormally high uterine prostaglandin production that occurs in many women with severe cramps (see Chapter 20 for more about prostaglandin hormones). These drugs can have adverse side effects such as intestinal upset, dizziness, and visual problems. Fortunately, the dose that most women need for relief of cramps is quite low and side effects have not been a serious problem.

The most extensively studied brands in this drug family are Motrin, Naprosyn, Ponstel, and Indocin (7). Some women find that one seems to work better than another, so it is worth trying a second brand if the first does not succeed. Several studies comparing brands with each other, with placebos, or with other pain relievers have been published (8).

Another new treatment for cramps now being investigated is dilation of the cervical canal with laminaria. Laminaria is a type of seaweed that expands gradually as it absorbs water. A slender (sterile, dry) laminaria rod is inserted into the cervical canal and left in place for about 6 hours. As the rod expands, it stretches the cervical canal painlessly. Laminaria insertion does not require anesthesia and can be done easily in an office setting.

Symptoms of premenstrual tension and fluid retention can be a real problem, and there are no simple medical answers. Some women are helped by diuretics (such as Spironolactone, Dyazide, or Diuril), but these typically reduce bloating without really treating the other premenstrual symptoms (2). Also, diuretics can have very serious side effects, and you would need close medical supervision with regular blood tests to check body salt balance. Tranquilizers may take the edge off your emotional symptoms, but they don't specifically treat the cause of premenstrual tension either. A few clinicians have suggested treatment with progesterone. Research on the safety and effectiveness of this approach, however, has not yet been published.

Cramps and premenstrual symptoms are very uncommon when a woman is using birth control Pills. If you need a method of birth control, you may want to include your cramps problem as one factor in choosing a method.

Irregular Menstrual Patterns

Regular menstrual periods are not as regular as you might think. Some women have a very predictable interval between periods, but most women have cycles that vary in length, and many women have variations of a week or more. Unpredictable cycle length is very common among teenage women whose periods have just begun and among women nearing menopause.

The average cycle is somewhere between 24 and 32 days long, counting from the first day of one menstrual period to the first day of the next period. Menstrual bleeding usually lasts three to seven days and totals 1 or 2 tablespoon(s) of blood and tissue loss. If your periods differ substantially from these averages, your clinician may use terms like *hypo*menorrhea (scant blood flow), *hyper*menorrhea (heavy blood flow), *oligo*menorrhea (infrequent periods), or *poly*menorrhea (very frequent periods).

Any vaginal bleeding that does not correspond to an average normal pattern should be reported to your clinician. If you are over 30, you must see your clinician promptly even if your unusual bleeding is not heavy or troublesome. Your clinician will want to evaluate you carefully for cancer of the uterus. If you are under 30, the likelihood of cancer is very remote; you may not need extensive evaluation unless the problem is persistent, bleeding is very heavy, you have cramps or other signs of infection, or you are trying to become pregnant. Any bleeding at all, even the tiniest trace, that occurs after menopause must be evaluated promptly.

MIDCYCLE SPOTTING

About 10% of women have spotting or light bleeding for one or two days at the time ovulation occurs. This bleeding is probably triggered by the temporary drop in estrogen production that coincides with ovulation. If this is the cause of your spotting, your next period should begin almost exactly 14 days later. Midcycle spotting is harmless.

LATE, HEAVY BLEEDING

If you don't ovulate, your uterine lining will continue to grow until it is so thick it sloughs away spontaneously; bleeding might begin, for example, six or seven weeks after your last period. Bleeding tends to be heavy and prolonged, or may have a stop-and-start-again pattern. A miscarriage (spontaneous abortion) can also produce this bleeding pattern.

PROLONGED OR HEAVY BLEEDING AT REGULAR INTERVALS

When the normal pattern of estrogen and progesterone production is disrupted, heavy, long periods can result. Your clinician might call this **dysfunctional uterine bleeding,** and it accounts for about half of all irregular bleeding problems. Dysfunctional bleeding is only serious if your total blood loss is large enough to make you anemic. Bleeding can be very heavy and can require hospitalization, transfusions, or even surgery in some cases.

Less common causes of prolonged or heavy bleeding include

uterine infection, uterine polyps (benign growths that arise from the uterine lining), fibroid tumors (see Chapter 30), adenomyosis (uterine lining tissue invades the muscle layer of the uterus), and an IUD. A woman who has diminished blood clotting because of medications, severe anemia, or a blood disorder such as leukemia may also have long, heavy periods.

UNPREDICTABLE, IRREGULAR BLEEDING INTERVALS

Persistent disruption in normal estrogen and progesterone patterns and failure to ovulate can cause irregular, unpredictable bleeding. You may bleed for five days, stop for five, bleed for seven, stop for twelve, bleed for three, and so on. Uterine infection, uterine polyps, birth control Pills, an IUD, thyroid deficiency, or ectopic pregnancy can also cause irregular bleeding. When persistent irregular bleeding occurs in a women over 30, the possibility of uterine or cervical cancer must be considered; irregular bleeding is the most common first sign of uterine cancer.

BLEEDING AFTER INTERCOURSE

Bleeding after intercourse is often an indication of cervical problems. Cervicitis (inflammation of the cervix, see Chapter 24), a cervical polyp, and eversion (cells from the cervical canal extend out to the surface of the cervix) are common causes. Bleeding after intercourse can also be caused by an IUD, uterine infection, or cervical cancer.

BLEEDING AFTER MENOPAUSE

If you have already passed menopause, you must report any bleeding of any kind to your clinician promptly. The decreased resilience of the vaginal lining after menopause can lead to pink discharge or light bleeding from the vaginal wall itself because of minor infection or the trauma of intercourse. Estrogen replacement therapy can cause bleeding, and may indicate that the estrogen dose you are taking is too high for you. Uterine cancer is also an important cause of bleeding during the postmenopausal years (see Chapter 28).

DIAGNOSIS AND TREATMENT OF IRREGULAR BLEEDING

If you are over age 30, or there is any question about the cause of your bleeding and your clinician is confident that you don't have a pelvic infection, she/he will probably recommend a D&C (dilation and curettage, scraping of the uterus, see Chapter 40) to be sure you don't have uterine cancer. The D&C may also serve as a treatment in some cases: heavy bleeding from almost any cause can usually be stopped, at least temporarily, with D&C, and endometrial polyps can be detected and removed during the procedure.

If the cause of your abnormal periods is a specific problem such as infection or fibroid tumors, your treatment will be directed to that particular problem. If you aren't ovulating and have abnormal hormone patterns, your clinician might advise hormone treatment. Progestin tablets or shots once a month can trigger a menstrual period and can correct an irregular cycle interval and decrease heavy bleeding. Your first progestin-triggered period may be quite heavy, but subsequent periods will probably be shorter and lighter. Birth control Pills can also produce a regular, light bleeding pattern. Neither of these hormone approaches treats the underlying cause of your ovulation failure, however. If you are trying to become pregnant, your clinician can prescribe drugs to induce ovulation (see Chapter 34).

If your clinician tells you that irregular bleeding is caused by *hormone imbalance,* she/he probably means that you have a temporary alteration in your estrogen and progesterone production that either delayed your period or caused it to start early. Stress or illness may have suppressed ovulation for one or two cycles; if this is the cause, your irregular bleeding is likely to resolve itself without treatment.

Serious hormone imbalance with persistent abnormality in one or more hormone levels is quite rare. There are at least 100 human hormones, and at least 20 of them specifically involve your reproductive system. Many of the body hormones are interdependent: if you have an abnormally high or low thyroid level, for example, your reproductive hormone patterns may be affected as well. It is possible that irregular bleeding could be a first indication of a serious hormone disorder, but it is not likely.

If your clinician does find evidence of one or more abnormal hormone levels, she/he will probably recommend further blood and urine tests to determine which hormones are involved, and may refer you to a hormone specialist (endocrinologist) for full evaluation.

No Menstrual Periods (Amenorrhea)

If you are between 15 and 45 and are not having menstrual periods, the first cause you and your clinician will think about is pregnancy; an examination and pregnancy test will be the first step in your evaluation. Almost every woman can expect to miss a few periods in her lifetime for reasons other than pregnancy, however. If unusual stress or illness has temporarily interrupted your hormone cycles, your periods should return spontaneously within a month or two. Short episodes of amenorrhea ("a" means without; "menorrhea" means menstrual flow) are so common that your clinician will probably not recommend any diagnostic tests unless:

- You have missed three or more periods in a row
- You have other symptoms such as nipple discharge, headache, vision changes, difficulty with coordination, or growth of body hair
- You are 18 years old and have never had a menstrual period
- You are 14 years old, have never had a menstrual period, and have not had any breast development or pubic hair growth

Menstrual cycles can be disrupted by problems in the uterus, cervix, or vaginal opening; the ovaries; the pituitary gland (located in the center of the brain); and the brain itself (hypothalamus). (You may want to review the hormone cycle that governs menstrual periods. See Chapter 1.)

Your clinician will probably follow a fairly standard step-by-step

Illustration 1   "Amenorrhea" means no menstrual periods.

procedure to determine the cause of your amenorrhea (see Illustration 2).

CAUSES OF AMENORRHEA

Absence of Ovulation. The most common cause of amenorrhea is absence of ovulation. When ovulation does not occur, your ovary does not produce progesterone; and without progesterone, menstrual bleeding may cease or become very irregular. Absence of ovulation is not directly harmful and is quite common. Some women ovulate only occasionally throughout their entire menstrual years.

Ovulation failure is a problem if you are trying to become pregnant. In this situation, your clinician can prescribe drugs to induce ovulation (see Chapter 34).

If you aren't having periods because you aren't ovulating, but you are not trying to become pregnant, your clinician may recommend that you take progestin shots or pills once every eight weeks or so to trigger a period. Some clinicians believe that taking progestin intermittently is important; there is some evidence that prolonged exposure to your body's own estrogen without any cyclic progesterone may increase your risk of breast or uterine cancer later on (9).

If you do not want to be pregnant, you do need to continue with birth control. Ovulation can occur at any time, and you will have no way to predict your return to ovulation in advance.

Problems in the Brain. Absent periods are often caused by a problem in the brain itself (hypothalamic amenorrhea). When hormone release from your hypothalamus is too low, the pituitary gland is not stimulated, and your ovaries in turn are not stimulated to produce normal estrogen and progesterone. There is no direct test for hypothalamic amenorrhea. Your clinician can confirm this diagnosis only by testing you for other causes of amenorrhea and determining that none of the others is present.

Illness, physical or mental stress, travel, a new job, rapid or extreme weight loss, beginning college, entering prison, and many other events can suppress hypothalamus hormones. Athletes often miss periods during serious training.

Amenorrhea that occurs after you stop using birth control Pills is usually caused by hypothalamus hormone suppression. If your menstrual periods do not return spontaneously within three to six months after you stop Pills, see your clinician for a full evaluation. The con-

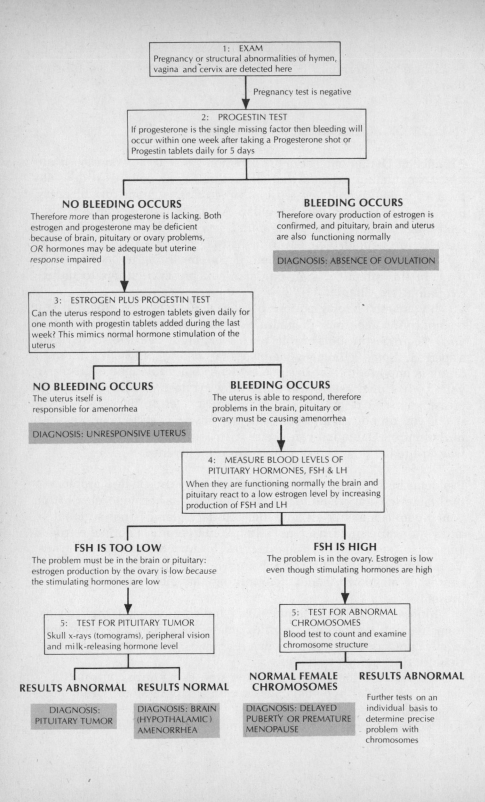

1: EXAM
Pregnancy or structural abnormalities of hymen, vagina and cervix are detected here

Pregnancy test is negative

2: PROGESTIN TEST
If progesterone is the single missing factor then bleeding will occur within one week after taking a Progesterone shot or Progestin tablets daily for 5 days

NO BLEEDING OCCURS
Therefore *more* than progesterone is lacking. Both estrogen and progesterone may be deficient because of brain, pituitary or ovary problems, *OR* hormones may be adequate but uterine *response* impaired

BLEEDING OCCURS
Therefore ovary production of estrogen is confirmed, and pituitary, brain and uterus are also functioning normally

DIAGNOSIS: ABSENCE OF OVULATION

3: ESTROGEN PLUS PROGESTIN TEST
Can the uterus respond to estrogen tablets given daily for one month with progestin tablets added during the last week? This mimics normal hormone stimulation of the uterus

NO BLEEDING OCCURS
The uterus itself is responsible for amenorrhea

DIAGNOSIS: UNRESPONSIVE UTERUS

BLEEDING OCCURS
The uterus is able to respond, therefore problems in the brain, pituitary or ovary must be causing amenorrhea

4: MEASURE BLOOD LEVELS OF PITUITARY HORMONES, FSH & LH
When they are functioning normally the brain and pituitary react to a low estrogen level by increasing production of FSH and LH

FSH IS TOO LOW
The problem must be in the brain or pituitary: estrogen production by the ovary is low *because* the stimulating hormones are low

FSH IS HIGH
The problem is in the ovary. Estrogen is low even though stimulating hormones are high

5: TEST FOR PITUITARY TUMOR
Skull x-rays (tomograms), peripheral vision and milk-releasing hormone level

5: TEST FOR ABNORMAL CHROMOSOMES
Blood test to count and examine chromosome structure

RESULTS ABNORMAL

DIAGNOSIS: PITUITARY TUMOR

RESULTS NORMAL

DIAGNOSIS: BRAIN (HYPOTHALAMIC) AMENORRHEA

NORMAL FEMALE CHROMOSOMES

DIAGNOSIS: DELAYED PUBERTY OR PREMATURE MENOPAUSE

RESULTS ABNORMAL

Further tests on an individual basis to determine precise problem with chromosomes

nection between your Pills and your missed periods could be only a coincidence.

> I started taking Pills after my daughter was born, and I stuck with them most of the time for about ten years. There were a couple of months when I didn't have any regular periods while I was off Pills, but I didn't think much about it until last year when I started using a diaphragm. When my periods *still* hadn't come back after six months of no Pills, I saw my doctor to see if I was having menopause or something. He told me it was common to miss periods after Pills; so I didn't worry about it. After we moved to Georgia, though, my new doctor made me have a lot of fancy tests and they found a *brain tumor*. After I had my operation, the surgeon told me that missing periods in my case had nothing to do with Pills; it was just a coincidence. He said the tumor was so large it must have been there at least five years!
>
> —*Woman, 34*

Structural Abnormalities. The other causes of amenorrhea are quite rare. If you have never had any periods, your clinician will look for structural abnormalities during your exam, such as a hymen that completely closes the entrance to your vagina ("imperforate" hymen) or an obstruction in your cervical canal. These problems are easily corrected by minor surgery or by dilating your cervical opening. Other structural abnormalities, such as a missing uterus or missing vagina, are extremely rare, and would be evident at the time of your first pelvic examination.

Problems with the Uterine Lining. If treatment with estrogen and progestin fails to trigger bleeding, your clinician will know that you have an *unresponsive uterus.* This condition usually means that your uterine lining tissue has been scarred or damaged by infection and/or scraping, such as with a D&C (see Chapter 40). Regrowth of uterine lining can sometimes be stimulated by hormone treatment, or your clinician may recommend an IUD to hold your uterine walls apart so that lining tissue has an opportunity to cover the inner walls completely.

Illustration 2   How your clinician will evaluate amenorrhea. (Reproductive Health Resources, Inc., used with permission.)

Pituitary Gland Tumor. A tumor in your pituitary gland can interfere with normal hormone production and stop your periods. A pituitary tumor may cause breast milk production because of excessive milk releasing hormone (prolactin) produced by your pituitary gland. Tumors may also cause symptoms such as headache or vision problems, and they are detected by measuring the level of prolactin hormone in your blood, special x-rays called tomograms and by careful measurement of your peripheral vision (visual fields). Pituitary tumors are almost always benign (not cancerous) and grow quite slowly. If you have bleeding after you receive progestin and you do not have breast milk production and your blood prolactin level is normal, then you can be confident that you do not have a pituitary gland tumor.

Menopause or Premature Menopause. At menopause your ovaries stop responding to hormones from the pituitary gland. If ovary response stops before age 45, you may have premature menopause, and there is no known treatment. If you are under 30 and premature menopause seems to be the cause of your amenorrhea, your clinician may recommend additional evaluation and also hormone replacement therapy. Premature menopause is very rare.

Delayed Puberty. Delayed puberty means that your ovaries fail to become responsive to pituitary stimulation at a normal age, and this condition is a possibility if you have not yet begun to have menstrual periods by age 18.

Abnormal Chromosome (Gene) Structure. Abnormal chromosome (gene) structure can result in ovaries that fail to produce estrogen and progesterone despite adequate pituitary hormone stimulation. Your clinician will be particularly concerned about this possibility if you have not yet started periods by age 18, or if you do not have breast and body hair development by age 14. Chromosome abnormalities are rare and require individualized evaluation and treatment.

SUMMARY

Thorough evaluation of amenorrhea is absolutely essential. It is a fairly complicated problem, and you may need to be patient and persistent as you make sure that you have all the necessary tests and that you understand your test results and recommended treatment. The main goal of evaluation is to be sure that you don't have a pituitary tumor.

Remember that you will need reevaluation at least once every 6 to 12 months as long as amenorrhea persists. A pituitary tumor can be very tiny and can grow so slowly that it is detected only after several repeated examinations. And remember to think about pregnancy; it is always a leading possibility.

REFERENCES

1. Ylikorkala O, Dawood M: New concepts in dysmenorrhea. *American Journal of Obstetrics and Gynecology* 130:833–847, 1978.
2. Friederich M, Labrum A: Evaluation and preferred management of premenstrual tension—pelvic congestive syndrome and allied states, in Reid DE and Christian CD, *Controversy in Obstetrics and Gynecology II.* Philadelphia, WB Saunders, 1974, pp 760–775.
3. Adams PW, Rose DP, Folkard J, et al: Effect of pyridoxine hydrochloride (vitamin B_6) upon depression associated with oral contraception. *Lancet* 1:897–904, April 1973.
4. Asplund J: The uterine cervix and isthmus under normal and pathological conditions: A clinical and roentgenological study. *Acta Radiologica Supplementum* 91:1, 1952.
5. Miller NF, Behrman SJ: Dysmenorrhea. *America Journal of Obstetrics and Gynecology* 65:505–516, 1953.
6. Pickles VR, Hall WJ, Best FA, et al: Prostaglandins in endometrium and menstrual fluid from normal and dysmenorrhoeic subjects. *Journal of Obstetrics and Gynaecology of the British Commonwealth* 72:185–192, 1965.
7. Drugs for dysmenorrhea. *The Medical Letter on Drugs and Therapeutics* 21(20):81–83, October 5, 1979.
8. Larkin RM, VanOrden DE, Poulson AM, et al: Dysmenorrhea: treatment with an antiprostaglandin. *Obstetrics and Gynecology* 54:456–460, 1979.
9. Speroff L, Glass RH, Kase N: *Clinical Gynecologic Endocrinology and Infertility,* ed 2. Baltimore, Williams and Wilkins, 1978.

27 | Abnormal Pap Smear Results

The primary purpose of a Pap smear is to detect the presence of abnormal cells on the surface of the cervix. It is a sensitive test that reliably reveals early, precancerous, or potentially cancerous cell changes, as well as true cervical cancer itself. Regular Pap tests are important, for cell changes that are detected *early* can be treated easily and very effectively. Cervical cancer usually progresses slowly. It begins with minimal precancer cell changes and evolves to true cancer over a period of years.

The Pap test does not reliably detect cancer of the uterus, vagina, or ovaries, but it can demonstrate cervical or vaginal infection in some cases and can sometimes provide a general idea of estrogen levels. Current recommendations for when, and how frequently, you will need routine Pap tests are discussed at the end of Chapter 21. If you have had herpes infection (see Chapter 22), abnormal Pap test results in the past, a family history of uterine or cervical cancer, or have been exposed to diethylstilbestrol (see Chapter 37), you will probably need more frequent Pap tests.

Techniques for obtaining and processing your Pap test specimen are described in Chapter 21. The pathologist or cytotechnician who examines your Pap smear slide looks at the shape, size, and structure of the cells; next she/he checks the number of cells of each type to assign a "reading" to your smear. If all the cells on your slide are types of cells that are present on the surface of a normal cervix, then your test result is normal. If abnormal cells are present, your Pap test report will show the type and degree of abnormality.

There are several different schemes for classifying Pap test abnormalities. One of the oldest and most common schemes divides Pap results into five classes: Class I is normal, and Class V is true cervical cancer. Class II designates abnormal infection cells (Class II abnormalities are not precancerous). Class III and Class IV indicate mild to severe precancerous cell changes.

A newer scheme, preferred by most experts in this field, divides Pap tests into three major categories: benign; precancerous (cell changes called cervical intraepithelial neoplasia, CIN); and malignant (cancer).

These schemes are confusing, the names are complicated, and it is not important to memorize them. To make this chapter simpler, only the "CIN system" terminology will be used. If your clinician uses a different scheme or different terms, you can substitute according to Table 1. The important point to understand about these schemes and grading systems is that cervical cell changes are a very gradual continuum. *If you have CIN, it does not mean that you have cancer.* It does mean that you need further evaluation and treatment, however.

Abnormal Pap test results are fairly common. Typical frequencies for Pap test results are shown in Table 2.

Understanding Your Pap Test Result

The principle of the Pap test is that cells collected from the surface of your cervix for study will accurately reflect what the surface of your cervix is like. The surface (epithelium) of the cervix is composed of several cell layers. There is constant cell growth and maturation within the cervical epithelium; new cells are produced at the bottom layer, then gradually mature and move up to the top surface as old cells are shed from the top. The Pap test scraper collects cells that are loose and ready to be shed from the top surface layer.

When precancerous cell changes occur, the cell maturation process is disturbed and immature cells move closer to the surface. Unusually large or distorted cells may be present. An *increased proportion* of immature and distorted cells is seen on the Pap smear.

Table 1   PAP SMEAR CLASSIFICATION SYSTEMS

Term Used in This Chapter	Class	Category	Other Terms
Normal	I	Benign	Negative
Inflammatory	II	Benign	Atypical; metaplasia
Mild CIN[a]	III	1) Mild CIN	Mild dysplasia
		2) Moderate CIN	Moderate dysplasia
Severe CIN[a]	IV	3) Severe CIN	Carcinoma in situ
Cancer	V	Malignant	Invasive cancer

[a]Cervical intraepithelial neoplasia.

Table 2   PAP TEST RESULTS[a]

Result	Frequency
Normal	90 in 100
Inflammatory	1 in 20
Mild CIN	1 in 30
Severe CIN	1 in 500
Cancer	1 in 1,000

[a]Based on tabulation of more than 500,000 pap smears evaluated by a large, private laboratory. Unpublished data, Cancer Screening Services, California. Pap test result rates depend on the age distribution, social, and medical characteristics of the group of women being evaluated.

PAP SMEARS AND CERVICAL BIOPSIES

In order to arrive at a precise and completely accurate diagnosis of cervical abnormalities, the pathologist also needs to evaluate the layered structure of the cells that make up the cervical surface. The Pap smear reflects the layered structure, but a biopsy gives the pathologist an actual tissue sample *with all the cell layers intact*, as shown in Illustration 1. The biopsy technique, in this case for removal of a shallow 1/16-by-1/16-inch piece of tissue from the surface of the cervix, is described in Chapter 21. If your Pap result is CIN, your clinician is almost certain to recommend biopsy. The biopsy site(s) is often chosen by careful examination of the cervix with a colposcope, also described in Chapter 21.

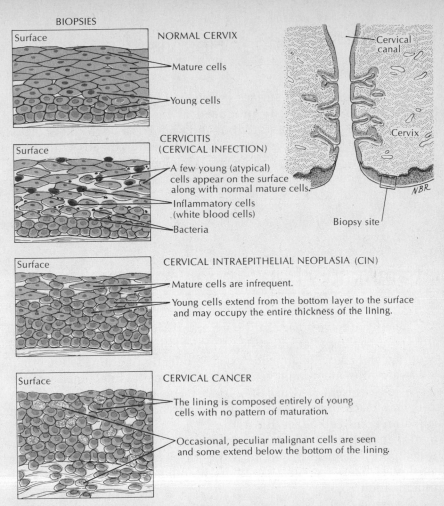

BIOPSIES

NORMAL CERVIX

Surface

- Mature cells
- Young cells

Cervical canal

CERVICITIS (CERVICAL INFECTION)

Surface

- A few young (atypical) cells appear on the surface along with normal mature cells.
- Inflammatory cells (white blood cells)
- Bacteria

Cervix

Biopsy site

NBR

CERVICAL INTRAEPITHELIAL NEOPLASIA (CIN)

Surface

- Mature cells are infrequent.
- Young cells extend from the bottom layer to the surface and may occupy the entire thickness of the lining.

CERVICAL CANCER

Surface

- The lining is composed entirely of young cells with no pattern of maturation.
- Occasional, peculiar malignant cells are seen and some extend below the bottom of the lining.

Illustration 1 The Pap smear reveals changes in cells that make up the surface of the cervix. The cervical biopsy provides a sample of cervical tissue with cell layers *intact*. (Reproductive Health Resources, Inc., used with permission.)

Normal Pap Smear Results

The normal cervical surface consists of about ten layers of cells. New cells are continuously produced at the bottom. These young, immature cells are small and round, and each has a large cell nucleus. All the cells at the top layer are older, fully matured cells with a flat, geometric "pancake" shape and a small nucleus. Your Pap smear slide contains only *mature* cells if it is normal (see Illustration 1).

Inflammatory Pap Smear Results

When you have a cervical infection or when your cervix is in the process of healing after infection or injury, the surface is disrupted by swelling, and many inflammatory cells—infection-fighting white blood cells—are present in among normal mature cells. Infectious bacteria may also be present. Because the surface layers are disrupted, immature cells may reach the surface and appear on your Pap smear. These are called **atypical** cells. (See Illustration 1.)

Inflammation of the cervix (cervicitis) is commonly caused by infection or chemical irritation, and is discussed in Chapter 24. Your Pap test is likely to reflect cervicitis no matter what is causing your inflammation.

Severe vaginitis (see Chapter 22) can cause your vaginal discharge to contain inflammatory cells and bacteria, and these cells can show up in your Pap smear even if infection has not truly invaded your cervix.

When your cervix is in the process of healing after severe infection or injury, your Pap smear may show inflammatory cells and occasional immature cells. This would be expected after a cervical biopsy or for several months after your cervix has been treated with cautery or cryosurgery (see Chapter 21).

An inflammatory Pap test is abnormal, but it has nothing whatsoever to do with cancer. Inflammatory cell changes are not precancerous and do not progress to cancer.

Inflammatory smears are undesirable, not because of what they mean, but because the presence of a large number of inflammatory cells can obscure the changes in cervical cells that your Pap smear is meant to detect; they interfere with accurate evaluation of your smear. Be sure that you have another Pap smear three to six months after an inflammatory result, once your cervicitis or vaginitis has been treated and cured.

Some women show unexplained inflammatory cells in their Pap smears that persist for long periods, and these women "routinely" have abnormal, inflammatory Pap test reports. This condition is not serious, and it is not an indication of cancer. It is inconvenient, because frequent Pap tests are required.

CIN (Cervical Intraepithelial Neoplasia)

CIN cell changes are restricted to the surface of your cervix itself, and usually to only a tiny area of the surface. Abnormal CIN cells do not invade other tissues.

These abnormal cell changes are precancerous, or potentially cancerous. In some 30 to 50% of **untreated** cases, abnormal cell development would gradually become more severe and would eventually result in true cancer of the cervix, which can invade other tissues (1). On the average, it takes about five years for CIN to become true cancer. If proper treatment is carried out, however, CIN can be cured in nearly all cases (2).

When CIN abnormalities are mild, your cervical biopsy specimen shows a disturbed maturation pattern, with a significant number of young cells in the top layers in among the mature cells. As the degree of abnormality becomes more severe the proportion of young cells increases. At the severe end of this progression, the entire thickness of the surface layers is composed of young cells, with no mature cells at all in your biopsy specimen or on your Pap smear slide (see Illustration 1).

If your Pap test report shows CIN, then the very first step is to be sure that the diagnosis is accurate. Your clinician will carefully prepare another Pap smear and will recommend biopsy. She/he will also recommend that you have a colposcopic examination of your cervix if possible (see Chapter 21) to pinpoint the most abnormal areas for biopsy and to evaluate the entire surface of your cervix.

If your clinician has been able to determine exactly where the entire abnormal area is with a colposcope and your biopsy report confirms CIN, then you have the information you need to assess the various treatment options. If there is any doubt about colposcopy findings or if your biopsy report does not agree with your Pap smear, then your clinician will probably recommend another biopsy or conization surgery to remove a major part of your cervical surface.

Before colposcopy became widely available, conization surgery was a routine recommendation for a woman with mild to moderate CIN, and in some cases severe CIN. Today, conization is recommended only for selected patients who have CIN, but who cannot be fully evaluated with the colposcope because the abnormal area extends up into the cervical canal beyond the view of the colposcope. If the entire extent of the abnormal area is not visible, it is impossible for a clinician to be certain, on the basis of colposcopy alone, that biopsy specimens represent the worst areas of abnormality. Conization surgery in this situation provides the information that colposcopically directed biopsies are usually able to provide: the assurance that CIN alone, and not cancer, is responsible for abnormal Pap smear results. Conization is also appropriate if biopsy results are not conclusive.

Because the entire surface of the cervix is removed in conization surgery, it may serve to eradicate the abnormal areas, thus providing treatment for CIN as well as diagnosis. Conization, however, would not be advised when treatment alone is the goal. Serious complications are more common with conization than they are with cryosurgery, the other treatment option for CIN. Also, conization surgery usually requires general anesthesia and is performed in a hospital or surgical center setting. Cryosurgery can be easily performed in an office setting and does not require any anesthesia.

For a conization procedure you would be given general anesthesia and then positioned as for a pelvic examination. The surgeon uses a vaginal speculum to see your cervix. After she/he places stitches on each side of your cervix to stabilize it and to diminish bleeding, she/he makes a circular incision through the surface of the cervix so that the entire abnormal area is included within the portion to be removed (see Illustration 2). The incision is extended deep into your cervix in a cone shape so that the lower portion of the cervical canal is removed along with the outer surface of the cervix. After the center cone of cervix is removed, the cut edges of the cervix are stitched.

Heavy bleeding is a common complication of conization that can occur during or immediately after surgery or about 10 days later when the cervix stitches are absorbed. One patient in ten may require treatment (transfusion and/or hospitalization and/or further surgery) be-

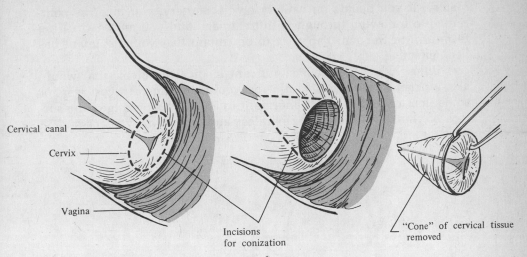

Cervical canal

Cervix

Vagina

Incisions
for conization

"Cone" of cervical tissue
removed

Illustration 2   Conization of the cervix is a major surgical procedure
that may be necessary when CIN is present, and the
abnormal area extends up into the cervical canal beyond the view of the colposcope. (Reproductive Health
Resources, Inc., used with permission.)

cause of hemorrhage. Infection and perforation of the uterus are other
immediate complications that can occur with conization, but they are
uncommon.

Long term effects of conization can also be serious. Cervical in-
competence, leading to premature delivery in subsequent pregnancies
is fairly common. Inadequate cervical mucus production after conization (which removes a substantial portion of the cervical tissue that
contains mucus glands) may be a cause of impaired fertility. Conization
can also cause scarring of the cervical canal. If the cervical canal is
blocked, menstrual blood may be trapped inside the uterus. Cervical
scarring can also interfere with proper cervical dilation during labor and
delivery in later pregnancies.

The goal of CIN treatment is to eradicate the abnormal cells, usually by cautery or cryosurgery (see Chapter 21). Hysterectomy would
also eliminate the abnormal cells, for the uterus and cervix would be
completely removed (see Chapter 41).

You and your clinician will want to consider several factors as you
decide on treatment for CIN. Your feelings about future pregnancies are
one factor, as well as your age, other medical problems, and your family

history. If you decide on cautery or cryosurgery, you must be committed to following through with treatment; and you must be willing to return for frequent Pap tests to be certain that your treatment has been effective.

Unless you have other significant medical problems that would also warrant surgery, most clinicians would recommend cryosurgery or sometimes cautery if your abnormalities are mild. Freezing of the surface of your cervix is almost painless and is extremely successful in treating mild or moderate CIN (see Illustration 3).

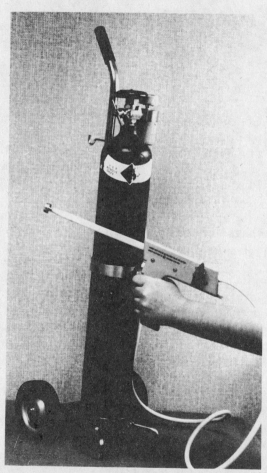

Illustration 3   Cryosurgery unit. (Photography by Rita R. Harris, Medical Photographer.)

If you have **severe CIN,** your treatment choices are less clear-cut. Most experts (3) believe that it is reasonable and safe to choose cryosurgery or cautery, and this would be a completely appropriate choice if you desire future pregnancies.

If future pregnancy is not a consideration for you, then you may want to consider hysterectomy. Some women find that repeated followup examinations are a hardship and a major source of anxiety. Hysterectomy allows them to deal with the problem once and for all and then forget about it.

Cervical Cancer

When cancer is present, the normal pattern of cell maturation is totally obliterated: young, rapidly growing cells fill all surface layers, and severely distorted malignant cells are present as well (see Illustration 1). Malignant cells do not behave at all like normal surface cells. Normal surface cells ordinarily exist **only** within surface layers. Cancer cells can move **beyond** the surface layers, deeper into cervical tissue, and can spread and grow in other body tissues as well.

Treatment for true cervical cancer is on the whole very successful. If it is detected and treated before malignant cells have spread beyond the cervix, it can be cured in about 90% of cases. If malignant cells have spread beyond the cervix but are confined to nearby tissue such as the uterus and vagina, the cure rate is about 60% (4).

Because early detection makes such a big difference, it is important to have regular Pap tests even if you are afraid. **Cervical cancer often does not have early symptoms that you would be likely to notice.** It is usually entirely painless and might grow undetected for several years if it isn't detected on a Pap test.

Treatment for cervical cancer is individualized. Surgery alone, radiation treatment alone, or radiation followed by surgery may be best in your particular case. Your clinician may refer you to a cancer specialist to help determine your best treatment options.

What Causes Cancer of the Cervix. There is no single, known cause of cervical cancer. Experts believe that environmental factors are of primary importance, as they are with many other types of cancer. Although the specific environmental factors have not yet been identified, the study of cervical cancer rates among different groups of women does provide some clues. Cervical cancer rates are quite low in some groups, and much higher in others (5).

Hereditary differences may make some women more prone to the development of cervical cancer, but cervical exposure to infectious agents (perhaps viruses we don't yet know about), injury, or chemicals seems to be an important common denominator. Extensive exposure that begins at a young age seems to increase cervical cancer risk, and exposure apparently occurs most often with intercourse. Women who have intercourse and pregnancy or miscarriage very early in their reproductive years, women who have multiple sexual partners (including women who are separated or divorced or who have multiple marriages), and women who have had herpes and other sexually transmitted infections have higher rates of cervical cancer. Women who choose the diaphragm or condoms for birth control may have a lower risk for cervical cancer than do women who use other methods.

Researchers used to suspect that women who had intercourse with circumcised men had less cervical cancer than women who had intercourse with uncircumcised men. Early research comparing the cancer incidence among Jewish women with that among other women seemed to show that circumcision was somehow a factor in low cervical cancer rates. More recent studies have determined, however, that factors other than circumcision must explain the relatively low rate of cervical cancer among Jewish women. Studies in other cultures that compared groups who practice circumcision with groups who do not have shown that *circumcision does not seem to affect cervical cancer rates* (6). Jewish social and religious values that dictate abstinence before marriage and sexual monogamy may explain the low cervical cancer rates.

As you evaluate your own risk for developing precancerous abnormalities or true cervical cancer, remember that the list of risk factors simply indicates a *somewhat* lower or higher risk than the average. Overall, the incidence of cervical cancer is about 1 in 100,000 for women aged 20 to 24, and rises with increasing age. For women aged 45 to 65, the incidence is about 50 in 100,000. It is reassuring to be in a group at very low risk, but this does not guarantee that you will not develop cancer. Similarly, the majority of women even in groups at highest risk will never develop the disease.

In either case, you need to have regular Pap smears in order to protect yourself. Regular Pap smears insure that precancerous abnormalities can be detected and eradicated before you ever develop true cancer.

REFERENCES

1. Hall JE, Walton C: Dysplasia of the cervix: A prospective study of 206 cases. *American Journal of Obstetrics and Gynecology* 100:662–671, 1968.
2. Nelson JH, Averette HE, Richart RM: *Dysplasia and Early Cervical Cancer: Detection, Diagnostic Evaluation, Treatment and Management.* New York, American Cancer Society, 1975.
3. Townsend DE: Detection and management of preinvasive cervical neoplasia. *Current Problems in Obstetrics and Gynecology* 1(2), October 1977.
4. Rutledge F, Bronow RC, Wharton JT: *Gynecologic Oncology.* New York, John Wiley, 1976.
5. Rotkin ID: A comparison review of key epidemiologic studies in cervical cancer related to current searches for transmissible agents. *Cancer Research* 33:1353–1367, 1973.
6. Coppleson M: Carcinoma of the cervix: Epidemiology and aetiology. *British Journal of Hospital Medicine* 2:961, 1969.

28 | Cancer of the Reproductive Organs

It is hard not to worry about cancer, and cancer of the reproductive organs is a major health threat for women. Today, however, most cancers of the reproductive organs *are cured* if they are detected and treated early. Your annual pelvic exams, Pap tests, and monthly self breast examinations, together with your prompt attention to cancer danger signs, are your insurance policies against the risks of reproductive system cancer.

Warning Signs

The warning signs that you and your clinician need to watch for are:
Breast Cancer
    A breast lump
    Nipple discharge
    A change in breast skin appearance: dimpling, red, or dry flaky skin
Skin Cancer on the Vulva
    A persistent sore or warty growth on the skin of the vulva
    Persistent itching, redness, or thickening of vulvar skin
Cervical Cancer
    Pap test results that show precancerous cell changes
    A persistent ulcer or growth on the cervix

410

Bleeding after intercourse
Abnormal bleeding or spotting
Abnormal vaginal discharge

Uterine Cancer
Abnormal bleeding in an irregular pattern or *any* bleeding after menopause
An enlarged or growing uterus, especially after menopause
Heavy mucus discharge
Pap test results that show uterine cancer cells*

Ovary Cancer
An enlarged ovary
After menopause, an ovary that is large enough to be felt during routine pelvic examination
Abdominal fullness or bladder or rectum pressure from an enlarged ovary
Pap test results that show ovary cancer cells*

Many of these signs can be caused by problems other than cancer, but the warning signs do mean that you need careful evaluation without delay.

Almost half of all cancers that occur in women involve the reproductive organs (see Illustration 1). Your age and many factors influence your own cancer risk. For example, if you are 22 years old, the likelihood that an enlarged ovary is due to cancer is very low; it is much higher if you are 72 years old. Similarly, breast cancer is extremely rare before the age of 25 but is the leading cause of death for women aged 40 to 44. Other factors that influence cancer risk, descriptions of symptoms you might have, and evaluation and treatment your clinician is likely to recommend for breast, cervical, and ovary cancer are discussed in Chapters 32, 27, and 29, respectively.

Cancer of the Uterus

The most common early sign of cancer in the lining of the uterus is *abnormal bleeding*. About 80% of all women with uterine cancer

---

*The Pap test is very reliable for detecting cancer of the cervix. Pap tests do not reliably detect any other kind of cancer, but in some cases, uterus or ovary cancer cells are visible on a Pap test slide.

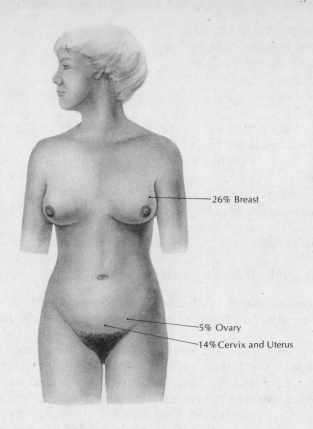

—26% Breast

—5% Ovary
—14% Cervix and Uterus

Illustration 1 Reproductive tract cancer sites in women: percentage of all female cancers diagnosed. Approximately 350,000 new cases of cancer are reported for women each year nationwide. Of these, 45 percent involve the reproductive organs. Overall about 175,000 cancer deaths among women are reported annually. Statistics do not include minor skin cancers or pre-invasive cancer of the cervix. (Edwin Silverberg: Cancer statistics, 1977, *Ca—A Cancer Journal for Clinicians* 27(1), January-February 1977, New York, American Cancer Society.)

report abnormal bleeding (1), and it is often the very first sign of a problem. Bleeding can be light and irregular, with spotting between normal periods or after menopause; or bleeding can be heavy with prolonged menstrual periods. Some women with uterine cancer have heavy mucus discharge. *Later* signs of cancer in the uterus include cramping, pelvic discomfort, pressure in the lower abdomen or bladder pressure, bleeding after intercourse, swollen lymph nodes, or lumps in the groin. Routine Pap tests detect uterine cancer cells in only 15 to 50% of women who have uterine cancer (1). The disease is more often discovered by dilation and curettage (D&C) that is performed to determine the cause of unusual bleeding. (See Chapter 40 for a description of D&C.)

As in the case of cervical cancer, researchers suspect that precancerous abnormalities may precede the development of true uterine cancer by months or even years. Abnormal cell maturation patterns in the uterine lining, called *endometrial hyperplasia,* apparently arise spontaneously in some cases, and in others are caused by exposure to estrogen drugs. Endometrial hyperplasia often causes abnormal bleeding or spotting and is therefore identified when a D&C or endometrial biopsy is performed because of bleeding. In some cases the uterine lining will return to normal when estrogen drugs are stopped or treatment with progestin is given. If this occurs, a follow-up D&C will show that the lining is normal. If the follow-up evaluation shows persistent hyperplasia, however, surgery to remove the uterus (hysterectomy) should be seriously considered because of the risk that true uterine cancer might later develop.

The likelihood that a 35-year-old woman will eventually develop uterine cancer is about 1.4%, or 1 in 70 (1). Some women have a lower or *higher* than average risk for uterine cancer, and there is substantial evidence that the incidence of uterine cancer has generally increased within the last eight to ten years (2). Researchers have linked the general increase in uterine cancer with increased use of estrogen drugs for treatment of menopause problems (see Chapter 36); they also believe that differences in the body's own estrogen levels may explain why some women have a higher risk for uterine cancer than others.

Some of the factors that may be associated with a higher than average uterine cancer risk are conditions that result in elevated estrogen levels or in prolonged exposure to estrogen without normal cyclic interruptions in exposure, such as:

• Menstrual patterns with prolonged intervals between periods, failure to ovulate, impaired fertility, or few or no pregnancies

- Presence of an estrogen-producing ovarian tumor (rare)
- Obesity
- Family history of uterine cancer
- Previous use of *sequential* birth control Pills (no longer marketed) containing high doses of estrogen
- Previous use of DES (diethylstilbestrol) during pregnancy—DES mothers (3)
- Previous use of estrogen drugs for menopausal symptoms (see Chapter 36)
- High blood pressure
- Previous benign tumors (polyps) of the uterine lining
- Diabetes

Uterine cancer is rare before the age of 40 and usually occurs after menopause. Most women who develop uterine cancer before age 30 or 40 have had clearly abnormal hormone patterns and have failed to ovulate regularly because of a hormone-producing tumor, generalized excessive ovary hormone production (Stein-Leventhal disease), or exposure to high estrogen levels in sequential birth control Pills.

Despite the apparent association between estrogen exposure and uterine cancer, there is as yet no definite proof that estrogen *causes* cancer; nor is there a clear understanding of how this effect might occur.

Diagnosis and Treatment of Uterine Cancer

A definite diagnosis requires microscopic evaluation of a sample of uterine lining tissue by the pathologist. Your clinician will probably recommend uterine scraping (D&C, see Chapter 40) to obtain shreds of uterine lining from each area of your uterus. In some cases, office procedures such as a vacuum scraping to obtain lining samples or endometrial biopsy (see Chapter 21) may provide sufficient tissue for diagnosis.

If you have uterine cancer, your clinician will probably refer you to a specialist in women's reproductive tract cancers for full evaluation and for help·with selecting your best treatment.

Depending on the location, extent, and microscopic appearance of the tumor, your treatment might include surgery alone (to remove the uterus and ovaries), radiation alone, surgery with radiation, or chemical or hormone drug treatment.

Overall, about 68% of women treated for uterine cancer are cured; that is, they are well with no evidence of disease after five years. If cancer has not spread beyond the uterus, the cure rate is about 76% (1).

REFERENCES

1. DiSaia PJ, Morrow CP, Townsend DE: *Synopsis of Gynecological Oncology*. New York, John Wiley, 1975.
2. Greenwald P, Caputo TA, Wolfgang PE: Endometrial cancer after menopausal use of estrogens. *Obstetrics and Gynecology* 50:239–243, 1977.
3. DES and breast cancer. *FDA Drug Bulletin* 8(2), March-April 1978. Food and Drug Administration.

 # Ovarian Cysts and Tumors

Symptoms

An ovary cyst (fluid-filled sac) or tumor (solid mass of cells) can develop with no symptoms at all; or you may notice a sensation of fullness in your lower abdomen, some discomfort, or pain during intercourse. You are most likely to find out about a cyst or tumor during a pelvic exam when your clinician notices an enlarged ovary.

Ovary cysts occasionally cause sudden, severe pain if the cyst ruptures, causes internal bleeding, or becomes twisted. Pain can even be mistaken for appendicitis, and you may also have weakness, nausea, and vomiting. You clinician might admit you to a hospital because of the severity of pain alone.

Infection in your uterus and tubes can cause similar symptoms; so if you are having pain and cramps, be sure to take your temperature at home, and tell your clinician if you have a fever (a temperature of 100.4 degrees Fahrenheit by mouth, or higher) or unusual vaginal discharge, or if you suspect that you have been exposed to gonorrhea.

Tubal (ectopic) pregnancy can also mimic ovary cysts or tumors. If you have pregnancy symptoms or think for any reason that you might be pregnant (see Chapter 4 for signs of pregnancy), be sure to tell your clinician.

416

Diagnosis

If you have an enlarged ovary, your clinician will consider your age, your medical history, your family history, your symptoms, and the size of your ovary as she/he determines what is causing your problem.

Cancerous ovarian tumors are very rare in women under 30. Cysts that arise from an egg follicle or a corpus luteum (called "functional" cysts) during a normal hormone cycle are very common among women under 30, and your clinician may simply recommend that you return for a second examination several weeks later to determine whether your ovary has returned to normal size. Most functional cysts simply disappear, and they are usually harmless.

If your ovary is larger than 3 inches (6 to 7 cm) in size, if you are over 40 years old, or if you are having bothersome pain, your clinician may recommend laboratory and x-ray tests or even exploratory surgery. It is usually impossible for your clinician to tell exactly what kind of cyst or tumor you have without surgery. Surgery allows your clinician to examine your ovary directly and remove a small piece of ovary tissue for microscopic evaluation. She/he will determine what further surgery you need, if any, on the basis of the appearance of your ovary and sometimes on the basis of microscopic evaluation.

If you are in your 30s and are not having bothersome pain, and your ovary is only moderately enlarged, your clinician may recommend one or more of the following tests:

- A sonogram (see Chapter 21) to provide a precise measurement of the size of your ovaries, and determine whether your enlargement is a cyst or a tumor;
- A pregnancy test to be sure that you are not pregnant;
- An abdominal x-ray to look for calcium or fatty deposits within your ovary that are common with certain types of tumors. Small cysts usually are not visible on an x-ray; a large cyst can sometimes be identified because it displaces other nearby structures that are visible on an x-ray.

Hormone suppression is sometimes recommended for a young woman who has an enlarged ovary less than 2 inches in size. If your ovarian enlargement is caused by a functional cyst, hormone medication to suppress your natural hormone cycle should cause your cyst to shrink and disappear. Clinicians often use one or two months of regular birth control Pills for hormone suppression. Your clinician will examine you after you have completed the hormone medication to see if your ovary has returned to normal size. If your ovary remains enlarged after hormone medication, you probably don't have a functional cyst. You may need surgery to determine the cause of your ovarian enlargement. Hormone medication is not recommended for women over 40 because of the possibility of ovarian cancer. Hormones might speed up growth of a cancerous tumor.

If hormone medication doesn't help your ovarian enlargement, your clinician may next try laparoscopy, a simple surgical procedure that permits your clinician to look at your ovaries through a lighted tube inserted through a 1-inch incision just below your navel. If your clinician wants a sample of your ovarian tissue for analysis, however, you will need exploratory surgery (laparotomy) with a 5-inch abdominal incision.

Types of Ovarian Cysts and Tumors

Functional cysts are responsible for ovarian enlargement in more than half the cases, and you probably won't need any extensive tests or surgery if you have a functional cyst. There are many other kinds of ovarian cysts and tumors, and overall about 75 to 85% are benign (not cancerous).

FUNCTIONAL OVARIAN CYSTS

A normal egg follicle is a small cavity that contains an egg and follicle fluid. After ovulation, the follicle cells rearrange themselves to form a corpus luteum. The corpus luteum often contains fluid surrounded by a layer of luteal cells. If an egg follicle is abnormally large, then it is by definition a cyst, a fluid-filled sac. An abnormally large fluid-filled corpus luteum is also a cyst. A corpus luteum cyst is shown in Illustration 1.

Follicular cysts and corpus luteum cysts are called "functional" cysts because they are the result of normal ovary functions.

Follicle cysts are quite common. Many women notice pain at the time of ovulation that is caused by rupture of a normal egg follicle as it releases the egg. If you have sudden, one-sided pain that occurs about

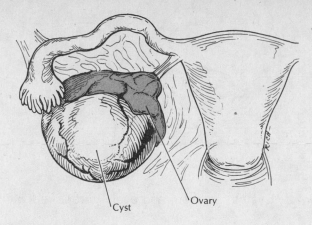

Illustration 1   Large corpus luteum cyst.

halfway between two menstrual periods and is gone within 24 hours, chances are that you had a follicle cyst rupture.

Corpus luteum cysts are even more common. You will most likely have at least one some time during your reproductive years. They are especially common during the early weeks of pregnancy when corpus luteum progesterone production is extremely high. You may notice an abnormally light or short period or irregular bleeding if you have a corpus luteum cyst, and you and your clinician may be worried about the possibility of pregnancy or tubal (ectopic) pregnancy. You may need to have a special pregnancy test sensitive enough to detect very early pregnancy or ectopic pregnancy (see Chapter 4). If there is any doubt about pregnancy, your clinician might recommend a sonogram or laparoscopy.

If you have really severe pain with a functional cyst, your clinician may recommend hospital observation. Internal bleeding can occur with a large functional cyst, and you may need surgery. It is almost always possible for your surgeon to remove the cyst and repair your ovary by stitching over the cyst area (see Illustration 2).

In most cases, surgery is not necessary. Your functional cyst will probably disappear on its own, or after one or two cycles of birth control Pills.

Functional cysts are rare in women who take birth control Pills on a regular schedule. If you are using Pills when your clinician discovers an enlarged ovary, you will need further evaluation.

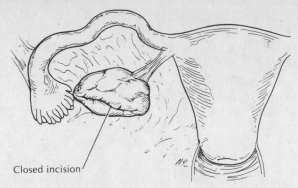

Closed incision

Illustration 2   Cyst is removed, and ovary is repaired with sutures.

BENIGN AND MALIGNANT TUMORS AND CYSTS

Benign (noncancerous) tumors usually require surgery and microscopic analysis to distinguish them from malignant (cancerous) tumors, as well as from each other. The likelihood of cancer as a cause of ovarian enlargement increases with your age, as shown in Table 1.

All the benign cysts and tumors cause similar symptoms if they cause any symptoms at all, and they require similar surgical treatment.

Table 1   OVARY TUMOR DIAGNOSIS BY AGE

Age	Tumors That Are Benign (Noncancerous) (approx. %)
Under 20	80–85
20 to 30	90–95
30 to 40	80–95
40 to 50	70–75
50 to 70	50
Over 70	66

SOURCES: Adapted from E Stewart Taylor, *Essentials of Gynecology*, Philadelphia, Lea and Febiger, 1962; and MF Fathalla, Factors in the causation and incidence of ovarian cancer, *Obstetrical and Gynecological Survey* 27:751–768, 1972.

It is important for you to know *what type* of tumor was found and whether you are likely to have another tumor in the future. You might want to ask your surgeon to give you a copy of your surgery report and pathologist's report to keep in your personal medical records. These reports may be helpful to any clinician caring for you in the future.

If your tumor is benign, it may be possible for your surgeon to remove just the tumor and leave your ovary in place. Even if your surgeon has to remove one ovary, your remaining ovary should be able to maintain your normal hormone levels. It is even possible to remove a substantial part of both ovaries without causing hormone deficiency problems.

If you have ovarian cancer, your surgeon will probably remove the tumor, both ovaries, and your uterus and tubes as well. Be sure to discuss your feelings about future pregnancy with your surgeon before your operation. If your malignant tumor is small and confined to one ovary, and the cancer is a slow-growing type, it may be possible for your surgeon to remove *just the tumor and one ovary.* This surgery will leave your uterus and one functioning ovary intact so that you may be able to become pregnant in the future.

30 | Fibroid Tumors of the Uterus

A fibroid is a noncancerous tumor that arises from uterine muscle and connective tissue. Technical names your clinician may use are fibro-myoma, myoma, or leiomyoma. *Almost all fibroid tumors of the uterus are benign.* In about 3 to 7 cases out of 1,000, fibroids are malignant (1). Fibroids are very common; 20 to 50% of women have at least some evidence of fibroids. The tumors are most often discovered among women in their 30s and 40s, but fibroids can occur in young women as well. They are much more common among black women than they are among white women (2), but the reason for this difference is not known.

Fibroid tumors are usually firm, spherical lumps that often occur in groups (see Illustration 1). The size of individual tumors varies widely; they can be as small as a pea or as large as an apple or even a cantaloupe. Fibroids that grow near the outer surface of the uterus create a firm bump or knob that can be easily detected during a pelvic examination. Fibroids near the inner lining of the uterus, however, may not be apparent during pelvic examination. The presence of fibroids often increases the overall size of the uterus. Fibroids sometimes extend from the outer surface of the uterus on a stalk and may be difficult to distinguish from an enlarged ovary.

422

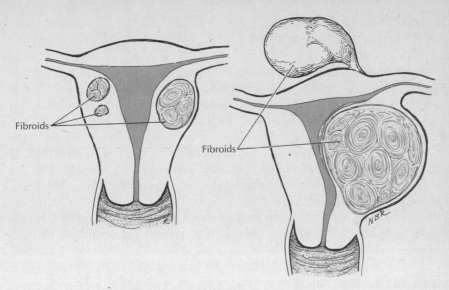

Illustration 1   The uterus on the left has three small fibroid tumors. On the right is an enlarged uterus with a large fibroid tumor and one fibroid tumor on a stalk (called a pedunculated fibroid).

Symptoms

Most women who have fibroids have no symptoms at all; their tumors are first discovered during routine pelvic examination. If you do have symptoms, they may include lower abdominal pain, a feeling of fullness and pressure in the lower abdomen, frequent urination caused by tumor pressure on your bladder, and in rare cases swelling of the lower abdomen. Fibroids can cause heavy menstrual periods, bleeding in between periods, and increasing menstrual cramps. If a fibroid grows rapidly, it can outstrip its nutrition supply from nearby blood vessels, with the result that oxygen-deprived tissue may degenerate and die; severe abdominal pain may result. Rapid growth is common in pregnancy when high estrogen levels stimulate tumor growth. Birth control Pills and estrogen replacement medication for menopause symptoms can also accelerate tumor growth.

Diagnosis

Your symptoms and your pelvic examination are the basis for diagnosing fibroids. If your clinician finds that your uterus is lumpy, enlarged, or irregular in shape, she/he may consider fibroids even if you have not had any symptoms. Additional tests can substantiate the diagnosis of fibroids:

A sonogram (see Chapter 21) can provide a picture of an irregular uterine shape and uterine enlargement. In some cases, a sonogram can also distinguish between an enlarged ovary and a fibroid. Pelvic x-ray sometimes reveals typical calcium deposits in the area of a suspected fibroid tumor. Your clinician may advise a D&C (see Chapter 40) if you have had abnormal bleeding. Your surgeon may even be able to feel the bumps within your uterus during a D&C if fibroids are present. She/he will also be able to examine you more thoroughly when you are anesthetized, because your abdominal muscles will be fully relaxed.

Treatment Options for Fibroid Tumors

Fibroids are unlikely to shrink or disappear on their own until after menopause. Before menopause, it is more likely that your fibroids will continue to grow and that you will gradually notice more and more symptoms. In the premenopausal years, fibroids usually do not improve with time; nor is there any effective medication.

Most clinicians would recommend that large tumors be removed as soon as they are discovered, because delaying could mean emergency surgery later; elective surgery is generally less risky than emergency surgery. Fibroids that are more than 5 inches (12 cm) in diameter are more likely than small fibroids to cause a significant medical crisis, such as degeneration because of inadequate blood supply or twisting of a fibroid stalk. Small fibroids, on the other hand, may remain unchanged for years with no serious symptoms at all; and once menopause occurs, they typically shrink in size so that they no longer can be detected even during pelvic examination.

The only risk with small fibroids is the very rare instance of a fibroid that is cancerous. Without surgery, there is no reliable way to

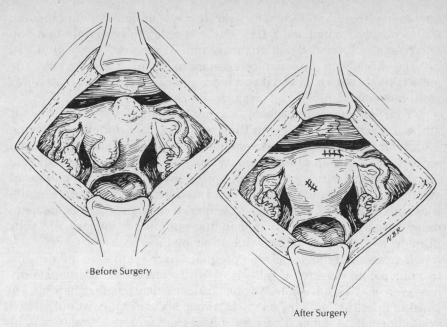

Before Surgery

After Surgery

Illustration 2 Surgical removal of fibroid tumors is called myomectomy.

distinguish malignant fibroids from fibroids that are benign. Malignancy is almost always detected at the time of surgery to remove what was **assumed** to be benign fibroids. The risk of malignancy is small, and most clinicians do not recommend surgery solely on the basis of cancer risk.

Treatment options for fibroid tumors are:

• Wait, and have frequent examinations to detect excessive growth.
• Have surgery (myomectomy) to remove only the fibroid(s) and repair the uterus as much as possible (see Illustration 2).
• Have a hysterectomy (see Chapter 41).

When your clinician first diagnoses fibroids, it is unlikely that you will need immediate surgery. Unless you have severe hemorrhage or unbearable pain, it will be safe for you to take time to think about your treatment alternatives.

The first step in planning your treatment is to be certain that fibroids are in fact the cause of your symptoms or abnormalities. If you are having irregular bleeding or your uterus is enlarged, your clinician will probably recommend a D&C without delay to be certain that you don't have an unrelated malignancy. Similarly, prompt evaluation will be necessary if your clinician feels a mass in the area of your ovary. The mass is likely to be a fibroid if you have other fibroids on your uterus as well, but your clinician will want to be certain.

Your clinician will probably recommend surgery if your uterus is grapefruit size or larger, if your tumors are large, or if they are growing rapidly. If your bleeding is heavy enough to cause anemia or you need repeated D&Cs, then fibroid surgery may also be recommended. You may decide that surgery is the best option if you have severe cramps or symptoms from bladder pressure that interfere with your normal activities. In any of these situations, however, it may also be reasonable to delay surgery if you expect menopause soon; after menopause, your fibroids will probably improve on their own.

If you would like to become pregnant in the future, you will want to consider hysterectomy only in a dire emergency. **Myomectomy,** however, may be advisable if your clinician suspects that fibroids are causing infertility or repeated miscarriage. Myomectomy would also be your appropriate choice if surgery is necessary for a very large tumor or heavy bleeding. Myomectomy surgery would involve a standard 5-inch abdominal incision and postoperative recovery similar to that for abdominal hysterectomy. If you have fibroids, it makes sense to avoid long delays in your plans for childbearing.

If future pregnancy is not a consideration, **hysterectomy** is usually a better surgery option than myomectomy. Hysterectomy ends your problem with fibroids, whereas myomectomy may be only a temporary solution; it is often impossible to remove all traces of fibroids during myomectomy, and tumor remnants may continue to grow and new tumors may develop as well.

If you decide against elective surgery, then you will need to have frequent pelvic examinations so that excessive tumor growth can be recognized early. There are no known medications that are helpful and no known steps for preventing fibroid tumors.

REFERENCES

1. *TeLinde's Operative Gynecology*, ed 5, Mattingly RF (ed). Philadelphia, Lippincott, 1977.
2. Novak ER, Woodruff JD: *Novak's Gynecologic and Obstetrical Pathology*, ed 7. Philadelphia, WB Saunders, 1974.

31 | Endometriosis

The lining of the uterine cavity is called the endometrium. The term endometriosis is used when patches of endometrial tissue implant *outside* the uterus. The most common locations for endometriosis implants—the outside surface of the uterus, the surface of the fallopian tubes, the ovaries, and the surface of the bladder and rectum—are shown in Illustration 1.

Symptoms

Endometriosis is very common, but as many as two-thirds of women with endometriosis patches have no symptoms at all. The most common symptom with endometriosis is excessive menstrual cramps. The endometriosis patches respond to changes in the hormone cycle just as normal uterine lining inside the uterus does; endometriosis patches grow and thicken, and they bleed at the end of each cycle. Endometriosis can also cause pain during intercourse, especially with deep penetration, and pain during bowel movements. Endometriosis is sometimes associated with irregular menstrual bleeding patterns, perhaps because of patches of endometriosis on the ovaries. It is a common cause of infertility. Bleeding from endometriosis sites inside the abdomen can cause scar tissue that obstructs the fallopian tubes, or a large clump of endometriosis tissue can cover part of one or both ovaries and interfere with escape of the eggs.

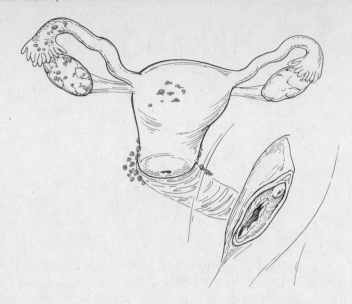

Illustration 1   Common sites of endometriosis.

Endometriosis symptoms may begin at puberty, but more commonly they start several years after menstrual periods begin. Symptoms tend to increase gradually over the years as the endometriosis areas slowly increase in size. Cyclic bleeding can sometimes occur within a mass of endometrial cells so that a blood-filled cyst gradually forms. This is called an endometrial or "chocolate" cyst and is a fairly common cause of enlarged ovaries (see Illustration 2).

No one knows exactly what causes endometriosis. One theory is that during menstruation, endometrial cells from the uterine lining are carried out through the ends of the fallopian tubes into the abdomen (this is called retrograde menstruation) where they implant and grow to form endometriosis patches. Another theory is that endometriosis patches originate from primitive cells that have been present in the abdomen since fetal development and undergo transformation into endometrial cells in the teenage or young adult years.

Diagnosis

It is essential for your clinician to be sure that you have endometriosis before any treatment is begun. Your symptoms may suggest endome-

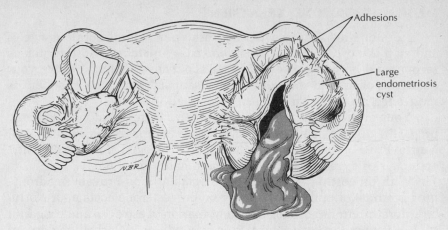

Illustration 2 Large "chocolate" cyst of endometriosis. The ovary is almost completely covered by an endometriosis cyst; old, dark blood is leaking out of the cyst.

triosis, and your clinician may find nodules on the surface of your uterus or in the wall between your vagina and rectum; but other problems, such as pelvic infection or fibroid tumors, can produce very similar symptoms.

There are no specific laboratory tests that will detect endometriosis. Laparoscopy (see Chapters 39 and 15) or perhaps exploratory surgery (see Chapter 39) will permit your clinician to see your pelvic organs; one of these procedures is almost always necessary to be certain that you have endometriosis.

Treatment

If endometriosis symptoms are mild, you may not need treatment of any kind; or perhaps your clinician will just recommend prescription pain medication to use during painful menstrual periods. If your symptoms are severe, if you have heavy internal bleeding, or if you are having difficulty becoming pregnant and your clinician is certain you have endometriosis, you may need either hormone medication or surgery to remove endometrial implants.

MEDICAL (HORMONE) TREATMENT

Hormone medication will suppress your natural hormone cycles and stop the cyclic growth of endometriosis patches. Most clinicians recommend hormone medication for about nine months to give your patches a chance to shrink or even disappear. Hormone treatment is most effective when the implants are small.

Your clinician may prescribe synthetic estrogen alone, synthetic progestin alone, a combination of estrogen and progestin such as birth control Pills, or male hormone (androgen). Estrogen alone was the first endometriosis treatment but is not commonly used today.

With progestin alone, such as injectable Depo-Provera (medroxy-progesterone) or oral Provera (medroxyprogesterone acetate) or Norlutate (norethindrone acetate), or a combination of estrogen and progestin such as is found in birth control Pills, you will need fairly high doses of hormones to stop your menstrual periods for such a long period of time. If you use birth control Pills, you will take the Pills continuously with *no* days off; and you will have to increase your Pill dose each time bleeding occurs. By the end of a nine month supression treatment you may be taking two, three, or more Pills each day. You are likely to have side effects such as nausea, breast tenderness, weight gain, and fluid retention. You cannot use birth control Pills for endometriosis if you have contraindications to the use of Pills. (Read Chapter 11 for Pill contraindications.)

A newly approved medication for treatment of endometriosis, danazol, is a synthetic male hormone (androgen) that suppresses your cycle effectively with relatively few side effects. Danazol is a very expensive drug (about $125 per month for the drug alone) and has not been widely used.

SURGICAL TREATMENT

Your clinician may recommend surgery if your endometriosis is extensive or your symptoms are severe, or if you have a large mass of endometrial tissue or a very enlarged ovary. Discuss your feelings and plans about future pregnancy with your surgeon beforehand. If you would like to become pregnant, your surgeon will remove scar tissue (adhesions) and as many endometriosis implants as possible. Small implant areas will be destroyed by electric cautery. Your surgeon will preserve your uterus and tubes and as much ovary tissue as possible.

If you don't plan any future pregnancies, your surgeon may recommend hysterectomy, or, if your ovaries are badly damaged, hysterectomy and oophorectomy (removal of your ovaries along with your uterus, see Chapter 41). Hysterectomy may be the best way to end your problems with endometriosis, since the problem can recur and require surgery again at a later time.

ENDOMETRIOSIS AND PREGNANCY

Gynecology textbooks often say that pregnancy is an ideal treatment for endometriosis, and it is true that women who have pregnancies fairly early in their reproductive years are less likely to develop endometriosis. Endometriosis often becomes progressively more severe over the years, and if you have endometriosis and delay pregnancy, you may find that you have impaired fertility. Pregnancy itself with its long menstruation-free interval may help your endometriosis. If you have endometriosis and plan to have children later on, you might consider beginning your childbearing earlier than you originally planned. If you wait, your fertility might be impaired.

32 | Breast Lumps

I found a lump in my right breast; a hard place, in the upper, outer part, that should have been soft. All morning and afternoon I pretended I hadn't found it; then I felt again in bed. Still there.

Not Betty Ford this time, or Happy Rockefeller. Me. I tried to remember the statistics: "Most lumps aren't cancer," but how many is *most*? "Only your doctor can tell for sure," but I didn't want to see a doctor. I wanted the lump not to be there.

Next morning I called my doctor. He found my lump, too. He said, "There's almost no chance this is anything but benign, but it should come out, just to be sure." He scheduled me for a biopsy in three weeks. I went straight from his office to the library and read about the statistics, but I couldn't connect myself with any of the numbers.

All I did was worry for three weeks. I told my friend Lynn, who said, "Don't worry," and then asked if I wanted her to keep my cat, "just in case." I decided not to tell anyone else.

I tried not to touch the lump, but I did, over and over. Especially at night, I found myself touching it unconsciously. Was it bigger? smaller? I realized I *loved* my breast. It was part of me, and I cried when I thought about losing it. But I didn't think I would die, not even at three in the morning.

I *didn't* water the plants, and I left enough cat food for only two days the day I checked into the hospital. Positive thinking.

Nurses ran tests, friends came by for short, awkward visits, and my surgeon talked to me about the surgery consent form. I wrote *"only"* next to Breast Biopsy—even though he had already promised to do *no more surgery immediately*, no matter what the initial lab report showed. "It's very important to me to have time to think," I said, even though I was *sure* I would agree to more surgery if it was cancer. I didn't want to be put to sleep—not knowing.

No breakfast on biopsy day. I got shots instead, and tried a few feeble wisecracks with the nurses. I remember being wheeled down a hall, masked faces, and someone saying, "This may sting a little." I recognized my surgeon and smiled at him.

I woke up in a room with bright lights and more masked faces.

"You're okay. It wasn't cancer."

I slept all day.

Adapted from Carol Comer, "The cold war between me and the tumor." Atlanta Journal and Constitution Sunday Magazine, *November 20, 1977. Used with permission of the author.*

There are few things more frightening for a woman than finding a breast lump. Most stories have happy endings like this woman's, because 75% of breast lumps that are biopsied are *benign* (1) and 65% of women who are treated for *malignant* breast lumps are alive and well five years later. Read Chapter 2 to learn how to examine your breasts and what kind of breast changes to look for. Even if you are tempted to wait and see if a lump will go away, call your personal physician or go to a clinic at once. *There is absolutely nothing to be gained by waiting.*

What to Expect If You Have a Breast Lump

Your clinician will examine your breast to confirm your findings. If you are under 30 and the lump feels like breast gland tissue, your clinician *may* believe that it is safe to wait about one month (one menstrual cycle) to see if the lump goes away. If you are over 30 or the lump persists, you will definitely need a full evaluation.

Your clinician may be able to remove fluid from a breast cyst while you are in the office, or she/he may recommend breast x-rays (xero-mammography) to help identify the exact location of the lump, to check for any other abnormal areas, and to give some indication of whether it is likely to be cancer. Even if your x-ray report says that the lump appears benign (not cancer), it is very likely that your clinician will recommend *surgical biopsy* to remove the lump anyway

In some cities, gynecologists usually perform breast biopsies and surgery, but in most areas, general surgeons assume this role. Your clinician will undoubtedly be able to recommend a surgeon; otherwise you might consult a breast screening clinic, your local National Organization for Women, a Planned Parenthood clinic, or a surgical nurse friend for suggestions.

Common Causes of Breast Lumps

It is likely that your tumor will turn out to be a lump of fibrous tissue (fibroadenoma) or will be due to fibrous thickening and cyst formation (fibrocystic disease). Breast injury or infection can cause a lump, and there are many other, less common types of noncancerous lumps; but the appearance of *a lump is also the most common first sign of breast cancer.* If you have had nipple discharge, be sure to discuss your symptoms with your clinician. Nipple discharge can be caused by several benign problems, but may also occur with cancer.

One breast change that you do *not* need to worry about is the relatively sudden appearance of a breast bud in a young adolescent. As the first stage of female breast development begins, a firm, round, movable, painless lump develops directly underneath the nipple; buds usually occur in both breasts at about the same time. A breast bud does feel like a lump; so if you are not certain, see your clinician.

FIBROCYSTIC DISEASE

Lumps are common with fibrocystic breast disease and often occur in several places simultaneously and in both breasts.

Fibrocystic disease can cause a dull, heavy pain and a sense of fullness and tenderness. Your symptoms and the size of the lumps will usually increase just before a menstrual period. You may notice the sudden appearance of a lump that wasn't there the last time you examined your breasts; the lump may feel like a balloon filled with water, and it may be tender. One research report has linked problems with fibrocystic disease to coffee, cola, tea, and chocolate. Thirteen out of 20 women who stopped consuming caffeine, theophylline, and theobromine stopped having problems with recurrent breast nodules, pain, tenderness, and nipple discharge within 6 months (2). Women who have fibrocystic disease do have a twofold increase in their chance of developing cancer of the breast in the future.

FIBROADENOMA

A fibroadenoma is a movable, solid, firm, rubbery, painless breast lump most often discovered in women between the ages of 15 and 40. Fibroadenomas often occur in clusters and can occur in both breasts. A fibroadenoma is **not** cancer; it is a benign tumor composed of gland cells and fibrous tissue cells. Fibroadenomas usually feel completely separate from your normal breast glands. It is common to develop a second fibroadenoma months or years after one has been removed.

CANCER

Cancer of the breast usually appears as a solitary lump. Cancer lumps occur most frequently in the upper, outer quadrant of the breast (see Illustration 1) and feel solid, hard, painless, and nontender. Most

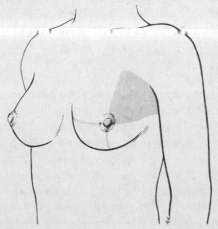

Illustration 1   Most cancer lumps occur in the upper, outer quadrant of the breast.

are irregular in shape and not easily defined. As the cancer becomes advanced, the nipple may draw up into the breast and the skin on the breast may appear dimpled. Some kinds of breast cancer cause dry, flaky skin around the nipple or red or inflamed skin.

Procedures for Evaluation of a Breast Lump

Once she/he has examined your breasts, your clinician is likely to recommend other tests and procedures in order to determine what kind of lump you have.

CYST ASPIRATION

If your lump feels like a fluid-filled cyst or if an x-ray shows that it *is* a cyst, your clinician may be able to drain the entire cyst by drawing out its fluid. She/he will use a local anesthetic to numb a small patch of skin and then put a needle into the cyst to withdraw fluid. The fluid can be sent to a pathologist, who will microscopically examine the fluid and any cells it contains. Usually a cyst will not recur once it has been drained. Your clinician may want you to have a mammogram to help determine whether a biopsy should be performed; and if the lump doesn't go away or if it recurs, you will probably need a breast biopsy (see below).

MAMMOGRAPHY

Mammography, x-ray of the breast, can be used to evaluate a lump. In some situations, it may be recommended as a routine test for a woman who does not have any obvious lumps. *Mammography is the only test currently available to detect cancer of the breast before a lump is big enough to feel.* Some experts estimate that mammography may detect cancer as much as two years before a lump could be felt. There are several large research studies that show that routine mammography can save lives by detecting breast cancer at a very early stage before it has a chance to spread.

If mammography had no risks, it would make sense for all women to have mammograms once a year or even oftener; the risk of breast cancer is so high that the expense and inconvenience probably would be justified. Unfortunately, mammography probably does have risks. X-ray is known to cause a number of problems, cancer among them, and it is always wise to avoid unnecessary x-ray exposure. Sophisticated x-ray techniques are being developed to give clear x-ray pictures with the lowest possible radiation exposure, but there is probably no dose of x-ray low enough to be completely safe.

So far, there is no evidence that mammography causes cancer, but researchers caution that large groups of women will have to be studied over a long period of time. There may be a long delay between exposure and the appearance of cancer. Experts estimate that any cancer increase will probably be small, probably on the order of 3–8/1,000,0000 women who have one mammogram. The cancers would probably become apparent 10–20 years later (3).

Experts agree that the risks of mammography are justified in many situations. The controversy about mammography concerns the use of breast x-ray for *routine screening.* Experts disagree about whether mammograms should be recommended for women who are young and do not have known breast disease. The following mammography recommendations are based on guidelines suggested by the American Cancer Society (4). These recommendations represent a middle position in the controversy and are designed to minimize unnecessary testing and yet provide adequate routine screening for women during the high-risk years.

Baseline mammogram: All women should have one routine mammogram between 35 and 40.

Women under 50: Consult your personal physician to determine if you need routine mammography because of risk factors such as personal or family history of breast cancer.

Mammography is almost never recommended for women under 25. For women age 25 to 34, mammography may be recommended for evaluation of breast disease or a lump, or for screening because of especially high risk (previous breast cancer, for example).

Women over 50: Mammograms are recommended as a routine part of your annual check up.

A mammogram can detect unsuspected breast disease, changes in breast structure, or a tiny lump that is too small to feel, and can also be used to pinpoint the exact location of a tumor deep inside the breast and to predict before biopsy whether a lump is likely to be benign or malignant.

THERMOGRAPHY

A thermogram is a visual display of the temperature in each area of the breast. When breast cancer is present, blood flow to that specific area is increased and the local temperature rises. Thermography is a safe procedure that avoids the use of x-ray. Its usefulness is limited, however. Thermography does not accurately detect cancer in its very early stages, and often does not pinpoint the exact location of a tumor. Since several diseases in addition to cancer can alter breast temperature, further tests are necessary to determine the cause of an abnormal thermogram. It can be helpful, however, to know whether the thermography results are or are not compatible with other tests, such as mammography.

BREAST BIOPSY

A breast biopsy is the surest and most common procedure for dealing with a breast lump. It is a surgical procedure in which abnormal tissue, usually the entire lump, is removed and sent to a pathologist for microscopic examination.

Breast biopsy is usually done in a hospital or surgical center. Either general anesthesia or local anesthesia can be used. Some women choose to have biopsy with local anesthesia in order to save money and to minimize risks of anesthesia complications. (See Chapter 39.)

Your surgeon will thoroughly clean the skin on your breast over the lump. She/he will make an incision, remove the lump, and then close the incision with stitches. The incision is usually only 1 or 2 inches long, and your surgeon will follow your breast contour if possible so that the healed scar will be as inconspicuous as possible (see Illustration 2).

If you have agreed to further surgery, if needed, your surgeon will ask the pathologist to evaluate the biopsy tissue *immediately,* while you are still asleep in the operating room. The pathologist can freeze a portion of tissue and examine it within about 15 minutes. One disadvantage of this approach, however, is that evaluation of frozen sections is not as accurate as evaluation after the routine procedure for preparing and examining biopsy tissue. If you are willing to have your biopsy and then wait 24 to 48 hours for the result, you may decrease the likelihood of incorrect results and possibly may avoid having an unnecessary mastectomy (removal of a breast).

More and more surgeons and patients are choosing to schedule

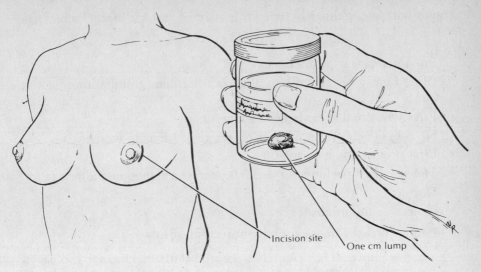

Incision site   One cm lump

Illustration 2   Breast biopsy incision site and biopsy specimen for evaluation. The entire lump is usually removed.

biopsy *only*, with plans for further treatment deferred until the pathologist's final report is completed. Discuss these options with your surgeon before your biopsy.

Determining Your Risk for Breast Cancer

Breast cancer is the leading cause of death for women aged 40 to 44. It is the most common type of cancer in adult women. About 7% of women, 1 out of 13, will develop breast cancer in their lifetimes.

The cause(s) of breast cancer is not known, but the risk for development of breast cancer is lower or higher than average for certain groups of women.

Women who begin menstruating after age 17, have menopause before age 45, or have surgery that removes the ovaries before age 40, Chinese women and Japanese women, all have a lower than average likelihood of breast cancer. Some of the factors that seem to be associated with approximately twice the average risk for breast cancer are (5):

- Previous cancer of the breast
- Close family history of breast cancer (mother, grandmother, sister, aunt)
- First menstrual periods before age 12
- No pregnancies (also unmarried women, infertile women)
- First pregnancy after age 30
- Menstrual cycles for more than 40 years, or menopause after age 55
- Obesity*
- Cancer of the uterus*
- Benign breast disease such as fibrocystic disease

The factors above all have widely-accepted statistical links to increased breast cancer risk. The possible relationship between exposure to estrogen drugs and breast cancer is more controversial. Some experts do feel that the following factors should be included on the breast cancer risk list (5):

- Birth control Pills for two to four years or more
- DES treatment during pregnancy (DES mothers) (6)
- Postmenopausal estrogen treatment for 10 to 15 years or more*

If one or more high-risk factors applies in your case, then you should seriously consider routine mammography screening beginning at age 35, and you will need to be particularly conscientious about monthly breast self-exams.

Treatment of Breast Cancer

About 65% of women who develop breast cancer are alive, well, and have no evidence of disease five years after treatment. About 83% of women who have tumors that are detected early and removed before there is evidence of spread are well five years later (7). Treatment is

---

*May be less than 100% increase in risk.

individualized and often combines surgery with radiation therapy and drug therapy.

There has been continuing controversy about what kind of treatment is best for breast cancer. The traditional recommendation has been **radical mastectomy,** which means removal of the entire breast and underlying muscle along with all the lymph nodes that drain the breast (see Illustration 3). More and more surgeons are recommending a less extensive procedure, called **modified radical mastectomy,** which removes the breast and some lymph nodes but does **not** remove any muscles and does not remove deep lymph nodes. The overall cure rate

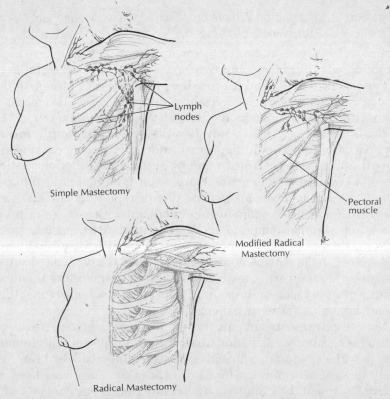

Simple Mastectomy

Lymph nodes

Pectoral muscle

Modified Radical Mastectomy

Radical Mastectomy

Illustration 3 Only breast tissue is removed in simple mastectomy. Breast and some lymph nodes are removed in modified radical mastectomy. Breast, underarm nodes, chest nodes, and pectoral muscle are removed in radical mastectomy.

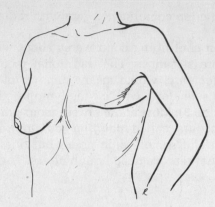

Illustration 4   Mastectomy incision. Some surgeons use an up-and-down incision instead.

after modified radical mastectomy seems to be as good as that following full radical surgery (8), and the modified radical procedure is unlikely to cause the problems with skin healing, decreased arm movement, and arm swelling that are common after radical mastectomy.

Modified radical mastectomy is quite similar to **simple mastectomy,** which removes only the breast and no lymph nodes. Healing, cosmetic appearance (see Illustration 4), and muscle function would be about the same for simple mastectomy as for modified radical mastectomy. The advantage some surgeons cite of removing surface lymph nodes is that a decision about further treatment with x-ray or drugs can be based on whether lymph nodes contain evidence of cancer spread.

For a limited group of patients whose cancer is very small and is located close to the surface, some surgeons have recommended surgery to remove only the part of the breast around and including the tumor. Even the most outspoken surgeons, however, do not believe that this is the best approach for most patients (9).

More innovative treatments that do not require extensive surgery are also being studied. Radiation treatment using special high-intensity x-ray machines and/or radioactive metal implants has been used widely in treatment of other forms of cancer, and has been used as a primary treatment for a limited number of patients with breast cancer. Drugs are also assuming a more important role in cancer management generally. Chemotherapy, drug treatment that kills cells that are growing rapidly, is often used in conjunction with breast surgery today. Drugs that enhance the body's own immune system so that *it* can destroy abnormal cancer cells are also promising. Progress in cancer management generally is in the direction of medical treatment, and it is likely that in the future there will be less emphasis on surgery as the primary therapy in breast cancer as well.

Comparative success rates for the various surgical, x-ray, and drug treatments used today are being studied. Current research findings are discussed at length in a recent review of the breast cancer treatment controversy by Consumers Union (10).

If your biopsy does show cancer, you may want to do some reading and investigating before you decide what treatment is best in your case. It makes sense to consider seeing a second physician for an independent opinion about your treatment options. Be certain that the physician you choose is a specialist in cancer and is able to work closely with specialists in radiology and chemotherapy in planning and undertaking your treatment. There are special cancer treatment (oncology) centers in many areas that are able to offer the coordinated services of all these specialized fields. *Further information about cancer is available at 18 cancer centers sponsored by the National Institutes of Health.* The center nearest you can give you the names of breast cancer specialists in your area. You can call 800-638-6694 toll free to find the center nearest you.

Future Hope for Early Breast Cancer Detection

Researchers studying human antibody responses (antibodies are proteins produced by the body's defense system to coat invading bacteria and other foreign proteins) have had initial success in detecting breast cancer with a simple skin test very much like the tuberculosis skin test (11). If further study confirms their findings, it is possible that this test could dramatically improve the likelihood of early cancer detection and permit treatment at a stage when breast cancer nearly always would be curable.

REFERENCES

1. Leis HP: The diagnosis of breast cancer. *Cancer* 27:209–232, 1977.
2. Minton JP, Foecking MK, Webster DJT, et al: Response of fibrocystic disease to caffeine withdrawal and correlation of cyclic nucleotides with

breast disease. *American Journal of Obstetrics and Gynecology* 135:157–158, 1979.
3. "Mammography screening for breast cancer." *The Medical Letter on Drugs and Therapeutics* 22(13):53–54, June 27, 1980.
4. Guidelines for the cancer-related checkup: recommendations and rationale: cancer of the breast. *Ca-A Cancer Journal for Clinicians*, American Cancer Society, 30(4):224–229, 1980.
5. Vorherr H, Messer RH: Breast cancer: Potentially predisposing and protecting factors. *American Journal of Obstetrics and Gynecology* 130:335–358, 1978.
6. *FDA Drug Bulletin* 8(2), March-April 1978. Food and Drug Administration.
7. Seidman H: *Cancer of the Breast.* Statistical and epidemiological data published by the Department of Epidemiological and Statistical Research, American Cancer Society. New York, 1972.
8. Wilson RE: The breast, in Sabiston DC (ed): *Davis-Christopher Textbook of Surgery: The Biologic Basis of Modern Surgical Practices.* Philadelphia, WB Saunders, 1977.
9. Crile G: Management of breast cancer: Limited mastectomy. *Journal of the American Medical Association* 230:95–98, 1974.
10. Breast cancer: the retreat from radical surgery. *Consumer Reports,* January 1981, pp 24–30.
11. Springer GF, Desai PR, Murty MS, et al: Human carcinoma-associated precursors of the blood group MN antigens, in Walborg EF Jr (ed): *Glycoproteins and Glycolipids in Disease Processes.* 175th National Meeting of the American Chemical Society, Anaheim, 1978.

33 | Pelvic Pain and Pain During Intercourse

Lower abdominal pain and pain during intercourse (dyspareunia) are very common symptoms that can be caused by many different problems. Often the two are linked: pelvic pain may be triggered or aggravated by intercourse, and pain that you first notice during intercourse can bother you at other times as well. Your clinician will ask you to describe what your pain is like, when it occurs, how it is related to your menstrual cycle and your daily activities, how long you have had it, and how it has changed since it first began. She/he will examine you to try to determine exactly where your pain is originating, and will evaluate you for any medical problems that may be related to your pain.

Pain Around the Entrance to the Vagina

Vaginal infection is the most common cause of burning, itching pain near the entrance to the vagina and on nearby skin areas. You are likely to notice pain first soon after intercourse because inflamed tissue is sensitive to any kind of friction or pressure. (Read about causes and treatment of vaginitis in Chapter 22.) Skin sensitivity or allergy to vaginal hygiene products can cause inflammation (see Chapter 3). Birth control foam and diaphragm jelly or cream are irritating to some women as well.

445

Another common cause of discomfort during intercourse is friction. If you and your partner begin intercourse before you are fully aroused, your normal lubricating response to arousal may not have a chance to moisten your vagina thoroughly. Intercourse may feel uncomfortable, and friction can irritate the entrance to your vagina and the vaginal walls as well. Your lubrication response may be diminished if your estrogen levels are low, such as immediately after a full-term pregnancy, especially if you are nursing, or after menopause. It may also be diminished by some medications, including antihistamines. Allowing time for your lubrication response may take care of the problem, or you may want to use extra lubrication, such as contraceptive jelly, cream, or foam, or a nonprescription water-soluble lubricant such as K-Y Jelly. Estrogen vaginal cream may be helpful after menopause or in the immediate postpartum period (see Chapter 36).

Pain Around the Urethra and Clitoris

Pain or tenderness in the area of your urinary opening (urethra) during intercourse can be caused by inflammation from a vaginal infection or a bladder or urethral infection, or by a pocket (diverticulum) that forms in the wall of the urethra. Estrogen deficiency during menopause can cause the urethra to become dry and fragile (see Chapter 36). See your clinician so that she/he can treat any infection and make sure your urethra is normal.

The clitoris is normally an exquisitely sensitive area. Many women find that direct clitoral stimulation is distinctly painful, even when the clitoris is perfectly healthy.

Vaginal Muscle Spasm

Painful spasm of vaginal muscles during intercourse or a pelvic exam is a problem that seems to be associated with traumatic sexual experiences in the past. Counseling and conditioning exercises at home can help you gradually become accustomed to vaginal manipulation and penetration. Pain or muscle tightness severe enough to make intercourse impossible (vaginismus) is rare, but often resolves with treatment. Similar problems in achieving intercourse can be caused by a small, rigid hymen opening. This can be easily corrected by exercises or in extreme cases by a minor surgical procedure.

Pain Deep in the Vagina or Abdomen

Pain deep in the vagina or lower abdomen can arise from the cervix, uterus, tubes, or ovaries, or from nearby intestines or the bladder. Most of the problems that cause deep pain can also cause pain during intercourse, especially with deep penetration or thrusting when your partner's penis bumps a tender cervix or jars your pelvic organs. If your problem is restricted to a small area, such as a cyst on one ovary, you may have pain with some intercourse positions but not with others. A generalized problem, such as infection in your uterus and both tubes, is likely to cause pain with any intercourse position. Deep pelvic pain and pain during intercourse can be caused by pelvic infection, cervical infection, bladder infection, ovary cysts, scar tissue, endometriosis, fibroid tumors, or narrowing and shortening of the vagina after hysterectomy. (All these problems are discussed in detail in other parts of this book.)

Appendicitis, infection in an intestinal pocket (diverticulitis), and inflammatory intestinal disease (ulcerative colitis and ileitis) can also cause deep pelvic pain.

Unexplained Pelvic Pain

Pelvic pain can be a devastating problem that interferes with normal activities and sexual functioning. In most cases, your clinician will be able to identify the cause of your pain and can plan appropriate treatment. In some cases, however, your clinician may not be able to find a cause for your pain. You might want to seek a second clinician's opinion. Surgery to remove "offending" pelvic organs is often an attractive idea when pain is really bothersome, but surgery is probably not a reasonable option. If the cause of your pain cannot be determined, there is no real reason to believe that surgery will cure it.

In the past, medical textbooks have linked complaints of pelvic pain with psychological problems. This link is probably unjustified in most cases, because pelvic pain is usually caused by real disease. In some cases, however, pelvic pain may be related to psychological or social stress, and some women may benefit more from counseling than they would from surgery or repeated evaluations. There is no reason to exempt the pelvis from the list of human body parts that react to stress.

34 | Fertility Problems

About 10 to 15% of all couples have impaired fertility. Fertility involves two people, and fertility evaluation should include both partners from the very beginning. Sometimes it is possible to identify one primary reason for impaired fertility. In 40% of couples, infertility is caused by a male factor, and in 40% the cause is a female factor (1). In the others, a combination of factors is involved, or it is impossible to identify one specific problem.

The goal of treatment is to increase your overall fertility level by improving as many factors as possible for both you and your partner. You might begin by reading the section on optimal pregnancy in Chapter 4.

When to Seek Medical Help

Experts define infertility as "the inability to conceive after trying for one year," and they usually counsel patience for couples who have been trying for only a few months.

In some situations, it doesn't make sense to wait. Seek help for fertility problems earlier if:

- You are over 30. Fertility declines with age, and childbearing is safer for you and your baby before you reach age 35.

449

- You aren't menstruating regularly. Irregular menstrual cycles may mean that you are not ovulating regularly; so trying to conceive before treatment is unlikely to help.
- You have had several miscarriages
- You or your partner had infectious diseases that can decrease fertility, such as pelvic infections for you and mumps (after childhood) for your partner.

How to Increase Your Chance of Pregnancy

If you don't fit into any of the above categories for immediate medical help, you might first try some of the following suggestions on your own. Many fertility experts agree with Masters and Johnson that some leading causes of fertility problems are not having intercourse often enough; not having intercourse at the right time in your cycle; and, not having intercourse in positions that enhance your ability to conceive (2).

1. *Keep a careful record of your menstrual cycles.* Use a menstrual calendar, basal body temperature (bbt) chart, and cervical mucus chart (see Chapter 8) to pinpoint your time of ovulation as accurately as possible. Watch especially for the "drop, then rise" pattern in your basal body temperature to be certain that you are ovulating.

2. *Avoid douching, and do not use lubricants on or before fertile days.* Lubricants can kill sperm. Don't even douche with plain water before intercourse.

3. *Have intercourse once every 24 to 48 hours during your fertile days.* Try to have intercourse three or four times during each fertile period: once about 24 to 36 hours before you expect ovulation, once on your ovulation day, and once 24 to 36 hours later. After each ejaculation, your partner's sperm production requires about 30 hours to return to peak fertility.

4. If your uterus angles toward the front of your body (anteverted, see Illustration 5 in Chapter 21), as it does in 70% of women, then your *best position for intercourse* is lying on your back with your partner above. Lie still after intercourse for at least an hour. If your uterus is angled toward your back (retroverted, see Illustration 6 in

Chapter 21), other positions may be better; you can check with a fertility specialist. Your goal is to insure that the pool of semen in your vagina stays in contact with the opening in your cervix as long as possible.

5. **Put a pillow under your hips** during and after intercourse to help semen stay in the back part of your vagina.

6. When your partner is about to ejaculate, he should stop thrusting and **penetrate as deeply as he can** so that semen is deposited deep in your vagina. Most of the sperm are in the first few ejaculated drops. Immediately after ejaculation, your partner should withdraw his penis carefully.

7. **Put your knees together and pull them up to your chest,** and keep this position for 15 to 30 minutes after intercourse.

Many couples find that trying to conceive is stressful, and you may worry that your anxiety and stress are contributing to your fertility problem. There is no evidence that resting, quitting a job, or even taking a vacation is helpful unless your frequency of intercourse increases as a result.

Your partner's ability to ejaculate is essential for fertility, but your ability to have an orgasm is not.

How Your Clinician Can Help

Your own clinician may be able to evaluate your fertility problem, or you and your partner may be referred to a fertility specialist. Your clinician will start by taking a complete medical, sexual, and social history for you and for your partner. Be prepared to answer many detailed and personal questions; your clinician will need to know, for example, your intercourse frequency and the positions and sexual techniques you use. You and your partner will need thorough physical exams, including routine blood and urine tests. After that, you and your clinician can plan for the tests that will be needed to determine the cause or causes of impaired fertility in your particular case.

Throughout your evaluation, your clinician will be looking for problems that might impair these essential components of fertility (3):

• Adequate sperm production and semen delivery (impaired for 35 to 40% of couples who seek fertility evaluation)

- Regular occurring ovulation (impaired for 10 to 15% of such couples)
- An unobstructed pathway (Fallopian tube) for sperm and egg (impaired for 20 to 30% of such couples)
- Receptive cervical mucus (impaired for 5% of such couples)

For some couples, multiple fertility problems may be identified. For about 20% of couples studied, no specific cause of infertility can be found; as yet unknown causes of fertility impairment may be involved. Your medical histories and examinations may pinpoint the most likely cause of your fertility problem, but other tests results will be important for confirming the cause(s) and for planning your treatment.

SEMEN ANALYSIS

Your partner will collect an entire ejaculate in a clean, dry container and take it to the laboratory within two hours. Semen volume and thickness will be measured, and a sample will be examined under a microscope. A normal semen specimen will total about ½ teaspoon (2 cc) or more. At least 60% of the sperm should be actively moving. The number of sperm in a normal ejaculate varies between 100 and 200 million, but there should be at least 20 million sperm. Semen analysis is a routine part of every fertility evaluation.

BASAL BODY TEMPERATURE (BBT) CHARTS

Your clinician will ask you to record your bbt each day and will review your bbt charts with you to look for a clear "drop, then rise" pattern that indicates ovulation. A drop of about 0.4 degrees (Fahrenheit), followed by a rise that is sustained for at least several days will pinpoint your most fertile time. (See Chapter 8 for complete bbt instructions.) Your clinician will ask you to record when you have intercourse so that you can determine whether you are timing intercourse correctly. If your bbt charts are not clear-cut, your clinician may recommend additional tests to find out for sure whether you are ovulating. Accurate bbt charts are very important for any fertility evaluation and will also be needed later, during treatment.

CERVICAL MUCUS TEST (HUHNER'S TEST)

The mucus in your cervical canal must be normal in order for pregnancy to occur. Mucus that is too thick, for example, can block sperm from swimming into your uterus.

The ideal time for cervical mucus evaluation is during ovulation and within two hours after intercourse. Your clinician will use an eyedropper or cotton swab to collect a few drops of mucus from your cervical canal and will examine your mucus under a microscope. (Mucus collection is painless.) She/he should be able to see sperm in the mucus, and at least half the sperm should be moving actively. Your clinician will also examine the consistency of your mucus, which should be abundant, thin, and slippery during your fertile days. If your mucus is scant, thick, and sticky, you may need more tests to be sure that you are ovulating and to find out when in your cycle ovulation is occurring.

If few sperm are present or they are not moving, you and your partner may both need more tests. Your partner's sperm count may be low, or sperm may not be reaching your cervix. Lack of sperm may mean that your cervical mucus is "hostile" or incompatible with your partner's sperm, and compatibility tests may be needed. Huhner's test is tricky to plan, but it is a simple, quick procedure that provides a great deal of information. It is a routine part of most fertility evaluations.

ENDOMETRIAL BIOPSY

A small shred of uterine lining (endometrium) can be examined by a pathologist to confirm that you are ovulating and to assess whether your cyclic uterine lining development pattern is normal (see Chapter 21 for a discussion of endometrial biopsy). Your clinician will schedule your endometrial biopsy for the last few days of your cycle just before you expect your period. Your clinician may recommend endometrial biopsy if your bbt charts are not clear-cut or if the remainder of your fertility evaluation has been normal.

MEASUREMENT OF HORMONE LEVELS

It is possible to measure the level of progesterone and estrogen in your blood, but these tests are expensive, sophisticated, and difficult to arrange. You would need a blood test each day for at least one whole cycle to provide an accurate picture of your hormone pattern. The range of normal hormone levels is wide, and levels change with the days of the cycle.

A single blood test to measure your progesterone level, taken several days after you think ovulation has occurred, may be helpful. Your clinician can use it to assess whether your progesterone production is adequate to support an early pregnancy, and a high progesterone level would confirm that ovulation probably did occur.

TUBAL PATHWAY TESTS

Your clinician will probably recommend a hysterosalpingogram to determine whether your fallopian tubes are blocked or scarred. This test will be scheduled one or two days after the end of a menstrual period, after you have stopped bleeding, but before ovulation. An x-ray specialist (radiologist) in the x-ray department of a hospital or in a special radiology facility will perform the procedure. The radiologist will position you on an x-ray table and insert a small tube into your cervical canal. X-ray dye is injected through the tube and into your uterus and tubes. The radiologist will watch the dye on the x-ray screen as it fills your uterus and moves out into your fallopian tubes. Abnormalities in the shape of your uterus or tubes will be apparent, and tubal obstruction will be evident as well. You may be asked to return for an additional x-ray a day later to check for scar tissue in your abdomen, because after 24 hours the dye should spread throughout the pelvis. A pocket of dye near the end of a tube may indicate obstruction or scar tissue near the ovaries.

There are two different types of x-ray dye that are commonly used for the hysterosalpingogram. Some fertility specialists recommend an oil-base dye, because women who have oil dye hysterosalpingograms seem to have a slightly higher fertility during the next six months. Water-base dye, on the other hand, may be safer, because it may be less likely to produce scar tissue, but it does not seem to increase fertility (1).

Rubin's test is an older procedure that can be used to detect obstructed fallopian tubes. Carbon dioxide gas is gently pumped through a tube into your cervical canal. If the gas flows freely at low pressure, your clinician can conclude that there must be an open pathway through your tubes. If your tubes are blocked, gas pressure will rise as soon as your uterus is filled. Rubin's test is inexpensive and can be done in your clinician's office, but it is less accurate than the hysterosalpingogram and does not detect abnormalities in the shape of your uterus or tubes.

Expect some discomfort during hysterosalpingography or Rubin's test. Your clinician will probably clamp your cervix to hold it steady during the procedure, and the clamp may cause cramps. Gas or dye pressure in your uterus and tubes may cause pain as well.

Hysterosalpingogram assessment of tube obstruction is about 75% accurate (4). If the results aren't clear or if obstruction does seem to be causing your fertility problem, your clinician will probably recommend laparoscopy.

LAPAROSCOPY

Laparoscopy is a simple surgical procedure that permits your clinician to look at your ovaries, tubes, and uterus through a lighted tube. The laparoscope is inserted into the abdomen through a 1-inch incision just below your navel (see Chapter 15). General anesthesia is usually required, but recovery is rapid and overnight hospitalization is rarely necessary. Your clinician will be able to see whether your fallopian tubes are scarred. She/he can inject dye during laparoscopy and watch the dye traverse your tubes and empty from the ends of your tubes. Any tubal obstruction or damage would be apparent. If you do have tube damage, your clinician can assess whether surgical correction is likely to be successful.

TESTS FOR SPERM INCOMPATIBILITY

If your clinician finds that sperm aren't moving in your cervical mucus test, she/he may recommend Duke's test to determine whether you have antibodies against your partner's sperm. A sample of your blood serum is mixed with a sample of your partner's sperm. If antibodies are present in your blood, they will attach to the sperm and immobilize them.

Fertility Treatment

The goal of fertility treatment is to maximize all the components necessary for pregnancy. Even if there seems to be one primary problem in your case, it is reasonable to do whatever you can to improve any other problems as well.

IMPROVING SPERM PRODUCTION AND SEMEN DELIVERY

If your partner's semen analysis is normal but your mucus test does not show sperm, your clinician will give you careful instructions on intercourse timing, technique, and positions. If you are still unsuccessful, you might consider artificial insemination with your partner's semen.

Many factors can cause abnormal semen analysis results, and analysis should be repeated after several weeks to determine whether the problem is persistent or whether an illness, medication, or drugs may have temporarily impaired sperm production. In some cases, a varicose vein in the testicle(s) (varicocele) can cause poor sperm production, and surgical correction of the vein defect will sometimes return sperm production to normal. Medication may be recommended in some cases, but there are no generally effective vitamin or hormone remedies.

If semen abnormalities cannot be corrected, you may want to consider donor insemination. Your clinician can find a semen donor who resembles your partner in coloring and body type and who has no known family history of inheritable disease. Your clinician would insert donor semen on the surface of your cervix at the time you are ovulating. About half of women do conceive after donor insemination treatment. About 20 to 30% of women who conceive do so after one donor insemination and 90% within six inseminations (5).

IMPROVING OVULATION

If you are not ovulating regularly, your clinician will probably recommend treatment with Clomid (clomiphene citrate tablets). Clomid is similar in structure to a synthetic estrogen, but has only very weak estrogen effects. It acts directly on the hormone regulatory process in the brain to cause increased pituitary hormone release which in turn triggers ovulation.

Clomid treatment involves taking Clomid tablets daily for 5 days beginning on the fifth day of a menstrual cycle. Ovulation should occur 5 to 10 days after the last Clomid tablet (on the 15th to 20th day of the cycle). Initially a dose of 50 milligrams daily ($2) is tried; if ovulation does not occur (as evidenced by a basal body temperature chart) then the dose is increased to 100 milligrams, then 150 and finally 200 milligrams daily.

An examination is necessary each month just before you begin the five-day Clomid treatment to check for excessive stimulation of the ovaries and to be sure that you have not already conceived. If your ovaries are tender or enlarged, then further treatment must be delayed until they return to normal. This problem is quite uncommon. Less serious side effects include: hot flashes (see Chapter 1); abdominal pain, soreness, and bloating; breast tenderness; nausea and vomiting; headache; and dry hair or hair loss. Side effects are not common and rarely are so severe that treatment must be stopped. Vision problems— spots or flashes or blurred vision—are uncommon, but stop Clomid and call your clinician should problems occur.

You should not take Clomid if you are already pregnant. There is no evidence that Clomid taken during pregnancy would cause fetal abnormalities in humans, but high doses given to animals during early pregnancy may do so. Pregnancies conceived after Clomid treatment, when ovulation is induced by Clomid, do not show an increased risk of congenital defects. The frequency of twin pregnancy (8% of Clomid pregnancies) is slightly higher than normal, but multiple pregnancy (quadruplets, quintuplets) is very rare (1).

If Clomid is not successful, then Pergonal (human menopausal gonadotropins), a more potent hormone stimulator may be a possibility. Pergonal should only be administered by an experienced specialist. You will need close medical supervision and frequent pelvic examinations while you are taking Pergonal. The dose of Pergonal must be adjusted very precisely, on an individual basis, to minimize the chance of multiple pregnancy and to avoid overstimulation of your ovaries, which could cause severe ovary swelling.

Clomid successfully induces ovulation in about 70% of women treated; about 40% conceive during treatment, usually within the first three cycles that ovulation occurs. Approximately 30% of women who do not ovulate with Clomid treatment, and are subsequently treated with Pergonal, can expect to conceive (1).

IMPROVING SPERM AND EGG PATHWAYS

Pathway obstruction most commonly occurs in the fallopian tubes or at the ends of the tubes near the ovaries, and is often the result of pelvic infection or endometriosis. Fibroid tumors in the uterus can also obstruct your tubes or interfere with pregnancy implantation. (Surgery to remove fibroid tumors is discussed in Chapter 30). When endometriosis is the problem, hormone treatment is sometimes effective, but surgery may be recommended for more thorough and quicker results (see Chapter 31). Scarring from infection or endometriosis can be surgically corrected in some cases. Success rates for tubal reconstruction are highest when microsurgery techniques are used and when your surgeon is a specialist in this field.

In many cases fallopian tube damage is irreparable. An embryo transplant procedure may offer the only possibility of pregnancy. The transplant procedure developed in England involved harvesting an egg surgically from the woman's ovary at the time of ovulation, providing a "test tube" mixture with sperm to permit fertilization to occur, and finally, implanting the early pregnancy into the woman's uterus surgically. Specialists in the United States will undoubtedly be ready to undertake similar procedures once the legal obstacles to artificial fertilization are overcome.

IMPROVING CERVICAL MUCUS RECEPTIVITY

Cervical mucus that is scant or sticky may be improved by your taking supplementary estrogen in the first two weeks of each cycle. If your cervical mucus is altered by cervix infection (see Chapter 24), treatment with antibiotic vaginal cream or cryosurgery (see Chapter 21) may be helpful. Artificial insemination performed by inserting your partner's sperm directly into your uterus may also be recommended.

IMPROVING SPERM COMPATIBILITY

If you have antibodies against your partner's sperm, your clinician may recommend the use of condoms for six months to prevent contact with sperm. Your antibody level may **drop,** during your vacation from semen contact, so that subsequent intercourse without condoms during your ovulation time may lead to pregnancy. If your antibody level remains high six months later, your clinician may suggest artificial insemination to insert your partner's sperm directly into your uterus and thus avoid sperm contact with cervical mucus. Insemination of donor semen to which you have no antibodies may be another option.

REFERENCES

1. Speroff L, Glass RH, Kane N: *Clinical Gynecologic Endocrinology and Infertility,* ed 2. Baltimore, Williams and Wilkins, 1978.
2. Masters WH, Johnson VE: Advice for women who want to have a baby. *Redbook Magazine,* March 1975, pp 70–74.
3. Behrman SJ, Kistner RW: *Progress in Infertility,* ed 2. Boston, Little, Brown, 1975.
4. Maathuis JB, Horbach JGM, vanHall EV: A comparison of the results of hysterosalpingography and laparoscopy in the diagnosis of fallopian tube dysfunction. *Fertility and Sterility* 23:428–431, 1972.
5. Sulewski JM, Eisenberg F, Stenger V: A longitudinal analysis of artificial insemination with donor semen. *Fertility and Sterility* 29:527–531, 1978.

35 | Sexual Problems

Almost everyone encounters problems with sexual functioning at some time in life. In many cases, the problem is temporary and the cause is obvious. For many people, however, persistent sexual problems are a source of continuing distress and difficulty. Clinicians who care for women report that sexual problems are extremely common complaints. It is likely that even more women would seek help if they knew how successful treatment approaches for some sexual problems have proved to be.

In the past, sex problems were considered to be symptoms of more general psychological or marital problems, and treatment was usually directed toward improving overall psychological functioning, with the hope that sexual problems would improve as a by-product of treatment. Long-term psychiatric treatment was expensive, and success in overcoming sex problems was not spectacular.

New approaches to treatment involve a more direct attack, for impaired sexual functioning is now considered to be a problem in its own right. Other psychological problems may be involved, either as the cause of sexual problems or as a result of the stress and anxiety that sex problems can cause. The new theory holds, however, that treatment designed **specifically** to improve sexual functioning can be successful even if overall psychological functioning is not perfect, and that other psychological and marital problems may even improve if sexual functioning is improved.

Short-term, specific treatment for some of the most common sexual problems has proved successful for both women and men. Early claims that, for example, premature ejaculation and inability to have an orgasm could be cured in an overwhelming majority of cases may have been somewhat exaggerated (1). However, these and other sexual problems have indeed been cured for a great many people in recent years.

A comprehensive discussion of sexual problems would require another whole book. This chapter is intended only as a brief introduction to normal sexual functioning and to some of the common problems and treatment approaches. If you are concerned about a sexual problem, you will probably want to read further. The "Suggested Reading" list at the end of this book may be helpful, and your clinician or therapist can also suggest reading that is appropriate for your needs.

Normal Sexual Functioning

It is difficult to describe **normal** sexual functioning, because one hallmark of human sexual behavior is diversity. There is no single normal pattern or even one average pattern. One person may be completely content with a form and frequency of sexual expression that another person finds inadequate or distressing. There are, however, themes of sexual expression that are almost universal, and there are physical responses during sexual activity that occur in quite predictable patterns for men and for women.

THE PHYSICAL EVENTS IN HUMAN SEXUAL RESPONSE

In their pioneering book, *Human Sexual Response*, Masters and Johnson (2) describe in detail the normal physical changes that occur during sexual activity. This section provides a simplified summary of their observations. They found it helpful to divide the sequence of physical events into four phases: *excitation,* the initial phase of sexual response; *plateau,* a middle phase of heightened sexual tension; *orgasm;* and *resolution,* the return to normal.

Excitation Phase. The initial female response to effective sexual stimulation is the appearance of vaginal lubrication. Tiny droplets of lubricating fluid are secreted by the vaginal walls within the first 10 to 30 seconds of excitation. Lubrication production continues as excitation continues, and after a few minutes is often noticeable as a distinctly wet sensation at the entrance to the vagina. The initial male response that parallels female lubrication is penile erection. Increased blood flow to the penis results in engorgement of the veins and spongy tissue in the shaft of the penis. Erection may subside partially or completely and then resume as stimulation varies or as distractions intervene.

Other physical changes that occur during the excitation phase include engorgement of blood vessels in the woman's inner vaginal lips (labia minora), spreading of the outer lips (labia majora) (see Illustration in Chapter 1) to uncover the vaginal opening, engorgement and enlargement of the clitoris, and engorgement of the veins of the breast. Nipple erection and an overall increase in breast size are often signs of excitation as well. As excitation increases, both men and women may show a generally increased muscle tension, heart rate, and blood pressure; and late in excitation a pink rash may appear that is caused by dilation of blood vessels near the skin surface. The rash appears first on the upper abdomen and spreads upward over the chest, neck, and face.

Plateau Phase. As sexual arousal increases to the plateau phase the clitoris retracts under the clitoral hood and is drawn back against the pubic bone. This change often makes it impossible to see the clitoris itself, which is usually prominent during the initial excitation phase. Retraction brings the clitoris close to the muscles of the vaginal outlet and to the junction of the labia, where stimulation of the clitoris by movement of the labia and muscles or by stimulation of the area over the pubic bone is likely to be effective.

The length and diameter of the vagina increase by as much as 1 or 2 inches during the excitation and plateau phases; during the plateau phase, the walls of the outer one-third of the vagina—nearest the vaginal opening—become engorged and firm to create a snug sleeve, while the inner two-thirds of the vagina remain dilated. Engorgement of the inner and outer lips also increases, and just before orgasm the skin of the inner lips may become deep red or wine colored. The uterus and uterine ligaments may also become engorged, shift forward in position, and increase in overall size.

During the plateau phase, engorgement of the man's testicles may increase their size by as much as 50%, and the testicles and scrotum draw up toward the base of the penis. Some men have nipple erection and breast congestion during this phase as well. Both men and women perceive increased muscle tension and often have a rapid breathing rate late in the plateau phase.

Orgasm. As male orgasm approaches, contraction of the seminal vesicles and prostate gland propels semen into the urethra. This contraction happens before ejaculation and gives the man a sense that ejaculation is imminent. Progression from this point to ejaculation is inevitable. Within moments the muscles of the urethra and penis forcefully expel semen (ejaculation) as orgasm contractions occur. Orgasm contractions occur rhythmically every 0.8 second for three or four contractions, followed by less frequent, milder contractions over the next few seconds.

As female orgasm approaches, the woman's heightened sexual tension may give her a sense that orgasm is imminent, but there does not appear to be a clear-cut preorgasmic phase comparable to the male's preorgasmic release of semen into the urethra. Female orgasm may begin with an initial sustained contraction of the muscles of the vaginal opening that lasts only a few seconds and is followed by a series of rhythmic contractions, or it may begin directly with rhythmic contractions occurring about 0.8 second apart. After an initial series of three to six contractions, the interval between contractions lengthens until a total of perhaps five to ten contractions have occurred.

> I get to a point where I feel as if there is no turning back—as if I were not in control anymore, but not in a scary way. At that point I'm not thinking about anything except my own body, and it seems as if nothing could possibly stop my body from moving to orgasm.
>
> —*Woman, 28*

Along with the primary genital muscle contractions of orgasm, both men and women may have rhythmic contractions of the muscles around the rectum, lower abdomen, and thighs. The intensity and duration of muscle contractions can range from mild, brief contractions localized in the genital area to powerful, spasmodic contractions involving muscles of the lower abdomen, thighs, and extremities as well. Orgasm intensity varies greatly, and may be related to individual differences, the level of sexual tension, and the duration of the preceding excitement and plateau phases. Masters and Johnson found that most people experience stronger muscle contractions and more intense orgasms with masturbation stimulation than with intercourse. The strength and intensity of orgasm contractions, however, are not necessarily related to the person's perception of satisfaction.

In addition to the physical events that Masters and Johnson were able to document with recording instruments, there are many other responses to orgasm that men and women report. Whole novels have been written about them. These responses include a sense of total absorption that blocks awareness of other parts of the environment, or a flood of pleasant warmth. Men often report an impetus to push for the deepest possible vaginal penetration and a tremendously satisfying release of pressure as ejaculation occurs. Responses after orgasm may include a sense of release, total relaxation, and serenity; often there is a sense of physical exhaustion similar to that after sustained, exhilarating physical exertion. Muscles throughout the body may feel heavy, warm, and weak. The rapid breathing (hyperventilation) of the late plateau phase and orgasm may cause a tingling sensation in the extremities, cramping of muscles in the hands and feet, and flashes of light (stars) in the visual field. Many people report overwhelming affection and emotional warmth toward their partner.

> Sometimes orgasm is a purely physical thing for me, pleasant and satisfying but not profound—just a good way for me to deal with a certain kind of tension. Other times, especially with my partner, it can be truly cosmic, overwhelmingly wonderful, and the physical part seems almost incidental.
>
> —*Woman, 36*

For women, the intensity of orgasm may vary on different occasions and in different circumstances. The physical events, however, appear to follow a uniform, predictable pattern. Similar muscular contractions occur with orgasm whether sexual stimulation has involved vaginal intercourse or has been restricted to other forms of stimulation such as masturbation or breast stimulation. Masters and Johnson's research **does not** support the concept that two different types of orgasm—vaginal and clitoral—exist.

Although orgasm and the immediate release of sexual tension are usually obvious to the man or woman himself or herself, orgasm often is **not** recognizable to a partner. The general high level of muscle tension during the plateau phase may make it impossible for a partner to identify with certainty the specific contractions of orgasm.

Resolution. Immediately after orgasm, both men and women often notice an interval of hypersensitivity. The clitoris and the tip (glans) of the penis may be so exquisitely sensitive that any form of stimulation is irritating or intolerable. Both men and women may notice the sudden appearance of perspiration on the face, trunk, and extremities within seconds after orgasm. As the resolution phase is established, there is a rapid decrease in blood vessel engorgement. Penis erection subsides by about 50%, and the clitoris returns to its normal unretracted position within seconds after orgasm. The thickened walls of the outer vagina and the engorged testicles gradually return to normal.

During the resolution phase, most men rapidly return to a low level of physical sexual tension, comparable to the early excitement phase. Women, on the other hand, often have a slower resolution in their physical level of sexual tension, more comparable to the plateau phase; some women are therefore able to resume sexual responsiveness and experience several orgasms within a short period of time. Most men, however, are not responsive to further sexual stimulation during the resolution phase and can return to the orgasm phase only after resuming sexual activity that reestablishes both the excitement phase and plateau phase physical events.

Control of Human Sexual Responses

Essentially all the physical events in the human sexual response cycle are controlled by the automatic (autonomic) nervous system, as are many other body functions, such as heart rate, blood pressure, and digestion. The autonomic nerve pathways, for example, cause the smooth muscle walls in the vessels (arteries) of the penis and vagina to dilate; thus, the rate of blood flow to these organs increases and blood vessels become engorged. You have no more voluntary control over the physical sexual response than you do over your blood pressure.

There are two distinct parts of the autonomic nervous system—the sympathetic ("fight") and the parasympathetic ("flight") systems—and each seems to have a distinct role in sexual responsiveness. The parasympathetic system plays the primary role in the physical events of the excitation and plateau phases, and the sympathetic system is responsible for orgasm (3). (See Illustration 1.) This division of responsibility may explain why many people can become aroused but are unable to have an orgasm.

Illustration 1   The arousal response and the orgasm response are
controlled by two distinct parts of the nervous system.
This concept is explained in HS Kaplan: *The New Sex
Therapy,* New York, Brunner/Mazel, 1974.

Although physical sexual responsiveness is not under voluntary
control, the conscious mind and the voluntary muscles nevertheless
hold **ultimate** control over sexuality. Physical sexual changes occur in
response to adequate sexual stimulation. Allowing an opportunity for
and being receptive to effective sexual stimulation are, for the most
part, **voluntary** factors. Stimuli may include conscious thoughts and
emotions as well as physical sensations.

For many people, the initiation of sexual tension and the physical
events of the early excitation phase typically occur in response to
voluntary, conscious thoughts or fantasies. Some people are even able
to achieve plateau phase physical changes solely by responding to
thoughts and fantasies. Most people, however, require direct physical sensations to achieve plateau responses. For some, nongenital
physical sensations are sufficient, but more typically both women and
men require effective stimulation specifically involving the clitoris or
penis in order to experience late plateau phase arousal and orgasm.

There is no simple universal formula for effective physical stimulation. Most women respond to direct pressure, such as stroking or
moving the shaft of the clitoris within the clitoral hood; most find that
all but the gentlest direct manipulation of the clitoris itself is unpleasantly sensitive. Most men respond to direct pressure, such as stroking
along the bottom side of the shaft of the penis; men often find direct
stimulation of the tip of the penis too intense to be pleasurable. The
range of individual responses is very wide, however, and the same
person may find one form of touching pleasurable on one occasion and
irritating on another. One of the important tasks in improving sexual
functioning is to learn through experimentation what is pleasurable
and effective for you and your partner.

Common Sexual Concerns and Malfunctions

Many of the problems described below are temporary and resolve spontaneously. You may already have a good idea about the cause of a problem yourself. If, for example, you find that your sexual functioning improves dramatically while you are on vacation, then you may want to consider changing your normal life routine to allow for more privacy, more relaxed time with your partner, and less physical fatigue. Success in overcoming even simple sexual problems will probably require recognition of the problems and their likely causes, discussion with your partner and mutual commitment to making the changes necessary. If you are concerned or feel uncertain about possible medical causes for a sexual problem, by all means discuss the matter with your clinician. She or he may be able to offer suggestions or information and reading material that can help.

It is especially important to discuss sex with your clinician when you or your partner has had a serious illness or surgery that temporarily interrupts sexual activity. You will need to learn from your clinician what is an appropriate convalescent period, when it is safe to resume normal sexual activity, and whether there are any particular precautions you need to observe. Your clinician may also be able to suggest specific sexual techniques to minimize discomfort or stress during the recovery period.

ALCOHOL, FATIGUE, AND PREOCCUPATION

Alcohol, fatigue, and preoccupation probably rank as the three most common causes of sexual problems. Sexual functioning requires physical and mental *energy*. Fatigue blunts your ability to be receptive to stimulation, as does alcohol. You may feel numb, and find that strong, prolonged stimulation is necessary to achieve a level of sexual arousal that seems effortless at other times. Fatigue may also interfere with your ability to be receptive to sexual thoughts, and may therefore diminish the likelihood of establishing even an initial level of sexual tension. You may perceive this as a decrease in sex drive or interest in sex.

I really love my husband, and I like to have sex with him, but somehow it's just not like it used to be. I'm tired a lot of the time, and I worry a lot about the children, bills, and my work. . . . And me—I don't think I'm as sexy as I used to be. When we start to make love, my mind often wanders off on a hundred different things, and Bob just gets discouraged and says he is tired of trying to make me turn on.

—Woman, 27

Preoccupation with problems or other nonsexual thoughts may also block receptivity to initial sexual stimuli, reducing both your interest in sex and your ability to respond to sexual stimulations.

INADEQUATE VAGINAL LUBRICATION

Inadequate vaginal lubrication is a very common problem among women. Often the problem is simply a result of beginning intercourse before the physical changes of the excitement phase have had a chance to occur. A little more time devoted to sexual arousal and some attention to improving techniques for achieving effective stimulation may solve the problem.

Some women notice that their lubrication response varies during the normal hormone cycle, and many find that using a water-soluble lubricant such as K-Y Jelly is helpful the first few days after a menstrual period when hormone levels are low and vaginal moisture tends to be scant. Vaginal dryness may be particularly troublesome if you have intercourse immediately after removing a vaginal tampon. A woman using decongestant cold medications may notice diminished vaginal lubrication along with the dryness in her nose and mouth.

Persistent problems with vaginal dryness are also common after menopause. When estrogen hormone levels are low, the vaginal lining becomes thinner and less resilient, and its ability to produce lubrication may be diminished. Treatment with hormones by mouth or in vaginal cream and/or use of vaginal lubricants are usually quite helpful (see Chapter 36).

TOO LITTLE INTEREST IN SEX

Many people worry about having too little interest in sex. Since people vary so greatly in what they consider an ideal amount of sexual activity, it is not hard to understand why so many couples feel that they are mismatched. Compromise is necessary in almost every partner relationship.

Diminished interest in sexual expression may simply reflect a stressful personal time in general. Unresolved marital conflict, serious personal problems, fatigue, intense involvement in school or work, illness or surgery, and fear of pregnancy are common underlying factors. Pain during intercourse or repeatedly frustrating sexual experiences may also result in diminished sexual interest. In some cases, medications are a factor; for example, birth control Pills, tranquilizers, antihypertensive agents, and sedatives may directly alter sexual interest for some persons.

If diminished sex drive is the result of an unrelated problem or a side effect of medicines, then initial treatment efforts might be best directed at solving the underlying problem itself. If unresolved marital conflict is a factor, you may need professional help to learn to improve communication and resolve conflict. For most people, sexual interest is also strongly influenced by factors within the realm of voluntary, conscious control; sex requires time, energy, and an appropriate physical and emotional setting. If a busy life style allows no opportunity for thinking about satisfying sexual experiences in the past, sexual fantasies, and the emotionally positive aspects of your relationship with your partner, then your interest in sexual expression may be diminished. A conscious decision to set aside time for sex in a relaxed, intimate setting may be surprisingly effective.

PREGNANCY AND CHILDBIRTH

Many women find that sexual function is at least temporarily altered after pregnancy and childbirth. In the first weeks after delivery, estrogen and progesterone levels are low, and many women notice that vaginal lubrication is diminished because of the low hormone levels. Many women find intercourse uncomfortable in the first weeks or months after childbirth. An episiotomy incision (requiring stitches at the bottom of the vagina) heals in about two or three weeks, but the area may remain sensitive to stretching or pressure for many weeks after that. Also, your genital structure itself (the size and length of your vagina, your genital muscle tone, and the position of your cervix) can be permanently altered to some degree by full-term pregnancy. Time, experimentation, and patience may be required for you and your partner to find intercourse positions and patterns that give you effective stimulation without discomfort.

In addition, life for both mother and father is dramatically altered by the presence of a newborn infant. Caring for a baby requires countless hours of work and involves a great deal of intimate physical contact. The new mother's need for rest, personal privacy, and time for herself alone may be more pressing than her sexual needs. Many couples find that their previous sexual patterns are not compatible with the baby's sleeping and waking schedule, and many are acutely aware of their loss of privacy as a couple. Time away from the responsibilities of parenthood is essential. Many mothers are reluctant to leave a 3-week-old baby with a sitter, even for short periods, but experienced mothers almost always recall the decision to have a sitter as an essential first step back to normal life. Even nursing mothers find that allowing for one or two bottle feedings each week, to give them time away from the baby, does not interfere with nursing once breast milk flow is well established during the first two or three weeks.

FERTILITY PROBLEMS

Sexual problems often arise when couples are anxious to conceive, especially if they suspect that they have a fertility problem or if fertility treatment is already under way. Both partners may find that the pressure to have intercourse at specific scheduled times blocks their normal sexual responsiveness and interferes with arousal, orgasm, or both.

Some couples find that a joint decision to take a vacation from trying to conceive is helpful. One or two months with no calendar records, no temperature charts, and no medical visits may be enough to overcome these sexual problems.

FEAR OF PREGNANCY

Fear of unplanned pregnancy may cause sexual problems for both men and women. Confidence in the high level of birth control protection afforded by birth control Pills may be one reason that many women and/or their partners experience increased sexual interest and responsiveness when they use this method of contraception. Similarly, some couples report increased sex drive and responsiveness after vasectomy or tubal ligation, procedures that do not alter hormone patterns but do provide extremely effective, permanent protection from pregnancy.

BIRTH CONTROL

Birth control methods may have a direct effect on sexual functioning, or an indirect effect through increased or diminished fear of pregnancy. Women using birth control Pills may have diminished sexual interest and responsiveness, probably a direct hormone effect in many cases, or they may have heightened sexual functioning, possibly because of a hormone effect and possibly because of diminished fear of pregnancy. Changing to a different Pill brand may be helpful (see Chapter 11). The IUD seems to result in improved sexual functioning for some women, and for others it causes problems; the IUD provides continuous protection with no need for paraphernalia or interruptions in lovemaking, but it can also cause prolonged vaginal bleeding and/or discomfort during intercourse. Some couples have no difficulty integrating a diaphragm, contraceptive foam, or condoms into comfortable sexual patterns, but others find them intrusive. (See the chapters on these methods for advice if using a diaphragm, foam, or condoms seems intrusive.) Couples who use natural family planning may find that they develop problems with *performance pressure,* similar to those experienced by couples who are trying to conceive; and their opportunities for sexual expression may be severely limited if they choose to abstain from all sexual activity on fertile days.

PAIN DURING OR AFTER INTERCOURSE

Discomfort or pain during or after intercourse often leads to diminished interest in sexual activity and to problems with sexual performance. Inadequate vaginal lubrication can result in genital and vaginal irritation, and painful symptoms of vaginal infection are often greatly aggravated by intercourse. Abdominal or pelvic pain during or after intercourse has many causes. These problems are discussed in Chapter 33.

Some women experience genital and lower abdominal pain when they are sexually aroused but do not have orgasm; if orgasm does not occur, the blood vessel engorgement of the inner and outer lips, vaginal walls, and uterus may be maintained for several hours. When pelvic pain is due to this prolonged congestion, the pain is dramatically and immediately improved by orgasm, either through intercourse or masturbation. Prolonged sexual arousal without ejaculation can cause similar discomfort for men.

CLITORAL ADHESIONS

Clitoral adhesions, strands of scar tissue between the clitoris and its hood, can cause pain during intercourse. Also, some experts believe that full mobility of the clitoral hood is important for optimal stimulation of the clitoris. Clitoral adhesions, however, are uncommon.

MEDICAL PROBLEMS

Sexual problems are common after surgery or after illness that affects the reproductive organs. A woman who has had breast surgery or hysterectomy may need to adjust psychologically to illness, and also to the physical changes in her sensory perceptions. Prostate surgery can damage nerve pathways essential for a man's sexual responsiveness and can have a psychological impact as well.

Medical problems unrelated to the reproductive organs can sometimes cause sexual problems. Pain, fatigue, worry, or just preoccupation with a serious medical illness or impending surgery can alter sexual interest and responsiveness. Diabetes may cause sexual problems, possibly through alteration in sensory nerve responses. Patients recovering from major surgery or heart attack may be fearful of the stress of sexual activity. Patients with nervous system disabilities or other chronic physical disabilities may have unique problems and may need specialized help to develop satisfactory sexual techniques.

Persistent Sexual Problems

If you are seeking sexual therapy, it is likely to be for a problem that is persistent, or because your sexual functioning has always been unsatisfactory to you. These problems share many features with the temporary malfunctions described above, and many people do have temporary episodes of more severe sexual distress. Reading and time alone, however, are not as likely to be successful aids in overcoming the problems described in the pages that follow.

Successful treatment of persistent problems usually involves substantial education about the physical aspects of sexual functioning, development of sexual skills, and help with communication between partners, as well as some reassessment of personal attitudes and of the emotional environment of sexual functioning.

This discussion is intended only as a brief overview of common problems; the causes and cure for persistent sexual disorders are not as simple and clear-cut as these brief descriptions might imply. Often there are multiple causes, and problems often occur in combination. Marital conflicts and psychological issues may be involved as well;

therefore, your therapist must be able to recognize and deal at least to some extent with the emotional and interpersonal factors, as well as the specific sexual problem.

INABILITY TO ACHIEVE ORGASM

Preorgasmia is very common among women and much less common among men. Women with this problem often are able to experience arousal and may achieve the physical responses of the excitement phase or even the plateau phase, but they do not have orgasm. Sex experts use the term *pre*orgasmia because treatment is successful for more than 90% of women who seek treatment. Often only a few weeks of therapy are required. It is such a common problem that relatively inexpensive group treatment is available in many parts of the country. Often women undertake therapy alone without involving their partners, at least during the initial phases of treatment.

In most cases, the treatment needed for preorgasmia is education. Many women have simply never had an opportunity to learn what kinds of emotional, mental, and physical sensations are sexually pleasurable and effective for them. Treatment includes thorough education about female reproductive organs and the physical sexual responses. Women learn through self-exploration about their own responses to a range of physical sensations, and they learn to develop *patterns* for effective stimulation.

In some cases, a woman who has been successful in achieving orgasm through masturbation finds that the transition to orgasm with a partner is no problem. Many times, however, this transition involves education for the partner as well, and joint therapy often helps to improve communication between partners.

It's really funny. For years I've been faking orgasms, and Harry never knew. Now I know how to have orgasms, and I know his technique is all wrong. I can't decide whether to tell him it's all been fake, and how I really need to be handled, or just forget the whole thing. He may be hurt, whichever I do.

—Woman, 34

A woman who has been orgasmic on only rare occasions or who has been orgasmic in the past but then develops lingering problems with orgasm may benefit from the education and training in skills that have been designed for preorgasmic women. Her problems, however, may also be aggravated by the vicious cycle of **performance fear** that is characteristic of a man's inability to achieve or maintain an erection.

INABILITY TO ACHIEVE OR MAINTAIN ERECTION

For men, difficulty in achieving erection is much more common than difficulty in achieving orgasm. Erection is the first physical event in the excitation phase for men. Erection is a nonvoluntary response. When sexual activity begins, a man cannot help but notice whether erection is occurring. If it is not, then **fear** is an almost universal reaction. Performance fear itself can create an almost unrelenting vicious cycle.

A man or woman who is worrying about sexual failure is unable to focus attention on sexual stimuli, and he or she is therefore unable to be receptive to stimulation that might otherwise be extremely pleasurable and effective. Treatment for this problem often involves exercises designed to help the person **interrupt** the performance fear cycle. The man or woman needs an opportunity to learn to enjoy and lose himself or herself in sensory experiences. This may only be possible when performance is out of the picture and the person is free to be a participant, rather than a spectator who is watching and evaluating performance. The term Masters and Johnson use for sensory enjoyment that is free of the need to perform is **sensate focus.** In many cases, men (and women) find that their own natural, automatic physical arousal responses resume when they are able to be receptive to sensory experiences through sensate focus.

PREMATURE EJACULATION

There is no clear-cut definition of premature ejaculation. In rare cases, control is so limited that ejaculation occurs as soon as 30 to 60 seconds after erection. More commonly, men have **some** ejaculatory control but have difficulty delaying ejaculation long enough for their partner to achieve orgasm during intercourse. Ejaculatory control can almost always be improved by simple approaches such as the squeeze technique or the pause technique. With the former, the man learns to signal his partner when he is approaching the point of ejaculatory inevitability. She then puts pressure on his penis with her fingers, which causes an immediate decrease in sexual tension level. With the latter, the couple simply pauses for a little while when the man feels he is nearing ejaculatory inevitability (4). After a brief period of time most men are able to control ejaculation themselves, and only need to rely on this maneuver from time to time in special situations.

INABILITY TO INITIATE SEXUAL ACTIVITY

Aversion or distaste for any form of genital exploration is an uncommon but distressing problem that primarily affects women. Some women may feel unable even to touch their external genital structures, and may have prolonged spasm contraction of all the genital muscles (vaginismus) when any form of vaginal penetration is attempted. This spasm response makes routine pelvic examination impossible or unbearable and may even make it impossible for a woman to use tampons or vaginal medications. As extreme as this condition seems, treatment is often dramatically effective. Treatment for the problem includes careful education and conditioning exercises that help the woman gradually to acclimate herself to vulvar and vaginal touching and to vaginal penetration.

Finding Help for a Sexual Problem

Your clinician may be a good person to see when you decide to tackle a sexual problem. Some gynecologists and family physicians have special interest and training in this area and can provide sexual therapy themselves. Many clinicians, however, choose to refer their patients to a specialist in sexual problems if it appears that more than brief counseling will be required. If you do not feel comfortable about discussing a sexual problem with your clinician or if your clinician is uncomfortable or unable to recommend a resource for therapy, then you might get in touch with a local family service agency, Planned Parenthood agency, or community mental health center for the names of reputable, experienced sex therapists.

The field of sexual therapy is new, and there is as yet no single acceptable credential or license for competence. Professionals working in the field have varied backgrounds, and professional degrees may include psychology, psychiatry, social work and others. You may not find it easy to select a therapist, but the effort to ascertain her or his professional reputation in your community is important. Not all who practice in the field of sexual treatment are equally competent or reputable.

Sexual therapy involves learning and personal change, but it does not mean abandoning your moral principles or becoming sexually indiscriminate. Reputable sex therapy *does not* include the therapist as a sex partner or sexual object. If you think your therapist may be taking advantage of you or that therapy techniques are inappropriate, then respect your own instincts. You are probably right.

Your therapy will probably begin with a thorough sexual history. You will be asked to describe the problems you are experiencing, and your therapist will also need to understand your past sexual functioning and any medical and social factors that might be related to the problem. You and your therapist can decide whether both partners should participate in all your sessions, some of the sessions, or not at all. Many therapists prefer to have both partners involved from the beginning, with individual sessions for each of the partners perhaps once or twice during the entire treatment. Therapy sessions consist of discussion and education. Sexual activity is reserved for "home work" assignments. Some therapy programs involve whole blocks of time, such as the two-week, full-time program that Masters and Johnson have developed. Most treatment approaches, however, require only weekly sessions of an hour or two.

REFERENCES

1. Zilbergeld B, Evans M: The inadequacy of Masters and Johnson. *Psychology Today*, August 1980, pp 29–43.
2. Masters WH, Johnson VE: *Human Sexual Response*, ed 1. Boston, Little Brown, 1966.
3. Kaplan HS: *The New Sex Therapy*. New York, Brunner/Mazel, 1974, pp 13–15.
4. Zilbergeld B: Lasting longer with a partner. *Male Sexuality*. New York, Bantam, 1978, pp 255–289.

36 | Problems During Menopause

Menopause itself (cessation of menstrual periods) is not a medical problem or a disease, but many women do have at least some troublesome symptoms associated with it. Common symptoms and their relationship to hormone changes that your body undergoes during the climacteric, the transition from the reproductive phase of a woman's life to the postreproductive phase, are discussed in Chapter 1. The subject of hormone replacement therapy is discussed at length in this chapter because it is both complex and controversial. Many women find, however, that they can manage their own menopause problems. Alternatives to estrogen therapy and recommendations for medical care after menopause are discussed in later sections of this chapter.

The Estrogen Replacement Controversy

There has rarely been a treatment as shrouded in misinformation as estrogen replacement therapy (ERT). Knowledge about the benefits and risks of estrogen is not yet complete, and the subject in confusing. It is not so complex, however, that a thoughtful woman will have trouble understanding the issues. On the basis of our knowledge about estro-

476

gen therapy at the present time, we believe that this therapy is appropriate only for a limited group of women with certain conditions:

- As a short-term treatment when menopause hot flashes are severe enough to be disabling, for women who wish to have help with this symptom of the transition period
- As therapy for severe vaginal and urinary symptoms caused by estrogen deficiency
- As one part of treatment for bone density loss (osteoporosis) when the loss is proved to be related to estrogen deficiency
- As replacement therapy for women who have their ovaries surgically removed, so that the transition from normal to low estrogen levels will be gradual rather than abrupt

Women who have taken estrogen for long periods are often surprised to find that they can stop their pills without any noticeable impact. Some women do experience a return of hot flashes if they stop their pills abruptly and may prefer gradually to decrease the dose over a period of months. They do not, however, suddenly appear older or become irrational or lose their memory.

It makes good sense for you to assume responsibility yourself for deciding whether menopause treatment is needed or for how long.

During the 1950s and 1960s, great public and medical enthusiasm was generated for routine use of estrogen after menopause. Menopause was viewed as an estrogen deficiency disease. Use of estrogen drugs intended for this purpose soared from an annual wholesale value of $15.4 million in 1962 to $82.8 million in 1975, a threefold increase when inflation is figured in. Estimates in 1975 indicated that annual sales in the United States provided enough estrogen for 6 million women. Since only about 1.5 million women undergo menopause each year, these figures indicate that a large number of women are continuing ERT for a prolonged period of time (1).

Medical enthusiasm for estrogen replacement therapy (ERT) was based on encouraging research regarding bone metabolism and on hopes that ERT would delay or prevent other changes associated with aging, and would preserve youthful psyche, libido, and skin appearance. In addition, the risk of heart disease and stroke was known to be lower for premenopausal women than for males of the same age. Physicians hoped to extend protection from cardiovascular disease by providing synthetic estrogen once natural estrogen production had declined.

Many of these hopes have not been realized. *Further research on the effects of estrogen has not demonstrated any protective effect against cardiovascular disease.*

Emotional problems do not respond specifically to ERT, and estrogen effects on skin are equivocal; some researchers conclude that estrogen causes loss of skin youthfulness (atrophy), and others conclude that it may cause skin swelling (edema) or apparent thickening for a more youthful appearance.

ESTROGEN AND BONES

The initially encouraging research on bone density loss (osteoporosis) has, however, been reaffirmed in subsequent research. *Low-dose estrogen replacement therapy can prevent osteoporosis.* Once osteoporosis has begun, estrogen replacement therapy may prevent further bone degeneration. It does not help other common orthopedic problems, such as arthritis or bone loss due to arthritis (osteoarthritis).

Approximately 20% of women who don't take estrogen will develop osteoporosis after menopause. The loss of bone minerals results in fragile bones that may fracture with minimal trauma. Fractures in the bones of the spinal column may cause pain, loss of body height, and spine curvature (dowager's hump). The problems caused by osteoporosis can be serious. Hip fracture, for example, is much more likely when osteoporosis is present and often leads to complications such as pneumonia that can be fatal for an elderly person. Prevention of osteoporosis remains as the strongest argument in favor of routine estrogen therapy.

Accurate height measurements are important in detecting osteoporosis, and x-ray studies of bone density can be used to assess its severity. Optimal treatment for osteoporosis is controversial. Estrogen, especially when used for prevention, is effective; estrogen, however, involves risks, and some women cannot use it at all. Experts feel that calcium, Vitamin D, and moderate exercise can also help prevent or retard osteoporosis.

ESTROGEN AND ENDOMETRIAL CANCER (UTERINE CANCER)

In 1975 and 1976, three separate medical researchers linked the risk of uterine cancer to long-term menopausal estrogen therapy. The three studies compared cancer rates in groups of women who had received ERT with the rates for similar women who were not treated. This type of research design (groups for comparison were chosen after the treatment had occurred) is not an ideal scientific approach. It is almost impossible to insure against bias in the way that control groups are selected and bias might entirely explain the difference in rates observed. For this reason, such studies cannot be accepted as conclusive proof that estrogen causes uterine cancer. Some researchers believe that estrogen replacement has been unfairly condemned.

The study findings, of course, may be accurate. The fact that three separate researchers reviewing separate population groups arrived at similar risk levels also adds credibility to their conclusions. They found that *women who received ERT were 4.5 to 8 times more likely to develop uterine cancer* than were women who did not receive ERT. This is an increase of 450 to 800% (3).

Proponents of estrogen replacement therapy used to say that ERT was safe because there had been no increase in overall uterine cancer rates; recently, however, an overall increase of 40 to 150% in the incidence of uterine cancer in the United States has been documented. The fact that cancer rates did not increase until several years after the popularization of ERT may be explained by a latent period between hormone exposure and development of disease, which is a common pattern in the case of cancer. The increase in cancer rates paralleled the increase in estrogen sales after a lag time of about ten years (see Illustration 1).

A statistical parallel does not prove that estrogen can cause endometrial cancer; it may be that some other environmental change is responsible for the increase in uterine cancer rates. The parallel, however, is not reassuring. Many experts in this field believe that there is a link between hormone exposure and later development of cancer, but that the specific woman's genetic background, previous hormone environment (natural or synthetic), and other factors such as obesity and diabetes also play a role in determining whether cancer will develop.

If the 1975 and 1976 researchers are correct, the anticipated increase in uterine cancer rates will be very significant. A sevenfold excess risk means that a 45-year-old woman whose risk for endometrial cancer would ordinarily be 1.6%, faces a risk of 11.2% if she chooses to use estrogen replacement therapy. Thus, *one woman out of every nine*

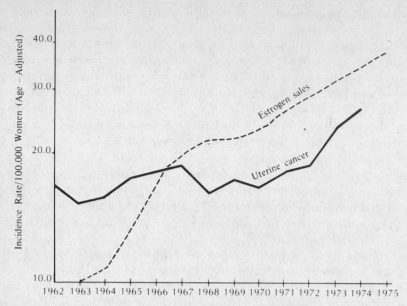

Illustration 1   An overall increase in uterine cancer rates in the United States (solid line) began in about 1970, and parallels the increase in sales of estrogen for replacement therapy (dashed line). (Adapted from P Greenwald, T Caputo, P E Wolfgang: Endometrial cancer after menopausal use of estrogens, *Obstetrics and Gynecology* 50:239–243, 1977. Used with permission.)

who receives menopause estrogen replacement therapy could expect to develop endometrial cancer (1). This is higher than the combined incidence rate for all breast, cervix, uterus, and ovary cancers among women who do not receive ERT.

ESTROGEN AND BREAST CANCER

Whether estrogen therapy has any effect on breast cancer risk is not known. Estrogen is known to trigger breast tumors in some animals and may accelerate tumor growth in humans if breast cancer is already present.

Initial research on breast cancer among women receiving ERT seemed to indicate no risk increase, and possibly even a protective effect. More recent reports suggest that the risk may be unchanged for some women, but increased for others. Specifically, women who develop benign (not cancer) breast disease while on ERT appear to have an increased risk of breast cancer at a later time (4). These results are not conclusive; they do mean that decisions about ERT should be made carefully even by women who have previously undergone hysterectomy and therefore have no endometrial cancer risk.

OTHER RISKS AND SIDE EFFECTS OF ESTROGEN THERAPY

The risk of significant gallbladder disease is increased among women who take estrogen after menopause, just as it is among women taking birth control Pills. (Estrogen side effects are discussed in detail in Chapter 11.) Other possible side effects include:

- Nausea
- Breast tenderness or swelling
- Marked thickening of the uterine lining (endometrial hyperplasia)
- Enlargement of uterine fibroids
- Liver problems, including yellow jaundice
- Possible increased risk of liver tumors
- Swelling or fluid retention (may aggravate asthma, epilepsy, migraine, heart disease, or kidney disease)
- Skin rash and chloasma (dark patches of skin on the face)
- Hair loss
- Inability to use contact lenses

CONTRAINDICATIONS TO ERT

A contraindication is a medical condition that renders a course of treatment inadvisable or unsafe that might otherwise be recommended.

Women who have had problems with estrogen in the past or have medical problems that might be aggravated by estrogen should avoid estrogen replacement therapy. These contraindications are quite similar to those for oral contraceptives, but many of the conditions are more frequently encountered among women of menopausal age than among young women. The reasons for each of the contraindications are discussed in Chapter 11.

- *Absolute Contraindications (Must not use ERT)*
  Current or past blood-clotting disorders
  Stroke
  Cardiovascular disease
  Undiagnosed abnormal vaginal bleeding
  Cancer of the breast, reproductive organs, or skin
  Pregnancy
- *Strong Relative Contraindications (Probably should not use ERT)*
  Impaired liver function
  Hypertension (high blood pressure)
  Diabetes
  Fibrocystic disease or fibroadenoma of the breast
  Sickle cell disease
  High blood serum lipid levels
  Elective surgery planned in the next four weeks
- *Relative Contraindications (Must be followed very carefully)*
  Fibroid tumor of the uterus
  Strong family history of diabetes
  Epilepsy
  Asthma
  Varicose veins

It is also important to remember that estrogens can interact with medications you may be taking for unrelated problems, for example, anticoagulants, insulin, promazine, meperidine, and tuberculin skin tests. Discuss this issue with your clinician, and be sure that any clinician you see is aware that you are using estrogen.

CURRENT RECOMMENDATIONS REGARDING ESTROGEN THERAPY

In March 1976, the Food and Drug Administration issued a drug advisory bulletin to all United States physicians recommending a conservative approach in the use of estrogen for menopausal symptoms. The FDA recommendations are (3):

1. Estrogen should be used only for management of specific problems, not routinely. These problems might include severe, disabling hot flashes; osteoporosis; and vaginal dryness or urinary symptoms due to estrogen deficiency.
2. Estrogen should be prescribed in the **lowest dose that is effective**

and for the *shortest interval possible,* with *reevaluation* of the need for estrogen *at least once every six months.* A typical low estrogen dose would be 0.3 to 0.625 milligrams of a conjugated estrogen (such as Premarin) a day.

3. Estrogen therapy should be viewed as a *temporary treatment* during a period of transition. The goal of therapy (except in the case of osteoporosis; see below) is to provide relief of disabling symptoms by creating a more gradual change in hormone levels. Ideally each patient can find a satisfactory schedule for gradually reducing her estrogen dose over a period of time without experiencing any intolerable symptoms.

4. Before estrogen therapy is begun a thorough review of *medical history and a physical examination are necessary* to determine that no contraindications are present, and this evaluation should be repeated *every six months* while estrogen is used. Special attention should be paid to blood pressure, breast examination, abdominal examination to detect liver enlargement or tenderness, pelvic examination, and Pap test. Measured height should also be recorded.

5. Patients using estrogen therapy should be instructed to *watch for and immediately report the danger signs* of estrogen complications: vaginal bleeding; chest pain, difficulty breathing, or cough; severe headaches, dizziness, faintness, vision changes; leg pain (calf); breast lump; yellowing of the skin or eyes (jaundice).

6. *Any vaginal bleeding that occurs during estrogen therapy, even spotting, must be thoroughly evaluated.* The Pap smear does not effectively test for uterine cancer. Further tests such as uterine scraping or dilation and curettage (D&C, see Chapter 40) are necessary to detect uterine cancer; these tests are *mandatory* if bleeding occurs. Experts in the field, participating in a 1979 conference sponsored by the National Institutes of Health, have recommended that all women receiving estrogen replacement therapy undergo such evaluation before beginning treatment and annually thereafter whether or not bleeding occurs (5).

7. If symptoms of estrogen excess such as breast tenderness, fluid retention, nausea, or bleeding occur, a *reduced dose of estrogen* should be considered.

8. *Estrogens should never be taken during pregnancy* or if pregnancy is suspected or possible.

9. The use of estrogen therapy for osteoporosis should be undertaken only by clinicians expert in this area *after thorough orthopedic assessment* and should be coordinated with other forms of treatment such as diet, mineral supplementation, and physiotherapy.

As of October 1977, the FDA required all estrogen manufacturers to provide a pamphlet for each woman purchasing estrogen. Be sure to read your pamphlet carefully each time your prescription is refilled and watch for new information that may be added as pamphlets are revised or that is reported in the press.

Most clinicians recommend that estrogen be taken cyclically with an estrogen-free interval of five to seven days each month. Many believe that it is advisable to add progestin along with the estrogen for the last week of each treatment cycle. These schemes may reduce the risk of excessive stimulation of your uterine lining and minimize the likelihood of abnormal bleeding and perhaps the risk of uterine cancer as well.

Many clinicians also feel that estrogen vaginal cream may be a better choice than oral tablets when the primary problem is vaginal dryness or urinary problems. Since estrogen in vaginal cream is absorbed into the bloodstream, the potential dangers are identical to those of oral estrogens, but a smaller overall dose of estrogen may be effective for controlling dryness symptoms when vaginal cream is used. After an initial intensive course of therapy (one-half to one applicator full of vaginal cream inserted in the vagina every night for 7 to 14 nights), one or two treatments a week may be sufficient.

Estrogen replacement is almost always recommended for women who undergo surgical removal of the ovaries because of infection or other benign disease. Often such surgery involves hysterectomy as well, so the major concern about uterine cancer is not applicable. The very abrupt hormone drop that occurs after such surgery commonly causes severe hot flashes and other menopausal symptoms. Recommendations vary as to the duration of estrogen therapy in such cases. Some clinicians believe that estrogen replacement should be continued until age 50 or even longer; others say that this plan may not be desirable in view of the potential side effects and complications other than uterine cancer. Many women find that prolonged therapy is unnecessary and are likely to stop taking estrogen after a process of gradual dose reductions.

Alternatives to Estrogen for Management of Bothersome Symptoms

Numerous drugs, diets, vitamins, and therapies have been suggested as alternatives to estrogen for management of menopause problems. Although none has achieved the uniformly high success rate of estrogen for controlling hot flashes and vaginal problems, one or more of these alternatives may prove helpful to you:

PROGESTIN THERAPY

If hot flashes are a severe problem but the use of estrogen is contraindicated, daily progestin pills or progestin shots every three months may be helpful. Although progestin too is a hormone normally produced by the ovary prior to menopause, it has a more limited list of contraindications (see Chapter 12 for a discussion of complications and contraindications for progestin).

VITAMIN THERAPY

Bioflavinoids and vitamin C have been suggested for treatment of hot flashes. Research evidence for their effectiveness is limited, but one published study reporting use of this combination (a drug called Peridin-C) did indicate some response to treatment (6).

ANTISPASMODICS AND TRANQUILIZERS

Antispasmodics and tranquilizers are widely used for menopausal symptoms. Some combination drugs like Bellergal that produce general relaxation of smooth muscle may be effective for managing flushes. Many clinicians believe, however, that the primary effect of these drugs and tranquilizers such as Valium and Librium is psychotropic. They blunt the emotional impact of symptoms, along with other life experiences as well. *Tranquilizers are not of any demonstrated value for ameliorating menopausal symptoms.* Tranquilizers may have significant side effects and are also potentially addictive. Many women prefer nonchemical approaches for improving psychic equilibrium, such as psychotherapy, yoga, or meditation.

PRACTICAL REMEDIES

Feel free to experiment with practical alterations in your daily routine that may help minimize the inconvenience or discomfort of symptoms that you do have. Some women find that an immediate drink of ice water can stop a flush reaction. A thermos of ice water on the bedside table may be helpful. Many women find that extra lubrication, such as K-Y Jelly or another water-soluble lubricant you can buy without a prescription, protects against irritation during intercourse.

Wardrobe planning that allows you to remove a jacket or sweater may be all you will need during the 6- to 12-months that severe hot flashes are likely to persist. You may find that 30 minutes of real exercise every day helps more with insomnia than sleeping pills or estrogen, and exercise may be beneficial for decreasing bone loss from osteoporosis as well.

MUSCLE TONE EXERCISES

Kegal's exercises are often very helpful for women who are having problems with bladder control because of loss of muscle tone. Try squeezing the muscles of your vagina as you would to stop a stream of urine. Squeeze and continue squeezing as you count to five, and then relax for a count of five. For another exercise, squeeze and relax five times as rapidly as you can. Repeat each of the exercises at least 100 times daily, while you are waiting in line or stopped at a traffic light.

Birth Control and Menopause

As menopause approaches, pregnancy is less and less likely. Nevertheless, you will probably want to continue with birth control until you can be certain that menopause has occurred. A woman who has had fairly regular menstrual periods in the past, is having other symptoms of menopause such as hot flashes, and is in the menopause age range (45 to 55) can reasonably assume that she is no longer fertile when six months have elapsed since her last menstrual period. If you are not certain about menopause and want to stop using birth control, then your clinician can arrange a pituitary hormone level test to determine whether your ovaries are still producing eggs and hormones.

Recommendations for Routine Care

It is easy to procrastinate about routine examinations, especially when you no longer have a need for birth control supplies. After menopause, however, examinations are more important than ever for early detection of serious problems. *A complete examination at least once every six months is recommended for women using estrogen.* Routine care for all women over 50 should include:

- Breast self-exam, monthly
- Blood pressure, height, weight, breast exam and pelvic exam; see Chapter 21 for recommendations on Pap test intervals
- Glaucoma test, annually
- Urinalysis, fasting blood sugar, and triglyceride level, annually
- Xeromammography (breast x-ray); see Chapter 32 for intervals
- Chest x-ray and electrocardiogram, every one to two years

More frequent examinations will be necessary if you are being treated for medical problems.

The value of a more elaborate annual "complete" physical exam and lab evaluation (a $150 to $200 checkup) for women who are not aware of any symptoms is controversial. Many clinicians believe that unless you have symptoms of some kind the likelihood of detecting a significant, treatable problem is so low that the expense and effort are not justified. It may be more sensible to use your personal and financial resources to implement your New Year's resolutions to take better care of yourself. Take your own preventive health inventory and do something about your needs: How close are you to your ideal weight? Is your daily diet what it should be? Do you need to stop smoking? Does your daily life provide for the physical exercise your body thrives on?

REFERENCES

1. Greenwald P, Caputo TA, Wolfgang PE: Endometrial cancer after menopausal use of estrogens. *Obstetrics and Gynecology* 50:239–243, 1977.
2. Drugs for postmenopausal osteoporosis. *The Medical Letter on Drugs and Therapeutics* 22(11):45–46, May 30, 1980.
3. *FDA Drug Bulletin* 6(1), February-March 1976. Food and Drug Administration.
4. Hoover R, Gray LA, Cole P, et al: Menopausal estrogens and breast cancer. *New England Journal of Medicine* 295:401–405, 1976.
5. Estrogen use and postmenopausal women: a National Institutes of Health Consensus Development Conference. *Annals of Internal Medicine* 91:921–922, 1979.
6. Smith CJ: Non-hormonal control of vaso-motor flushing in menopausal patients. *Chicago Medicine* 67:193–195, 1964.

37 | Exposure to Diethylstilbestrol (DES)

Diethylstilbestrol (DES), the first synthetic estrogen, became available for medical use in the 1940s. On the basis of an encouraging research report, physicians prescribed DES for some pregnant women in an attempt to prevent miscarriage. Later research showed, however, that DES does not effectively prevent miscarriage (1), and its use declined somewhat after 1955. The dangers of DES were not documented until the 1970s, when the first study was published that demonstrated the link between DES and vaginal cancer in daughters of women who took DES during pregnancy. In November 1971, the Food and Drug Administration recommended that DES no longer be used during pregnancy. We now know that DES exposure may have harmful effects on **daughters, sons, and the DES-treated mothers** themselves.

DES and two similar synthetic estrogens, dienestrol and hexestrol, were the main drugs used for pregnancy treatment. The term "DES exposure" is used for all three drugs, and they all appear to have had similar harmful effects. Newer synthetic estrogens such as those now used in birth control Pills have a somewhat different chemical structure and have never been extensively used during pregnancy. It is not known whether DES effects are unique for the specific chemical structure of DES, hexestrol, and dienestrol, or whether similar problems would occur with the newer estrogens as well.

How to Determine DES Exposure

Between 1940 and 1971, about 2 million pregnant women were treated with DES (2). DES treatment was most common between 1950 and 1955, when as many as 5 to 10% of pregnant women who received care at some medical centers were given the drug (3). DES use declined after 1960, but cases of DES exposure as late as 1975 have been reported.

Consider the possibility of DES exposure if:

- You were pregnant or were conceived between 1940 and 1975, especially between 1950 and 1960
- You (your mother) had bleeding during early pregnancy, or previous miscarriage (spontaneous abortion), or diabetes
- You (your mother) took oral medication (tablets) during pregnancy. DES treatment usually started early in pregnancy and continued with increasing doses until about one month before delivery. It was usually given in tablet form, not by injection, and was marketed under many brand names. (See Table 1 for common brand names.)

It may be possible to confirm DES exposure by checking medical records from the time of pregnancy or by identifying abnormalities that are common with DES exposure if you are a DES daughter or son. Even if you cannot find old medical records, *if you suspect that you may have taken DES during pregnancy or you are a daughter or son who may have been exposed, then you require special medical attention.*

DES Daughters: Possible Effects of Fetal Exposure

As with most drugs, harmful effects on the fetus are more likely if DES exposure occurred early in pregnancy. Daughters exposed to DES during the first five months of fetal life are more likely to have DES problems than are daughters exposed only in the later months.

Table 1   DES-TYPE DRUGS THAT MAY HAVE BEEN PRESCRIBED TO PREGNANT WOMEN

Nonsteroidal estrogens		Nonsteroidal estrogen-androgen combinations	
Benzestrol	Mikarol		
Chlorotrianisene	Mikarol forti	Amperone	Teserene
Comestrol	Milestrol	Di-Erone	Tylandril
Cyren A.	Monomestrol	Estan	Tylosterone
Cyren B.	Neo-Oestranol I	Metystil	
Delvinal	Neo-Oestranol II		
DES	Nulabort	*Nonsteroidal estrogen-progesterone combination*	
DesPlex	Oestrogenine		
Diestryl	Oestromenin		
Dibestil	Oestromon	Progravidium	
Dienestrol	Orestol		
Dienoestrol	Pabestrol D.	*Vaginal cream—and suppositories with nonsteroidal estrogens*	
Diethylstilbestrol	Palestrol		
Dipalmitate	Restrol		
Diethylstilbestrol	Stil-Rol		
Diphosphate	Stilbal	AVC cream with	
Diethylstilbestrol	Stilbestrol	Dienestrol	
Dipropionate	Stilbestronate	Dienestrol cream	
Diethylstilbenediol	Stilbetin		
Digestil	Stilbinol		
Domestrol	Stilboestroform		
Estilben	Stilboestrol		
Estrobene	Stilboestrol DP.		
Estrobene DP.	Stilestrate		
Estrosyn	Stilpalmitate		
Fonatol	Stilphostrol		
Gynben	Stilronate		
Gyneben	Stilrone		
Hexestrol	Stils		
Hexoestrol	Synestrin		
Hi-Bestrol	Synestrol		
Menocrin	Synthoestrin		
Meprane	Tace		
Mestilbol	Vallestril		
Methallenestril	Willestrol		
Microest			

SOURCE: US Department of Health, Education and Welfare Information for Physicians: *DES Exposure in Utero*. Publication No (NIH) 76-1119, pp 10–11.

VAGINAL CANCER (CLEAR CELL ADENOCARCINOMA)

Vaginal cancer is uncommon, even among DES daughters.* About 400 cases worldwide had been reported as of mid-1980. Experts estimate that somewhere between 1 in 700 and 1 in 7,000 DES daughters develops vaginal cancer (0.14 to 1.4 per 1,000 DES daughters) (4). All the DES daughters who developed vaginal cancer were exposed to DES before the 18th week of pregnancy, and almost all cancers became apparent when the DES daughters were between the ages of 14 and 24 (3). This cancer, called vaginal clear cell adenocarcinoma, can be successfully treated with surgery and x-ray, and interim reports show that three out of four women who have been treated for vaginal cancer are alive and well. Many DES daughters have not yet completed five years of observation after surgery, however (4). Danger signs for vaginal cancer are *abnormal vaginal bleeding and thickening or lumps in the wall of the vagina.*

DYSPLASIA OF THE CERVIX

Some researchers have reported that dysplasia, precancerous cell changes on the surface of the cervix (see Chapter 27), is five times more common among DES daughters than among other women (5). Other experts do not believe that dysplasia risk is linked to DES exposure. Nevertheless, since dysplasia is known to precede development of cancer of the cervix, researchers are concerned that DES daughters may prove to have higher than average cervical cancer rates. Statistics probably will not show whether there is a link between DES and cervical cancer until more DES daughters reach the age when cervical cancer is more common (about age 35 to age 50). Pap smears are very reliable for detecting dysplasia and cancer of the cervix. Cervical cancer (squamous cell carcinoma of the cervix) is completely different from vaginal cancer, but like vaginal cancer, it is curable in most cases if it is detected early.

STRUCTURAL ABNORMALITIES OF THE CERVIX AND VAGINA

As many as 40% of DES daughters have obvious alterations in the

---

*Vaginal clear cell adenocarcinoma can occur on the vaginal walls and even on the cervix. Clear cell cancer was very rare before the DES era, and is distinct from the common type of cervical cancer, called squamous cell carcinoma of the cervix. DES, however, may also increase the likelihood of squamous cell carcinoma of the cervix.

Normal Cervix

Abnormal collar

Abnormal mucus-secreting glands
that cover the surface of the cervix
and extend onto the vaginal wall

Abnormal bump

Illustration 1   Your clinician may suspect DES exposure if your cervix has an abnormal shape. (Reproductive Health Resources, Inc. Used with permission.)

shape of the cervix (see Illustration 1) (6), the vaginal walls, or the uterus. In most cases these structural abnormalities seem to cause no symptoms, but in some cases they might impair fertility (7).

ADENOSIS

The normal outer surface of the cervix and the vaginal walls is smooth, shiny tissue (squamous epithelium) composed of flat, pancake-shaped cells. The term "adenosis" means that patches of abnormal cells appear on the surface of the cervix and/or walls of the vagina. Adenosis surface cells are tall and velvety (columnar epithelium), similar to cells that line the cervical canal, and adenosis tissue contains a rich supply of mucus-secreting glands (see Illustration 2). Adenosis is extremely common among DES daughters. You might have adenosis with no symptoms at all, or you might have a heavy, mucus-like vaginal discharge. Your vagina may not look *at all* unusual to your clinician during your routine pelvic exam. Clinicians use iodine staining of the vagina and colposcopy (examination of the cervix and vagina through magnifying lenses) to detect adenosis (see Chapter 21 for details on these procedures). Adenosis was very uncommon before the era of DES daughters, and long-term effects of adenosis are not yet known.

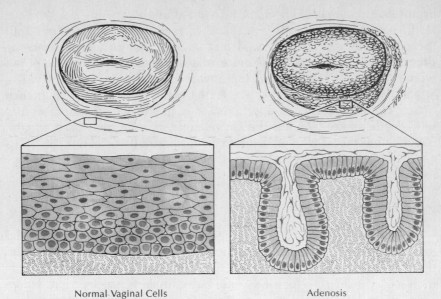

Normal Vaginal Cells   Adenosis

Illustration 2   Adenosis means that glandular, mucus-secreting cells, normally present only in the cervical canal, extend onto the surface of the cervix and/or vaginal walls. (Reproductive Health Resources, Inc. Used with permission.)

Some researchers are concerned that a woman with adenosis may have an increased risk for cervical (squamous) cancer. Cervical cancer almost always arises from the "transformation zone," a circular area on the surface of a normal cervix where two types of surface cells meet—*squamous* cells from the outer surface of the cervix and *columnar* cells from the lining of the cervical canal. Women with adenosis have a transformation zone that is much larger than normal: columnar, mucus-secreting cells can extend over the whole cervix and out onto the vaginal walls themselves. There is as yet no evidence that women with adenosis have an increased risk for cervical cancer, but it makes sense to have Pap smears regularly, *including Pap smears from the vaginal walls* themselves (see routine care recommendations later in this chapter).

MENSTRUAL IRREGULARITIES AND FERTILITY

Studies comparing DES daughters to unexposed women of the same age indicate that DES daughters are more likely to have irregular or infrequent menstrual periods, infrequent ovulation, and very serious fertility problems as well (8,9,10). Two recent studies confirmed all these findings and also showed that DES daughters who do become pregnant have substantially more miscarriages than do unexposed women. In one of the studies there were 106 DES daughters who did attempt pregnancy: only 58 live births occurred. Overall pregnancy losses, from spontaneous abortions, ectopic (tubal) pregnancies, and fetal deaths, were 37% for the DES daughters who became pregnant. Among unexposed women this rate would normally be about 15%. DES daughters who had vaginal adenosis or cervical hoods had pregnancy losses of 53% (9).

PROBLEMS OF DES SONS

DES-exposed sons have not yet been studied as extensively as DES daughters, and DES-related problems have only recently been identified and reported for young men. To date, there is no evidence of any increased cancer risk for DES sons, but clinicians are worried. Undescended testicles are an important risk factor for testicular cancer, and DES sons have higher rates of undescended testicles than do unexposed men.

More than 30% of DES sons in one study had abnormalities such as testicle cysts, underdeveloped or undescended testicles, or abnormal placement of the urinary opening (see Illustration 3). Similar abnormalities were found in only 8% of young men who had not been exposed to DES (10,11).

In the same study, about 40% of DES sons had low sperm counts

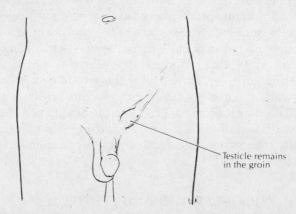

Testicle remains in the groin

Illustration 3   A young man who was exposed to DES during fetal development may have an undescended testicle.

and abnormally shaped sperm cells. In half of these young men (20% of all DES sons), sperm production was impaired enough to interfere with fertility (10,11).

PROBLEMS OF DES MOTHERS

Preliminary study results released by the Food and Drug Administration in 1978 indicate that adult women who were treated with DES during pregnancy may have a higher risk for breast cancer, cervical cancer, and ovarian cancer than do similar women who did not take DES (1). Further study will be required to confirm this finding and to determine how much the cancer risk is increased for DES mothers, if at all.

Treatment for DES Problems

Some DES problems, such as undescended testicles or vaginal cancer, require surgical treatment. You may need surgery to correct uterine or cervical abnormalities if they are causing infertility. Some clinicians have treated adenosis with hormones, surgery, or cryosurgery (see Chapter 21 for a description of cryosurgery), but there is no evidence that adenosis treatment is beneficial. Most experts believe that treatment is not justified unless Pap smears and/or biopsies show precancerous cell changes.

Guidelines for Medical Care: DES Mothers, Daughters, and Sons

Whether you are sure about exposure or only suspect DES exposure, DES mothers, daughters, and sons must be aware of the harmful effects that we now know about, must be faithful about routine examinations, and must be alert for new information about DES problems and any unusual symptoms they may experience.

DES SONS

Make sure that you are evaluated at least once a year by your clinician. You might try to find a pediatrician or urologist who is specifically interested in and experienced with DES problems.

DES DAUGHTERS

Try to arrange for ongoing routine care with a gynecologist trained in the use of colposcopy (see Chapter 21) and experienced with DES problems. Begin having routine exams when your menstrual periods start or at age 14, whichever occurs earlier. Prompt examination is essential if vaginal bleeding or discharge occurs, even if you are very young. Have a routine exam once a year. If your clinician finds any DES-related abnormalities, you will need more frequent exams. In addition to a routine pelvic exam, your annual examinations should include:

- A two-slide Pap test: one slide from the cervix and one or more slides from the walls of the vagina
- Colposcopic examination of the cervix and vagina
- Iodine staining of the cervix and upper vagina
- Careful palpation (feeling) of the walls of the vagina and cervix to detect thickening, lumps, or roughness
- Biopsy (a tiny tissue fragment removed for microscopic evaluation, see Chapter 21) of any abnormal areas on the cervix or vaginal walls

DES MOTHERS

See a gynecologist, an internist, or a family physician annually for routine exams. Self breast examination every month and Pap tests at least once every year are especially important.

Long-Term Effects of DES Exposure

The long-term effects of DES are not yet known. DES mothers are now reaching peak ages for breast, uterine, and ovarian cancer, but the oldest DES daughters and sons are only approaching their 40s.

The most serious DES consequence known at this time—vaginal cancer—appears to be quite uncommon. DES daughters may also have a higher risk for squamous cell cancer of the cervix, but we cannot be sure until more DES daughters reach the peak age groups for this kind of cervical cancer.

It is possible that no further harmful effects of DES will be found. It is also possible, however, that DES exposure may increase rates for cancer in other female or male reproductive organs, as well as the vagina, and the answers will not be known for many years.

Many DES daughters ask whether it would be safe for them to use birth control Pills. There is no evidence to date that DES daughters should avoid Pills or that Pill risks for a DES daughter are higher than they are for other women, but the FDA-approved patient leaflet for Pills advises that DES daughters who choose Pills should be followed very carefully by their clinicians. Long-term effects of Pills are not known, and neither are long-term effects of DES. Other birth control methods may be safer than Pills.

Further Information About DES

The National Cancer Institute sponsors ongoing research about DES and adenosis in the DESAD Project, a multicenter effort to monitor the consequences of DES exposure. The DESAD Project centers and project directors are:

Dr. Duane E. Townsend
DESAD Project
8631 West Third Street Suite 215E
Los Angeles, California 90048 (213/657-1040)

Dr. Robert B. Bowser
Project Officer, DESAD Project
Division of Cancer Control and Rehabilitation
National Cancer Institute
Blair Building, 8300 Colesville Road
Silver Spring, Maryland 20910 (301/427-8648)

Dr. Ann Barnes and Dr. Stanley J. Robboy
Massachusetts General Hospital, DESAD Project
32 Fruit Street
Boston, Massachusetts 02114 (617/726-8883)

Dr. Kenneth Noller
Mayo Clinic, DESAD Project
Rochester, Minnesota 55901 (507/284-8358)

Dr. Raymond H. Kaufman
Baylor College of Medicine, DESAD Project
1200 Moursand Avenue
Houston, Texas 77025 (713/790-4405)

DES action groups in a number of cities offer information and referral for DES problems. Some action groups are:

DES ACTION
Coalition for the Medical Rights of Women
1638 B Haight Street
San Francisco, California 94117 (415/621-8032)

DES ACTION
5426—27th Street, NW
Washington, D.C. 20015 (202/966-1766)

DES ACTION
P.O. Box 126
Stoton, Massachusetts 02072 (617/828-7461)

DES ACTION
19 Laurel Lane
Plainview, New York 10803 (516/681-6496) (212/343-9222)

DES ACTION
P.O. Box 12092, Holiday Park Station
Portland, Oregon 97212 (503/232-3088)

DES ACTION, NATIONAL HEADQUARTERS
L. I. Jewish-Hillside Medical Center
New Hyde Park, New York 11040 (212/470-2847)

REFERENCES

1.   DES and breast cancer. *FDA Drug Bulletin* 8(2), March-April 1978. Food and Drug Administration.

2. Schmitt A: The stilbestrol story. *Bulletin of the Society of Pharmacological and Environmental Pathologists* 2(2), 1974.

3. Herbst A, Cole P, Colton T, et al: Age-incidence and risk of diethylstilbestrol-related clear cell adenocarcinoma of the vaginas and cervix. *American Journal of Obstetrics and Gynecology* 128:43–50, 1977.

4. Herbst A, Cole P: Epidemiologic and clinical aspects of clear cell adenocarcinoma in young women, in Herbst A (ed): *Intrauterine Exposure to Diethylstilbestrol in the Human.* Proceedings of Symposium on DES, 1977. Chicago, American College of Obstetricians and Gynecologists, February 1978. (Monograph.)

5. Mattingly R, Stafl A: Cancer risk in DES exposed offspring. *American Journal of Obstetrics and Gynecology* 126:543–548, 1976.

6. Townsend D: Techniques of examination and screening of the DES-exposed female, in Herbst A (ed) (see ref. 4).

7. Kaufman R, Binder G, Gray P, et al: Upper genital tract changes associated with exposure in utero to diethylstilbestrol. *American Journal of Obstetrics and Gynecology* 128:51–59, 1977.

8. Herbst AL, Hubby MM, Blough RR, et al: A comparison of pregnancy experience in DES-exposed and DES-unexposed daughters. *Journal of Reproductive Medicine* 24:62–69, 1980.

9. Schmidt G, Fowler WC, Talbert LM, et al: Reproductive history of women exposed to diethylstilbestrol in utero. *Fertility and Sterility* 33:21 24, 1980.

10. Bibbo M, Gill W, Freidoon A, et al: Follow-up study of male and female offspring of DES-exposed mothers. *Obstetrics and Gynecology* 49(1):1–8, 1977.

11. Gill W, Schumacher G, Bibbo M: Genital and semen abnormalities in adult males two and one half decades after in utero exposure to diethylstilbestrol, in Herbst A (ed) (see ref. 4).

38 | Rape

Rape is a violent crime of aggression that happens to resemble a sexual act. It is an assault on a person's whole being and leaves most victims feeling vulnerable, naked, and powerless.

Being careful helps, of course, but careful behavior won't always prevent rape. As long as people express violent aggression in a sexual mode, we will be coping with the aftermath of rape.

The aftermath of rape is much like the grieving period after a loved one's death; the victim's sense of inviolable personhood may literally die. Most victims experience typical grieving emotions, such as denial, anger, and depression. With time, with good emotional support, and with access to competent counseling when it is needed, most victims can resolve rape and leave the experience in the past. "It took 11 months, but now I think I can stop being a rape victim," one woman said.

Most rape victims aren't seriously injured, because most rapists (about 85%) (1) are either armed or threaten to use physical force if the victim doesn't cooperate. Most women* realize that arguing with a gun, a knife, or a person who outweighs her by 30 pounds or more is

---

*We refer to rape victims as women and to rapists as men because that is by far the most common situation. In prison settings, men frequently express dominance by raping other men, and women rapists are not unheard of. There is no intention to slight male victims, whose problems and needs are much the same as those female victims experience.

folly, so they submit, bargaining with rape in return for staying alive. Most victims feel lucky to be alive; it is common to feel numb and shocked, as you would after a brush with death of any kind.

If you don't know where to find help after rape, look in the telephone book or ask an operator for a *24-hour crisis line.* In some cities, rape crisis centers have 24-hour telephone counselors of their own, and most cities have crisis lines operated by a community center, health department, or mental health association. Crisis line counselors can advise you about getting medical care and about the police procedures for reporting rape. They can discuss the pros and cons of prosecuting your attacker and help you through the court process if you decide to prosecute. They can also talk with you about your emotional needs.

Medical Care for Rape Victims

It didn't hurt, and it didn't feel any different from any other pelvic exam. Maybe it took a couple of minutes longer. I was really tense about it, though. I was *afraid* it would hurt, and I really didn't want *another* strange man looking at me naked, you know? That already happened once tonight.

—*Woman, 35*

The medical examination for rape is essentially the same as a routine pelvic exam (see Chapter 21), with several additional simple procedures specifically relating to rape. **Make sure that you are examined by a physician who is trained to handle rape evidence properly.** All potential physical evidence must be dealt with in a rigorous chain of custody procedure, signed into the safekeeping of a physician or police officer and stored under lock and key.

EXAMINATION FOR INJURY

If you have been beaten or injured in any way, your clinician will care for your injuries first. She/he will carefully record all injuries, including minor ones, in your medical record.

TESTS FOR DETECTING SEMEN

During your speculum examination, your clinician will collect a routine Pap test specimen and ask the pathologist to examine the slide for sperm cells (see Chapter 21). She/he will also wash your cervix and vaginal walls with about a tablespoon of saline solution and then draw the fluid back up into a syringe. Part of the fluid sample can be tested for acid phosphatase, a chemical produced by the male prostate gland, and the remainder will be used for microscopic examination to detect sperm cells. Your clinician will record on your chart the number of sperm and whether the sperm were moving.

These routine tests do not distinguish between an attacker's sperm and your partner's sperm, and they may show no sperm at all, although in fact you have been raped. Your attacker may not have ejaculated, or could possibly be sterile. One important reason for having your exam promptly is that *evidence of sperm may disappear in eight to ten hours.*

TESTS FOR SEXUALLY TRANSMITTED INFECTION

Tests performed immediately after rape will not reveal whether you caught an infection from your attacker. Your clinician will test you for gonorrhea and syphilis anyway, but you must have both tests repeated. *Have another gonorrhea test within no longer than 2 weeks. Have another blood test for syphilis in 6 to 12 weeks.* Neither gonorrhea nor syphilis produces reliable symptoms in women in the early stages, so you cannot rely on how you feel to tell if you have an infection. Tell the clinician who performs your repeat exam if you were orally or anally raped; if so, she/he can collect specimens from your throat and/or rectum for gonorrhea culture and examine you carefully for evidence of syphilis. (Symptoms and treatment for gonorrhea and syphilis are described in Chapter 22.)

COLLECTION OF EVIDENCE

A thorough medical exam for rape includes a careful check for any substances on your body or your clothing that might be used as evidence. Some examples are:

- Dirt, blood, or grass stains on clothing
- Scrapings from under your fingernails, especially if you struggled with your attacker
- Pubic or scalp hair that looks different from your own, with samples of your hair for comparison
- Anything clinging to your hair or clothing that might be matched with the scene of your attack. You may be asked to leave your

clothing with your clinician if she/he thinks it might be needed as evidence.

ASSESSING YOUR PREGNANCY RISK

You may want to consider "morning-after" emergency birth control. The likelihood of conception after a single act of intercourse and your "morning-after" options are discussed in detail in Chapter 13. Your clinician can help you weigh the pros and cons in your case. *If you decide to use "morning-after" estrogen, you must begin taking it within 72 hours after the rape, and the sooner the better.* You must not use estrogen if you have a breast lump or unexplained vaginal bleeding, or if there is any chance you could already be pregnant.

Most clinicians believe that the IUD is not a good "morning-after" birth control choice for a woman who has been raped. You may have a higher than average risk of infection; if your attacker had a sexually transmitted infection, the IUD insertion process could carry those germs up into your uterus.

Reporting Rape to the Police

In addition to arranging for medical care, you may also want to report your rape to the police. You can report the rape immediately and decide later whether you want to prosecute. If you do decide to prosecute, you'll have a stronger case if you have reported the rape promptly. Reporting rape only means giving the police a full account of what happened, what your attacker looked like, and all other details you can remember. Most rape specialists believe that it is advisable at least to report your rape. Prosecuting your attacker means that the police will try to arrest him so that he can be tried on your charges. *Whether or not you bring charges against your attacker is completely up to you.*

Recovering From Rape

Emotional reactions to rape can be profound, and many women find that professional counseling is extremely helpful, whether rape occurred three hours or three years ago.

Counselors who work with rape victims report that it is common for a woman to work through phases of denial, anger, and/or depression before she can resolve the rape experience and put it to rest (2).

DENIAL

> I went to work the next morning as usual and didn't tell *anybody* what happened. After three months I had broken up with my boyfriend and was practically becoming an alcoholic. I called the rape crisis center. I talked to them on the phone three or four times and finally figured out that it was never going to *go away* until I could admit it was *there.*
>
> —*Woman, 23*

It can be hard to admit you need help getting through a crisis, especially if you are an independent person. If you don't feel like talking to a friend, partner, or family member, try a rape crisis center, mental health clinic, psychologist, or psychiatrist.

DEPRESSION

> I started crying in class, and I couldn't stop. It was about two weeks after I was raped. I was *so tired* of being brave and strong and picking up the pieces and all that crap. I felt *sorry* for myself, by God, and I think I had a right to!
>
> —*Woman, 19*

Depression, fears, nightmares, and feelings of alienation and helplessness are common after a few days, or even months later—whenever the full impact of what has happened really hits you. Most women are acutely aware of a loss of control, and it is a terrifying feeling.

ANGER

> About six weeks after they raped me, I started getting really mad at the whole world. I yelled at my secretary, my husband, and everybody else. My husband said, "Why don't you get mad at those punks who did it? I'm on your side, remember?"
>
> —*Woman, 40*

Counselors say that anger can often be a very good sign of healing, especially when it is directed—appropriately—at the rapist. Anger means that your internalized feelings are finding a way out. Try to channel your anger where it belongs; misdirected anger won't help you in the long run.

RESOLUTION

The day eventually comes, sooner or later, when you can stop being a rape victim. Emotional wounds do heal in time for most women. You can help yourself by relying on trusted friends and competent counselors to help you clarify your feelings. **Don't hesitate to get professional help** if your feelings are more than you can handle, even if it means long distance calls to a rape crisis center a hundred miles away.

> It took me a long time to admit I couldn't get over it by myself. *Everybody* knew I needed help before I could admit to it myself! I started seeing a psychologist once a week, and I read some things she recommended. It was a relief to learn it was *normal* to check every closet twice a night, and *normal* to worry that he'd find me, even though we'd moved to a different apartment.
> I'll never forget it, that's for sure. But it no longer haunts me.
>
> —*Woman, 50*

How Family and Friends Can Help

When someone you care about has been raped, you will want to help and support her. She will probably have a lot of powerful feelings she needs to express, so make sure she knows you are willing to listen. You can help her best if you know the facts about rape in general. There are many myths about rape ("no woman can be raped against her will," for example), and if you aren't certain about your own perceptions about rape, do some reading or get in touch with a rape crisis center for advice.

Rape affects you too, and you may have very distressing feelings of your own to sort out. You could feel angry or even guilty, as though her rape were somehow your fault. You may be uncertain about how to handle your own relationship with her, especially if the two of you are sexual partners. Make sure she knows you are willing to put her needs first during this diffucult time. She could want and need sexual intimacy with you very much, or she may not be interested in sex at all. Talk with her and ask her what will help her most. No one expects you to be a professional therapist, so don't hesitate to seek help from a rape crisis center or a mental health center when you need it.

REFERENCES

1. Brownmiller S: *Against Our Will: Men, Women, and Rape.* New York, Simon and Schuster, 1975.
2. Burgess AW, Holmstrom LL: *Rape: Victims of Crisis.* Bowie, Maryland, Robert J. Brody Company, 1974.

39 | Basic Facts About Surgery

Don't be surprised if you feel anxious or even fearful when your clinician has recommended surgery. These feelings are common and normal. Most people find that a detailed understanding of their particular health problem, and of the treatment possibilities involved, helps relieve anxiety. It is usually easier to cope with specific fears based on clear information about possible risks and complications than it is to ease the fear of something unknown. You may feel genuinely relieved after your clinician has reviewed the worst possibilities with you in detail.

Before you make a decision about surgery it is essential for you to know what all your options are, both surgical and non-surgical. You need to know enough about each option that you can weigh them rationally. Be sure you understand, *for each option,* the likely benefits you can expect, the precise procedure or treatment proposed, the possible complications that might occur immediately or later on, and what follow-up treatment, if any, you will need.

Once your decision is made, you will probably find the whole surgery process easier if you understand in advance exactly what will happen. Even pain is easier to bear if you know what is causing it, how it can be treated, and how long it will last.

A clear understanding of your problem and of your treatment is also important for your future medical care. You may want to write down the details of your surgery so you will be able to report them accurately to clinicians caring for you in the future. It may be hard to *remember ten years after surgery whether your right or your left ovary was the culprit, exactly what was removed, or what the technical name for your cyst was. Your clinician may be able to give you a copy of your surgical record and the pathologist's report to keep in your personal health files.*

Deciding About Surgery—Informed Consent

Deciding whether or not to have surgery is your decision, and no one else's. Your clinician will help you evaluate your options and will probably give you her/his clear recommendations, but you yourself are the one who must make the decision. No matter what kind of surgery your clinician has recommended, you will probably have many questions, not only about your specific medical problem and the surgery you are considering but also about hospital procedures, anesthesia, and how to plan for your recovery after surgery. You will give proof of your understanding and of your decision to have surgery by signing your surgical consent form. Be sure that you have clear, complete information about all your options, a detailed understanding of the recommended surgery, and a clear idea of the problems, complications, or risks involved, both in the surgery and in the other treatment alternatives. It is your right to have a full explanation and to have all your questions answered before you give your consent. ***Your responsibility*** in assuring that your consent to surgery is truly informed is to ask questions. Your clinician can't read your mind! You must ask—and keep asking—until you understand the answers, no matter how busy your clinician seems to be. (And by all means ask about costs if you want to know.) Remember that you have the right to change your mind any time before surgery.

Surgery is the best alternative for many problems discussed in this book, either to confirm a diagnosis or to treat your problem. Nevertheless, any surgery, and especially major surgery, has the potential for serious complications and even death. You will certainly want to make your decision carefully.

The following suggestions on how to avoid unnecessary surgery are summarized and adapted from Herbert S. Dennenberg's *A Shop-*

per's Guide to Surgery: Fourteen Rules on How to Avoid Unnecessary Surgery (1).

1. *Go first to your primary care clinician; ideally, your internist or family doctor.* Your own doctor may be able to treat you without surgery in many cases.

2. *Make sure that your surgeon is Board certified and a Fellow of the American College of Surgeons or the American College of Obstetricians and Gynecologists.* These organizations certify your physician's competence as a surgeon by oral, written, and clinical examinations. An appointment on the faculty of a medical school may also be an indication of competence. You can check at a large public library or a medical library in the *Medical Specialists Directory* for information on where your surgeon went to medical school and had specialty training. When you are selecting a surgeon, ask for at least two names from your primary care physician. Friends (possibly an operating room nurse), other doctors or nurses, or organizations such as the National Organization for Women or Planned Parenthood may also be able to recommend specific surgeons. *Talk to your surgeon.* You must have confidence in her or him. If you do not, find another surgeon.

3. *Get a second opinion from another physician before you agree to major surgery.* A second opinion from an independent source (rather than your surgeon's office partner, for example) may reveal other treatment options or clarify questions for you. Reputable, competent surgeons are *always* comfortable about a second opinion. If your surgeon seems unwilling for you to seek a second opinion, you may want to consider finding another surgeon. Be sure that you have a clear idea from your first surgeon about the urgency of your proposed surgery; you need to know how much time you have to get a second opinion.

4. *Make sure that your surgery is performed in an accredited hospital.* A list of accredited hospitals in your area is available from the Joint Commission on Accreditation of Hospitals, 645 North Michigan Avenue, Chicago, Illinois 60611.

5. *Don't push a doctor to perform surgery.* If you insist on a surgical solution to your problem, you will usually be able to find a surgeon willing to go along with you, even if surgery is not needed.

6. *Make sure that you understand your consent forms completely before you sign them.*

7. *Make sure that your surgeon knows and is willing to work with your primary care physician.* If you are over age 60, you need an internist as well as a surgeon or gynecologist involved in your postoperative care. If your surgeon belongs to a medical group that includes an internist, it may be easier to involve other specialists in your postoperative care if needed. Make sure that you know any other physicians your surgeon works with for night coverage.

8. *Select a surgeon who is not too busy to give you enough time and attention.* Good surgeons are busy, but they should answer all your questions and take the time to oversee your care before and after surgery.

9. *Be especially watchful if your surgeon recommends hysterectomy, hemorrhoidectomy, or tonsilectomy and adenoidectomy (T&A).* These are often cited as the most common unnecessary operations. Be certain that you understand whether your surgeon believes your operation is *necessary* or whether it is *elective*. Remember that except for cancer, uncontrollable infection, and uncontrollable hemorrhage, surgery is almost never truly necessary. Elective surgery may be desirable and in your best interest (hernia repair, for example); but unjustifiable, unnecessary surgery does occur. Be wary of a surgeon who seems to be pressuring you into elective surgery. Take the time to think it over, talk with your family or friends, obtain another opinion, and do some reading.

10. *You are entitled to make the final decision about surgery.* Don't let anyone else make the decision for you.

Anesthesia

Local anesthesia is often sufficient for minor surgical procedures that are short and technically simple. An anesthetic drug (similar to dental Novocain) is injected into the surgical site and blocks pain nerves in the area for about 30 to 60 minutes. Adverse reactions to local anesthesia are rare. Rash, hives, swelling, or asthma symptoms can occur because of allergy, and fatal allergic reactions are possible but are extremely rare. Local anesthetics can also cause heart rhythm changes,

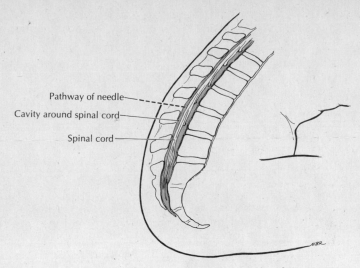

Pathway of needle
Cavity around spinal cord
Spinal cord

Illustration 1   Pathway of spinal anesthesia injection. Anesthetic enters the space that surrounds the spinal cord.

seizures, stroke, or even heart arrest if large or repeated doses are used. Local anesthesia is not recommended for long procedures that would require repeated injections of anesthetic drug, or when anesthesia of an extensive body area is needed.

General anesthesia is a term that includes the many different techniques that produce anesthesia sleep or complete nerve block in large areas of the body (regional anesthesia).

Regional techniques such as **spinal, epidural,** or **caudal block** anesthesia are commonly used for full-term delivery, D&C, and other relatively minor surgical procedures. An anesthetic is injected into the space surrounding the spinal cord (see Illustration 1) or in the area of a major nerve. The anesthetic drug blocks all nerve messages from the area supplied by that nerve, making a large portion of the body numb. If you have spinal anesthesia, for example, the entire lower half of your body, including your legs and feet, will be temporarily numb and paralyzed (see Illustration 2). You will be fully conscious and alert during regional anesthesia surgery. You may be given a sedative so that you won't be anxious or bothered by any discomfort that does occur. Regional anesthesia is most effective for blocking pain from superficial tissues like skin and muscle, and to some degree it also diminishes pain sensations from pelvic organs inside the abdomen.

Headache is the most common side effect with spinal anesthesia. It

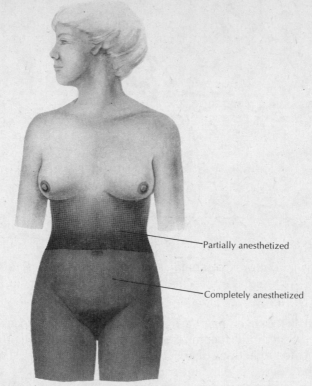

Illustration 2 Areas anesthetized by spinal anesthesia.

is less likely to occur if anesthesia is administered by an experienced anesthesiologist who uses a small needle to inject the drug, but head-aches can be severe enough to delay discharge from the hospital and may persist for as long as two weeks. Injury or infection that damages the spinal cord could cause permanent paralysis, but is extremely rare. It is important that your anesthesiologist watch you carefully until the regional anesthesia effects have worn off, for muscle relaxation in the anesthetized area can cause a sudden drop in blood pressure. Your blood pressure and heart rate will be checked frequently, and your anesthesiologist will use drugs to raise your blood pressure if it drops to a dangerous level.

General anesthesia to induce *anesthetic sleep* is usually recom-mended for major operations such as hysterectomy (see Chapter 41) and laparoscopy tubal ligation (see Chapter 15). Your anesthesiologist will use a combination of anesthesia drugs and gases to induce sleep and block pain sensations. You will probably be given drugs by injection about 30 minutes before surgery to relax you and to dry up mucus and saliva production. A typical preoperative drug combination is atropine and a narcotic such as Demerol (meperidine). Your anesthesiologist will use an intravenous tube in your arm to administer drugs during surgery. After you are in the operating room and positioned on the operating table, your anesthesiologist will probably inject a rapid-acting barbiturate such as Pentothal to induce sleep. Pentothal takes effect within seconds and produces sound sleep almost immediately. You will not be able to say more than one or two words before you fall asleep. After you are asleep, a tube will be placed through your mouth into your windpipe to insure a clear pathway for breathing. Anesthetic gas that you breathe along with oxygen will block pain sensations. The anesthesiologist may use muscle-paralyzing drugs to insure complete muscle relaxation, in which case the anesthesiologist will breathe *for you* by pumping oxygen and anesthesia gas from the anesthesia machine into your lungs. As your surgery is nearing completion, the anesthesiologist will stop the anesthetic gas and Pentothal, and you will be awake before you leave the operating room. You probably will not remember the operating room, however, and are more likely to remember waking up in the recovery room, where you will be under close observation for about two hours after surgery.

If anesthesia sleep is brief, as for a tubal ligation or D&C, for example, you will recover quickly from the anesthesia. Most women are fully awake, able to walk comfortably, and fairly alert within four hours after a tubal ligation or D&C. Anesthesia drugs do slow reflexes and impair coordination, however, so it is essential that you avoid driving or operating dangerous machinery for at least 24 hours after any general anesthesia.

Anesthesia sleep is less risky than you might imagine, but complications are possible. The overall death rate for complications of anesthesia sleep and regional anesthesia is about 2.7 per 10,000 procedures for women (7.1 for men) (1). The risk of serious problems that could lead to permanent damage or death, such as stroke, or heart or breathing arrest, is low for young, healthy women and higher for older women or women with serious medical problems such as heart disease or emphysema.

The anesthesiologist will probably visit you the evening before surgery or will take time just before surgery to review your medical history, answer your questions, and discuss the type of anesthesia she/he plans in your case. Be sure to tell her/him about any drug allergies or adverse reactions you have had, and answer all questions honestly and completely.

Just before surgery, the anesthesiologist will ask you if you have had anything to eat or drink in the last eight hours. Be sure that your answer is accurate. Anesthesia risk is greatly increased if you have anything in your stomach, for you could vomit and inhale fluid into your lungs. If your surgery is not an emergency, your anesthesiologist may even recommend that surgery be delayed long enough for your stomach to empty.

Preparing for Surgery

It is very important for you to undertstand and follow instructions for preparing for surgery. If you are late arriving at the hospital or have not had the proper lab tests in advance, for example, hospital rules may force your surgeon to cancel your surgery appointment.

A blood count and urinalysis are usually required before any general anesthesia surgery. If you are having a hysterectomy or other major surgery, additional tests to determine your blood-clotting time and blood type, and a blood cross-match for transfusion may also be required. Your surgeon or anesthesiologist may recommend more thorough evaluation, including a cardiogram and a chest x-ray if you have had previous medical problems or are over age 40.

If you will be having an abdominal incision, a nurse will probably wash your abdomen carefully and shave your entire abdomen, including any pubic hair that covers your lower abdomen. Vaginal surgery preparation will require shaving all your pubic hair and your upper thighs as well. Shaving is not always necessary for D&C or laparoscopy tubal ligation. Your surgeon may also order an enema the evening before major surgery.

Just before major surgery, a narrow rubber tube (catheter) will be inserted through your urinary opening (urethra) into your bladder. The catheter insures that your bladder will remain empty throughout surgery and therefore will be less vulnerable to injury. Insertion of the catheter is quick, but if you are not already under anesthesia, you may have a slight stinging sensation for a second or two.

What to Expect After Surgery

The major effects of general anesthesia subside gradually over the first two to six hours, but you may have fatigue, mild nausea, drowsiness, and impaired reflexes for 24 to 48 hours. The length of time you need to allow for recovery from surgery depends on what kind of surgery you had and on the kind of medical problem that necessitated your surgery. Recovery is rapid after minor procedures such as D&C or tubal ligation, and you can safely plan to resume normal activities within the first week; many women are fully recovered within two or three days after surgery.

Major surgery such as hysterectomy will require about *six weeks* for full recovery, assuming that you do not have any serious complications. During the first two days after surgery, you will probably have narcotic pain shots, and you may not remember this time clearly. You will be getting out of bed to urinate as soon as your catheter is removed, usually the morning after surgery. During the first three or four days, your pain will subside so that pain injections can be replaced with milder pain pills; and your intestines will gradually resume normal functioning. You will first be given clear liquids to drink and can have normal foods once you begin to have bowel contractions, rectal gas, and bowel movements. You will not *feel* hungry until your stomach and intestines have resumed normal contractions, and if you do eat solid food too soon, you will probably have bloating and nausea. Once your bowel function is normal, perhaps with the aid of an enema, you are ready to go home. Most women go home five or six days after major surgery.

SURVIVING IN THE HOSPITAL

With a little planning and good information, you can make any hospital stay less unpleasant.

- *Have a clear idea of what is going to happen.* If you know beforehand what kind of incision you will have, whether or not a catheter will be used, how long you will need intravenous tubes, and what medications you will be given, you can avoid surprises once you are in the hospital.
- *Remember that your doctor or surgeon must write all orders.* If something doesn't happen when you want it to, it is probably be-

cause there is no order in your chart. Nurses can only carry out your doctor's orders and provide routine nursing care. If you need something, be sure that your doctor knows about it, including simple things like taking a shower or having your hair washed.

- *Gain the support of the nursing staff.* Thoughtfulness and courtesy do pay off. Ask for what you need, but let your surgeon be the one to make demands or settle any problems. If you are labeled a "difficult" patient, your hospital stay can be miserable.
- *Have your doctor talk to an appointed family member or friend after your surgery.* When you wake up, your family member or friend can tell you how your surgery went and how you are doing. Your surgeon probably won't see you until the evening or even the next morning.
- *Order the food you want.* If you are a vegetarian or have a special dietary need, make sure that you talk to the dietary department before you enter the hospital. If your hospital has a reputation for bad food, you might try the vegetarian meals; often they are of higher quality than the regular meals.
- *Bring something simple you like to do.* You will probably be able to rent a television set for your hospital room, but you will also enjoy having several good books or a portable hobby.

HOME RECOVERY

Before you leave the hospital, your surgeon will remove the clips or stiches from your incision and will give you instructions on caring for your incision, taking medications, bathing, eating, exercising, and other activities. In some cases, absorbable stitches are used on the skin, and these do not have to be removed. Your incision will seal closed within about three to four days, and after it seals you can safely bathe or shower. Your incision will be prominent, a deeper red than the normal skin, and will have a firm lump or cord of fibrous tissue just underneath. The fibrous lump and deep color of the incision gradually subside over the first one to two months. Numbness in the incision area is also common and may persist for several months.

Think of your home recovery time after major surgery as three separate two-week periods. During the first two weeks you will need complete rest; do not plan any activities outside the house, and do *no* cleaning, cooking, lifting, or housework. Take your temperature three times each day (at 2, 6, and 10 P.M.), drink plenty of fluids, and plan a mild, bland diet. Do not put *anything* in your vagina.

During the second two weeks at home (three to four weeks after surgery), you can begin limited activity. Short walks in your yard, a short ride (do not drive yourself), or a trip out to dinner would be reasonable. You may begin to resume limited household activities, but avoid heavy lifting or prolonged standing. Rest if you feel tired, and take your temperature at least once a day or any time you feel feverish.

During the last two weeks (five to six weeks after surgery), you can gradually increase all your activities to normal. Do not put anything in your vagina (no intercourse) until after your postoperative checkup, which will probably be scheduled during this two-week time.

In other words, someone else must do the cooking, cleaning and shopping, and take over any child care responsibilities you have for at least four to five weeks after your surgery. During the first two weeks or so you will need someone available to help take care of you during at least part of the day and in the evening. Unless you have unusual medical problems or complications, however, you will not need professional nursing care at home.

Common Surgery Procedures

Bartholin's Cyst Removal (Cystectomy) or Marsupialization: Surgery to remove an enlarged Bartholin's gland or to create a permanent opening in the gland so that gland secretions cannot accumulate. Although general anesthesia is often recommended, this is a fairly minor surgical procedure, involving only external structures. Recovery in two or three weeks can be expected (see Chapter 22).

Conization of the Cervix: Surgery to remove the surface of the cervix. Preparations are similar to those for vaginal hysterectomy, but recovery is more rapid (three to five weeks) (see Chapter 27).

D&C (Dilation and Curettage): Scraping of the uterine lining with instruments inserted through the dilated cervical canal. No incision is required. (See Chapter 40.)

Exploratory Laparoscopy: The laparoscopy tube is inserted through a 1-inch incision below the navel and permits the surgeon to see the uterus, tubes, and ovaries inside the abdomen. Preparations, procedure, and recovery are similar to those for laparoscopic tubal ligation (see Chapter 15).

Exploratory Laparotomy: Abdominal surgery for diagnosing a problem; for example, when ectopic pregnancy is suspected. An abdominal incision permits the surgeon to examine the uterus, tubes, ovaries, and abdominal organs and to correct abnormalities discovered. Preparations, procedure, and recovery are similar to those for abdominal hysterectomy.

Hysterectomy: Surgery to remove the uterus through an incision in the abdomen (abdominal hysterectomy) or in the vagina (vaginal hysterectomy). (See Chapter 41).

Oophorectomy: Surgery to remove one or both ovaries, or part of an ovary. An abdominal incision is used. Preparations, procedure, and recovery are similar to those for abdominal hysterectomy.

Pelvic Repair: Surgery to correct impaired pelvic muscle support damaged by childbirth, often performed in conjunction with vaginal hysterectomy. Preparations, procedure, and recovery are similar to those for vaginal hysterectomy.

Tubal Ligation: Abdominal, postpartum, laparoscopy, vaginal, and mini-laparotomy techniques are described in Chapter 15.

REFERENCES

1. Dennenberg HS: A shopper's guide to surgery: fourteen rules on how to avoid unnecessary surgery. Unpublished paper. See Suggested Reading for instructions on ordering this paper.
2. Phillips JC: Public health aspects of critical care medicine: Anesthesia mortality. *Clinical Anesthesia* 10:220–244, 1974.

40 | Dilation and Curettage (D&C), Uterine Scraping

Dilation and curettage (D&C) is one of the most frequently performed of all surgical procedures. About 4% of all women undergo D&C each year, and it is likely that you could need a D&C at some time in your life. The goal of D&C is to scrape away part of the uterine lining (endometrium) (See Illustration 1).

Uterine scraping may be recommended to stop vaginal bleeding, to determine the cause of abnormal bleeding or spotting, or to remove retained fragments of fetal or placental tissue after full-term delivery, miscarriage, or abortion. Shreds of tissue scraped from the uterine lining during D&C can be microscopically examined by a pathologist for an accurate determination of whether or not uterine cancer is present. Your surgeon can locate and remove uterine polyps (benign tumors that arise from uterine lining tissue) during D&C. Heavy vaginal bleeding is usually greatly reduced or completely stopped by a D&C procedure unless the bleeding has been caused by a traumatic injury to the uterus.

The D&C Procedure

General anesthesia (anesthesia sleep) or spinal anesthesia is usually recommended for a D&C. Local anesthesia similar to that for abortion

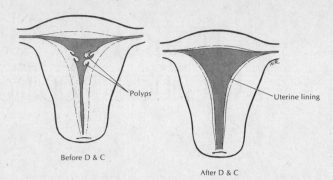

Before D & C

After D & C

Illustration 1 The D&C procedure removes most of the uterine lining and any polyps that arise from the lining.

can be used for D&C (see Chapter 20), but local anesthesia does not fully eliminate pain. Since the goal of D&C is careful, thorough exploration of the entire uterine cavity, it is important that patient discomfort not be an obstacle to performing the procedure properly.

Once anesthesia is complete, you are placed in the standard pelvic examination position. Your vulva, inner thighs, and vagina are thoroughly cleansed, and the entire area is covered with sterile towels to leave just your vagina exposed. Some surgeons recommend that your pubic hair be shaved, and others do not.

The first step is careful pelvic examination. Your abdominal and pelvic muscles are completely relaxed under anesthesia, and your surgeon can use this opportunity to examine your uterus, tubes, and ovaries very carefully.

Next, a speculum is placed in your vagina so that your surgeon can see your cervix. The cervix is held steady with a clamp (tenaculum), and the angle of your cervical canal and depth of your uterus are determined by inserting a thin metal rod (uterine sound) through the canal and up to the top of your uterus.

At this point, your surgeon may obtain some tissue specimens from your cervical canal lining itself. A very narrow rod (curet) that has a sharp, spoon-shaped tip is used for the scraping.

Next your surgeon will widen (dilate) your cervical canal by inserting tapered rods (dilators) in graduated sizes until the canal is about ½ inch in diameter (see Illustration 2).

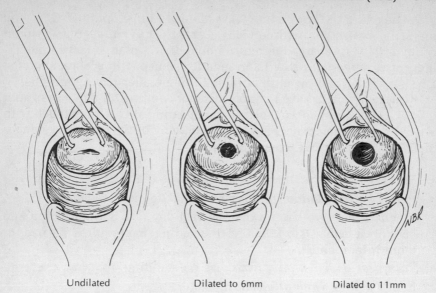

| Undilated | Dilated to 6mm | Dilated to 11mm |

Illustration 2 The first step of a D&C is dilation of the cervical canal. Graduated metal rods are used to widen the cervical opening.

After dilation, your surgeon locates and removes any polyps that you may have on the uterine lining and then uses a slightly larger curet to scrape each area of your entire uterine lining (see Illustration 3). All the shreds of tissue that are removed are carefully collected so that they can be microscopically examined. When scraping is completed, the curet, clamp, and speculum are removed.

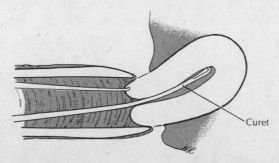

Curet

Illustration 3 The surgeon scrapes away uterine lining with a sharp, spoon-shaped curet.

The entire D&C procedure takes about 10 to 20 minutes. Once you are fully awake, you will be ready to return to your regular hospital room or to be discharged to return home. If you plan to leave immediately after surgery, be sure to arrange for someone to accompany you. Don't try to drive a car until at least 24 hours after having anesthesia.

It is common to have light bleeding or spotting for a few days after a D&C, although some women have no bleeding at all. Get in touch with your surgeon immediately if you develop any of the following danger signs for possible D&C complications:

- *Fever:* oral temperature of 100.4 degrees (Fahrenheit) or more
- *Persistent abdominal pain* or severe abdominal *cramps*
- *Bleeding* heavier than on the heaviest day of a normal period and lasting more than 6 to 12 hours, or bleeding that requires five pads or more in one hour
- *Faintness or weakness;* dizziness on standing up
- Foul-smelling *vaginal discharge*

Most surgeons advise women to avoid intercourse, douching, and tampons for the first two weeks after D&C until the cervical canal has had a chance to shrink back to normal size. These precautions may help avoid contaminating the uterus with bacteria that might cause infection.

Be sure to see your surgeon for your postoperative checkup about two weeks after surgery. This visit is almost always included in her/his surgical fee, and it is very important. Your surgeon will check for tenderness in your uterus or tubes that might indicate infection, and will check to be certain that your cervical canal has returned to normal size. The pathologist's report on your D&C specimen will be completed about one week after your surgery. Your clinician may call you to give you the results by phone or may discuss them with you at your checkup visit.

Risks and Complications

D&C is a simple procedure, and complications are rare. The overall death rate for healthy women under 50 years of age undergoing D&C is about 2 deaths per 10,000 procedures (1). In addition to complications of anesthesia (see Chapter 39), the possible problems you should be aware of are:

INFECTION

Infection inside the uterus and tubes is the most common serious problem following D&C. Infection can occur any time instruments are inserted into your uterine cavity and is usually caused by bacteria carried into your uterus from your own cervix, vagina, or bowel. The risk of infection is greatly increased if you have gonorrhea, have recently been exposed to gonorrhea, or have had pelvic infections in the past. Infections usually resolve quickly with antibiotic treatment, but they may be serious enough to require further surgery, including total hysterectomy, and can even cause death.

HEMORRHAGE

Heavy bleeding during or after a D&C is possible if your uterine walls are injured during scraping, if a polyp or fibroid tumor is only partially removed, if your cervix is injured by the clamp, or if you have abnormal bleeding tendencies. Hemorrhage is rare; more often, D&C will decrease or stop abnormal bleeding.

DAMAGE TO THE UTERUS OR OTHER PELVIC ORGANS

Puncture (perforation) of the uterus by a surgical instrument is a possible complication of D&C, although it is very rare. If the puncture damages only the uterus, chances are good that the defect will close and heal spontaneously without further treatment. Damage to nearby blood vessels, bladder, or bowel is possible, and immediate surgery to repair the injury could be necessary. If your surgeon suspects that you have a perforation, she/he may want you to stay in the hospital for observation, and may recommend laparoscopy (see Chapter 15) to assess whether there is any damage to your uterus or internal organs that needs surgical repair.

SCAR TISSUE FORMATION IN THE UTERINE CAVITY

A very rare complication of a D&C is formation of scar tissue that partially or completely blocks the uterine cavity. This problem, called

Asherman's syndrome, can cause infertility and the absence of menstrual periods; it most commonly occurs among women who have a D&C at the time they have an infected uterus, but can occur after a routine D&C or uncomplicated vacuum abortion procedure as well.

Contraindications

A contraindication is a medical condition that renders a course of treatment inadvisable or unsafe that might otherwise be recommended. Because D&C is a procedure of great importance for detecting uterine cancer as early as possible, there are no absolute contraindications to D&C. There are several medical conditions, however, that may mean that D&C should not be performed unless it is absolutely necessary:

- Uterine infection, tubal infection, or cervicitis. It is highly desirable to treat and cure infection before surgery.
- Pregnancy. D&C must be avoided if you wish to continue your pregnancy. D&C *is* an abortion technique, but the vacuum technique is safer and more effective when abortion is your goal (see Chapter 20).
- Serious medical problems, such as heart or kidney disease, that increase anesthesia risk.
- Blood disorders that impair blood clotting or cause excessive bleeding.

REFERENCE

1. Moses L: Comparison of crude and standardized anesthetic death rates, in Bunker JP, Forest WH, Mosteller F, et al (eds): *The National Halothane Study: Report of the Subcommittee on the National Halothane Study.* Washington, DC, US Government Printing Office, 1969, Chapter IV-2.

41 | Hysterectomy

Hysterectomy is one of the most common of all surgical procedures ("hyster" means uterus; "ectomy" means surgical removal). It is often cited as an example of unnecessary surgery. A 1973 nationwide study showed that if current surgery rates continue, more than half of all women will have had hysterectomies by the time they are 65 years old [1,2]. Hysterectomy rates are highest in geographical areas where surgeons are plentiful and among poor women who receive care at large teaching hospitals [3,4].

As you assess the issues of hysterectomy and unnecessary surgery, however, it is important to remember that in most cases the woman undergoing surgery is doing so voluntarily, and often is very eager to have the surgery. There are many situations in which hysterectomy, although not necessary to preserve or save a woman's life, does add greatly to the quality of life. A woman who has incapacitating menstrual cramps for seven days each month because of endometriosis may feel that the risks and expense of surgery are justified, even though hysterectomy is not medically necessary in her case.

Reasons for Hysterectomy

The four situations in which hysterectomy is necessary to preserve or save a woman's life are:

1. To remove cancer originating in the vagina, cervix, uterus, fallopian tubes, or ovaries
2. To stop severe, uncontrollable hemorrhage
3. To stop severe, uncontrollable infection
4. As part of surgery for life-threatening problems affecting the intestine or bladder when it is technically impossible to correct the primary problem without removing the uterus as well

Hysterectomy in any other situation is elective and not truly necessary. In many cases, however, elective hysterectomy can be well justified. Surgery may be appropriate treatment for serious problems when other treatment is not available or has been ineffective. Surgery may also be justified for problems that are likely to become more severe at some future time. Surgery that is delayed until a simple problem becomes a severe problem or until emergency surgery is necessary incurs a higher overall surgery risk than does elective surgery. Some problems that may justify hysterectomy are:

- Recurrent attacks of pelvic infection
- Extensive endometriosis
- Large or extensive fibroid tumors; fibroids causing bladder pressure or disabling symptoms
- Loss of pelvic muscle support from childbirth injury that is severe enough to interfere with bladder or bowel function
- Vaginal bleeding that is excessive enough to cause anemia and cannot be controlled with hormones

Hysterectomy may be a wise choice in other situations as well, but when medical reasons for surgery are vague and other treatment alternatives with lower risks are available, it is especially important to consider surgery carefully. Many clinicians believe, for example, that hysterectomy is not appropriate when the main goal of surgery is sterilization; tubal ligation and vasectomy are safer alternatives. Problems such as pelvic pain, backache, pelvic pressure, menstrual cramps, and heavy discharge often can be managed effectively without surgery.

Unless you have a life-threatening problem, such as cancer, hemorrhage, or infection, you have time to think about hysterectomy before you make a final decision. You may find it helpful to do some reading and see a second clinician for an independent assessment of your treatment options.

Hysterectomy Procedures

There are several different hysterectomy techniques (see Illustration 1). Be sure that you understand exactly which procedure your surgeon plans to use and why.

Total Abdominal Hysterectomy (TAH): Removal of the uterus and cervix through an incision in the lower abdomen. The fallopian tubes and ovaries are not removed.

Total Abdominal Hysterectomy and Bilateral Salpingo-Oophorectomy (TAH and BSO): Removal of the uterus, cervix, fallopian tubes, and ovaries through an incision in the lower abdomen.

"Complete Hysterectomy": A lay term sometimes used for removal of the ovaries in addition to the uterus, fallopian tubes, and cervix. "Complete hysterectomy" is the same as TAH and BSO.

Vaginal Hysterectomy: Removal of the uterus and cervix through an incision inside the vagina. The fallopian tubes and ovaries are not removed.

Subtotal Hysterectomy: Removal of the uterus but not the cervix. The fallopian tubes and ovaries are not removed. This procedure is rarely used because without the uterus the cervix has no essential functions and does pose a future cancer risk.

If you are under 40 years of age when you have a hysterectomy, your clinician will probably recommend that your ovaries be left in place unless you have cervical, uterine, or ovarian cancer, or extensive pelvic infection or endometriosis that affects your ovaries. Your ovaries are your source of estrogen and progesterone, and if they are removed, you are likely to develop menopause symptoms.

Removal of the ovaries (oophorectomy) is usually recommended

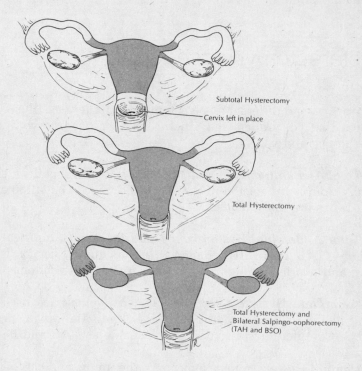

Subtotal Hysterectomy

Cervix left in place

Total Hysterectomy

Total Hysterectomy and
Bilateral Salpingo-oophorectomy
(TAH and BSO)

Illustration 1   Subtotal hysterectomy leaves the cervix in place. Total
hysterectomy means that all of the uterus (including the
cervix) is removed. The operation for removal of the
uterus, tubes, and ovaries is called total abdominal hysterectomy and bilateral salpingo-oophorectomy (TAH-
BSO).

for women over 40 who have hysterectomy (5). The rationale for this
recommendation is that ovarian hormone production will soon cease in
any case with menopause and that removing the ovaries is a cancer
prevention measure. Of all women who develop cancer of the ovary,
about 44% previously had a hysterectomy between the ages of 40 and
50 (6). If you have already reached menopause, you would not notice

any difference whether your ovaries were removed or not. If you are over 40 but have not reached menopause, your surgeon will discuss this issue with you and should be willing to respect your feelings. Synthetic hormones can be used to prevent disabling menopause symptoms if your ovaries are removed before menopause, but synthetic hormones themselves have disadvantages and risks to consider. (See Chapter 36 for a discussion of the estrogen replacement therapy controversy.)

Vaginal hysterectomy is only recommended when your ovaries will be left in place. This operation is popular because the incision scar is inside your vagina, out of sight, and because recovery after surgery is often quicker and less painful than with abdominal surgery. The vaginal approach is especially appropriate if repair of pelvic muscle support is the reason for your surgery. Vaginal surgery may not be advisable if your uterus is very large or if you have extensive scarring from infection or endometriosis. The risk of postoperative infection is higher with vaginal surgery than it is with abdominal surgery.

Any form of hysterectomy is major surgery and requires general anesthesia. You can expect to stay in the hospital for at least five or six days and then at home for about six weeks. Read Chapter 39 carefully to review preoperative procedures for major surgery, anesthesia, and what to expect after surgery.

Total Abdominal Hysterectomy and Total Abdominal Hysterectomy and Bilateral Salpingo-oophorectomy (TAH, and TAH and BSO)

After surgical preparations and anesthesia are complete, your surgeon makes a horizontal 5-inch incision across the middle of your lower abdomen (see Illustration 2). If you have had previous surgery with a vertical incision, your surgeon will follow your old incision line in order to remove the original scar tissue and leave you with one vertical scar. The incision is extended through the muscle and connective tissue layers of your abdomen and through the thin translucent membrane (peritoneum) that lines your abdominal cavity. Once the ab-

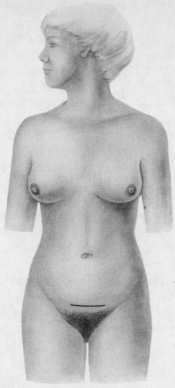

Illustration 2   Hysterectomy is often performed with a horizontal (Pfannenstiel) abdominal incision.

dominal cavity is open, your surgeon inspects all your pelvic organs,
intestines, and bladder and checks your kidneys, liver, and gallbladder
with her/his fingers to detect any abnormalities. Then, instruments are
used to hold your incision open and hold your intestines out of the way
so that your uterus, tubes, and ovaries can be seen clearly (see Illustration 3). Your surgeon removes your uterus (or uterus, tubes, and
ovaries) by first placing clamps across the ligaments and blood vessels
that attach these organs to the rest of your pelvis. Each clamp site is
then carefully cut and stitched to prevent bleeding. The juncture of the
cervix with the back of the vagina can be stitched closed, or in some
cases left partially open to allow fluid from the surgery site to drain out
during healing; in that case, the deep vaginal incision site will close on
its own within two or three weeks.

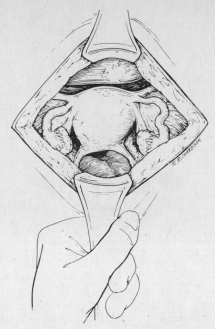

Illustration 3   Your surgeon can see all your pelvic organs clearly during abdominal hysterectomy.

After your uterus and cervix (and sometimes ovaries and tubes) are removed, your surgeon repairs each layer—the peritoneum, connective tissue, muscle, and skin—to close your incision.

Vaginal Hysterectomy

After anesthesia, you will be placed in the pelvic examination position and your vagina and thighs will be cleansed. Your surgeon holds open the walls of your vagina with special specula and makes an incision through the inside of your vagina where the vaginal walls meet the cervix (see Illustration 4). The incision is extended through muscle, connective tissue, and peritoneum into your abdominal cavity. Your surgeon uses a clamp to pull down on your cervix in order to locate, suture, and cut the ligaments and blood vessels that attach the uterus to other pelvic structures. As your uterus is cut free, uterus and cervix are

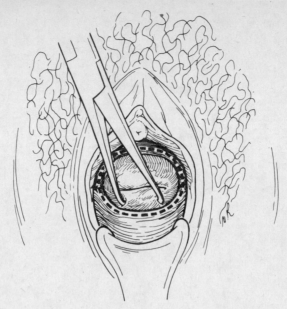

Illustration 4   Incision for vaginal hysterectomy.

removed through the opening in your vagina. Finally, your surgeon repairs each of the incision layers and closes the incision.

Hysterectomy Complications and Risks

The risk of death or serious complications with hysterectomy depends on your age and general health status, the competence of your surgeon, the quality of hospital care, and the specific procedure used in your case (7). For relatively healthy women under 45, the death rate for hysterectomy is about 50 in 100,000 cases (8). The death risk is increased about 15-fold for a woman over 50 who has high blood pressure.

Deaths are rare, but serious complications are not rare. About 40% of hysterectomy patients have one or more major complications (5,7).

INFECTION

Infection is the most common serious hysterectomy complication. About 30 to 40% of women who have hysterectomy require treatment for infection (5,7). In most cases, infection is mild and involves only the bladder or the surface of the incision, so it responds readily to antibiotic treatment. Infection problems can be severe, however. An abscess might require further surgery, and uncontrolled infection is a major cause of the few deaths that do occur with hysterectomy.

Infection risk is 50% higher after vaginal hysterectomy than after abdominal hysterectomy (7), and many surgeons prescribe antibiotics before and after vaginal hysterectomy to reduce infection rates.

HEMORRHAGE

Bleeding can occur during surgery, and about 15% of women who have hysterectomy have blood transfusions (7). Heavy bleeding can also occur after you go home and is most common about 7 to 14 days after surgery when your internal stitches begin to dissolve. Less than 1% of women require hospitalization or transfusion because of late bleeding, however.

URINARY PROBLEMS

Problems with urination are quite common during the first few weeks after hysterectomy, but usually are not serious. About half of all women have bladder or kidney infection after hysterectomy. About 5% of women are unable to urinate on their own as late as 12 days after surgery, and hospitalization is prolonged until difficulty with urination resolves and the urine catheter can be removed (5). Damage to the bladder or the tubes (ureters) that carry urine from the kidneys to the bladder occurs during hysterectomy in about 1 out of 200 cases (5,7).

BOWEL PROBLEMS

Bowel problems are rare, but can occur if your intestines are damaged during surgery or if scar tissue interferes with intestinal contractions. Later surgery to remove scar tissue may be required in as many as 2% of hysterectomy patients.

ABNORMAL BLOOD CLOTTING

Thrombophlebitis occurs in about 1% of women who have hysterectomy (7) and can be a potentially fatal problem because an abnormal clot from a leg or pelvic vein could break loose and travel to the lung. Block in circulation by a clot could cause a stroke with permanent brain damage or even death.

LATE COMPLICATIONS

Among the late complications of hysterectomy are shortening or narrowing of the vagina; damage to ovary blood circulation that results in impaired hormone production or development of ovary cysts; persistent vaginal discharge because of improper healing of a vaginal incision and protrusion of the cut end of the fallopian tube; and loss of pelvic muscle support. All these problems are rare.

DANGER SIGNS

Any of the following danger signs may indicate complications after hysterectomy. Get in touch with your surgeon immediately.

- *Fever* (temperature over 100.4 degrees Fahrenheit by mouth)
- *Pain* not relieved by the medication your surgeon has given you
- *Bright red vaginal bleeding* that soaks two pads in an hour, or forms large clots
- More than three days without a normal bowel movement
- Persistent bladder discomfort, burning with urination, blood in your urine, or inability to urinate
- *Pain, swelling, tenderness, or redness in your leg*
- *Chest pain, cough, difficulty in breathing,* or coughing blood

Other Effects of Hysterectomy

A hysterectomy can provide advantages unrelated to the problem that necessitated your surgery, for the uterus and cervix are the source of many problems. After hysterectomy you will have no further menstrual bleeding or cramps; no pregnancy risk; no risk for cervical or uterine cancer; no risk for serious pelvic infection; and a reduced chance for vaginitis or abnormal vaginal discharge.

Hysterectomy does not alter your normal hormone patterns unless your ovaries are also removed. As long as your ovaries aren't removed, there is no medical or chemical reason that you should feel different or that your sex drive should be altered. If your ovaries are removed, and you have not already undergone menopause, then your supply of estrogen and progesterone hormones (produced by the ovary) will abruptly end. You are likely to have hot flashes and possibly other symptoms associated with menopause unless you are able to take synthetic estrogen hormone replacement beginning soon after surgery.

There is very little good research about the effects of hysterectomy on sexual functioning, however. The uterus and cervix are not necessary for arousal or orgasm, and it is possible that you will notice no change at all in your sexual functioning after hysterectomy. If the gynecologic problems that necessitated surgery were interfering with your sexual activity or if fear of pregnancy was a major concern for you, it is likely that hysterectomy will improve your sexual functioning.

It is not accurate to say that hysterectomy has no effect on a woman's sexuality, however. The uterus and cervix do *participate* in sexual arousal and orgasm responses. After hysterectomy, the shape and length of your vagina will be slightly altered, and you will have a scar line in the back of your vagina. It is possible that you will notice physical differences during sexual activity. Because emotions are so important in sexual functioning, it is also possible that your feelings about loss of fertility may have an impact on your sexuality. You may find that your partner has reactions as well.

> I didn't have any trouble having orgasms after my hysterectomy, but I certainly was *afraid* I would. My orgasms do feel a little bit different now. There is definitely something *missing* that I used to feel—a kind of muscle contraction deep inside during orgasm. It doesn't really bother me at all, but I do notice it sometimes.
>
> —*Woman, 37*

Many women are concerned about weight gain after hysterectomy. If hysterectomy is necessary because of prolonged infection, it is likely that you will feel better after surgery and your appetite may increase. Whether or not your ovaries are removed, however, there is no evidence that hysterectomy can cause weight gain.

REFERENCES

1. *Surgical Operations in Short Stay Hospitals: United States, 1968.* National Center for Health Statistics, Department of Health, Education and Welfare, Publication No (HSM) 73-1762, January 1973.
2. *Surgery in Short Stay Hospitals: United States, 1973.* National Center for Health Statistics, Department of Health, Education and Welfare, Publication No (HRA) 75-1120, vol 24, No 3 (suppl), May 30, 1975.
3. Bunker JP: Surgical manpower: A comparison of operations and surgeons in the United States and in England and Wales. *New England Journal of Medicine* 282:135–144, 1970.
4. Wennberg J, Gittlesohn A: Health care delivery in Maine: I. Patterns of use of common surgical procedures. *Journal of the Maine Medical Association* 66:123–130, 1975.
5. *TeLinde's Operative Gynecology*, ed 5, Mattingly RF (ed). Philadelphia, Lippincott, 1977.
6. Terz JJ, Barber HR, Brunschwig A: Incidence of carcinoma in the retained ovary. *American Journal of Surgery* 113:511–515, 1967.
7. Ledger W, Child M: The hospital care of patients undergoing hysterectomy: An analysis of 12,026 patients from the Professional Activity Study. *American Journal of Obstetrics and Gynecology* 117:423–433, 1973.
8. Bunker JP, McPherson K, Henneman PC: Elective hysterectomy, in *Costs, Risks and Benefits of Surgery*. New York, Oxford University Press, 1977, pp 262–276.

Suggested Reading

General

The Alan Guttmacher Institute: *Eleven Million Teenagers: What Can Be Done About the Epidemic of Adolescent Pregnancies in the United States*. New York, The Alan Guttmacher Institute, 1976.

A comprehensive report on the problems of teenage pregnancy with extensive statistics and thoughtful analysis.

Anderson, Barrie, Connell, Elizabeth, Kaplan, Helen Singer, et al.: *The Menopause Book*. New York, Hawthorn Books, 1977.

Changes of menopause discussed in detail from the perspective of women authors who view menopause as a normal transition rather than a disease.

The Boston Women's Health Book Collective: *Our Bodies, Ourselves*. (Revised and expanded edition.) New York, Simon and Schuster, 1976.

A pioneering book that covers a wide range of women's physical, emotional, and social issues with excellent annotated bibliographies for further reading. Also available in Spanish.

The Diagram Group: *Woman's Body: An Owner's Manual*. New York, Bantam Books, 1978.

Brief but clear descriptions of normal physical structures including all internal organs, together with discussion of common problems that women encounter.

539

Eagan, Andrea Boroft: *Why Am I So Miserable If These Are the Best Years of My Life? A Survival Guide for the Young Woman.* Philadelphia, J. B. Lippincott, 1976.

Sensible, practical, explicit information for the adolescent woman.

Gordon, Sol: *Let's Make Sex a Household Word.* New York, The John Day Co. (10 E. 53rd Street), 1975.

Help for teens and parents trying to communicate about sex. Also see books by Sol Gordon written for young women and men in the adolescent years.

Birth Control, Abortion, Sterilization

Callahan, Daniel: *Abortion Law, Choice, and Morality.* New York, Macmillan, 1970.
A humanist examines ethical, social, moral, legal, religious, and medical implications of abortion law.

Hatcher, Robert, Stewart, Gary, et al.: *Contraceptive Technology, 1980–1981.* New York, Irvington Publishers, 1980

A handbook for medical professionals in the family planning field. Many lay readers appreciate the wealth of detail.

Howard, Marion: *Only Human.* New York, The Seabury Press, 1975.

Written for the adolescent who faces a decision about an unwanted pregnancy; the personal stories of six teenagers and their decisions.

Nofzieger, Margaret: *A Cooperative Method of Natural Birth Control.* Summertown, Tennessee, The Book Publishing Co. (156 Drakes Lane), 1976.

Detailed information about using a combination of calendar calculations, temperature charts, and cervical mucus changes to prevent conception.

Seaman, Barbara, and Seaman, Gideon: *Women and the Crisis in Sex Hormones.* New York, Rawson Associates Publishers, 1977.

Extremely comprehensive and fascinating account of the history and current status of sex hormone medications, with strong emphasis on the known and potential dangers of hormones.

Shapiro, Howard I.: *The Birth Control Book.* New York, St. Martin's Press, 1977.

A lively and very readable overview of birth control options presented in question-and-answer format.

Task Force on Concerns of Physically Disabled Women: *Toward Intimacy.* New York, Human Sciences Press, 1977. Available from Reproductive Health Resources, Inc., 1507 21st Street, Suite 100, Sacramento, California 95814 ($2.50).

Practical advice on family planning and sexuality concerns of physically disabled women.

Common Problems

Barbach, Lonnie Garfield: *For Yourself.* New York, Doubleday and Co., 1975.

An excellent starting point for preorgasmic women.

Burack, Richard: *The New Book of Prescription Drugs.* New York, Ballantine Books, 1976.

Consumers Union: *The Medicine Show.* Mount Vernon, New York, Consumers Union, 1980. (By the Editors of Consumer Reports Books.)

Comprehensive and cogent discussions of common medical problems ranging from colds and sore throats to constipation. The chapter on estrogen replacement therapy after menopause is exceptional and includes a thorough discussion of research findings in this area.

Kaplan, Helen Singer: *The New Sex Therapy: Active Treatment of Sexual Dysfunctions.* New York, Brunner/Mazel, 1974.

Theoretical and quite technical descriptions of sexual therapy approaches; intended for professionals who provide therapy.

Kaufman, Sherwin A.: *New Hope for the Childless Couple.* New York, Simon and Schuster, 1976.

Masters, William H., and Johnson, Virginia E.: *Human Sexual Response.* Boston, Little, Brown, 1966.

A detailed description of the physical events in human sexual response written primarily for the professional.

Menning, Barbara Eck: *Infertility: A Guide for the Childless Couple,* Englewood Cliffs, New Jersey, Prentice-Hall, 1977.

Woman's Day Magazine: "The Revolution in Breast-Cancer Care." *Woman's Day,* May 19, 1978.

A brief but excellent review of new approaches to breast cancer treatment with sound recommendations for any woman facing this problem.

Zilbergeld, Bernie: *Male Sexuality.* New York, Bantam Books, 1978.

An excellent starting point for couples or men struggling with ejaculatory control and other common problems with sexual functioning.

Surgery

Annas, George J.: *The Rights of Hospital Patients: The Basic ACLU Guide to a Hospital Patient's Rights.* An American Civil Liberties Handbook. New York, Avon Books, 1975.

Bunker, John P, Barnes, Benjamin A, and Mosteller, Frederick: *Costs, Risks, and Benefits of Surgery.* New York, Oxford University Press, 1977.

Dennenberg, Herbert: *A Shopper's Guide to Surgery: Fourteen Rules on How to Avoid Unnecessary Surgery.* Address for ordering: Pennsylvania Department of Insurance, Harrisburg, Pennsylvania.

Galton, Lawrence: *The Patient's Guide to Surgery.* New York, Avon Books, 1976.

Pregnancy

Bing, Elisabeth and Colman, Libby: *Having a Baby After 30.* New York, Bantam Books, 1980.

A thoughtful, human and comprehensive discussion of the psychological, social and medical concerns facing couples who are considering parenthood after 30. Couples who are undecided about parenthood will also find this book helpful.

Ewy, Donna, and Ewy, Roger: *Preparation for Childbirth: A LaMaze Guide.* New York, New American Library, 1970.

Prenatal exercises and LaMaze techniques for natural delivery.

Kelly, Marguerite, and Parsons, Elia: *Mother's Almanac.* New York, Doubleday and Co., 1975.

Practical suggestions, joyously written for parenthood; infant through toddler.

Kitzinger, Shiela: *The Experience of Childbirth.* Baltimore, Penguin Books, 1975.

Understanding and coping with pregnancy, birth, and early parenthood.

Klaus, Marshall H., and Kennell, John H.: *Maternal Infant Bonding.* St. Louis, C. V. Mosby, 1976.

The importance of early, intimate contact between newborn infant and parents.

Rozdilsky, Mary Lou, and Banet, Barbara: *What Now?* Order from *What Now*, 3415 NE 50th Street, Seattle, Washington 98105. ($1.25).
Physical and emotional aspects of the first six weeks of parenthood.

Shneour, Elie: *The Malnourished Mind*. New York, Anchor Press/Doubleday, 1974.
The impact of nutrition on mental development of the fetus and young child.

Index

Abdominal pain:
  and birth control pill use, 188
  and cervicitis, 371
  and ectopic pregnancy, 58, 147
  and fibroid tumor, 423
  during intercourse, 445-448
  and IUD expulsion, 148
Abdominal tubal ligation, 236, 243-245
Abortion, 278-314
  amniocentesis type, 296-300
    pain, 299
  anesthesia for, 285-286, 289, 290, 296,
    305, 306, 308
  and birth control choice, 71
  complications:
    danger signs, 312
    of illegal abortion, 280
  contraindications, 308-309
  cost of, 288
  counseling, 284
  deaths from, 281, 302-303
  and dilation and curettage, 524
  dilation and evacuation, 287-288
  and drug reactions, 306-307
  in early pregnancy, 60-61
  early vacuum, 286-287, 289-295
  emotional response to, 313
  followup/emergency care, 283, 287-288,
    304, 310-312

and future fertility, 307-308
herbal remedies for, 300
incomplete, 304-305
infection, 302, 304
  pelvic, 376-377
with intact-IUD pregnancy, 59, 146
legal aspects, 278-282
legal vs. illegal, 280-281
menstrual extraction, 221, 295-296
parental consent for minor, 274, 279
preparations for, 288-289
private physicians and, 286-287
prostaglandin:
  injection, 287, 297, 305
  vaginal tablet, 299-300
repeated, 313-314
and Rh-negative factor, 309-310
risks, 302-308
  with delay, 302-303
  vs. full-term pregnancy risk, 279-280
saline, 297
  risks, 287, 305, 308
second trimester procedures, 287
selecting a physician or clinic, 284-288
special clinics, 286
spontaneous, see Miscarriage
Supreme Court decision, 278
urea, 297
world pattern, 280-281

Felicia H. Stewart, M.D., practices obstetrics and gynecology in Sacramento, California. She is a clinical lecturer in obstetrics and gynecology at the University of California School of Medicine in Davis, California. She has published clinical research based on her four years' work with the Planned Parenthood Association of Sacramento, and is an active public speaker on women's health care issues. She enjoys her children, racquetball, and music.

Gary K. Stewart, M.D., M.P.H., F.A.C.O.G., practices obstetrics and gynecology in Sacramento, California. He is medical director of the Planned Parenthood Association of Sacramento, and assistant clinical professor of obstetrics and gynecology at the University of California School of Medicine in Davis, California. He was a Peace Corps physician for three years in East Africa, and his interests include African art and photography.

Felicia J. Guest, B.A., develops and conducts training courses at the Regional Training Center for Family Planning, Emory University School of Medicine, Atlanta, Georgia. For six years she wrote and produced patient education materials as the health educator with the Emory University/Grady Memorial Hospital Family Planning Program. She has written *To Comfort and Relieve Them,* a manual for counseling rape victims, and writes a bimonthly health education newsletter for the National Clearinghouse for Family Planning Information. She plays the clarinet and believes the Atlanta Braves will win a pennant in her lifetime.

Robert A. Hatcher, M.D., M.P.H., F.A.A.P., has directed the Emory University/Grady Memorial Hospital Family Planning Program since 1968. He is associate professor of Gynecology and Obstetrics at the Emory University School of Medicine in Atlanta, Georgia. He is the senior author of *Contraceptive Technology,* which is co-authored by Gary Stewart, Felicia Guest, and Felicia Stewart. This basic textbook for physicians, medical students, family planning counselors, and nurse practitioners is now in its ninth edition and has sold more than 500,000 copies. He is active in his local church and community, where he and his wife Carolyn often conduct sex education programs for parents and teens. He is an enthusiastic tennis player and gardener.